CW00525252

Voices of Scotswomen in Peace and War

Other books by Ian MacDougall include:

Voices of Scottish Librarians (edited with notes by Alan
Reid and David Fletcher) (Edinburgh, 2017)

Voices from Lilliesleaf (Edinburgh, 2015)

Voices of Scottish Journalists (Edinburgh, 2013)

Through the mill (Edinburgh, 2009)

*All Men Are Brethren: Prisoners of War in
Scotland, 1803–1814* (Edinburgh, 2008)

*Mid and East Lothian Miners' Association Minutes
1894–1918* (ed.) (Edinburgh, 2003)

Onion Johnnies (East Linton, 2002)

Voices of Leith Dockers (Edinburgh, 2001)

Bondagers (East Linton, 2001)

'Oh! Ye Had Tae Be Careful' (East Linton, 2000)

Voices from Work and Home (Edinburgh, 2000)

Hoggie's Angels (East Linton, 1995)

Mungo Mackay and the Green Table (East Linton, 1995)

Voices from War (Edinburgh, 1995)

Hard Work, Ye Ken (East Linton, 1993)

Voices from the Hunger Marches (2 vols) (Edinburgh 1990–1)

The Prisoners at Penicuik, 1803–1814 (Dalkeith, 1989)

Voices from the Spanish Civil War (Edinburgh, 1986)

*Labour in Scotland: A Pictorial History from the Eighteenth
Century to the Present Day* (Edinburgh, 1985)

Militant Miners (Edinburgh, 1981)

Essays in Scottish Labour History (ed.) (Edinburgh, 1978)

*A Catalogue of some Labour Records in Scotland and some Scots
Records Outside Scotland* (comp. and ed.) (Edinburgh, 1978)

Minutes of Edinburgh Trades Council, 1859–1873 (ed.) (Edinburgh, 1969)

Voices of Scotswomen in Peace and War

Spoken Recollections of Home Life,
Employment and 1939–45 War Service

Ian MacDougall

First published in Great Britain in 2019 by
John Donald, an imprint of Birlinn Ltd

West Newington House
10 Newington Road
Edinburgh
EH9 1QS

www.birlinn.co.uk

ISBN: 978 1 910900 32 1

Copyright © Ian MacDougall 2019

The right of Ian MacDougall to be identified as the author
of this work has been asserted by him in accordance
with the Copyright, Designs and Patents Act, 1988

All rights reserved. No part of this publication may
be reproduced, stored, or transmitted in any form, or
by any means, electronic, mechanical or photocopying,
recording or otherwise, without the express written
permission of the publisher.

British Library Cataloguing-in-Publication Data
A catalogue record for this book is available on request from the British Library

Typeset by Biblichor Ltd, Edinburgh
Printed and bound in Malta by Gutenberg Press

Contents

List of Illustrations

16. Timber Corps Girls standing at ease. Alexina McGlinn (later Mrs Bolger) is third from the left in the rear row.
17. More than half a century after the war, Agnes (Nessie) Lawrie lays flowers at the graves of RAF airmen in Scopwick cemetery, Lincolnshire.

Places Shown on the Map of Scotland

1. Aberdeen
2. Barney Hill farm, East Lothian
3. Blairgowrie
4. Bonchester Bridge
5. Bridge of Earn
6. Brora
7. Buckie
8. Cleland
9. Clydebank
10. Cowdenbeath
11. Crail
12. Cruachan Hydro-Electric Scheme, Argyll
13. Dalkeith
14. Dingwall
15. Donibristle
16. Drem
17. Dumfries
18. Dunbar
19. Dundee
20. Dunfermline
21. Dunoon
22. Dyce
23. Earlston
24. East Barns, East Lothian
25. Edinburgh
26. Falkirk
27. Firth of Clyde
28. Firth of Forth
29. Flotta
30. Fodderty
31. Forfar
32. Fort George
33. Forth Bridge
34. Fraserburgh
35. Galashiels
36. Garelochhead
37. Glasgow
38. Glenrothes
39. Golspie
40. Grangemouth
41. Greenock
42. Hebrides (Outer)
43. Helensburgh
44. Howwood
45. Hoy
46. Inverness
47. Kailzie
48. Kelso
49. Kelton
50. Kirkcaldy
51. Kirkwall
52. Kirriemuir
53. Leith
54. Lewis
55. Linlithgow Bridge
56. Loch Etiveside
57. Lyness
58. Manderston
59. Melrose
60. Mull
61. Newbattle Abbey
62. Newtongrange
63. North Sea
64. Oban
65. Orkney
66. Oxenfoord Castle
67. Paisley
68. Peebles
69. Penicuik
70. Perth
71. Peterhead
72. Port Seton
73. Rogart
74. Rosyth
75. Rothesay
76. Sauchie
77. Scapa Flow
78. Shandford Lodge
79. Skye
80. St Andrews
81. Stirling
82. Stornoway
83. Stranraer
84. Stromness
85. Taynuilt
86. Thurso
87. Tiree
88. Tobermory
89. West Barns, East Lothian
90. West Linton

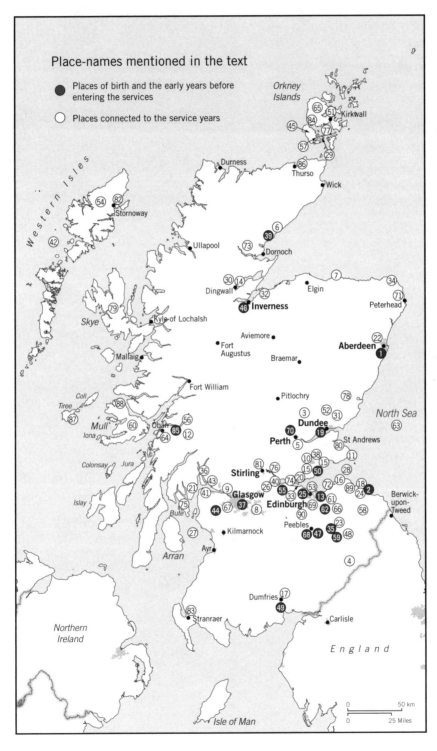

Place-names mentioned in the text

● Places of birth and the early years before entering the services

○ Places connected to the service years

Orkney Islands

Kirkwall

Western Isles

Durness

Thurso

Wick

Stornoway

Ullapool

Dornoch

Dingwall

Elgin

Inverness

Peterhead

Skye

Kyle of Lochalsh

Aviemore

Fort Augustus

Aberdeen

Braemar

Mallaig

Fort William

Pitlochry

North Sea

Coll

Tiree

Dundee

Mull

Oban

Perth

Iona

St Andrews

Colonsay

Jura

Stirling

Glasgow

Edinburgh

Islay

Berwick-upon-Tweed

Bute

Peebles

Arran

Kilmarnock

Ayr

Northern Ireland

Dumfries

Stranraer

Carlisle

England

Isle of Man

0   50 km

0   25 Miles

Introduction

This book presents the personal, spoken, recorded and edited recollections of 19 Scotswomen in peace and war. Their recollections are of their girlhood and families, their housing, schooling and employment in the 1920s, 1930s and early 1940s, and of the coming of the 1939–45 War and their service during it in the Auxiliary Territorial Service (ATS), Women's Auxiliary Air Force (WAAF), Women's Royal Naval Service (WRNS) or Timber Corps.

Almost all 19 recall also, if more briefly, some of their experiences in the post-1945 years. Of the 19, nine during the war were in the ATS, four in the WAAF, five in the WRNS and one in the Timber Corps. Their recollections were recorded in one-to-one interviews between June 1998 and June 2005. All but four of them either offered themselves for interview or were suggested by members of their family or by friends or neighbours. The other four were known to me long before the project began in 1998.

All 19 women were born between 1918 and 1926. Esther Cowper, the oldest of them, and Margaret Campbell, the second oldest, were both born in 1918, weeks before the end of the Great War in November that year. The youngest of the 19, Williamina MacNab, was born shortly before the General Strike of May 1926.

These 19 women belonged to cities, towns, villages, hamlets or farmplaces throughout Scotland. Margaret McLeod came from Golspie in Sutherland, Christina Chisholm from Inverness, Nancy Cowe from a farm near Dunbar in East Lothian, Jean Crosbie from Howwood village in Renfrewshire, Isobel Cumming from Kailzie in Peeblesshire, Esther Cowper from Linlithgow Bridge in West Lothian, May Kerr

1

from Edinburgh, Williamina MacNab from Perth, Ann Baird from Glasgow, Isa Dougan from Edinburgh, Nessie Lawrie from Dalkeith, Elizabeth Weston from Newtongrange in Midlothian, Jean Robertson from Aberdeen, Margaret Campbell from Taynuilt in Argyllshire, Isa Allan from Galashiels/Melrose, Elizabeth Stewart from the hamlet of Kelton in Dumfriesshire, Christina Millaney from Kirkcaldy, Olga Matthews from Edinburgh, and Alexina McGlinn from Dundee.

For the presentation of their recollections in the pages below, the 19 are arranged in four groups. First comes the largest group among them, those nine who were in the ATS. Second come the four who were in the WAAF. Third come the five who were in the WRNS. Finally comes Alexina McGlinn, who was in the Timber Corps. Within each of the first three groups the recollections are presented in the chronological order in which each interviewee joined that service.

These recollections are essentially oral history, spoken history, history from the mouth, rather than history based mainly or entirely on documents such as minutes, diaries, letters, financial accounts, notes, photographs. Two of these 19 interviewees (Nancy Cowe and Jean Crosbie) refer to diaries that, at least for a time, they kept during the war; two or three others of the 19 believed they might still perhaps possess a Services paybook, or a few contemporary notes made about their experiences; and almost all of them, or their families, retained a photograph or photographs of themselves in uniform. Christina Chisholm (Mrs Morrison) was an exception in having already written, before her recorded and edited interview in the pages below, two type-script booklets, the first about her pre-war experiences in Inverness, the second about her wartime experiences. But also she afterwards wrote a book covering her whole life to the end of the war in 1945. Sadly, Christina died in January 2016, a few weeks before her book, of 160 pages and titled *Yesterday's Child*, was published.

That this present project, begun in 1998, has taken so long to complete has been due mainly to two factors. First, from 1996 until 2012, I was already committed, as the research worker for the Scottish Working People's History Trust, to giving priority to its oral history, documentary and other projects. Second, from 2006 until 2012 a succession of attacks of myasthenia gravis put me from time to time *hors de combat*. But successful counter-attacks by the highly skilled forces of the NHS Western General Hospital, Edinburgh, enabled work to resume and continue.

Oral history was once described by the distinguished historian A.J.P. Taylor as 'Old men drooling about their youth.' Whether he would have included elderly women, too, in his rejection of recorded interviews of spoken recollections as a means of learning more about the past, is uncertain; but it seems more likely than not. The vast majority of so-called ordinary people never write anything down about their lives. So there is surely a mass of information and insight about the past (at least about the past *within living memory*, and above all about the past as lived by ordinary folk) which often remains unexplored. If investigated, recorded and published it would help further to illuminate and promote greater understanding of that more recent past. The recollections of these 19 Scotswomen about their experiences in peace and war in the 20th century make, it is hoped, some contribution toward that end.

Especially within the 1920s and 1930s, when the 19 were growing up, they provide some vivid spoken memories of their family life, touch on some consequences of the 1914–18 War, describe housing conditions, poverty, diet, ill-health, unemployment, their schooling, and their girlhood interests, activities and ambitions, employment, pay and working conditions, holidays or the lack of them and, by the late 1930s, some memories of the shadow of approaching war. One aspect of that past which does not attract much comment among these recollections is the political. Christina Chisholm says that in the late 1930s she had 'a leaning towards the Scottish Nationalists'; Esther Cowper, that she became a Scottish Nationalist while still at primary school. Jean Robertson appears to have been well aware of at least some of the dangers Nazism posed by 1939 and, not being herself a Nordic blonde, could not sleep for worrying about her prospective annihilation. Jean Crosbie, who could clearly remember the declaration of war by Chamberlain in September 1939, added: 'But I had really no idea what it was about, not a clue. I wasn't political at all.' By the end of the war in 1945, however, Jean's interest in politics had markedly developed. As the General Election results that summer were reaching a roomful of Jean's fellow ATS officers, all of whom were lamenting the great Labour victory as 'the end of England', Jean burst into tears and declared: 'I have to tell you that I am a socialist!' If readers may find a certain paucity of political comment or commitment and activity in these recollections, it is hoped they

3

will keep in mind that, even as late as at the outbreak of war in 1939, 16 of these 19 women were still teenagers, their ages then ranging from 13 to 19.

But are these recollections of that relatively recent past, including not least the 19 women's memories of their service in the 1939–45 War, accurate and reliable accounts? After all, they are attempting to recall events, people and places from 70 or so years earlier. The accuracy and reliability of memory obviously varies between one person and another. Some people, at least for certain events or places or persons, have, or appear to have, almost photographic memories. Others frankly admit (as will be found here and there in the pages below) that of certain matters, aspects, places or people even within living memory they have no recollection whatever. It is above all when the interviewee is recalling some event, person or place with which or with whom she herself was directly involved, and especially if she speaks as an eye witness, that the recollection is likely to be most accurate and reliable. (Mere hearsay is not good evidence, though it may sometimes prove helpful provided it can be thoroughly investigated.)

Thus Isobel Cumming, training at a camp at Hereford in December 1941 to become an ATS driver, recalls in her contribution how the camp authorities, convinced all the Scots girls there would 'go wild' on Auld Year's Night, put them on 'tae peelin' tatties. I resented that very much. No' that ah wanted tae go wild on Auld Year's Night. . . . [But] That's the only time ah remember peelin' tatties in the ATS. Ah'll no' forget it!' Isobel's experience then hardly amounts to a significant historical event, although it seems to reveal the ignorance of some people in one part of the United Kingdom, about the customs or habits of those belonging to another part. Yet it is a small example of an event with some historical interest – and one unlikely to have been recorded in any contemporary documentary source.

So oral history, preferably recorded in systematic and comprehensive interviews, and especially if recorded by a reasonably sized group of people recalling subjects or periods they have experienced in common, can and often does provide the general reader, the school pupil, the college and university student, and the historian, with useful, even unique, information and insights. Above all, where oral history, checked as carefully as possible for accuracy, can be combined or interlarded with history based on contemporaneous trustworthy documents, it is likely to be at its most accurate and helpful.

Notes provided towards the end of this book include, first, brief explanations or amplifications of passing references to events, people or places that may be unfamiliar to the general reader; and, second, corrections to any clearly inaccurate statements. An attempt has been made throughout to preserve and present the actual words spoken by the interviewees. For recollections spoken wholly or partly in dialect or in an accent likely to be unfamiliar to many readers, a glossary is also provided. And words within square brackets [ ] in the texts are editorial insertions.

Each of the three main periods which these recollections cover provides the reader with a wide range of aspects and experiences to explore. If there are some general similarities in the 19 women's war experiences, particularly in their induction, training, appointments to particular jobs or trades, and their postings to particular camps, airfields, offices, or barracks, and even in their struggles to find seats on trains taking them to or from those places or on or from leave, there are also some differences reported by them about their Service billets and beds, food, degree of subjection to enemy bombing, posting abroad or to service on a troopship, and about their ranks. Of the 19, two – Jean Crosbie in the ATS and Margaret Campbell in the WRNS – eventually became commissioned officers, and several others among them became warrant officers or non-commissioned officers (NCOs).

Unsurprisingly, the 19 women came from a variety of family backgrounds and experiences. Margaret McLeod's father had followed his own father's trade by completing his apprenticeship as a boot and shoe repairer, then he ran his own repair and retail shop first at Kirriemuir then at Golspie. Jean Crosbie's father was a skilled engineer but for a time in the 1920s ran a bus in Renfrewshire, and was then also subject to spells of unemployment. Isa Dougan's father was a highly experienced and punctilious train driver and foreman at Haymarket railway depot in Edinburgh, who 'drove the Royal train quite a few times'. Elizabeth Weston's father worked in the main coal pit at Newtongrange, where he shared a contract with another man. Margaret Campbell's father had inherited a sheep farm on Loch Etiveside in Argyll. But he 'wasn't keen on farming' and was, though never a professional academic, 'a Gaelic scholar'. Elizabeth Stewart's father was an officer in the merchant navy. Christina Millaney's father, whose health is understood to have been badly affected by his involvement in the 1914–18 War, was a skilled cabinetmaker who had a shop in Kirkcaldy. But from the age of 11 Christina never saw him again. Olga Matthews's father had been a regular Royal Navy officer, was at the battle of Jutland in 1916 and was recalled as a reservist to the navy in the 1939–45 War. In the 1920s he had become a partner in an Edinburgh law firm. Olga's mother had worked at the Foreign Office in London during the 1914–18 War, was present at the Peace Conference at Versailles in 1919 and became secretary to the British ambassador at Constantinople (Istanbul), where she met and married Olga's father. These families, though obviously not without their varied difficulties at least at times, could be seen as a bit, or more than a bit, better off than the families and circumstances of many of the other 11 women who relate their experiences in the pages below.

Of these 11 others, Christina Chisholm's father, a Regular soldier and pipe major in the Cameron Highlanders, had been in the Sudan Campaign in 1896–9, the Boer War in 1899–1902 and the 1914–18 War, at the end of which he became a railway clerk in Inverness. The fathers of Nancy Cowe and Isa Allan were farm workers, although, like Christina Chisholm's father, Isa's had earlier been a long-serving Regular soldier, in his case in the Scots Greys. Isobel Cumming's father was a sawmill and forestry worker; Esther Cowper's a wages clerk at a paper mill at Linlithgow Bridge. May Kerr's father, 'a man wi' many jobs', had been in the army at age 16, but hated it and was bought out; worked at Rosyth naval dockyard in the 1914–18 War; then was often unemployed between the wars, but worked when he could as a gardener, grave-digger and laundry van driver; from the 1939–45 War onwards until he retired he worked at Rosyth dockyard. Williamina MacNab's father, an orphan, trained as a bootmaker but worked mainly as a shoe repairer; badly wounded in the 1914–18 War and, like several others among these fathers, a Military Medallist, he was unemployed in the early 1920s until he found a job as a cobbler at Bridge of Earn, the 4½ miles between which and his home (itself hardly 'Fit For Heroes') in Perth he walked each way daily, despite his bad leg. Ann Baird's father was a boiler-maker in the Glasgow shipyards; Nessie Lawrie's was a coal miner, but also worked part-time at weekends in a fish and chip shop. Jean Robertson's father, badly wounded in the 1914–18 War, worked as an

Aberdeen tram and bus driver. Alexina McGlinn's father, a building labourer in Dundee and an army volunteer in the 1914–18 War, was often afterwards unemployed, so that Alexina's mother became the family breadwinner by going out to work in the city's jute mills.

Other aspects of family history these 19 women touch upon include the number of brothers and sisters they had, and infant mortality. In cases of the latter, Nancy Cowe lost her only brother to measles when he was aged 3½; Jean Crosbie, an older brother stillborn; Elizabeth Weston, an older brother to pneumonia when he was aged 18 months; and Alexina McGlinn, an older sister at age 4 to scarlet fever. Almost two thirds of the 19 interviewees were members of families of between one and four children. Elizabeth Stewart was the only one among the 19 who was an only child. Six of the 19 belonged to families of between six and ten children. Christina Chisholm and Elizabeth Weston were members of the two largest families of the 19, each of which had ten children.

There are also references to the lives, employments and activities of brothers and sisters of the 19, as well as to grandparents and even, in a few cases, to great-grandparents. Isa Dougan's maternal granny, for example, though apparently only about five feet tall, appears as a remarkable character. She had had nine children, but all of them except Isa's mother had died in childhood. Granny had never had any schooling and could neither read nor write, although she had her own bank account and signed with a cross. She could be found every afternoon except Sunday in one or other of half-a-dozen cinemas near where she lived in Elm Row, Edinburgh, and always with a bag of sweets in her pocket. One day when a man with drink taken had ignored her warnings not to put his arm round her waist, she knocked him flat out with a single pile-driver from her fist. Esther Cowper never knew either of her grandfathers, but she was fortunate in having two remarkable grannies. Esther's maternal grandmother was widowed when her husband died aged 44 in the Mauricewood pit disaster at Penicuik in 1889, along with two of their sons aged 14 and 12, and 60 other miners. She was left with six dependent children under the age of 11, the youngest a month-old baby – and brought them all up successfully. Esther's paternal grandfather, a plater, had been killed on the railway at Penicuik in his thirties, leaving his widow with four boys and two girls to bring up, which she, too, did successfully.

Almost all the 19 have clear memories of their housing, particularly during their girlhood but also during their wartime service. Williamina MacNab, for instance, recollects in detail the house in the Watergate in Perth where she, with her parents, her sister and brother, lived until she was about nine years old, when the family moved to a wonderful newly built council house with all the mod cons that had been so lacking in the Watergate. Alexina McGlinn recalls how similar conditions existed in the tenement flat in Brook Street, Dundee, where, until she was about 12 in 1934–5, she and her parents, three sisters and three brothers lived in a room and kitchen. The children – girls first or boys first – got a bath in a big tub in front of the fire every Friday night. 'But it wis the same water for us a'. Ma mother and father couldnae afford tae keep bilin' the kettle.' Her parents slept in the kitchen, all seven children in the room, where a curtain divided the boys from the girls.

Their schooling is recalled by all 19 women. Unsurprisingly perhaps in that era, some of their teachers appear to have varied from the excellent and the charismatic to the incompetent and the sadistic. Jean Crosbie, always first in her class at Camphill Secondary School in Paisley, had found one of her teachers at primary school 'terrifying'. Esther Cowper loved both her time at her local primary at Linlithgow Bridge and later her six secondary years at Linlithgow Academy. But in her early years at primary in the 1920s, to punish her for fidgeting with her gymslip girdle, her teacher tied Esther's hands behind her back with the girdle, but forgot to untie her at the lunch break. So Esther arrived home still struggling to untie her hands, and with 'red raw weals' on her wrists. Williamina MacNab felt, when she went, aged 12, to Stormont Street Roman Catholic School in Perth that 'Most of the teachers weren't really qualified, but they were Catholics.' And at St Andrew's School in the Overgate in Dundee, Alexina McGlinn found one of the women teachers not only '. . . whacked the children' [but] 'She used a stick on our hands.'

Two of the 19 women had experience of schooling rather different from that of the other 17. Until she was aged eight, Margaret Campbell, living up Loch Etiveside six miles from the nearest school, was taught at home by her parents. She then had two successive qualified tutors at home, and passed the Qualifying exam at age 10 (the usual age was 11 or 12). From the age of 11 Margaret then spent six successful years at Oban High School. Olga Matthews began at what seems to have been a private school in Edinburgh. Then when her mother found a teaching job at Oxenfoord Castle boarding school in Midlothian, Olga became a day pupil there. From age 13 or 14 she became a pupil at St George's girls' private school in Edinburgh, then, with several Highers passes, and just as war broke out in September 1939, began what proved to be a year as a student at Edinburgh College of Art.

The largest group of the 19 women – nine altogether – left school at the age of 14. A further five left at age 15, one at 16, another at 16 or 17, and three at 17. At least four, but probably five, of the 19 left school with some Highers and Lowers. Isa Dougan, whose ambition was to become an office worker, left school before she could sit any Highers or Lowers but had already become well qualified in shorthand and typing. Margaret McLeod, who wanted to study domestic science, catering and hotel work, and seems likely to have had some Highers when she left school at 16 or 17, found she could not begin a college course in those subjects until she was 18. With a pass in commercial subjects among her five Highers, Christina Chisholm was well equipped for office work. Though Jean Crosbie, Isa Hall and Williamina MacNab left school before they could sit Lowers or Highers, they then enrolled in evening classes, in Jean and Isa's cases, for shorthand and typing, and in Williamina's for book-keeping. Elizabeth Weston left school at age 14 but was directed by her parents to attend for a year a private commercial college in Edinburgh, where she successfully took a course in shorthand, typing and book-keeping. Similarly, when Margaret Campbell left Oban High School aged 17 with Highers passes, she enrolled at the West of Scotland Commercial College in Glasgow and successfully completed a commercial course there.

The first jobs that these 19 women found on leaving school reflected more or less their age and their qualifications (if any). Nancy Cowe's first job, at age 15 in 1935, was as a live-in housemaid in a big house in East Lothian, a first step towards realising her ambition to become a cook. Nancy recalls the long hours she worked, from rising at 5.30 am until finishing about 7pm, though with breaks for breakfast, lunch, high tea, and an hour or so of relaxation in the afternoon. Sunday work was until 12 noon; and Nancy got an afternoon off once a week from about 2pm. She could not recall how much her pay was. She left that job after a few months, to start as a live-in table-maid at another big house nearby, where she was much encouraged by the resident cook towards fulfilling her ambition. Williamina MacNab, prevented, when she left school aged 14 in 1940, from starting as an apprentice hairdresser by the need to pay fees, began work with a printing and bookbinding firm in Perth. Williamina lasted a week. She found she was expected to clean the toilet, which was used almost exclusively by men. She told her mother: 'I'm not cleaning the lavatory for the men,' and didn't go back. Her mother supported her decision. Isobel Cumming's first job proved even more distressing, and longer-lasting. Isobel's girlhood ambition was to become a driver – of a taxi. That being beyond her reach when she left Peebles High School aged 14, she started work instead in a local tweed mill. 'Ah didnae want tae gaun intae the mill. Ah think ah wis dragged tae the mill in tears! . . . And at first ah had tae go in ma school gymslip because ah hadnae a peenie!' The date of her starting at the mill remained branded on Isobel's memory 60 years later: 19 October 1936. Christina Millaney's ambition from the age of 10 was to become a teacher of sewing. She passed the Qualifying exam at that early age in 1934 at St Mary's School in Kirkcaldy – but the absence of any Catholic secondary school there meant Christina had to remain at St Mary's as her mother could not afford the daily bus fares to the nearest Catholic secondary eight miles away at Cowdenbeath. When she left St Mary's aged 14 in 1938, her mother found her a job as an apprentice French polisher at Alexander's bus company factory in Kirkcaldy. Christina found she was one of only four girls or women there among a hundred men. For a five-day but apparently almost 48-hour week, Christina's wage per week was 7s 6d (37½p). She didn't like the work and 'hated all the men at Alexander's. They were always trying to get you in corners. I was only a wee girl, and very naïve.' She left after a year and began as an apprentice tailoress in a shop in Kirkcaldy. When Margaret McLeod left Golspie High School aged 16 about 1937 she found she could not begin a course in domestic science and hotel and catering at the Atholl Crescent College in Edinburgh until she was 18, so she remained at home helping her mother until, having joined the Territorial Army/ATS in December 1938, 'I went away to the war in September 1939.'

Each of the 19 women recalls how, why, where and (in a few cases only approximately) when they joined one of the three Services (or, in Alexina McGlinn's case, the Timber Corps). Ann Baird, employed in a baker's shop in Glasgow, appears to have been unique among the 19 in having a six-month deferment. When in 1940 Elizabeth Weston was told by her father to leave her office job in Edinburgh because her mother, with husband and five sons at home who were all miners and on different shifts, needed help at home, Elizabeth did as she was told. Matters, however, developed very differently from what Elizabeth and her family had expected. For in October 1942 she found herself en route to Gloucester to join the WAAF. With the introduction of conscription for single women and childless widows aged between 20 and 30 Elizabeth was deemed eligible for call-up, not least because she was considered by the Labour Exchange to be unemployed. She had no medical examination before, along with about 50 other WAAF recruits, she was marched from the Assembly Rooms in Edinburgh down to the Waverley station to board the train for Gloucester. Elizabeth paints a memorable picture of their march and their departure. But she always remained convinced she would never have been in the WAAF or any other women's Service during the war had she had a medical examination at the outset of her call-up, because, left-handed as she was, she had been born with a deformed right arm, could not turn or use her right hand, which she had to raise up, though even then only to a limited height, with her left hand. Her conclusion: 'Ah definitely should have been rejected on medical grounds.' When she pointed out during her medical examination after arrival at Gloucester that she could not salute with her right hand, she was told, 'Oh, that won't matter. You can type. We need you to type.'

The 1939–45 War, no doubt like all or most wars before or since, drew masses of women away from their normal daily lives, and thrust upon them a wide range of experiences. Thus Ann Baird, from her job selling bakeries at a shop in Byres Road, Glasgow, and having never been further from home than Barrow-in-Furness, found herself early in 1945, along with other ATS girls, on a troopship heading for Naples. Ann then went on to Rome, Rimini, Padua and Venice, and in September that year to Trieste, where she met and later married her husband, who came from Edinburgh. Margaret Campbell, as an officer in the WRNS, who had never been abroad before, began towards the end of the war to sail on troopships as a member of the cipher staff, and crossed the Atlantic three times in each direction aboard the requisitioned pre-war French passenger liner *Ile de France*. Some 26 of Jean Crosbie's ATS friends and colleagues were killed in their hut at Yarmouth by a

German bomber, and Jean herself would almost certainly have been killed, too, had she not been home on leave at the time. Christina Chisholm, posted in 1941–2 to top secret work (for MI6, as it seemed to her and her colleagues there), two storeys down in the basement of the War Office in Whitehall, and not far from the underground Cabinet War Rooms, once encountered 'this big fat man', clad in his pyjamas and dressing gown, trudging towards her about 4 am along one of the underground passages. 'Good evening,' said Winston Churchill, Prime Minister, to Christina, who politely returned his greeting. Isa Dougan was delighted in autumn 1943 to learn that, for her seventh posting since joining the WAAF in August 1941, she was going from Gloucester back to Scotland. Her destination, however, the Inner Hebridean island of Tiree, she had never heard of and had no idea where it was. Her odyssey by train from Gloucester and ferry to Tiree terminated in an RAF ambulance that 'always came down from the airfield and waited there' to uplift seasick and exhausted passengers like Isa.

These 19 Scotswomen formed friendships with other young women they met during their wartime service, and in some cases also with local people who befriended them where they happened to be stationed. Not a few of those friendships lasted a lifetime. Nessie Lawrie of Dalkeith, very hard-working, and who in girlhood had not enjoyed perhaps the easiest of upbringings, was in no doubt of the importance in her life of being in the wartime WAAF. In retrospect, she declared: 'The four and a half years ah wis a WAAF were the happiest in ma life. Ah've remembered people ah wouldnae have seen or met or heard o' if it hadnae been for the war: Canadians, Americans, New Zealanders, Belgians, a Polish boy and Germans. . . . [And] ah would never have been to Lincolnshire, Bridgnorth, Digby, or anywhere else in England that I got tae or passed through durin' the war. Oh, ah loved every minute ah wis in the WAAF. . . . Ah've never had any regrets.'

Out of the masses of women in Britain who during the 1939–45 War served in the ATS, WAAF, WRNS, or in the munitions and armaments factories, the Land Army, the Timber Corps, or as nurses, Civil Defence workers, on the railways, or in a multitude of other organisations official or voluntary, such as the WVS (Women's Voluntary Service), and also those millions of women who as housewives kept, in a host of ways, the home fires burning as their contribution to the defeat of Nazism and Fascism, these 19 Scotswomen may seem a tiny group. But their experiences in, and recollections of, both peace and war are there for the reader to explore.

* * *

Thanks are due to all those who have contributed to the making of this book. To the 19 contributors of their recollections warmest thanks are due. Alas, those thanks are now in so many cases posthumous, for it is sad indeed that, because of the long delay between recording the interviews and publication of the book, few of the 19 have lived to see their recollections in print. Those of the 19, or of their families, who were able to provide relevant photographs, or some further information, have been additionally helpful. Thanks are also due to local studies and reference librarians, archivists, museum curators, registrars, local history groups, friends, as well as members of my own family. The list is a lengthy one: Paul Adair, Perth Museum; Robin and Muriel Bald; Alayne Barton and colleagues, The Islands Book Trust; Caroline Boyd; Richard Breese; David Buchanan; Jessica Burns; Alison Cameron; Roy and Ann Dow; Alastair Duncan; Edinburgh Southside Heritage Group; Mrs Argyro Francis, Lisa Simmonds, and colleagues at the Commonwealth War Graves Commission; Ron and Alan Herriot; Charlotte Johnson; Rev Jack Kellet and Mrs Ena Kellet; Dorothy Kidd, National Museums of Scotland; Hazel Lorimer, Perth Registrar; Fiona MacDougall; George and June MacDougall; Hugh K. Mackay; Ross Macphail; Shoji Masuzawa; Jane McTavish and colleagues, Edinburgh Public Libraries Reference and Scottish Departments; Mrs Marion O'Hara, David Oswald, Local Studies, Aberdeen Central Library; David Powell, Archive Manager, D.C. Thomson & Co. Ltd, Dundee; Mr Preece, Archivist, Inverness Royal Academy; Evelyn Purves; John Rae; Charlene Rankin, Royal Incorporation of Architects in Scotland; Dr Hanita Ritchie and colleagues, East Lothian Archive & Local History Service, John Gray Centre, Haddington; Steve and Maureen Rooney; Mark Ryan; Mrs Jean Simpson; Pauline Smeed, Dunbar & District Local History Society; David and Edit Smith; Mrs Margaret Strand; Andy Wilson; Mrs Jess Wilson. Particular thanks are also due to Neville Moir and Mairi Sutherland from the publisher, John Donald (an imprint of Birlinn Ltd); the typesetter Gavin Peebles; the cartographer Helen Stirling; and the designer Mark Blackadder, who designed the plate section.

Generous donations to help meet the cost of publication were made by Robin and Muriel Bald; Sir Robert Clerk, Bart; Fire Brigades Union, Scottish Regional Committee; Laurie Flynn; the late Dr Norman Godman and Mrs Trish Godman; James T. Howat Charitable Trust; Kay Hamilton, Dowager Duchess of Hamilton; Baroness Helen Liddell of Coatdyke; Professor Alexander McCall Smith; George and June MacDougall; Sally Magnusson; Nancie Massey Charitable Trust; Musicians' Union; Dr Gordon Prestoungrange, MBE; RMT Scotland Regional Council; Scotland Inheritance Fund; Gary Smith, GMB Scotland Secretary and Scotland Regional Committee; Rt Hon. Dr Gavin Strang; Mrs Jean Smith; UNISON: Mike J. Kirby, Scottish Secretary, and the following branches of the Union: Housing and Care Scotland, Falkirk Council, Glasgow City, North Lanarkshire, South Lanarkshire and Moray.

Above all, without the steady encouragement and practical help throughout of Sandra, my wife, the work would have taken even longer to complete. Whatever sins of omission or commission that may remain in the pages below are to be blamed on me alone.

Ian MacDougall
Edinburgh

Margaret McLeod

I think it was the 6th or the 9th of December 1938 that aged 17 I joined the Territorial Army. I think I joined because my father was in the Seaforth Highlanders as a volunteer in the TA before the First World War.[1]

I was born in Kirriemuir in Angus on the 2nd of March 1921. My father was a shoemaker and shoe repairer there. Born about 1895, he was in the 5th Seaforths in the 1914–18 War. About 1917, I think at Ypres, he was badly wounded in the spine. He got a pension, a very small pension: I think it was only ten bob [50p] a week or something. He didn't speak much about the war. Well, when he came out the army he bought this shoemaker business in Kirriemuir.

My mother came from Carlisle. She was a trained nurse, and that's how she met my father – when he was recovering from wounds in Bangour Hospital in West Lothian. I had one sister, Jean, a few years younger than me. My grandfather McLeod was also a shoemaker and shoe repairer. He was born in Golspie in Sutherland and that's where he had his shop, and where my father had done his apprenticeship.

I began school at Kirriemuir, but I don't remember my schooling there at all. In 1928, when I was seven, my grandfather McLeod retired from his shop in Golspie. My father then left Kirriemuir, came to Golspie with my mother, my sister Jean and me, and carried on the shoemaking, repair and retail business at Golspie until 1960. He died aged 66 a year later.

So I had begun at Golspie Junior School when I was seven. I suppose I liked the school, but I can't remember much about my Junior School days at all. I sat the Qualifying exam there and went on to the Higher

Grade, which was in a separate building. Now it's called Golspie High School. There wasn't then commercial subjects like book-keeping and typing. There was French, but I didn't take it. It was just more or less the same subjects I'd had at the primary stage. I left in the fourth year when I was 16 – or was it 17? I can't remember, nor can I remember if my parents encouraged me to stay on longer at school than most pupils who left at the minimum age of 14.

As a girl my ambition was to go to Atholl Crescent [the Edinburgh School of Cookery and Domestic Economy]. I didn't have to have a Higher Leaving Certificate, because I didn't want to be a teacher. I just wanted to study domestic science, hotel and catering and that kind of work. That's where I was wanting to go when I left school. But they didn't take people then till they were 18. So I never got to the stage of applying to Atholl Crescent, because I was too young. When I left school in or about 1937 I don't think I did anything. I was just at home helping my mother, with a bit of housework, going for the shopping, that sort of thing, till I went away to the war in September 1939.

When I was growing up in Golspie I was in the Brownies, then Guides, and then Rangers.[2] I loved uniform – at least you would think I lived uniform! I was a regular Sunday School attender and church-goer. My parents were also regular attenders at the Church of Scotland. I don't remember as a girl reading a lot of comics, but *The Children's Newspaper* rings a bell,[3] and though I couldn't tell you the name of it I suppose I had a comic. I don't think reading books was a major interest for me. I played tennis. But I wasn't otherwise into sport.

Well, as I've said, I joined the Territorial Army on, I think it was, the 6th or the 9th of December 1938. What prompted me to join the TA, I think, was because my father had joined it before the 1914–18 War and was in the 5th Seaforth Highlanders (TA) during the war. But I wasn't influenced by him at all directly. Nor by any of my friends; none of them were already in the TA. I just think it was something to do. Honest to goodness, I really don't know. I think at that time I was the only girl from Golspie in the TA. There were one or two from Brora and Rogart came along.[4]

We assembled, I think it was on a Thursday night, every week at the drill hall in Golspie. Before the summer camp in 1939 five of us, I think, went down to Fort George near Inverness.[5] At that stage you didn't have much choice in the Territorial Army what you wanted to do. It was all cooks at the beginning. The five of us went then by train or car to Fort George for three or four days' training in the cookhouse. I suppose with my interest in learning to cook that interested me; but that wasn't a reason for me joining the TA.

The first TA summer camp I went to must have been in June or July 1939. It was a tented camp at Strathpeffer, about five miles west of Dingwall in Ross and Cromarty. My parents weren't in the habit of going away from Golspie for an annual holiday. So that was probably – apart from the training course at Fort George – the first time I'd really been away from home. I don't think I felt nervous or apprehensive about that. Of course by then I'd made friends with the other girls from Rogart and Brora at the TA at Golspie. I honestly can't remember if the summer camp at Strathpeffer was a week or a fortnight. I suppose it was enjoyable. It must have been all right. If it wasn't, I wouldn't have carried on!

Then on Saturday, the 2nd of September 1939 we got our calling-up papers. We had to report to the drill hall in Golspie on the Monday. It's difficult to remember now whether it was on Sunday, 3rd September, or since then that I heard the broadcast by Neville Chamberlain announcing the declaration of war.[6] But I think I was in our living room with my parents that morning and we were going to church.

Anyway those of us in the TA reported for duty in the hall here in Golspie on the Monday. Then the same day – big deal – we went to Dornoch [8 miles south of Golspie]. There was no train to Dornoch. So how we got there I honestly don't know. But we must have gone in lorries or buses. Anyway we got there. We were just the girls – the men were already away.

At Dornoch we were billeted in what used to be the stables belonging to the Sutherland Arms Hotel. It was upstairs. We had just to fill our palliasses, and that's what we did. We slept on the floor. And the cookers they were just trenches in, I suppose, the sports field. The men just dug trenches. I can't remember what we were using for fuel. Anyway it just had grids and we put the dixies on top.[7]

Each morning we were up about four o'clock, and we marched to the cookers at five o'clock. For an 18-year old it wasn't . . . But anyway we were marching through Dornoch in the pitch dark. The place where we did the cooking was a good bit away from our billet and, oh, it took us ten minutes anyway to get there.

We were at Dornoch a couple of months, I think. And then we went on to Evanton [as the crow flies, more than 20 miles southwest of Dornoch]. We were in billets there – empty houses, I suppose, they were. I can't picture where the men were – the Seaforths, because we knew all the men. They must have been tented. I do remember there was no hot water in our billets. The hotel used to give us a bath – but we had to pay a shilling for a bath. That was a lot of money. We got paid 7s 6d [37½p] or 7s-and-something. So that was about 15 per cent of our weekly wage for a bath! And at that time we didn't have great-coats. We only had what we would call waterproofs there – a raincoat. And at Evanton I just remember the bedrooms. We had each an iron bed. I don't think we even had a hot water bottle. And I don't remember a recreation room or anything. I can't even remember a kitchen in the billet – I suppose we ate on the field where we did the cooking and the men ate. It was the same at Evanton as it was in Dornoch. I suppose it'd be standard army rations: beef, potatoes, rice pudding, soup. Oh, I think we had reasonable enough amounts of food, and plenty tea. We were only maybe several weeks at Evanton when in December 1939 we were all shoved down to Leeds.

Long before this we girls and women were just called the Auxiliary Territorial Service, the ATS.[8] In those early days we weren't called Privates. The word was Volunteer. And when you got your first stripe you were a Chief Volunteer. Then later on, in 1940 or 1941, we came under Army rule, military orders – King's Regulations. And that's when we learnt to use army ranks like corporal and private.

Anyway, we went down by train from Evanton to Leeds in December 1939. At Leeds we were in Beckett Park Teachers Training College. Oh, it was a marvellous place to be billeted: beautiful buildings, and a swimming pool. It was just what the student teachers had had. And now it was the Royal Army Medical Corps that took it over. That was us finished with the Seaforth Highlanders. We became attached now to the Medical Corps.

At Beckett Park I went on to administration. I wasn't cooking. But I was still in the catering line. At first I was in the Other Ranks' mess. I was just a general factotum, seeing the place was clean and that the food was there.

Though I wasn't there at the time – I was home on leave – it seemed that some folk came there from the Dunkirk evacuation in May-June

1940.[9] But honestly I don't remember any details of that. The reason I missed all that was because I took my finger off or something and was sent home. Och, I was just stupid. I was in the cookhouse and I was feeding the mincer. Instead of using the thing what did I do? I put my finger in. The tip of my finger came off. Och, there was nothing to it. But that's what happened. Believe it or not I was in hospital for ten days, even just for a little thing like that. I was in hospital in Leeds to begin with, and then I came home. I can't remember how long that was. When I went back to Beckett Park it seemed men had arrived from Dunkirk during my absence. I don't remember seeing any of those men at all, and I don't remember what happened. I wasn't there, and they must have been there very briefly. By the time I returned all the Dunkirk men would be into proper hospitals. As I say, I never saw any wounded Dunkirk men, I just heard about them. When I went back to Beckett Park it was maybe in the later part of June. I then remained at Beckett Park until 1945.

It was when I came back from sick leave in summer 1940 that I think I got my lance corporal's stripe. I was a lance corporal for about a year, then I became in 1941 a corporal. I moved then to working in the sergeants' mess. I have not a clue how many sergeants there were, it's so long ago now. There'd maybe be scores, but, oh, not hundreds. They were, or most of them were, in the Royal Army Medical Corps. But they – and we ATS – weren't attached to a military hospital. They dealt with stores, medical stores, rather than with patients. And there used to be junior officers came in for training – doctors who had maybe just graduated and joined the army – and they came to Beckett Park for training. They weren't dealing there with patients. I think there was just a small hospital as part of the unit.

I got my third stripe when I was 21. So that would be in 1942. I had to leave the sergeants' mess then and move to dealing with the officers' mess. It was the same sort of work I did there as in the other ranks' and sergeants' messes. It was all admin work. I was in charge of the order-lies and the women that cleaned the billets. The billets, as I've said, were the rooms previously occupied by the student teachers. They were beautiful buildings that had to be maintained to a high standard. The swimming pool, which was mostly in use, had nothing to do with me. My responsibility was the sleeping quarters, the dining area and the offices. I suppose I was a kind of supervisor of those who did the cleaning and kept the place neat and tidy. I wasn't involved with ledgers or ordering stores of food, etc.

Beckett Park was a friendly place in which to work. Everyone was very friendly. And I often think of how the men respected the ATS women. You wouldn't get that today I don't think. You know, all this swearing and everything: you didn't get that between the men and the women at the daily work or off duty in the evenings and at weekends. The men's and women's quarters were always quite separate – oh, not an awful lot of distance between them but, I mean, they were quite separate.

With the promotions from volunteer or private to lance corporal, corporal, then sergeant, oh, I was better off. As a sergeant I was reasonably well off. In fact, I often think a senior NCO is one of the best ranks in the army. And sergeants are one of the most important ranks. You get that bit of respect and you get your own mess. The sergeants' mess at Beckett Park was quite a friendly group. I would say we all got on well together.

Of the original girls from Golspie, Rogart and Brora who came with me to Beckett Park in December 1939 one or two were posted off from there to different units. I can't remember who they were. But there weren't many of the originals left in Beckett Park by the middle of the war.

I never considered applying for a commission in the ATS. I was too young and inexperienced. I couldn't order women about. Oh, I can order anybody now! And, well, in those days you had to have a bit of a Morningside accent to become an officer. I found that.[10] There was a class consciousness. I know that your accent and your background maybe still counted in 1940–1. I was convinced of that. Not that it put me against . . . But, I mean, I never thought of applying for a commission. I wasn't capable – although sometimes now I wonder! Well, I was only 18 when I went away to the war. And I was never approached about applying for a commission.

* * *

At Beckett Park we could go into Leeds any time we liked in our free time. And, oh, I did so. The cinema would be the main thing, and I did like the theatre. Though I loved dancing, I never went dancing. And though there were regular sort of Saturday night dances in the camp, I never went to them funnily enough. And then there was many a night you didn't go out. In the blackout you couldn't go out. I don't remember how often we were on duty at nights but, oh, we were on duty, though the ATS didn't do guards – the men would do them.

Looking back, you wonder what we knew during the war. We never knew at Beckett Park there was a war on. Leeds had a few air raids but nothing like Sheffield or Hull, London, Coventry . . .

Then as far as the army discipline was concerned, well, really some found it a bit irksome, a bit troublesome. But I can't say I ever did. I must have been army mad! During those five years from 1940 to 1945 I was at Beckett Park I never applied to be posted elsewhere, and nobody ever suggested I should be posted. I was quite happy there.

And during those years I had regular leaves home three times a year. I usually planned the leaves sometimes for New Year, then about Easter, and then about August or September. I came up by train all the way from Leeds to Golspie. They were terrible journeys when I think of it. I must have travelled overnight. I used to get in to Golspie on the morning train anyway. I left Leeds on, say, an afternoon, just squashed in a corridor or into a seat. I would say that Servicemen going home were generally gentlemanly in my experience. I mean, if they saw a girl standing they would give her a seat.

On the return journeys I went from Golspie to Inverness, changed there for Glasgow, then from Glasgow to Leeds. And I always had a sleeper. I left Golspie at 6pm. It took three hours in those days to go to Inverness. I think I got a sleeper train from Inverness about 10-something pm. I was always booked just as Sergeant McLeod. So when I got into the sleeper this night there was a man already there! I said to the attendant, 'Just the two berths?' 'Just the two berths,' said the attendant. 'Well,' he said, 'I didn't know you were an ATS sergeant.' I thought, 'Oh, well, I'll take a chance.' So I did. I remember the man was well-dressed, and he was very nice, and we spoke to each other. So I slept there in one berth and he in the other one. You wouldn't do that today would you?! Though nowadays I suppose I might be listed as WSgt McLeod or something.

I don't remember air raids taking place while I was making those journeys by train, the train stopping, the lights going out, and that sort of thing. But, oh, the trains were cold and overcrowded.

* * *

When in May 1945 the war at last came to an end I think it was just a quiet time at the Beckett Park depot. If there were big crowds in Leeds on VE Day at the celebrations of peace I didn't go there myself. I was quite early being demobbed out of the ATS as one of the first into it. I was home in Golspie before Christmas, I would say about November. I don't think the Servicewomen, unlike the men, got a demob suit. I think we were allowed to keep maybe our underclothing, which wasn't . . . , and our shoes maybe. We didn't get anything else except a gratuity of some sort – Did we get ten bob [50p] in our pockets? What it was I have no idea, but it wouldn't be very much. I don't remember any protests by the ATS. But, God forbid, if there were a war tomorrow and at the end of it Servicewomen were differently treated from Servicemen there would be a great outcry nowadays.

So when I came home I had already thought of my next step: I wanted to go to Atholl Crescent College of Domestic Science in Edinburgh. I had actually been in touch with Atholl Crescent before the war ended. They wrote back and said, yes, there would be so many vacancies for ex-Service people. But when I actually applied at the end of 1945 or beginning of 1946 there were no vacancies. So I said, 'Right. Stuff it.' So I applied for Aberdeen, and got into Aberdeen Dough School – Robert Gordon's School of Domestic Science – and did a year there. The course was only one year: I didn't want to teach, I just wanted hotel management or something like that. In Aberdeen I lived in the YWCA in Dee Street.

Then I became housekeeper in an ex-Servicewomen's club in Edinburgh, where the women were permanent residents, mainly women who were at college or university or in jobs. I had two assistants there and I enjoyed that work – I enjoyed most things I did. I was there about three years. Then, in 1951 after the Korean War had broken out, I went into the Territorial Army full-time! They were forming TA in Aberdeen, Glasgow and Edinburgh, were looking for officers, and I was asked if I would go in as a commissioned officer – Quartermaster Lieutenant, to the Seaforth Highlanders, 4th Battalion, which was the Edinburgh unit but covering also the Borders: Hawick, Galashiels, Dumfries, and all these places. There was no promotion: you went in as a lieutenant and came out as a lieutenant. So I did my six years in that. I lived in digs.

When I came out the TA I didn't know what I was going to do. But I saw an advert: the Edinburgh College of Art was looking for a warden. I thought, 'Right, I'll have a go at that.' And I got that job and was there for three years. Then I had to come home to Golspie for family reasons: my father was ill and died a year later in 1961. So I came home and took over the shoe shop business and ran it until 1971, when I had a health problem myself. So we sold the business then.

When I came home to Golspie in 1960 the Women's Voluntary Service started here. I was organiser here for quite a while. There was one year when we had a tremendous blackout for a week, with no electricity in the village, and we also had a terrible snowstorm. And that was an experience, going round as WVS with people helping us organising food. I thought that was a tremendous experience, in some ways reminiscent of the war years, when people tended to muck in and help each other.

Well, I was in the TA/ATS from December 1938 until about November 1945. It was an important phase in my life. I've no regrets. And if I was young and the same thing happened again I'd be off again.

Margaret McLeod (Mrs Margaret MacLennan) died on 28 December 2012.

Christina Chisholm

I volunteered into the ATS in May 1939. My father was a Regular soldier, a pipe major, in the Queen's Own Cameron Highlanders.[1] He had retired from the army in 1918, and I was born on the 20th of February 1919.

My father and my mother both belonged to Gravir, a village near Stornoway on the Isle of Lewis in the Outer Hebrides. My father was about 12 years older than my mother. They first met in Edinburgh, when my father was stationed in the Castle, and my mother had left Gravir when she was about 18 to work, either as a domestic servant or a receptionist, for a doctor in Edinburgh. The doctor – Dr MacDonald – was an army surgeon who'd been many years in India, and he was a great one for having recitals. My mother said Scott Skinner, the famous fiddler, used to come to the house, and my father would be invited down from the Castle to play his pipes.[2] So that's how my parents met. And Scott Skinner used to get hold of my mother when he heard she was from the islands. He would put her in a corner and he'd say, 'Now, Johan, sing me a Gaelic song.'

My mother had at first been a monitor – a pupil teacher, but she'd never done teacher training. But in the islands there wasn't much employment for them to do, and I understand that she and a cousin went to Edinburgh because they both had sisters working there and they would look out jobs and accommodation for them.

My father was born in 1874, and I think he joined the army when he was about 21. Before then he'd been a poor sort of crofter-fisherman. Probably he hadn't seen a train in his life till he went off to the army. He was always in the Camerons. He had a Long Service and Good

Conduct Medal. He fought in the Sudan War and was at the battle of Atbara; he told me it was fought against Dervishes. And he was in the South African War. He had five medals for the South African War and several of them had bars on them. There was the battle of Diamond Hill, I remember hearing about that.[3] And I remember him saying they were put off the boat at Cape Town, and they had to walk all the way to the Sudan once. He said they were turned into the fields to eat the ears of the corn sometimes when their transport wasn't coming up cooking it. Well, after he left the army in 1918 he was employed as a stores clerk on the Highland Railway in Inverness.

Both my grandfathers were crofter-fishermen in Lewis. I never met my father's father or mother. But I've traced my father's family to 1770 – all of them were crofter-fishermen. And I knew and remember my mother's parents. My grandfather passed away about 1931 when I was 12; my grandmother died during the 1939–45 War, when I was in London.

I was the sixth in a family of ten children: seven boys and three girls. My parents married in 1909. Angus, my oldest brother, was born in 1910. And the three or four oldest of my brothers and sisters were brought up in the Barracks in Inverness. So they were army children. It was only after my father left the army in 1918 that . . .

Angus began work as an apprentice draughtsman in the Rose Street foundry in Inverness, like the welders that in the 1939–45 War did the Pipe Line Under The Ocean.[4] But he always wanted to join the army. The recruiting officer came to my father – this is the story my father told me – and said, 'Angus has been at the recruiting office today and he wants to join the army. But,' he said, 'you can stop it, because he's just 18.' My father said, 'If that's what he wants to do . . .' So Angus joined the army in 1928. He was sent to India in 1929, then he was posted to Egypt, and then posted back to India. When he came back from India I didn't recognise him. I thought he was a Silkada Jump – Indians who came round with silk jumpers: a silk and a jump. He was in India and Egypt during the war. He lost his left eye in the Libyan campaign when they were driving across this minefield and they were blown up. At the time his boss was General Wavell (I think he had lost his eye, too), and for a while Angus was General Wavell's aide-de-camp.[5] Angus was a major in the Camerons. Then in India he was posted to the Ministry of Economic Warfare in Bombay – what

Churchill used to call the Ministry of Dirty Tricks. It was like the SOE, Special Operations Executive. Angus's work was clandestine. But they blew up several enemy submarines based at Goa, then a colony of Portugal, which was a neutral country.[6]

My older sister Marion, born about 1911, was the second oldest in our family. Kenneth was third, then came Ian, Callum, me, Alex, Jack, my younger sister Marie, and then Patrick. Patrick was born about 1925–6, so he'd be seven or eight years younger than me. I was number six in the family. In our family all the names were traditional. The first son was called after one of the grandfathers, the second son after the other grandfather. The first girl was called after a grandmother, the second one after the other grandmother.

My brother Kenneth became an electrical engineer, and during the war he was a district engineer in a reserved occupation at Stowmarket in Suffolk. I used to go down there for weekends when I was in the ATS. Kenneth was in charge of the electricity supply to the American air bases there. Ian was in the Territorial Army Cameron Highlanders during part of the war. But he was also an electrical engineer, so he left the Camerons and was in the Royal Engineers. Ian got the Belgian Croix de Guerre and Bar. Callum was in a reserved occupation as a telegraphic installer on the railway. He went to the recruiting office to join the navy, but of course he wasn't allowed to leave his civilian job. Alex, who worked in Inverness as a clerk, was also in the Territorial Army. He was in the 51st Highland Division at the beginning of the war, and was wounded – shot in the left arm – at Saint-Valery-en-Caux. You see, all these Territorial Army fellows knew each other. My brothers knew the Skye boys because they'd meet them at the annual camp. Alex was only 18 when he was wounded, so some of the boys – the older men down our street – hid him in a wood. The Germans didn't get him, the Red Cross got him.[7] Alex was reported missing, but my mother got a letter from him in Bangour Hospital in West Lothian before she got word from the War Office. Fortunately, as a sedentary worker Alex just carried on after he was discharged from the army, and became an assessor of rates for houses and that. Then my brother Jack started off as a lab assistant in the infirmary, but he became a mechanic. He was too young to go overseas with the Camerons, so they transferred him to the Sherwood Foresters or the Green Howards, I can't remember which. But he had a big, big green patch on his back. He was artillery and fought mainly in the Middle East. He joined the Edinburgh Police after the war. Patrick, the youngest of our family, was working in the Ministry of Labour when the war started and was too young to join up. But when he became old enough he joined the navy. All five of my brothers who were in the wartime Services were volunteers, as I was – well, Angus of course was a Regular from 1928 onwards. Then of my two sisters, Marion, the older one and second oldest in our family, was married before the war and had a child. Bill, her husband, was in the Forces. Marie, my younger sister, worked in Inverness County library during the war and drove the library van round the country districts. When from the end of 1941 single women became subject to conscription Marie worked as a civilian in a precision factory in Glasgow.[8]

* * *

My earliest memories are of growing up in Inverness. Though I was born in Rosebery Place in The Haugh at Inverness I don't remember being there. But I remember the house in Innes Street where we were brought up when we were younger. We were in the second flat of three storeys in what was like a tenement. These houses in Innes Street would probably be old mansion houses, because there were bells and that as well. There was a woman down on the ground floor, and there was actually a shop there, too – Baikie's shop we called it. A woman doctor owned several of the houses and was my parents' landlady. I used to go with my mother sometimes to pay the rent.

We'd three rooms there and two sort of attic rooms. But the attic rooms were big, maybe about 16 feet square, and it was dormer windows. As there were only three girls we only had one room. My oldest sister Marion, eight years older than me, had a bed for herself. My younger sister Marie and I shared a bed. As I've said, my oldest brother Angus went to India in the army when I was 10, and my youngest brother Patrick would be only about two or three years old. Often big families coped because the older sons joined the Forces and the oldest girls maybe went away into domestic service. The wee ones got more space then. But as we had five rooms in the house in Innes Street we weren't badly overcrowded.

We didn't have a sitting-room so-called. But we had what we called The Room. But the odd thing was we children took our friends into

The Room; my parents took their friends into the big kitchen-living room. We just called it the kitchen. That was where we ate our food, unless there was anything special on and we would do something in The Room.

There were fires in all the bedrooms. And we weren't like some people that had to go outside to the toilets. We had an extension down below with two toilets, one of them for us. And it was a flush toilet. We didn't share a toilet with other families. It wasn't a bathroom, just a toilet, and we had a key for it. The key was necessary because people could come in the front door.

We had a range but we didn't have hot water. My mother also got a gas cooker. We must have had gas lighting. In fact, I remember we had gas lamps, because we had them also in the street. And then with the boys being electricians we were the first in Innes Street to have electricity. My brothers installed it for my mother. Once my mother said to me about paying for the electricity, 'Oh, we were on the contract' – whatever that meant. But I also remember paraffin lamps. I don't know if it was a paraffin or a Tilley lamp,[9] but I do remember a lamp in our bedroom when my father, who was great for Gaelic singing, would come and sing to me if I had a cold or anything. I still sing when I hear some of the Gaelic songs. It takes me back to my father singing.

My father and our family were, oh, very musical. We had a piano in Innes Street. You see, that's the entertainment you had. We'd go to each other's houses and sing, things like songs from the American Civil War – *Marching Through Georgia*, and all these things, But my first musical instrument we had in the house was an autoharp. It was like a zither. I played that before I started on the piano

* * *

A bit before the war, in the middle 1930s, when I was 15 or 16 and still at school, we moved from Innes Street to a new house in Columba Road, Inverness. It was a council house, one of the earliest in Inverness, oh, a lovely house. It's still there. We were the first tenants. And in these days people didn't look down on council house tenants. In fact, they were rather thought to be a bit . . . because the Provost of Inverness, a fellow Ross, was living there. He had a pub in Tomnahurich Street or somewhere. And there was such an outcry about the

Provost occupying a council house.[10] A lot of businessmen, too, lived in council houses.

In Columba Road we had electricity from the beginning, hot and cold water, a bath, a big sink and a little sink, and a big gas boiler. In Innes Street I think my mother had had a boiler of some sort to do the washing in. But at neither house was there an outside washhouse, there was nothing like that in Inverness – at least I don't remember seeing that in Inverness. With all us children, doing the washing was a big job for my mother. But she had a woman, Annie Murchison from Kyle of Lochalsh, that used to come in and help her and whom she paid. She wouldn't have paid very much in these days – maybe half a crown [12½p] or something.

Oh, I remember as a child eating well. My father had a garden – well, at Innes Street not much of a garden – and he also had near the harbour a plot or allotment from the railway. You see, at Innes Street you didn't keep coal in the house and the garden was nearly all taken up for our coal sheds. But I remember there was a lilac tree, and there were gooseberries and an apple tree. And, even in Innes Street, my father would come with lettuce from the garden and we would have lettuce and tomatoes. But at the back of the Innes Street house it was like a yard. In his allotment my father used to grow vegetables like marrows and all that. So that helped the family economy with food. In Columba Road we had a garden at the back and front of the house. My father was very particular in his garden, and wouldn't let any of us do anything in it. But he used to give me a packet of marigolds, and I was allowed to plant them round the lawn. Oh, I don't remember ever going hungry as a child. And my mother was a great manager.

My father – you know how the islanders, as he was, are so hospitable – if he met anybody on the railway who came from Lewis they would come down to our house. Sometimes we would vacate our beds for folk, and just sleep three in a bed. Our own aunts and uncles in Lewis didn't visit us very much. Most of them went to Glasgow or something like that. But we visited them in Lewis, and at first we needed an interpreter, an older one of our cousins, to interpret, because they didn't speak English and we didn't speak Gaelic. There wasn't much Gaelic spoken then in Inverness. But, oh, I had a very happy childhood.

* * *

I started school in Inverness at the age of five. The school was Farraline Park Primary, called colloquially Bell's School because a Dr Bell founded it. I went right through the school for the usual six or seven years until I sat my Qualifying exam there. Of the subjects at Farraline Park that interested me, oh, English particularly did. I got the prize in English: a big thick book, *The Sword of the North*, all about the First World War, written by a man who was a minister and whose father had been a minister in Inverness. Oh, a marvellous book which I really appreciated when I'd been in the Second War myself.[11] But when I got the book presented I thought, what a stupid thing – why didn't they give me a medal? Maybe they'd have known I had army connections. And then I loved history, too, and I was second in the class for maths. So I liked the primary school, got on well there, passed the Qualifying exam and went on to Inverness High School.

In those days the main meal – dinner – was at midday. You see, my father went out early in the morning to his work as a railway stores clerk, but at Innes Street he was near enough (it was within walking distance) to be able to come home for his lunch – his dinner. He came home for the day about five o'clock. He never had a car, he had a bike. But when we were young and came home from school in the late afternoon we got pieces, as we called them. You see, Marion, my older sister, eight years older than me, was like a second mother to us. Marion worked in a builder's office, so maybe she got off early from work. Anyway, she always seemed to be there at home when we came in from school, and she saw to our pieces. She would be sitting there at the kitchen table with a loaf and a bread knife, and would say to us: 'White or brown, double or single, thick or thin, butter or jam?'

By the time I left Farraline Park Primary School I had developed some girlhood ambitions. I wasn't interested in teaching – I wouldn't have the patience – and I certainly couldn't do nursing. So I had three other ambitions. First, I wanted to be a concert pianist. That was killed stone-dead when during the war I went to London and heard Dame Myra Hess playing in St Martin-in-the-Fields.[12] Second, I wanted to be an author. We had no school magazine. But I used to write by hand schoolgirl stories. Then I decided I would like to be a secretary to an MP. I was cured of that during the war, when we used to visit the House of Commons!

So when I passed the Qualifying exam at primary school and went on to Inverness High School, I could have gone instead to Inverness Royal Academy because I had passed for a bursary there. The Academy (unlike the High School) was fee-paying (until 1953).[13] But more important, I discovered the Academy didn't start teaching shorthand until the second year. So I decided to go to the High School because they started shorthand in the first year. You see, this business of becoming a secretary to an MP was one of my ambitions as early as the age of 11 or 12. And I fell in love with shorthand.

I found Inverness High School lovely and I enjoyed it very much. Again there was English, history, maths, and I took French, but not Latin. An odd thing about Farraline Park Primary had been that before we left we had had six months of Latin, because they said, 'Now you might be taking languages when you go on to the big school.' So I remember bits: dominus, dominum, domino. Anyway, then the High School would be a bit like a later junior secondary school: they only had three years. So I would either have had to leave school then or go on to the Royal Academy. Of course, I had got a bursary for the Academy and that paid the fees there. At the Academy, as at the High School, we didn't have to wear a uniform, but we used to do so. My parents seemed to be able to afford that. You see, my father had a pension from the army. He had also his pay from the railway, though that wouldn't be very much. But he also taught piping after he left the army. It was often a sticking-point that youngsters would win a place at the Royal Academy but they didn't go because their parents couldn't afford to buy uniform or pay bus or train fares.

The transition from the High School (where in my third, or last, year I had passed what they called the Day School Highers) to the Academy was quite easy. There I took an academic-commercial course. The academic subjects were the same as at the High School; the commercial part was shorthand, typing, book-keeping, accounting and business training. We were put in for Royal Society of Arts certificates as well, and I got several of these. So I left school aged almost 17½ in 1936 with five Highers: English, French, history, maths and commercial subjects. I could do 120 words a minute in shorthand and I could touch-type about 50 words a minute. I then applied for my first job.

As a girl many of my spare-time interests actually lay outdoors. I was a hockey fiend. Nearly every Saturday I'd be playing hockey. I was vice-captain of the school team, and later on, when I went to the ATS, I was captain of the hockey team there. I played tennis, and we went out of Inverness to play badminton. I wasn't a swimmer, yet I'd always been messing about in boats; and we went climbing and cycling. I had my own bike. When I was a teenager at school we used to cycle every Saturday to Beauly – about 12 miles – or Nairn: pretty flat roads. Sometimes our friends' mothers would come, but my mother couldn't come because of the younger children. We had two pairs of ice skates among our whole family and we used to go ice-skating. But I was always falling. However, I used to be great at roller-skating down in the street – a lovely street with concrete pavements and not a break in them. They said I was a tomboy; maybe they were right. At Farraline Park Primary School we girls were taught to play football. That was unusual in these days. But I never went to a football match: I thought it was infra dig! But some of my friends went. Then although I liked sports I didn't like the gym. I didn't like somersaults. But I liked being out of doors. We were really out-of-doors people. And I liked walking. Then we used to gather wild berries. We'd go to Bunchrew between Inverness and Beauly – about four miles away – and gather blueberries and raspberries. And I was a keen reader. Our house was full of books. In our bookcase in Inverness you'd get *A Life Of Schubert* next to *Treasure Island* or maybe *The First Hundred Thousand* by Ian Hay. I used to read all these boys' books like *The First Form At St Dominic's* or something.[14] You see, with all these brothers of mine . . . I didn't get comics. My brothers had comics: *Film Fun, The Wizard, The Beano* and *The Dandy* and things like that. However, we had friends in America that sent comics to us. So I used to read comics.[15] I got the *Schoolgirls' Own*! Then every Sunday I went to Sunday School and to the church service. My parents were Free Church of Scotland, and I was brought up in the Free Church. I don't know if you would call them broad-minded, but my parents allowed us to go to other churches. We children went to each other's – our friends' – churches. I had two school pals. Rose was a Methodist and years later became the president of the Methodist Women's Guild in Inverness. Rene was a Brethren – so I was allowed to go to her church, but she wasn't allowed to come to ours. My parents themselves would go to the Free Church, and then a crowd of them after the Free Church would go up to the Baptist Church to the afternoon Fellowship there. So they weren't narrow-minded.

* * *

As I've said, when I left Inverness Royal Academy in 1936 I applied for and got my first job – as a junior shorthand typist in Inverness Town Clerk's office. I thought I knew everything. But by the time my first afternoon there was over I discovered I knew nothing. I was told off for putting on a postage stamp upside down! The Town Clerk in those days was a lawyer. So that was the beginning of my training in law. If I'd thought of it I could have gone into law. But at that time I had no thought of going on to university. You see, we couldn't get grants.

At the Town Clerk's office I got 15 shillings [75p] a week. My working hours were 9am till 5pm, with an hour for lunch. I went home for lunch. You didn't work on a Saturday – just a five-day week. Well, I was there in the Town Clerk's office for about two years and getting on very well, with lovely colleagues and a good boss, James Cameron, a Gaelic speaker. One day Miss MacRae, the chief shorthand writer, took me aside. She was the one that had told me off for sticking that stamp on upside down. 'It's insulting to the monarch,' she'd said. So anyway she took me aside one day and said, 'I can see you're very ambitious.' (Little did she know I was taking a correspondence course for becoming a secretary. And I also went to evening classes and got a Higher National Diploma in business training or whatever they called it.) But Miss MacRae said to me, 'Now the government are opening up a new office in Inverness: the Council for Physical Training and Recreation, Northern Regional Committee, and,' she says, 'they're looking for a competent shorthand typist. I think it would do you if you apply for it.' So I applied and got the job. I think I got about £2 10s 0d [£2.50] or something a week, which was much better than at the Town Clerk's office. The hours were just about the same. We didn't work there either on a Saturday morning.

That was in the earlier half of 1938. The Northern Regional Committee, which had a suite of rooms in Academy Street in Inverness, acted for the whole north of Scotland in encouraging people to apply for village halls, to keep fit, and all sorts of things. The Committee was composed of very public-spirited people. Kurt Hahn, the founder of Gordonstoun School, was one of the leading lights.[16] My boss, James McConnel, was a retired major from the Seaforth Highlanders.

Later in 1938, after Munich,[17] the government decided they would set up this WATS, as we were called at first: Women's Auxiliary Territorial Service. So Major McConnel came to see me one day and said, 'Miss Chisholm, the government says we'll have to set aside part of our office for the use of the WATS, as the government wants us to help these ladies.' The leading lights as commanders of the WATS or ATS in the Northern Area were county ladies, including Lady Maud Baillie of Dochfour and Mrs Fraser-Tytler of Aldourie Castle.[18] I was giving them a hand with typing and that. And then – this was the catch – Major McConnel said to me one day, 'Miss Chisholm, you get three weeks' paid leave from the government because you're working here for the Council for Physical Training and Recreation. Now,' he says, 'what about joining the ATS? And you'll get another paid fortnight's leave to go to camps.' So I was hooked. But I didn't go into the ATS then. I went in May 1939.

I think it was once a fortnight we went up to the Cameron Barracks in Inverness to do a couple of hours or so of square-bashing. I'm very round-shouldered, sloping shoulders. And Adams the colour sergeant used to say to me: 'Keep your head up, Chisholm, love. I've lifted all the thrupenny bits off the barrack square this morning.' I just laughed. Adams knew my father of course and, oh, my oldest brother Angus, who'd come back from India and done a tour of duty at Inverness just before the war. And I used to meet the pipers at the barracks who would come down to my father sometimes. But Angus wouldn't let me go to the barrack dances. You see, in those days it was a crippling thing. You thought soldiers would have . . . But when we went up there in the ATS I realised they were just a cross-section of everything.

The ATS didn't have weapons, so we didn't get weapon training. And I don't believe in that, women in the front line. Neither did Churchill. And when I hear all these girls that say they were on a gunsite, they weren't allowed to fire guns. I can't understand the sex that gives life wanting to take it away. There's no need for Servicewomen to have weapons. We were pleased to do a job in the ATS that was releasing a man for the Forces, like I know I was releasing a man from the Foreign Office to go to the front line. I wouldn't shoot a human being.

As soon as we joined the ATS at Inverness we were issued with khaki uniform. But we were told we had to be measured for Cameron tartan skirts. Just before the war there was a lot of Poles and Lithuanians came as refugees to Inverness. They could maybe be Jews. Cymbalist was this fellow's name and he was a tailor. We were sent to him and we had lovely Cameron tartan skirts – thick, more a worsted – made for us.[19] And we got a cheese-cutter hat. Mrs Fraser-Tytler said to us: 'I'm going to give you Cameron Highlander buttons.' And she gave us them at her own expense. She also gave us a real silver badge for the ATS, for wearing when we were in mufti. When we got these Cameron buttons we took off the GS, General Service, buttons. But once war broke out we were told: 'Take off those Cameron buttons.' So we had to put back on the GS ones. Of course, later on in London I wore my tartan skirt only when I was off-duty. We weren't issued with trousers, though the drivers would have been. We were issued with a thing like an overall – like what they call safari suits. But I never had to wear it, or a hat or anything. We had a standard khaki tunic, lacing shoes with flat heels, and lisle stockings. I think we just got one set of uniforms. Probably we got other underwear, shirts and that, but I don't remember these things really.

We had different ranks. I was made up to a corporal. But I wasn't called a corporal: I was called a sub-leader.

When I joined the ATS in 1939 we were told in June that, instead of going to camp like the men did, we would go up to the barracks and do the jobs we would do if war broke out. So that actually happened. I was in the orderly room with the colonel. And it meant we were called up two days before the war broke out.

At the end of August 1939 I came back from holiday on Lewis with my fiancé Donald Morrison. Donald was from the same village, Gravir, on Lewis as my parents belonged to, and they had met him. I met him on the ferry when he was a boat crew man – and I hated the sight of him when I saw him at first! I thought he was so arrogant. But he made me laugh. Anyway, when I came off the train at Inverness my younger sister Marie was waiting for me with my calling-up papers. That would be the 1st of September, when Hitler invaded Poland. That's when they needed me! So I was called up two days before the declaration of war by Mr Chamberlain. I was actually working in the barracks when war was declared, and I remember hearing the declaration.

I felt exhilarated about the coming of the war. My experience of the war reminded me of what Wordsworth said about the French Revolution: 'Bliss was it in that dawn to be alive, But to be young was very heaven!'[20] It was exciting. Before then I hadn't had any political views – well, I had a leaning towards the Scottish Nationalists. Then we had a fellow in Inverness – I knew him very well – who was a Blackshirt. I can see him just now with this black shirt. Fowler was his name. Oh, he was very active in Inverness. I don't think there was a sizeable number of Blackshirts in Inverness. And Fowler seemed to be treated with contempt generally. He was an architect. He had a business of his own. And he built a most unusual house. It's still there, in quite a nice part of the town, and he called it *Over and Above.*[21]

But I'll tell you what I remember most about the political situation then, and it was strange to me. I remember my parents discussing Pastor Martin Niemöller. What connection did he have with my parents, because they would talk about him? Martin Niemöller was the one that said that first the Nazis came for the Jews. 'But I wasn't a Jew, so I didn't speak out. Then they came for the trade unionists.' And he goes on like this. 'And when they came for me there was nobody . . .' And of course there was Dietrich Bonhoeffer, who was killed by the Nazis too. And I used to hear my parents speaking about him. They were aware of Hitler and of these Christian opponents of Hitler.[22] Then I knew about the Spanish Civil War, but it didn't make me feel Fascism should be opposed.[23] I wasn't political at all. I realised the danger of Hitler. But I didn't go deeply into politics. Then John MacCormick used to come a lot to Inverness, and we had Wendy Wood and all that. And the boys used to cheer them round the town. It was quite exciting. And they would have to come in to the Town Clerk's office to get permission sometimes to hold their meetings.[24]

Oh, we knew about the dangers of another war. But I remember being in Lewis when I was a teenager in the 1930s, and the door of every house was open to you. You would just sit in what they called the seis. It was like a garden seat. And they were discussing if there was another war with Germany, and they said: 'The Germans have a secret weapon. They've got this death ray. When it shines on somebody it melts them and they die', and whatnot. So of course it must have lodged in my subconscious mind, because a few nights afterwards I woke up in the middle of the night with a light shining in my face. And I thought it was the death ray. But it was only my brother Callum, who'd been out sailing late at night. My granny always locked the door when we went to bed. So Callum was knocking at my bedroom window and shining his torch, for me to get up and open the door to him!

* * *

Well, at Cameron Barracks, Inverness, I was in the orderly room as a shorthand typist, with the colonel. But then a call went out for these lazy officers! They found it was great having us: they could dictate. So I was sent down to Highland District Headquarters in the Palace Hotel in Inverness, to work for Colonel Mitchell, the Commander, Royal Engineers (CRE), who was an architect. There I was given a typing pool of four girl civilians. Later one of them went to the Women's Royal Naval Service (WRNS), and two to the ATS.[25] Some things I remember clearly, others I don't. But I think in the couple or so years I remained in Inverness I got promoted to sergeant.

Anyway, the Commander, Royal Engineers, was in charge of all the fortifications in the north of Scotland. I don't think we were involved in Scapa Flow, but just on the mainland.[26] And we had civilian surveyors and architects on the staff. But I found the work dead boring. I had to type out reeds and screeds of specifications – technical stuff and repetitive. Once I typed them they went to surveyors' clerks – some civilians, too – and what they did was called squaring the dimension, using duodecimals, which I hadn't a clue about. Though one great thing was they used to give us starched plans, and we'd take them home, boil them, and make tablecloths and things like that!

Well, before the war, when we joined up we had a choice: General Service, which meant you could be sent anywhere; or Local Service – you couldn't be sent away from your home. So we lived at home. But I noticed some of the girls that joined General Service never left Inverness, though they had to leave their own homes there and go and live in huts round about Inverness. I lived at home all the time I worked in the barracks and then with the CRE. I was Local Service. So they couldn't send me away. But one day, bored as I was, I said to my subaltern Gillian Mitford from Lentran near Inverness, 'Could you find me an interesting job to do elsewhere?' You see, I thought, 'What are we doing here? A civilian could do the job I'm doing, and I'm not really helping.' And I thought about the 51st Highland Division and my brothers and everything, how they were fighting so hard. Of course, my parents and my friends thought I was daft, because I was really in a cushy job in Inverness. So Gillian Mitford came to me one day and said: 'There's a telegram. You have to go to London next Friday. You're going on a cipher course.' I suppose my parents minded my going off to London, but they didn't stand in my way.

So it was some time in 1941–2 I left Inverness and went down to London by train. It wasn't the first time I'd been away from home. Och, I'd been in Lewis, Glasgow, and all these places. Anyway, when I arrived in London I didn't go on a cipher course. I was sent straight to the War Office and I was told, 'Now you'll learn as you go along, and after three months you'll be put on the permanent staff and you'll be made up to warrant officer.' That was two ranks above sergeant.

I'd never been in London before, and it was a laugh when I arrived and said to the taxi driver, 'Can you take me to Cadogan Gardens?' He said to me, 'What?' I said, 'Cadogan Gardens.' 'Spell it.' So I spelt it. 'Oh, *Ca-duggen* Gardens,' he says. So the next morning I was taken to the War Office by one of the other girls. My instructor was Bunny Lisle. Her husband was Lord Lisle, an Irishman.[27] She was lovely and a scream. I couldn't say if girls like me arriving in the job were not normally sent on courses of training. Anyway, we sussed out that it was MI6 that we were working for. That's probably why we weren't allowed to wear identifying flashes. The other girls, in the Central Cipher Office (CENCIPH), another branch in the War Office, they had great publicity, even their names in the paper. They were attached to the Royal Signals. We weren't. But I think we were employed really by MI6, Military Intelligence, because our two bosses were retired naval officers from the Foreign Office. And the traffic we were dealing with was mostly with our ambassadors and our agents overseas. But nobody ever told us we were employed by MI6. It was very hush-hush.

A big house in Cadogan Gardens in Chelsea was where we lived. I shared a room with two other girls. The room was very basic. The beds weren't like ordinary camp beds. They were like a piece of wood cut out of a tree trunk, with a sort of dip. No slats, no nothing, just wood – and three biscuits or palliasses. I couldn't sleep the first night, the bed was so hard and uncomfortable. But I didn't mind it after the first night. One of the girls who became a friend had a cheque book and was very well-off. A lovely girl, she used to say to me, 'Oh, Chris, I'm missing my Slumberland mattress.' I said, 'The mattresses we had at home were flock mattresses made by the blind.' Then she would say, 'I'm missing my gowns.' And I was thinking how at home we used to make our own summer frocks.

There was a mixture among the girls. Betty Grail's father was the chief engineer or something in Cairo. Another, Ann Lever, her father was the ambassador to somewhere. I met a lot of people like that. But I didn't feel lacking in confidence. We Highlanders we're classless. We always think we're as good as anybody else, and we can mix! I was still only about 22 or 23 when I went to London. But in the ATS at Inverness I'd met with Lady So-and-So. And before that I'd met so many people at the Town Hall, because they used to have civic receptions and I would have to send invitations to all the County folk. And a lot of people like hotel owners would come in to the Town Hall if they wanted late licences. So I sort of felt I knew everybody in Inverness, people of various social classes. Then there were all those I'd met through the Council for Physical Training & Recreation, such as Kurt Hahn and sons of the Duke of Hamilton.[28] So all that probably gave me a sense of confidence when I went down to London in 1941–2. But the girls at Cadogan Gardens were a fine lot and we mingled quite well together. You were never stuck for a companion.

Another girl I shared with was from Kettering in Northamptonshire. She invited me up to her house there. It was a huge house. Her father had a factory. But what amused me was the bathroom, a big room with a big, big tank. You know what they had in the kitchen? A pump. There was obviously signs of wealth in their place. But my house in Columba Road in Inverness was so modern and our facilities there were far better. Then some of the girls at Cadogan Gardens would ask me, 'What are the streets like in Inverness?' Because they were very ignorant about that. 'Have they got cobbles?' But the girls were lovely. I got on with them. I never felt inferior to anybody.

But my impression was and is that most of the girls working in my section in the War Office were drawn from higher social classes. I felt my background was a bit different from theirs. Some of the girls had come from ordinary working class families. They weren't all like the one from Kettering. There were one or two Cockneys, for instance. Then one of my best friends was an Irish girl – from southern Ireland, a neutral country during the war. She couldn't go back home in her ATS uniform or she'd have been interned. She was educated in a convent in England and had an upper class accent. But she was the only one of us who sent money home. 'You know,' she said to me, 'when I go home I don't know why I'm working here. My mother is often invited to receptions at the German ambassador's in Dublin.'

As far as I was aware there was no check made on us – questioning, examining our background – from the point of view of security. I was never aware of any questions being asked about us or about our families having any political views, or being members of the Communist Party, Blackshirts – or Anarchists! Though we were in a job where secrecy was the order of the day.

In the section of the War Office where we worked it was enciphering, deciphering, encoding and decoding. I never set eyes on a typewriter. We had nothing to do with it – or with shorthand. Well, the messages would come down from Signals. We had a chute operation – like one of those things they used to have in the big stores: brass tubes and ssshhhooo. And sometimes when the tube had caught in the air – what an upset and loss. Then the difference between code and cipher was, well, we got such a message as: 'The invasion of Europe will be referred to as Overlord.' Now Overlord is a code.[29] A cipher is different. A cipher is usually in groups of letters, and each letter stands for another letter. That's the difference between them. I didn't have to learn it. It was all automatic: the machines did it for us. So when I was enciphering or deciphering I sat at a cipher machine. You touched certain keys. It was the Enigma – we were working with Enigma too.[30] But we called our standard machine Type X. It was like a teleprinter. It was a heavy machine. We had ticker tape.

In early June 1944 I was on duty the night immediately before D-Day. People nowadays talk about what's D-Day. It's Decision Day. Well, as far as we were concerned it wasn't: it was Departure Day, because the decisions had been taken. So on duty that night my job was doing duds. Duds were cipher messages that came over the air but had not been properly enciphered by the signallers, or for other reasons. So they could be deciphered only laboriously. So we had to go through a process we called The 39 Steps. I often wonder if John Buchan, author of the book of that title and who was working in the Foreign Office in the 1914–18 War, was the source of our description – or was it vice versa?[31] We had the morse code of other machines to refer to, and you would say the code you were given – there would be figures for the code to open the cipher. The ones most likely to be mixed up were A and N. One is dot-dash, the other dash-dot. Or B and V: one is da-da-da-da, the other is the opposite. So you would try that, then all sorts of things. Well, as I say, the night preceding D-Day I had a whole bunch of duds to do. It was like doing a crossword; it would take you hours to get through them. The last one took me about two hours. But eventually I got through them all. The problem was if you didn't decipher the message and you got in touch with the signaller, then if he or they repeated it the Germans could maybe break it down. So we had all sorts of tricks. Anyway this message – I always remember it – was about a cargo of ghee.[32] During this I had heard some noise in a corner of our work room, but didn't pay much attention to it. I thought, 'It'll be somebody's engagement or something.' Then my friend Joan said to me, 'It's great news, isn't it, Chris?!' I said, 'What's great news?' It was D-Day. Oh, I can remember plenty of other dramatic signals or messages. One that I was very sad about was Rommel's death. I admired him. You know, General Montgomery used to call him 'My friendly enemy.'[33]

* * *

In the main building of the War Office in Whitehall, opposite Downing Street, we were right down in the basement. It was quite deep down, about two storeys down. It was air-conditioned. There was a lift. But we never took the lift. We just went down the steps. And down there there was a labyrinth of passages. Now we went in by a side door in Northumberland Street, and two policemen would be standing there at a table to examine your War Office pass. That was the first time I ever saw policemen with holsters and pistols in them. So we would go away down below to our office. I think it was Room 40 and Room 36 we had. The size of each room would be roughly 16 feet or 20 feet square. Then sitting outside our door we had veterans – ex-soldiers, old Regulars, I think they were – ready to carry urgent messages.

We worked in shifts. You would have the day shift. The night shift was a long shift. And you'd have shift people who were off work. The day shift was from 9am to 5pm – or 4pm: I can't remember. We got a break for lunch. On day shift we mostly fed at a vegetarian restaurant in Leicester Square. You didn't necessarily go outside though. You could go instead to a place called QMG House – Quarter Master General's House – which was reached through a labyrinth of passages.

We had no afternoon or back shift. There were just the two shifts, day shift, night shift. Wait till you hear how long the night shift was: 16 hours. We went in at 5pm and we didn't get off till 9am in the morning. But we were allowed an hour and a half during that time to sleep in bunks that were down there. It was staggered, so that some of us slept while the others remained at work: there was always somebody on duty. And we could get supper in QMG House. But we used to go to The Strand Lyons Corner House.[34]

The bunks we slept in down there were double, one above the other. Fortunately, I never slept in a bottom bunk, because one of the girls said there was a rat ran over her one night. You see, with the rats about sometimes we'd take turns to make the tea. We just had a kettle. I was terrified of rats. Well, before I put on the light I used to throw the kettle lid in, so that all rats would scatter away before we did the tea! I didn't see the rats, but I heard them. Don't forget, we were near the Thames. We had these huge flood doors.

Although I wasn't in the Cabinet War Rooms they weren't far from us underground. And that's when I saw Mr Churchill, the prime minister, in one of these underground passages one night when I was on night shift. I was going along to waken those having their one and a half hour's sleep, so that the rest of us could go for ours. It would be about four o'clock in the morning. And I saw this big fat man trudging along in his pyjamas and his dressing gown. When I got level with him he said, 'Good evening,' and I said, 'Good evening.'[35] I didn't ask him for his autograph or anything. But manys a time I enciphered a message which said, 'For Mr Churchill's eyes only.' Now Mr Churchill's eyes couldn't read that message till I put it in plain. But I didn't run with it to him. The veterans – ex-soldiers, old Regulars, as I've said – sitting outside our door, they'd be sitting there for urgent messages.

So our office was never empty. With the result that our Mrs Mopp had to clean up and take all the secret waste and all that away. I don't know her name. We just called her Mrs Mopp.[36] And she said to me once that she had been bombed out of her house four times. Would she leave? Not for all the tea in China, she said. So I said to her, 'Do you like your work?' 'Yes,' she said, 'but I think some of the girls here are awful snobs.' I said, 'Oh, I don't think so. Which ones?' She pointed to this one who was one of my friends, not a particular friend but she was from Coventry. She had one of these accents as if she had a bad smell under her nose. But she wasn't really . . . So I said to Mrs Mopp, 'Oh, I'm sure you get your own back.' 'Yes,' Mrs Mopp said. 'What do you do?' I asked. 'Well,' she said, 'when she's passing I always splash her legs with dirty water.' Well, I never got my legs splashed.

But I found that if you wanted to go to the theatre or the Proms or whatever, or go away for the weekend, there was always somebody willing to go with you. So you weren't short of friends there. And most of my friends were English girls because (I say this with a bit of trepidation) there's a big difference between a Highlander and a Lowlander. And I found that I had more in common with the English girls than with the Lowlanders. Though I also found that the English in general were very class conscious. They didn't like regional accents. They looked down. But the odd thing is they didn't object to Scottish accents – because they probably couldn't guess what strata in society the Scots came from.

I think there might have been about 60 of us girls altogether. We called ourselves The Belles of C6 Tels. Now the C – that's the clue to MI6. The C branch was called after the first commander of MI6 in the First World War, a Scotsman called Cumming. He was referred to as C.[37] Nobody ever told us, but that gave us a clue to the sort of work we were doing. We just had to suss it out. There'd be about 26 of us on each shift – day and night shift. And maybe about eight or 10 on leave or off sick.

Well, I got through my three months' probation. There were no examinations. It was just doing the work efficiently, and then you were established as a member of the group. There was one Inverness girl who was told what I was told: 'You'll be on probation.' Her father was in charge of all the buses in the north of Scotland. She'd probably gone to one of the private schools in Inverness. She had been in the FANYs [First Aid Nursing Yeomanry], because she was a driver before she came down to the War Office. She was in my section there. When I asked her how she had got on during her probation, 'Och,' she said, 'I didn't pass. I didn't pass.' So she went back home.

Then another one who had to leave was the girl from southern Ireland, who had this English upper class accent. But when she was annoyed with the English she would say to me, 'Oh, these English. You know, Chris, my mother slept in a barn during the revolution.' I said to her, 'Do you mean the 1916 Rising?' 'Yes,' she said.[38] But she got involved with this solicitor's clerk, who was married and had children. She used to ask me to make up a table for four at Claridges – very upmarket.[39] But we were always nagging her about this solicitor's clerk. Oh, I was so disappointed in her. She was the only one of our friends who had to leave under Paragraph 11 – having a baby. She was a Catholic. Her mother wouldn't take her home, but one of the London girls took her into her home. We went to see her once the baby was born. I said to her, 'Can we see the baby?' She said, 'I'm not supposed to see the baby. It's for adoption. But,' she says, 'one of the nuns'll bring the baby.' What a sad business. But when you think of it there were no or hardly any contraceptives available then to speak of. Well, that was the only girl I knew who found herself in those circumstances, and she was a particular friend of my own. But if a [unmarried] girl had to leave the ATS for that reason there was a notice under Para 11 put up on the board. It wasn't kept confidential, everybody would know, and it must have been humiliating for the girl concerned. It certainly must have been humiliating for that Irish girl. Her mother wouldn't take her home, though she was the only one of our group that used to send 10 shillings a week out of her pay home to her mother. When I had asked my mother if I could send her some of my pay, she said, 'For all you get, you don't need to.'

Incidentally, under war conditions some of the girls weren't always faithful to their fiancé or their husband. I used to nag them and say to them, 'See your wedding ring? That's his safety catch.' I explained to them: 'There was an old advertisement, *Clothes Make The Man.*' What put me wise to these things were the tinkers coming up to Cameron Barracks in Inverness. When you saw them in their uniform what a change they made! And I used to say to the girls, 'You watch, particularly the Americans, because you might end up with a hobo in a shack. Watch it!' Somebody said to me about the war: 'Did you feel hedonistic – you know, eat, drink and be merry, for tomorrow we die?' I myself didn't feel hedonistic ever, and I said, 'No, we did not, because we never envisaged losing the war.' We knew there were two prominent people, Lord Halifax and Joseph Kennedy, the American ambassador. They thought we wouldn't win the war. But we did our best to win the war.[40]

* * *

The system of pay at the War Office was we got flat pay, rank pay, pay as a cipher operator, then an extra 10d [4p] (which was most peculiar) for every day we actually attended the War Office. When we were on leave we didn't get that attendance pay, and I wonder if that was meant to be danger pay! Anyway, that added quite a bit to our pay if we worked five or six days a week: that was 10 to 12 shillings [50p to 60p], which was quite a lot of money in those days.

I'd arrived at the War Office in 1941–2 as a sergeant. But I was promoted once I'd passed my three months' probation there. I missed staff-sergeant then and went straight to being Warrant Officer Class II. So I think my pay would be £3.50 a week. We also got free food – marvellous food – and free accommodation, and our warrant officers' mess fees were minimal. Mind you, we were vain when you think of it. We went to Moss Bros to buy stiffer hats – cheese cutters (we had forage caps, which I didn't like very much);[41] and we also bought Kayser Bond silk stockings. We were young women and wanted to look our best! Incidentally, the mess where we got our food was in Draycott Place.

In our section there were no men at all, except for our two bosses, the two retired naval officers from the Foreign Office. They were both Scotsmen – with English accents. The rest of us were all girls, mainly sergeants, but no staff-sergeants at all, some warrant officers, as I became, and about six or eight women commissioned officers.

As I've said, when I left Inverness for London in 1941–2 my parents didn't stand in my way. But after I was in London I used to get awful letters from my mother because I wasn't writing. I kept in touch – I would write her all right – but I don't think I was writing as often as I should have. Partly the reason was that in 1943 Donald Morrison, my fiancé and I got married, and I was writing to my husband every day.

And I got regular home leaves. I can't remember how often they were, but I didn't see my husband: I couldn't go. He was in Northern Ireland, in the RAF. I remember going home to Inverness though. But, so that I could get a couple of extra days, sometimes I used to have my leave made out to Lewis, where my parents had been born and grew up. Inverness was a protected area during the war. I used to go home on the sleeper train straight from Euston to Inverness. Sometimes there would be air raids on the way, and the train would stop, and that.

Speaking of air raids, I don't remember ever going into an air raid shelter during the war. In the War Office of course we were two storeys underground. And I never went into an air raid shelter at our billets in Cadogan Gardens. I remember the first night I was orderly officer I thought, 'What do I do here? I'll have to look for the stirrup pump.'[42] I found this pail with sand, went down to the basement and sat there about quarter of an hour. Nobody came down. So I went back to bed after that.

But we used to hear the Americans next door with their big tackety boots, running out to the air raid shelter. They were in the Air Corps. We wondered what airmen were doing in billets next to us. But we discovered they were doing mosaics. That meant that when aeroplanes went over on reconnaissance and they took photographs, these men were placing them together like a jigsaw. They were very nice. They used to come into our mess and we would go into theirs. And they used to get films before they were generally released in the UK. So we used to see them. But one morning later in the war a doodlebug – a German V1 bomb – fell, and 80 of these Americans were killed. They had been in trucks going for their breakfast down the street. We knew many of those who were killed.

When I went to London in 1941–2 there was no Blitz.[43] We had plenty of raids, but not so Blitz-like. But in the last year of the war, in 1944–5, we had the doodlebugs – V1 flying bombs – and the V2 rockets. 'Oh, for an old-fashioned raid,' we used to say. Usually, in ordinary raids, you'd hear Jerry going home. But the V1s were nerve-racking because you could hear one coming. I thought the V1s were the worst. They began just after D-Day. It was so sinister. When the girls coming on duty told us, 'Oh, it's a pilotless plane,' you thought it was something devilish. But we couldn't understand why the siren was going all night. Anyway you would hear the V1 coming over: ddrrr ddrrr ddrrr. Then when the engine stopped it fell straight down. That's what made it so nerve-racking. Once it stopped, fell flat and exploded you would breathe a sigh of relief. Then you would see another one coming in the distance.

They came over in lots of numbers. With the V2 rocket, as light travels quicker than sound, you would see the light in the sky and you would know it had exploded. They said they were at random. But I don't believe that, because Chelsea Barracks near us were hit twice and a whole lot of people were killed.[44]

* * *

Well, as I've said, I had met my husband Donald Morrison before the war, when I was 17. He belonged to Lewis, the same village – Gravir – that both my parents came from. Donald was a house painter by trade and set himself up in business in Skye. We became engaged at New Year 1939, just before the war. I was 19 then. When the war came we decided we wouldn't get married until after the war ended. We just thought it was an unfortunate time to get married. And during the war we couldn't meet, or it wasn't easy for us to meet. Sometimes I didn't see Donald for over a year. When I had got my calling up papers in September 1939 and had to go to war, Donald had volunteered into the Royal Air Force and remained in it right through the war. He went on a pilots' course. But he never went on operations, because he was struck down with muscular rheumatism, and landed in the Morecambe Hydro. He worked on Sunderland flying boats, did direction work, and for a while did police work. He had trained at Padgate. After we were married in 1943 he was in a place called Wig Bay [Luce Bay?], near Stranraer. Then Donald was posted to Northern Ireland. And for a while too he was outside Carlisle – Newton Arlosh was the name of the place there. Donald used to tell me the laugh when he was there. One night when he was in Carlisle he missed the bus back to the base at Newton Arlosh. And he couldn't see any other buses. In wartime of course you couldn't easily ask people, 'Where's such and such a place?' But eventually he thought he'd ask this man. 'I'm looking for the bus back to Newton Arlosh and I can't find it. And,' Donald says, 'could you tell me which way to go?' 'Oh,' the man said, 'I'll take you along and you'll find out.' So he took Donald straight along to the police office! The man said to the policeman, 'Excuse me, sergeant. But I think this man is a German spy.' Donald, you see, was a native Gaelic speaker and had a strong Lewis accent. So what a time Donald had, because they were all English policemen. Eventually they'd to send to some other village for a Scottish policeman, who, when he arrived, asked Donald, 'Where are you from?' And they brought Donald a map! After D-Day Donald was posted to a Polish squadron, and went through north-west Europe and into Germany. Anyway, despite our earlier decision not to get married during the war, we thought, 'When is it going to end?' So we got married in October 1943. At my wedding you could only invite 30 people, because of [food] rationing. And there were hardly any young people among the 30, because they were all away in the Forces. We were married in Inverness, had a brief honeymoon at Pitlochry, then Donald returned to his RAF posting and I to the War Office.

Every Sunday in London that I was off-duty I went to the Pont Street Church of Scotland services. The church was round the corner from us. All the big shots went to that church. I remember, for instance, Sir Archibald Sinclair. There was an awfully good minister there, Dr Scott.[45] But then the church was bombed, and the services were held in Jehanjer Hall, the Hall of India, in Kensington. But once a month I went to the Church of Scotland in Covent Garden, because they had a Gaelic service. At that time I didn't have much Gaelic. But I would sit there and I would sort of feel the way you feel when you hear *I'm Longing For My Ain Folk*. And when they sang the Gaelic songs my tears would be coming down. Much earlier on, when I first joined the ATS and when I was asked to work on a Sunday, I didn't want to. That was not entirely out of religious principle. I thought we could all do with a rest on Sunday. So I said to my then boss, 'I don't want to work on Sunday. You should get one of the civilian typists to do the work, because they'll be paid overtime.' My boss, a wee fellow in the Royal Engineers – his wellingtons were almost up to his waist – said to me, 'Well, that's all very well. But remember our boys. They can't stop work or anything like that.' So he made me see the sense of it. Well, even the code and cipher work I was doing we couldn't stop on a Sunday. It was going all the time. But maybe my religious upbringing and principles saved me from quite a lot of things, because I used to say to myself, 'Would my parents like to see me here?' I was so confident maybe because I was a Christian and believed in God. It wasn't so much that I was afraid . . . It was a kind of fatalism.

We were crossing Westminster Bridge one day and a land mine fell, and everybody threw themselves on the ground. Then you'd be in the theatre and a doodlebug stopped and that meant it was going to come down and explode. The stage manager would come running out and shout, 'Everybody down on the floor!' Well, we would look at each other. But we wouldn't lie on the floor or anything: I always think at Easter time about the Cockneys. Because I went down the city one day and there wasn't a building to be seen but St Paul's Cathedral. It was the only building still standing. When I reached the grounds of St Paul's, what was growing in the rubble but London Pride.[46] The Cockneys were marvellous. You read books that say the people wanted to give in. That's a lot of rubbish. And there was a marvellous feeling of camaraderie.

* * *

Toward the end of the war I was given the chance to be posted to the British Military Mission in Washington. But I declined to go, because I wouldn't have got back to the War Office, and also I would be reduced from Warrant Officer 2nd class to the rank of sergeant. And of course as I was from an army family the rumour would go around that I'd done something terrible! But also my husband was by then serving in Europe. I was afraid something would happen to him and I wouldn't be able to get back from America. Somewhere around that same period I was to go on a course at the School of Military Intelligence at Herne Hill in London. I turned it down. The object of the course was just passing the time as the war neared its end. And it was low grade cipher, which we didn't do. What we did was high grade cipher.

Then, too, some of us had a chance of going to OCTU (Officer Cadets Training Unit), to become officers. When my friends and I worked it all out we thought that the ones that went to be officers wouldn't necessarily come back to the War Office. And the ones who did become officers never got any promotion. They remained subalterns – 2nd lieutenants, the lowest rank. And they had to pay private mess fees, whereas ours were minimal. As commissioned officers we would also have to pay for our uniforms instead of getting them free. And we warrant officers had orderlies that we shared. They were marvellous. I had one, Joyce, from Cromer in Norfolk. When I came off night duty she would have a bath and a hot water bottle ready for me. And, of course, we were called ma'am. So I and my friends didn't see we would gain anything by becoming commissioned officers.

I was also put up for promotion from Warrant Officer [WO] 2nd class to 1st class. But this was only about a month before I was to be demobbed at the end of the war. However, I was conned into letting someone else get that promotion, not that it mattered really. It just meant that maybe I got £100 less than I would have got. And the girl who was promoted to WO 1st class was one of my friends anyway.

An odd thing was that shortly before the war ended we were asked about jobs post-war. It wasn't the official time for demob: you just don't down tools. For instance, my ambition to become an MP's secretary: it could have happened, because I'd had a letter from the Inverness Town Clerk to say, 'Now, Chrissie, you're being demobbed and Sir Murdoch Macdonald needs a secretary.' Sir Murdoch was MP for Inverness-shire.[47] I met him shortly after I came home and he said I would get a letter from a solicitor in Inverness. He wrote me, but I wrote back and said no, I wasn't interested. Mr James Cameron, my old boss at the Town Council, asked me, 'Why didn't you take that job as secretary? It would just be in Inverness.' 'Well,' I said, 'it's like this. I don't want it, for I worked all during the war. Sir Murdoch wanted me to start before the official demob. And I was disillusioned enough of MPs.' But I didn't want to go anyway. Och, it was a shame, because that had been one of my earliest ambitions. But, you see, my friends at home were all having children and I wanted to do the same.

I can't remember the actual date of my demob. It'll be in my discharge [book], but I can't find it. I've lost it some way. But we were told, 'First in, first out.' I was in the first group out not only of women but also the men. It was before VJ [Victory over Japan] Day in the middle of August 1945.[48] I got a reference at my discharge. It said: 'Behaviour exemplary. Has a lot of common sense.' Much later on, our kids thought that last bit was hilarious. Anyway, in true British muddled fashion our train taking us for demob to Dreghorn or Redford Barracks in Edinburgh duly left Euston station in London – and the next thing was we were told we were on the wrong track. So we had all to get out the train and go back to London and start again! After that the journey was very quiet till we got to the Border. Then the train erupted! There were bagpipes and . . .

I was given three options when I was demobbed. First, to stay on as a civilian in the same branch C6 at the War Office. The work was going on, our machines weren't destroyed, though people say Churchill said all cipher machines had to be destroyed at Bletchley Park. Second, I could be put to any university I wanted. Third, demob. So I chose demob. As I say, I was married, wanted to have children and to set up home in Inverness. Although I loved London I didn't fancy living there. Donald, my husband, and I really wanted to live in the country.

When we were demobbed at the barracks in Edinburgh we didn't get an overcoat, a suit and a hat as the men did. We didn't get any civilian clothing. We got clothing coupons. But we were allowed to keep our uniform if we wanted. And of course we got a gratuity. In my case the gratuity was a few hundred pounds. It depended on rank, length of service, and all that.

Donald was demobbed from the RAF in September 1945. We lived for a while with my mother in Inverness. Then Donald managed to get a painter's shop in Dunkeld in Perthshire. I worked in the shop and Donald worked as a painter and decorator on contracts. We lived in Perth at first, then at Kinloch near Amulree, where my first child was born. We were there two years then we went back to Inverness because my father had died. Donald got a job with the council, and we got a council house. In 1959, by which time I had all my five children, we exchanged our house in Inverness for one in Skye. In 1979 we retired and went to Lewis, but after four years Donald died there. I remained a further four years, then came back to Skye.

Well, looking back on my ATS years from 1939 to 1945, I have no regrets, none. I'm pleased I had the experience and about all the different people I met. I wouldn't have missed it for anything.

Christina Chisholm (Mrs Christina Morrison) died on 10 January 2016, five weeks before her 97th birthday and the publication of her autobiography, *Yesterday's Child* (Islands Book Trust, Laxay Hall, Laxay, Isle of Lewis HS2 9PJ).

Nancy Cowe

Ah wis just over four years in the ATS, from the end o' 1940 tae the beginnin' o 1945. Oh, ah thoroughly enjoyed it. Ah wouldnae have missed it for anythin'.

Ah wis born at Barneyhill farm, near Dunbar, East Lothian, on 27 November 1920. Ma father, a ploughman, worked on that farm all his days, and his father before him on the same farm. Ah remember ma grandfather Cowe very, very well, and what a rare man he was. The first time ah ever got tae bake girdle scones, when ah wis jist a wee girl at the school, he sat in the chair and watched me that ah did it right. He was 84 when he died. Ah wis only a girl then, ah think it wis 1935. So he wis born about 1851. He got that medal, the Long Service Medal, for farm workers. As far as ah can remember he'd left school and started work on the farm and ah never heard o' him doin' anythin' else. Oh, he worked there more than 50 years.

Ah don't remember anythin' about ma great-grandfather Cowe. Ah've got a feelin' that he came fae the Berwickshire area. But ah couldnae tell ye what he did. Ah don't remember ma grandfather speakin' about his father. And ah never met ma grandmother Cowe, that ah'm called after. She died when ma dad was only aboot 19 or 20, long before ah wis born.

Then ma mother's father, he was somethin' tae do wi' shepherdin'. Ah think it wis in East Lothian, but ah'm no' positive about that. Ma mother used tae talk a lot aboot her mother and her granny. She was very, very fond of her grandmother. She wis fond o' her mother as well. But she seemed tae have a lot tae do wi' her grandmother. Ma mother wis jist a girl when she used tae walk with her grandmother intae

Dunbar tae pay the bills monthly. Oh, it would be about four miles tae Dunbar – so eight miles there and back. But ma great-grandmother she wis fit. She was tall like me. Ah don't remember her, ah just heard about her from ma mother. Ma mother spoke about her so much ah felt ah knew her. And ah seen photiegraphs o' them. Then ma grandmother, ma mother's mother, ah cannae remember very much about her workin'. But ah know that when they needed anybody tae milk the cows she did it. Ah wis taught tae do that when ah wis young and ah enjoyed it very much. There wisnae machines then, it wis your hands. Well, ma granny died when ah'd be about 11 or 12, in 1931–2.

Ma mother – her maiden name wis McCraw, a Berwickshire name, ah think – before she married she wis in domestic service. She looked after children, like a nanny, with the Bows at Skateraw, right on the coast, four miles fae Dunbar. The locals used tae call Mr Bow, the farmer, Tattie Bow, because he had something to do with potatoes. Ma mother didnae do that work immediately she left the school, because she looked after her grandmother for a while at home. Ma mother was quite a clever person actually. She had a big family o' brothers and sisters. Ma dad had three sisters, no brothers: it wisnae a big family.

Ah had a sister aboot two years older than me. Janet she was christened, but she always got Jen. John, ma brother, was younger than me. And he would be aboot jist over 3½, ah think, when he got the measles. And ah lost ma brother John wi' that measles.

* * *

Our house at Barneyhill farm was a very happy house, a very happy home. It was two bedrooms, a livin' room and a kitchen – but not kitchens like they are now. And to do the washing there was a coal-fired boiler jist in the corner o' the kitchen. Ma first recollection is that we didn't have cold water taps, we didn't have a bath, and the toilet was outside. We got our water from a well outside a few yards away. Everybody carried their own water from the well. And it was very good water: lovely, clear. I've never tasted water like it again. At the beginning you put your bucket under a pump at the well; later it was a tap and you just turned it on then. Occasionally, as a girl ah had tae carry the water intae the house. That was one o' ma tasks; that wis common among children. The water was brought intae the house whenever it wis needed. Ah never drunk milk, because seemin'ly when ah wis young ah had the measles, and ma mother had squashed medicine powder in the milk, and ah never drunk milk again. And ah can always remember runnin' home from school at 11 o'clock at playtime, fillin' ma big jug wi' cold water from the well, standin' drinkin' it, puttin' the jug back in the house, and runnin' back to the school jist down the road.

O' course, havin' tae carry a' the water intae the house gave ma mother a lot o' work, oh, it definitely did, especially on washin' days! Ah remember the washin' days. They had come on a bit by that time, and ma mother didnae have an old sack as an apron. What they did was they used tae bleach flour bags white and make aprons for themselves. Then for baths, well, there wis a big tin bath and we had that in front o' the fire. After John ma brother died there wis jist the two o' us girls. Every Friday night wis our bath night. And we got oor hair washed, sometimes twice a week, sometimes thrice a week, it all depended.

The lighting, well, it wis paraffin lamps at first. Then ma mother got a Tilley lamp before the war, and, oh, we thought this was marvellous this Tilley lamp. You used tae pump it up. And it hung; then she got another one later and it stood. That made everything a lot lighter. But before that it was paraffin lamps and candles. There wis always dangers wi' candles, but you were well trained and well taught. Oh, Jen and me werenae allowed to go up to bed wi' a candle. Ma mother took the candle up for you and then took it away once we were in bed. Jen and me had a room to oursels and we slept together. Ma mum and dad slept in the livin' room. The kitchen was where the work was done, the cookin' and a' that, and that's where we ate wir food.

Ah cannae mind the toilet so well, but as we didnae have runnin' water in the house, it must have been an outside dry toilet. We didn't share it wi' other families. It wis a wee bit away fae the house, in the garden at the back o' the house.

The garden wis quite big, and ma father, oh, he was a great gardener. He grew a lot o' vegetables. Ah'll never forget the onions, because when he cut the onions and hung them up tae dry ma mother had a great big fryin' pan, and if ye took down one onion and sliced it up it filled the fryin' pan. And there were carrots, turnips, cabbages, Brussels sprouts, cauliflower, shallots, potatoes, beans, peas – you name it, he had everything. Of course, it was good red soil. So a' that definitely helped our family diet! Oh, we ate well as children.

And ma father kept a pig. And there used tae be what they called the pig-killins, when ma mother had the big white damask tablecloth out, and the table was a' set. And a few o' them at the pig-killin' would bring their half-bottles. Occasionally, ma sister Jen and I got tae stay up a wee while longer in the evening. We never got tae see the pig-killin' itsel' o' course. They used to bring in their half-bottle to our house, as ah say, and there were only wee glasses then. They didnae put lemonade or water or anythin' in, it was neat. And there was this old man, Peter Fife. He was really old. And ah used tae say tae ma sister Jen, 'Watch Peter, watch him.' And they would fill up wi' whisky, and Peter shook all the time but he never spilt a drop! Jen and me used tae laugh, and ma mother said: 'Bed!' So it was a great occasion, the pig-killin'. And then ma dad cured the pigmeat himself. He did it wi' that stuff – och, nearly forgotten: what is that stuff? – saltpetre. The liquid and the pigmeat wis contained in a long stone place, like slabs or a trough, and ma dad turned it. So you had the ham, the pork and the bacon. This steepin' went on for a while, and then they used tae hang the meat from the ceiling on cleeks. When ye wanted ham in the pan ye took it down and cut the ham into slices. It wis lovely.

And then if a sheep or a lamb got killed, well, everybody on the farm got their bit meat. And we had our own hens as well. So you'd get the odd chicken to eat and plenty of eggs. We didn't have our own cow, but there was a big dairy at the farm and, oh, we got cheap milk. Oh, we ate well, we did, we were really well fed.

Then ma mother wis a lovely cook and baker. She cooked at first on jist the open fire, and it wis slow, very slow. And then it was a range that wis installed. Ah think ma mother's range had a wee water tank wi' a wee tap. But when it wis the open fire there wis a swee, and she used tae put on the swee the soup pot and the girdle for the scones. It made lovely scones and lovely soup. Then ma mother at one stage had a paraffin ring and then she got a paraffin oven. And she discovered that if she put so many ply o' brown paper on top o' her oven she got more heat. And she used tae make her sponges and everythin' in it.

So ah had a very, very happy childhood with ma sister Jen, we did. We played together, and there were other children on the farm. There wis four houses there with upstairs as well as downstairs. And then there wis three jist single, ground floor only: they were like cottages, and the bedroom windows had diamond panes. They were quite old houses. Oh, Barneyhill was one of the biggest farms in East Lothian. There'd be aboot seven ploughmen if there wis seven houses. Oh, there were more than seven ploughmen because then there wis East Barns farm tae: some o' the ploughmen lived there. East Barns had the most pair o' horse, but ah cannae mind the number now. It wis the biggest farm in East Lothian. So there was more than a dozen or 14 ploughmen at East Barns. It's demolished now, because the Blue Circle Cement crowd came. But ah can't remember the right story about what happened aboot East Barns, because of course ah wis away fae there a' these years.[1] Your people die and you lose touch. But East Barns wis a very big farm. I remember there used tae be 50 Irishmen come tae it. And there wis one year ah remember ma dad sayin' there wis 100 Irishmen there, but only for a short time – for the hay, the grain harvest, then they stayed for the tattie howkin', and some o' them would stay on for the turnips. The farmer, James Hope – he became Sir James Hope – was a big, big farmer. And he took in fields in Oldhamstocks, further south in East Lothian, and at Lowlyn. And he had Spott farm and Spott House – he stayed there. Then he had a place up in – ah think it wis in Perthshire. Ma dad went up there two or three times. Oh, Sir James Hope wis a big, big farmer, a very wealthy man in his heyday, definitely a powerful man.[2]

* * *

Ah wis only 4½ when ah started school – a bit younger than others, because one day ah jist chummed ma sister Jen there. And the teacher sent Jen oot tae ma mother tae say that ah wis there wi' ma sister, and that the teacher wis jist goin' tae keep me. Ah wis a keen scholar – until ah took rheumatic fever when ah wid be aboot six, and ah wis off a while wi' that. It wis East Barns School, a wee village school, and there wis some words on it: *Disco Vale Discere*. Ma mum said, 'That means, *Leave Come Depart*.'[3] Barneyhill wis very near it on the other side o' the road. As ah've said, ah used tae run home up the road at playtime for a drink o' water.

Oh, ah loved the school. Ah did like writin' stories, essays. Ah wisnae sae keen on the sums, though ah wis until ah took that rheumatic fever. And we got a lot aboot wild life, nature studies. Mr MacCallum, our head teacher, he stayed in the house right next tae the school. He was Highland of course, and he used tae recite bits tae us. He actually taught us in Gaelic, but ah cannae remember it now: *My heart's in the Highlands a-chasing the deer; but it isn't here.*[4] Oh, ah got on grand at the school. Then when we were aboot 11 or 12 we sat the Qualifying exam in our own wee school. Ah passed the Quali, and then ah went tae Dunbar Grammar School. If ah hadnae passed the Quali ah would have stayed at East Barns School till ah wis 14.

Tae begin wi' ye felt a bit nervous aboot goin' tae Dunbar Grammar School. But ah liked the Grammar School. By that time old Stark he'd started the taxi and bus services.[5] So there wis a school bus used tae come out from Dunbar and pick us up and take us tae the school. They went as far as away beyond Skateraw and maybe tae Thorntonloch. Some o' the children fae Thorntonloch went tae Innerwick School and the bus picked them up. But the bus also picked up Grahame Budge and thame – Grahame later played rugby for Scotland, he wis the same age as me and ah went tae school wi' him.[6] So the bus went as far as the holdins or tae Cove near Cockburnspath. We used tae have tae be at the end o' the road, because we got the bus when it came back fae thae places. It would be aboot quarter o' an hour for us on the bus tae Dunbar.

At the Grammar School, well, ah can tell ye ah hated algebra, absolutely hated it! It wasnae well explained tae us. But ah liked art, ah wis very fond o' art. Ah loved the PT, which they call PE now. Ah liked science and domestic science as well. We were taught of course how tae do washin' and ironing, cooking, and ye got a bit o' dressmakin'. Of course, ma mother had encouraged us wi' thae things when Jen and me were very small. If ma mother wis makin' scones we'd get a wee bit o' dough each. So ah liked the Grammar School and got on well there.

Outside the school, ma interests as a girl were, well, ah wis in the Brownies, ah wis in the Guides. I liked swimming. We learned to swim in the sea of course: at Barneyhill we were only aboot a mile and a half fae the North Sea. And ah think ah would be aboot eight or nine when ah got a bike. Ah cycled anywhere and everywhere, oh, as far as Dunbar. And we used tae cycle tae East Linton, which wis further than Dunbar – East Linton wid be aboot 12 miles fae Barneyhill. It wis a long run there and back, but we enjoyed it. So ah liked tae explore the countryside roond aboot, and there wisnae the cars and stuff then that there is now.

Then at the harvest time we used tae help the farm workers wi' the stooks. And then, when it came tae the feenishins – the last bit they were cuttin' – there wis always rabbits in there, and we used tae chase the rabbits. Eventually ah caught one: ah fell on it!

And ah climbed trees. Oh, ah wis a first-class climber o' trees! Ma mother always said I wis a tomboy. But it wis a grand life for children: freedom and fresh air. And our school holidays wis never long enough: we had too much we wanted tae do. We could be at the sea one minute, then we were away up by The Brunt and Thurston Glen and Doon Hill near Spott. Of course, Barneyhill farm wis jist next tae where the Battle o' Dunbar wis fought wi' Oliver Cromwell.[7] And we used tae guddle in the wee burn and a' that.[8] We had so much that we did. The days were never long enough.

Oh, as a girl ah wis a reader. We were brought up tae read books. Ah liked *Black Beauty*, that wis one o' ma favourites, and *Pegasus*, the winged horse.[9] And of course when Jen and me were younger it was fairy tales. And ma dad, if he walked the six miles tae and back fae Dunbar to get his hair cut, he would bring ma mother sweeties and bring Jen and me sweeties and fairly tales, wee booklets. But ah can never remember gettin' a comic, no' regular. There wis a comic aboot girls, ah've forgotten what they called it, but we didnae get it regular. But we did get books at East Barns School. Ah remember the boxes o' books comin'. You could borrow a couple o' books fae the boxes and read them, then exchange them the next time the boxes came. Ah wisnae in the public library as a girl.

But ah used tae go tae Grant's Operas in Dunbar when ah wis young. Grant wis the chemist in Dunbar, and he wis the man that started off Grant's Operas. Ma big cousin Margaret Ainsley used tae take Jen and me there. Ah loved it, it wis the whole thing. The girls Winter – one o' them wis Violet, ah've forgotten the first name o' the other one – young women fae Dunbar, they participated in them. It wis light operas – Gilbert and Sullivan, no' Verdi or Wagner. *The Pirates o' Penzance* wis one. They had a performance once a year. It wis really great.[10]

Oh, ah loved music. Ah used tae play the violin and the piano by ear. And ah could play the organ, but it wis the kind where ye peddled wi' your feet. And ah played the mouth organ! Ah never went tae private music lessons, but we had a music teacher at the Grammar School.

Ma sister Jen and me got pocket money. At first we used tae get a ha'penny [c. ¼p]. Then we got a penny [½p] – and you could buy a bar o' Highland Cream toffee! Then it came up tae tuppence [2d: approx. 1p]. So after they put the bus service on we sometimes took the bus tae Dunbar for tuppence. We used tae look in the shop windows in Dunbar, meet some o' oor friends and talk away wi' them, go tae the harbour, then we walked home the three miles. We never thought anythin' of it. The time passed quick. But that wis our pocket money gone.

Then ah remember when the shows came tae Dunbar at the time o' the Hirin' Fair for farm workers. The 28th o' March, ah think it wis. We used tae like it when the shows came. Then ye heard the farm workers at the Fair bein' spoken tae by the farmers, what the arrangements wis, and things like that. We used tae see some o' them spit on their hands and then shake hands wi' them. That meant they were hired. Ah cannae remember now how many farm workers would be at the Hirin' Fairs. At Barneyhill, the farm ma dad wis on, there were very few would leave tae go tae other farms. Like ma dad, they stayed on year after year. The man he, and ma grandfather before him, had wis a good boss. But ah remember bein' in Dunbar and seein' the folk standin' there at the Hirin' Fairs. Ah cannae really mind where they got hired but ah think it wis in the main street. You'd get that fae an old *Haddington Courier* – that wis the paper we got a' the time.[11] But really a' ah wis interested in wis the shows. There wis roundabouts, steamboats, things like that, and coconut stalls and what have ye. All ye wis lackin' wis money tae have a go! But, well, ye met a lot o' folk – some o' them your relatives that ye hadnae seen for a while. We had aunts and uncles livin' and workin' on farms round about Dunbar. As ah've said, ma dad didnae have any brothers, only sisters: ma Aunty Meg, Jess and Ag. But on ma mother's side it wis a big family. So at the shows you'd be more likely tae see ma mother's relatives than ma dad's.

For holidays ah used tae stay for a week or a fortnight wi' ma Aunty Meg, ma dad's sister, in Edinburgh, at 17 West Preston Street, a tenement. But ma sister Jen never went, she never wanted tae go there. She wid come there wi' ma mother when ma mother came tae take me home. But Jen and me never went wi' ma mother and dad for holidays tae the seaside at Burntisland or Spittal or anywhere like that. No, there were nothing like that. I remember the first holiday ma dad had wis durin' the war – and they went tae Kinnettles, near

Forfar. Ma dad and ma mum stayed there wi' the gamekeeper and his wife that had moved there fae East Barns. They'd never had a holiday away anywhere before that. Ah remember ah wis in the ATS when ah got the letter fae them sayin' that they were going tae Kinnettles on holiday. It wis marvellous! Ye see, ma dad worked six days a week at Barneyhill farm. He never had a Saturday afternoon off work, no' then before the war, never.

The farm workers' union wisnae a strong union then.[12] Ah remember when ah wis a wee girl, only six, and it wis the 1926 General Strike. Ah remember the miners' comin' and playin' melodeons at Barneyhill and collectin' money. Oor parents and that put money in the hat. And ah remember this man comin' tae see ma dad, tae talk ma dad intae joinin' the farm workers' union. Ma dad didnae want tae join it, but the man eventually talked him intae it. So when the Strike came about ma dad came intae the house – he wis an awfy quiet man, and ah never ever heard him talkin' aboot anybody or bein' annoyed aboot anythin' – and he wis very angry aboot somethin'. It wis the first time ah'd seen him like that. And he said tae ma mother, 'Well, that's it.' Ah discovered after that he overheard this man that had talked him intae joinin' the union tellin' the boss what wis goin' tae happen. By 'the boss' ah think ma dad meant, no' the farmer, but the grieve or steward. They called him the grieve in those days. So ma dad came out the farm workers' union.

Another thing ah remember: we had tae go faithfully every Sunday tae the church, the Sunday School, the choir – the junior choir, and then as we got older the senior choir. It wis Innerwick Parish Church, ah think it wis more than a mile away tae walk fae Barneyhill. It wis a' uphill, ah remember that. The Sunday School wis first, then we met our parents for the church. The services were both in the church, the one followed on the other. Sometimes we had tae stay behind on a Sunday for choir practice; but it wis usually a Wednesday night we would have tae go for choir practice. If there wis a cantata or whatever ye had tae go for it. Ah loved it really. Ma mother wis a lovely singer. Ah remember ah had tae sing solo, so had ma sister Jen. Ah sang *What a creature is the rose. Silently she buds and blows.* Ah sang that when ah wis still at East Barns School.

* * *

As a girl what ah really, really wanted tae be was as good a cook as ma mother – and ah also wanted tae drive a car! Oh, ah dreamed o' becomin' a professional cook, working in a restaurant maybe or a big house. When ah wis 14 and still at Dunbar Grammar School ah went tae work. Ma first job wis in Dunbar in Greco's ice cream shop and restaurant.[13] Greco wis Italian. Ah worked on Saturdays and in the evening, and when ah got ma school holidays I worked there then too. Ah worked in the big shop and at Greco's café at the open-air swimmin' pool, right next tae the sea. Ah used tae work at the café wi' Mary Greco – she wis the oldest daughter – and Betty Henderson, a pal o' mine. There wis sometimes a swimmin' gala on there at night. Ah liked watchin' the swimmin' and the water polo and what have ye. You could watch it from the café. In the big shop ah used tae serve the tables and the counter and make up sandwiches and what have ye. They sold sweeties, ice cream, sandwiches, biscuits, coffee, tea, Oxo and Ovaltine. It wis good experience for me and gave me confidence in dealin' wi' people. Ah liked it. Then when the work was over ah used tae cycle home. And sometimes on a Sunday ah went in the ice cream van to country places, and sold cones and sliders and what have ye. The van went away down by the coast as far as Cockburnspath, and sometimes it went up more tae the hill side, and came round and back tae Dunbar. Before Greco had the van they used tae go really on bikes wi' the ice cream. Alex Smith, who worked in the lemonade factory in Dunbar, drove the van for Greco on a Sunday – a spare-time job for him.[14] Ah cannae mind now how much ah got paid at Greco's – maybe a shillin' or two [5 or 10p] a week. Ah gave ma money tae ma mum, and she gave me ma pocket money.

The Greco family were Italians, husband, wife, and there wis Mary and Anna and Arthur. Then the wee one came to the shop after ah started there. They brought her over from Italy, she wisnae at the school and she couldnae speak English. When the war came Mr Greco wisnae interned, none o' the Grecos wis interned. Ah lost touch wi' them when ah went away tae the ATS. There wis one Italian ah knew in Dunbar, a nice man, ah liked him. He wis in the Blackshirts in Edinburgh, gave himself up, and wis interned. Nobody in Dunbar knew. His family were very, very nice and some o' them were in the British Services helpin' this country. But there wis a ship, the *Arandora Star*, goin' tae Canada wi' internees that wis torpedoed and he wis on that and wis killed. Ma mother used tae tell us that he and his brother came over here after the 1914–18 War, and he used tae go tae the fields and pick the chats – small potatoes, put them in bags, and that's how they started off, makin' chips for a wee shop they got.[15]

Ma mother would have liked us tae stay on at school and maybe sit our Highers. But ah really jist wanted tae get a job, work and get some money. So ah didn't follow ma parents' advice about stayin' on at school. And it wisnae that ma parents couldnae afford to leave me on at the school. When now ah think back we were pretty well brought up and we never really wanted for anything. And ma dad wis never unemployed. So ah could never say we were hard up as a family. So though ma dad wouldnae have a big pay as a farm worker, we had everything.

When ah left the Grammar School at 15 in 1935 ah didnae have a job tae go tae. So ah started then lookin' for a job. But ah wis unemployed for a wee while, maybe two or three weeks. Ma first job wis wi' Sir James Hope in his Big House at East Barns. Ah didnae apply for the job. It wis ma aunty, ma dad's sister, she'd worked in the Big House, she came and said what about starting there? So when ah first began I made the beds and did the rooms – dustin' and cleanin' and so on. And ah had a' the paraffin lamps tae dae and, God, there were a lot of lamps! They were beautiful lamps. But they didnae have electricity, no' at that time. Ah wis the housemaid, and there wis a cook, a table-maid and a milkmaid. We a' lived in at the Big House.

Ah got up at half-past five in the mornin', got washed, and jist started in tae the work. Then aboot eight o'clock we got a good breakfast. We got half an hour for that, though you could actually take more than half an hour and nobody said anything. Then ye jist went on wi' your work. About ten o'clock we got a cup o' tea, then carried on workin' until lunch-time. If Sir James Hope wis at home – he wis away quite a lot – lunch wis at 12 o'clock tae one. Even a' the farm workers wis the same.

Ah've heard that farm workers on other farms often had a two-hour break at midday – no' tae rest theirsels but tae rest their horses. Well, ah'm afraid they didnae have that there at East Barns or Barneyhill. And ah can remember that ma dad wis up long before four o'clock in the mornin', because as First Ploughman he had tae go up tae the horses before five o'clock. And it wis a long day. Ma dad could ha' been the grieve but he didnae want the job, he wisnae interested in promotion. But, oh, he wis away early tae his bed every night about nine o'clock.

So at the Big House we had a complete break frae work at lunch-time and had our main meal then. After our lunch break we worked on again till, oh, maybe three o'clock or ha' past three – it a' depended on how much work we got done in the mornin'. Oh, we were workers, we did it. But there wis no hard and fast rule that ye worked the whole afternoon. So in the afternoon ah could sit for maybe an hour or so wi' ma sewin' or ma knittin', or whatever we were doin' – writin' letters or whatever. Then usually aboot ha' past five we had the high tea. We got an hour's break then, and then we jist washed up. Ah used tae help wi' the washin' up. Then maybe about seven o'clock that wis us finished for the night.

Ye got a half-day off, usually on a Wednesday, from aboot two o'clock. On a Sunday ah jist used tae work tae 12 o'clock, and the rest o' Sunday wis mine. Ah went home tae Barneyhill on the half-day and on Sunday.

Ah cannae mind how much ah wis paid. It's such a long time ago you cannae remember the details. But Sir James Hope wis a great man tae work for. He wis very down-tae-earth. And he treated me as if ah should know everything. He used tae phone up and say, 'There's so many gimmers comin' in at Dunbar station. Phone ma brother Robert and tell him.' The first time he said gimmers, ah thought, 'What's a gimmer?' And it wis sheep![16] And then he would bring a handful o' wheat: 'What dae ye think o' that?' Well, ah'd grown up on a farm, so ah had a good idea what tae say. At breakfast time he used tae come intae the kitchen, and he'd say tae me, 'Now don't bother settin' the table in the dinin' room. Ah'll jist have ma porridge here.' But he always had his main meal at lunchtime and he had it in the dinin' room. And he used tae have a lot o' Irish cattle dealers – Dubliners they were – come across tae sell cattle. Oh, there wis a lot o' cattle and a lot o' sheep as well on East Barns farm. Sir James wis away quite a lot, but if he wis at home he always had his lunch at 12 o'clock tae one, the same as the workers. Then sometimes if he'd been away somewhere, he'd say, 'Ah'll have a cup o' cocoa' – and then away tae his bed.

Well, ah remained workin' in the Big House at East Barns aboot seven months. Then ah went to work at Miss Marrow's house at West Barns. Ah changed ma job because ah wanted tae really get a chance tae learn things aboot cookin'. Ma ambition wis tae be a cook. Ah heard there wis a vacancy at Miss Marrow's and ah applied for the job and started tae work there as a table-maid aboot the beginnin' o' 1936.

Miss Molly Marrow stayed in a house rented from local gentry – West Barns House. West Barns wis aboot two miles fae Dunbar. Miss Marrow wis English. Ah cannae mind now where she belonged to in England. She never got married – well, she wis engaged but he wis killed in the First World War, and she never married. She wis a very clever woman. She'd been a volunteer in the war, in the VAD. She was the type that would pick up medical work without any bother, and of course she could drive. She would be middle-aged, well intae her forties, when ah worked at West Barns House.[17]

Every chance ah got ah used tae be in the kitchen wi' the cook, Tibby White – Miss Marrow called her Bella. Tibby wis a marvellous wee woman. She wisnae five feet tall. Tibby wis the most marvellous cook ah've ever met. Her father had a baker's shop in Dunbar. Ah knew Tibby before ah got the job wi' Miss Marrow. Well, ma future husband's oldest sister (I knew him long before we got married) had worked with Miss Marrow and of course she knew Tibby, and that's how ah first met Tibby. Well, Miss Marrow had a lot o' dinner parties. A' the aristocracy roond aboot used tae come tae her dinner parties. Oh, the Duke o' Hamilton used tae come.[18]

As a table-maid you had tae clean the silver. When ye cleaned it – and there wis a lot o' silver – ye washed it, ye dried it, ye polished it. Then Miss Marrow used tae have shootin' parties, and there were big hampers got packed for them tae take, wi' a' the delicacies and what have ye, and the bottles and the glasses. We had a' that tae do tae – that wis Tibby and masel', and sometimes George Porteous the gardener. George wid give us a hand.

Oh, Miss Marrow wis a very well-connected woman, and definitely, definitely from quite a wealthy family. Some very interestin' people used tae come up from London as well. One old titled lady that came from London – ah wish ah could remember her name – she brought her personal maid with her. She also brought her Pekinese wi' her, and its special bath kit. Then ah wis taught tae valet the gentlemen as well. When they came and stayed you were taught how tae lay out their clothes, everything. Oh, it wis a lot tae learn. Ah had no previous experience o' that, but it wis good learnin', and I enjoyed it. And ah wis meetin' different people. They were friendly. Ye see, the people that are well off they're not snobs. Ye only get the snobs among the people that have been self-made or have got some money.

At Miss Marrow's again I lived in. Up at five o'clock in the mornin' and down the stairs ye went. That wis the beginnin' o' your day. If a shootin' party went out they took everythin' with them. But if it came bad weather they came home early. So the dinner had tae be on at night. Wi' the stuff that wis in hampers there wis very little that ye could have done anythin' about. Ye had tae start fae scratch again. But Miss Marrow's was a very good meat house. Ye got the very same food as they got, oh, very good food. She really was good tae us.

Before we began work in the mornin' about half-past five, we had a cup o' tea. Then we usually had oor breakfast aboot eight o'clock – a cooked breakfast, and we got half an hour tae sit down and eat it. Oh, there were never any problems aboot that. Ye started work again aboot half-past eight and worked on till we got our lunch maybe about half-past eleven. We had our lunch before Miss Marrow had hers. And then Miss Marrow would have her lunch, maybe a light lunch. In the evening she always had dinner, even though she was just on her own. And of course as table-maid ah wis busy when she wis having her food. She taught me how to decant the port and the other wine. And in those days it was two muslins, and things like that, ye know, because it came up fae the cellar. Then, if it wis a dinner party, they would be there for eight o'clock and sit down at half-past eight or nine o'clock. After dinner, the ladies left the room and the gentlemen stayed for their port and their cigars. The ladies went tae the drawin' room upstairs. So you went in wi' coffee or whatever they were havin' there. The men joined them later. And if they were in a talkative mood – if it wis politics they were talkin' aboot – it could go on and on and on. It might be eleven o'clock before they finished. So we had oor main meal late, maybe midnight. But we enjoyed it, and we used tae ask George the gardener in for his. When Miss Marrow wis havin' large dinner parties ma future husband's oldest sister used tae come in and help. And there wis another woman fae West Barns that used tae come in and help wi' the washin'-up. They were long, long hours from bein' up at five o'clock in the mornin' till after eleven at night. But we never thought anythin' about it – and it didnae happen every day of course, maybe jist once or twice a month

Although Miss Marrow did a lot o' entertainin', there wis times when she did no entertainin', and life wis jist normal. And she would go away on holiday, and would be away for weeks. She would go tae Monte Carlo and places like that. So there wis a lot less for us tae do at West Barns House.

But Miss Marrow wis thought a lot o', she really was. She'd done a lot o' work in the VAD in the war, she really did. She had a lot o' pictures, drawins, o' French soldiers she'd worked wi'. Some o' the drawins she'd done herself. But there wis somethin', ah can't remember it now, but ah've an awfy feelin' that she might have been injured or hurt somehow, somethin' tae do wi' her breathin'. It wis as if she had asthma, jist like me. There wis times when she wis quite breathless. She wis clever tae at inventin' things. She patented a sort o' support for big flowers in herbaceous gardens, and a bucket where ye pressed the pedal. She was a very interestin' woman. Oh, ah got on great wi' her. She wis very generous. All the staff got Christmas gifts fae her. Ma first Christmas wi' her she bought me a beautiful green quilted dressing gown and slippers tae match.

Ah can't remember what ah wis paid by Miss Marrow. But ah wis better off when ah think on it. Ah gave ma mother an allowance, oh, definitely. Ah had a half-day off, usually a Thursday, and ah had Sunday off – but ah didnae finish there till about two o'clock: some days ah wis goin' walkin' out that road jist before four o'clock. And ah had a good bit tae walk, because it wis much further fae West Barns tae where ah stayed at Barneyhill. Though ah had tae walk the one way ah always got a bus back at night. Ah didnae sleep at home on the half-day or Sunday, but went back tae Miss Marrow's. Then holidays: ah'd had four days paid holidays when ah wis wi' Sir James Hope at East Barns, and ah jist stayed at home. At Miss Marrow's ah think ah got a week's paid holidays, and ah went tae Edinburgh tae ma Aunty Meg.

Another thing ah remember about Miss Marrow. She wis active in the Conservative Party. So at her dinner parties there wis a lot o' political discussion. When ah wis waitin' at the table ah used tae hear the conversations, and ah wis quite interested actually. But of course ah wis never interested in becomin' a Tory. Although ma dad didnae believe in what happened wi' that [trade] unionist thing, ma mother always used tae say ah wis a Communist! But ah wisnae a Communist. Because ma mum and dad wis Liberal. Anyway, ah remained wi' Miss Marrow at West Barns until after the war broke out.

* * *

As a young girl, oh, ah wis very interested in politics. And ah remember Chamberlain runnin' back and forward tae Munich, and there wis fear war wis goin' tae break oot in 1938. Well, we did actually feel war wis likely tae come before it actually happened. From aboot 1937 the young people that ah mixed wi' then we all felt that there wis goin' tae be a war. Ah think after Edward VIII abdicated, a lot o' us got that strange feelin', listenin' tae the wireless and readin' the newspapers and what have ye that there wis goin' tae be somethin'.[19] Ah liked readin' newspapers. Ah used tae read *The Scotsman* actually because it came tae Miss Marrow's house and she passed it on tae us. But ah wisnae politically active masel', ah never joined a political party before the war, no, ah never joined anythin'. Ah wis only 18 when the war broke out in September, then 19 in the November.

Stewart Dickson, ma future husband, wis called up. He wis in the army reserve, and he went away down tae England in August. Stewart's two sisters were friends o' mine and, oh, ah knew Stewart from ah wis 15½. We actually started goin' out together when ah wis jist over 16. And then he wanted us tae get married when the war came. But ma mother said no, ah wis too young and we should 'Wait until the war's over.' So we got engaged in September 1939. Stewart went away tae France in November. Tae begin wi' he wis in the RAOC [Royal Army Ordnance Corps], then he wis put in the REME [Royal Electrical & Mechanical Engineers], and he wis attached tae the Royal Artillery, repairin' guns and what have ye. He wis in France eight months then got leave and came home. He'd only been home four days when they were ordered tae go back. Stewart said, 'Well, ah've waited eight months tae get leave and ah'm stayin' here until the end o' ma leave.' Ah thought, oh, he'll get it when he goes back. However, it wis ma future brother-in-law Ebenezer went back tae Lille – and walked straight into Germans. He wis in a prisoner o' war camp for the rest o' the war.

Well, Stewart was not at Dunkirk. He couldnae rejoin his regiment: they had moved on. And he came out o' France at Brest, a fortnight after Dunkirk. He wis lucky tae get away then. He got a leave – then he wis away tae Egypt. He wis in the Eighth Army and went right through the North African campaign, then intae Sicily and Italy. He came back fae Italy in August 1944 and we got married then.[20] It wis a shame we were separated for so long. They're so different nowadays;

they couldnae have done that, no' now, they couldnae do it. Well, that wis the only reason ah joined up. Until ah did, ah remained wi' Miss Marrow at West Barns. And she wis still there after the war, tae aboot 1948 or '49. Then the family that owned her house wanted it. She got a house in Haddington. Miss Marrow died in Haddington, and Tibby White the cook wis still wi' her and lookin' after her till then. Tibby hersel' lived on well intae her 80s and died aboot 1970.

* * *

Well, wi' Stewart bein' away ah wis jist fed up, and ah jist thought, as ah've said, och, ah'll jist join up. Ma sister Jen and three o' ma friends, the Thorburns, and me all five o' us decided tae join up. The oldest girl Thorburn wis already in the FANYs [First Aid Nursing Yeomanry]. When she'd been a civvy and ye asked her, 'How are ye gettin' on, Nellie?', she'd say, 'Fed up.' She wis always fed up then. So when she was home on leave from the FANYs and ah asked her how she wis gettin' on, she said, 'Fine.' She said she wis surprised at me no' joinin' up as ah could go in as a driver since ah'd learned tae drive. So ah did think then aboot it, and the five o' us were a' goin' thegither tae join the WAAF.[21] But ah didnae want tae join the WAAF! Ah wis jist goin' along wi' them. So we got intae Edinburgh tae join up. Ah think it wis in the Music Hall in George Street. We were walkin' along this corridor, the rest o' them were sort o' walkin' in front o' me. And there was a sergeant standin' outside this door. He said somethin' like, 'Wouldn't you like tae join the ATS?' So ah jist said, 'Right.' So ah went in, and away the others went: they never even knew ah wisnae there! So when we a' met up again, they said, 'What did you do that for?' Ah said, 'Ah jist decided ah would.' It wis jist on the spur o' the moment and because Stewart wis away in the army that ah volunteered intae the ATS at the end o' 1940.

So ah went first tae Craigmillar Park in East Suffolk Road, Edinburgh. It wis Edinburgh University student residences there: Carlyle House, Darroch House, Playfair House. Later on, ATS recruits in Scotland went first tae Newbattle Abbey near Dalkeith.[22] At Craigmillar Park they had big market gardens and they employed gardeners. Well, ma diary says we did six weeks' trainin' at Craigmillar Park when we joined up. And you never got out the place for six weeks.

Ah'm tryin' tae remember when later on it became an OCTU [Officer Cadet Training Unit]. Anyway, ah wis kept on there in Headquarters Company. And there wis sergeants and sergeant-majors came in. But there were women came in in uniform wi' no army ranks or anythin'. But they must have been volunteers. They wanted tae be officers, and they trained as officers.

When ah joined up and volunteered intae the ATS ah joined up tae be a driver. That wis what ah asked tae be trained as. But when I went in ah wis told there wis no vacancies at that moment. Was there anythin' else ah could do? And ah said, 'Yes: cooking.' And that wis the worst thing ah ever did. Because ye never get out o' it again. Ah used tae go tae the office every Monday tae see if ah could get tae be a driver. Ah could actually drive already. But needless tae say ah never ever got tae be an ATS driver, though ah did get a shot now and again.

So ah wis always an ATS cook. But ah did very well out o' it. Eventually I wis a lance-corporal, then ah wis a full corporal, and then ah wis an actin' sergeant. It wis ma own fault that ah wis never made a full sergeant. Ah wis goin' on a course tae Aldershot tae be made a war substantive sergeant, but ah cancelled it because by then it wis 1944 and Stewart, ma husband, wis at last comin' home. However, that didnae matter. And ah really enjoyed ma job as an ATS cook and enjoyed the people ah worked wi'. And another thing ah wis trained tae do wis field kitchens, a different form o' cookin'. Aye, it was a different kettle o' fish: wellin'tons, trousers, oh! And much more basic cookin' equipment. Then once fae Craigmillar Park ah wis sent to London tae Gower Street holdin' camp, because ah wis goin' on a cookin' course tae the Guards' depot at Caterham in Surrey. And ah passed that wi' flyin' colours. Oh, ah felt really well trained as a cook in the ATS.

At Craigmillar Park it wisnae Nissen huts we lived in, it wis bedrooms.[23] Oh, home comforts! And ah got home to Barneyhill on ma weekend leaves, ma 48 hours. Ah could go home, which ah did always. It wis an hour in the bus tae Dunbar, and then the other side o' Dunbar. And ah liked when ah wis stationed in Edinburgh. We used tae go tae the dancing. We went tae the Palais de Danse at Fountainbridge and the Cavendish at Tollcross. We thoroughly enjoyed it, 'cause ah loved dancin'. That wis one o' ma interests definitely. And at the New Victoria picture house at St Patrick Square they had every Sunday night what they called the Garrison Theatre. When ah joined the ATS ah met this girl Molly Easton. The pair o' us shared a room together at Craigmillar Park. She lived at Galashiels. And we're still friends. Her father wis a miner in Arniston in Midlothian, then they lived at Tranent in East Lothian, then they went tae Cardenden in Fife and it wis from Cardenden that Molly came as a volunteer intae the ATS. She wis a cook, tae. But it wis another girl, Elsie Davidson, an Aberdonian, and I that were walkin' from Newington Station, just along fae Craigmillar Park, tae the Garrison Theatre at the New Victoria one Sunday night, when this big posh car – would it be a Bentley or a Rolls Royce? – chauffeur-driven of course, stopped and this gentleman in it asked where we were goin'. So he says, 'If you'd like to get into the car we'll take you there.' So he kept talkin' tae us on the way up, asked oor names and how long we'd been in the ATS and if we liked it, where we came from, and a' this. When the car came tae the Garrison Theatre, 'Now,' he said, 'here's the card, and you'll show that card and it won't cost you anything to go into the Garrison Theatre. And when you come out from the show you'll be taken back-stage to have a cup of tea and a sandwich or whatever, and meet with the cast.' And it turned out the gentleman was either Will Y. Darling, the Lord Provost of Edinburgh, or the Chief Constable. I think it wis Will Y., because we used tae get him tae dinners when ah cooked at Craigmillar Park.[24] Oh, we had a number of VIPs came there tae inspect us. Royalty visited there as well. And we had a lot of big parades. And of course ah wis always the marker on parade because ah wis tall. Ah participated in a lot o' parades along Princes Street, the main street in Edinburgh. Then our officers at Craigmillar included Lady Margaret Egerton and Miss Celia Sprot, who later wis married on William Whitelaw. We were invited tae their weddin'. Ah liked Celia, she wis nice. Oh, Craigmillar Park definitely wis a very important centre for the ATS.[25]

Well, ah wis there a year and so many months. Then ah wis posted tae Garelochhead, No. 1 Military Port.[26] It would be some time in 1942. Ah wisnae really upset, because the Signals wis takin' over at Craigmillar. And then when they changed the intake o' new ATS recruits tae Newbattle Abbey a lot o' our friends at Craigmillar went away tae Newbattle. Ah never heard that Newbattle had been the base for ATS recruits from the beginnin' o' the war. But anyway ah enjoyed Garelochhead. But it wis Nissen huts we lived in, which we hadnae had at Craigmillar.

At Garelochhead No. 1 Military Port troopships were by then comin' in, big ships, some from America.[27] It wis also a trainin' place for divers. And the troopships used tae leave fae there. It wis a very interestin' port really. Shandon Hydro wis our headquarters at Garelochhead. It was a big change for me, but ah got on fine. Ah wisnae upset that ah wis much further away fae home, no' really. And we used tae get weekends in Glasgow occasionally. Some other weekends ah wid go home. There wis quite a lot o' entertainment there, tae. We used tae go tae the dancin' or a theatre or somethin'. It wis quite a big camp. It wis mixed, soldiers – Royal Engineers – as well as ATS. We were a' in the same camp, but the men were all in their own bit and the ATS in their bit, quite separate.

Ye could get very bad winters there. Ah think ah must have gone there in the winter, because ah remember they had tae drop some o' the stuff by plane because they couldnae get through by road. They brought a big crane up fae Liverpool. A lot o' the men that worked there wis Liverpool and Birkenhead blokes. They did work hard, they did. And we had great concert parties up there, a lot o' really good Yorkshire and Fife men. Two fellows fae Fife played the accordion and they became quite famous after the war.

Then from Garelochhead ah got posted tae Irvine Moor Camp, on the way tae Kilwinnin' in Ayrshire. It wis a big camp. Again it wis a mixed camp, ATS and a' English Royal Engineers men. They were experimentin' wi' amphibious tanks and those flame-throwers and flail things for the tanks.[28] And of course we had there the camp followers that had come up fae England wi' them. Ah had never experienced that! They were women that came wi' the soldiers – loose women.

* * *

Well, Stewart, ma fiancé came back, as ah've said, fae Italy in August 1944. We both got leaves, and we got married in Belhaven Church at Dunbar on the 25th o' August. We'd been engaged by then for five years. Ah got posted back tae Irvine Moor Camp, but ah wanted a postin' nearer home. So ah got posted tae Dreghorn Barracks at Edinburgh, which ah enjoyed. It would be aboot three months, ah think, ah wis at Dreghorn. And then ah got posted tae Redford Barracks at Edinburgh, which ah didn't like. Oh, it wis a huge place. Ah never liked it. But it wis only weeks, thank goodness, ah wis there.

What happened was, Stewart had been posted tae Birkenhead. He'd been out for a walk and met this padre that said tae Stewart, 'You're a stranger in this camp.' Ma husband said, 'Yes, sir, ah am.' Stewart told him his home town wis Dunbar, 'But we usually say Edinburgh.' The padre said, 'Well, what are you doin' down here at Birkenhead?' 'That's what I would like to know,' says Stewart. 'I was supposed tae get a home postin'.' 'Well,' said the padre, 'would you like a home postin'?' 'Yes,' says Stewart. So they posted him to Redford Barracks.

By then I was at Redford Barracks. I'm lying on top o' ma bed there readin' one Sunday, when in came the orderly officer and the orderly sergeant: 'Get your kit packed. You're goin' tae Galashiels.' 'Today?', ah said, 'on a Sunday?' 'Yes,' she said. 'A utility [car]'ll take you to the bus station and you'll get a bus. You've been posted to the Maxwell Hotel in Galashiels.' And that wis because ma husband wis gettin' posted tae Redford Barracks. And, husband and wife, ye couldnae both be in the same place. So Stewart wis left at Redford and ah wis sent away tae Galashiels! But that wis the rule, husbands and wives were kept separate. But ah got out the ATS in February 1945 because I was pregnant. Any o' the girls expectin' were able tae leave right away. So that wis the end o' ma army career. It wis jist before the war in Europe ended in May 1945.

Ah wis sorry tae leave the ATS, 'cause ah'd played tennis, basketball, cricket, everythin'. Ah'd made a lot o' friends. Ah wis in the ATS for jist over four years and, oh, ah thoroughly enjoyed it. Ah wouldnae have missed it for anythin'. It wis everythin'. Ah mean, the company: what ah missed when ah came out wis the company. The best friends you ever had wis durin' wartime. Ah think it wis because o' the atmosphere, ye know, the times we were livin' in. You were all in it together. And ye missed them. Oh, ah definitely felt at the end o' the war ah wis a more experienced and mature person. You grew up, ye did.

But there were girls that didnae like the army. And some o' them did terrible things, ah mean, tae try and get out o' the army. Of course girls like me were volunteers, but those other girls were conscripts and a lot o' them didnae really want tae go intae the army. So there were some sad experiences as well.

Well, after the war ah didnae work until ma youngest son wis about six. Then ah went tae work at Rosslynlee [Mental Hospital, Midlothian]. When ah left Rosslynlee ah came tae work at Larry's Lunchette at

Surgeon's Hall in Edinburgh. Larry wis Laurence Di Marco, he wis only 20 when ah went there workin'; his dad put him in that job. Ah did griddle cooking there – you cooked in front o' the customers. But as time went on ah got fed up wi' it. Then ah went tae work in the Carlton Hotel in the Bridges in Edinburgh. So ah more or less worked always as a cook in cafés, hotels, hospitals, and in school meals, whatever. Wi' school meals ah started off at St David's High School, Dalkeith, and ah worked in practically every one in the holiday time. Then ah wis made supervisor at Lugton Westfield School in Dalkeith, till ah finished up there. Before that ah wis drivin' a butcher's van for W.G. Adams, the butchers in Dalkeith. Ah used tae deliver in Edinburgh – deep freezes and what have ye, a' the posh bits! Ah went as far oot as near the Forth Bridge, and ah used tae go up tae Broughty Ferry near Dundee for stuff for Adams and a' that. Oh, ah loved gettin' oot and aboot in the van. So ah retired fae Lugton School. Ah took a year's early retirement because ah wisnae well. Then ah took breast cancer. But ah'm still here.

Nancy Cowe (Mrs Nancy Dickson) died on 1 June 2013.

Jean Crosbie

When Hitler marched into Poland on 1st September 1939 I can remember my big sister Margaret saying, 'That means we will be at war.' Oh, I remember the declaration of war by Mr Chamberlain clearly. But I had really no idea what it was about, not a clue. I wasn't political at all.

Well, oddly enough, I was born in July 1923 in Windsor, Ontario, in Canada. My mother and father, with my brother Charles and my sister Margaret, both older than me, had gone to Canada. But my father, a bit of a hypochondriac, thought he was dying and that he must get home to Scotland to die. So we came home to Scotland shortly after I was born.

My father, born in Glasgow in 1889, was an engineer. But he did a lot of different things. When he was in Canada I think he worked for a while as a joiner. And I know he ran a bus here in Scotland for a while. I can remember as a small child under five sitting beside my father as he drove his bus. At that time we lived in Howwood, near Johnstone, in Renfrewshire. A man named Young and my father had buses independently of each other. I don't quite know what went on, but Young went on to have a fleet of buses, and my father didn't. Anyway my father went back to ordinary engineering. His mother had died when he was quite young and one of his two sisters had brought him up. He was very good at everything. He made wonderful bogies when we were children; my brother always had the best bogie in the village. But I remember my father being unemployed from time to time when I was quite young. I do remember a kind of worrying time; and of course no family allowances in those days. But we always had food. Then my father was an avid newspaper reader; I think he got the

Daily Express, and he liked the *Evening Citizen* because it was a Glasgow paper.[1]

My mother was a very reserved lady. Her parents were from the Highlands – Dunvegan in Skye, so they were Sgitheanachs, persons from Skye. My mother wasn't a fluent Gaelic speaker, she had only some words of it. She was one of a large family. She left school at 14. She should have been a teacher. Her teachers had wanted her to become a pupil teacher. But the family needed her wage. She lived at Neilston and before her marriage, worked, I understand, in a mill there.

My brother Charles was the oldest in our family. There had been another boy after Charles, but stillborn. Then came my sister Margaret, then me, then my sisters May, Anna, Kathy and Norma: six girls and one boy. Even in those days it was considered a large family. There would be three or four years between Charles and Margaret, and about two years between each of the rest of us. So there'd be about 14 years between Charles and my youngest sister Norma. Charles was born about 1916 or 1917, and I remember he used to say that he wasn't going to get married until he was 30. We girls thought this was hilarious, because anybody would be past it by that time. Charles was a clever lad and at school took his Highers. After he left school he did a lot of different things; for instance, he ran a fish lorry – really it was a horse and cart but it was called a lorry. But he also got his Higher National Diploma and became a draughtsman. My older sister Margaret also passed her Highers at school. She worked first in a shop, then in the office of J. & P. Coats, the threadmakers in Paisley.[2]

I didn't know my father's parents at all: they'd both died. As I've said, his mother had died when my father was quite young. But I can remember very clearly my mother's father. He lived in Lugton in North Ayrshire. I don't know what he did all his life, but latterly he worked on the railway. When we got bigger and got bikes we used to cycle over from Howwood to visit Grandpa. He had a very Highland accent, and I would think he would be a fluent Gaelic speaker. He was known as Donald the Bard. I think he had a lot of poetic accomplishments. He married a second time, and both my mother and her sisters always called the new wife Mrs Ferguson, because we were not allowed to call her granny.

* * *

My earliest memory is of I think it would be a room and kitchen in Paisley. When we came back from Canada we went to Neilston, and then went from there to Paisley. So we were maybe a couple of years at Neilston and then a couple of years at Paisley. Now I can remember quite clearly being at Paisley and my big sister Margaret going to the school there and going in. One day I had walked to the school by myself and a teacher brought me into Margaret's classroom: 'This is Margaret Crosbie's wee sister.' And Margaret was furious about it. Of course, I was only four when we left Paisley, so I was too young to begin school there.

From Paisley we moved into the country at Howwood, to a two-roomed cottage – a room and kitchen. But each room was enormous. And there were beds galore. The cottage was on the main street of the village. The sleeping arrangements were that I always slept with a sister. I can't remember where my brother slept. But we girls slept in the room, two to a bed as the younger ones came along. My parents slept in the kitchen.

We started there with paraffin lamps – no electricity. Then we got gas in. I think my mother cooked on a range, with an oven at one side of it. I don't remember a wee water tank in the range. But I think there must have been a gas ring, I can't truly remember. But I remember my mother cooking a lot, because she baked cakes for the shop.

My parents had very quickly opened a little shop, which was just sort of built on to the cottage. I don't think it was a shop before we went there. Maybe my dad built that. He was very clever. So my mother ran the shop. She worked out how much the ingredients for the cakes cost, then added on a little bit for mark-up. But she didn't think of paying herself for her labour. My father remained working as an engineer, periodically unemployed, which was serious. My mum had a hard time. But then after my brother Charles left school he ran the shop for a while. That would be in the early 1930s, because we were so hard up. As I've said, Charles also ran a fish lorry.

Then the toilet at our cottage at Howwood was round the back. It was part of the cottage, but to get to it you had to go out the back door, along the cottage wall – which was quite long – then round the next corner, and there it was. Oh, it was a flush toilet, and we didn't share it with anyone. Opposite the toilet was the washhouse, which I don't think my mother was in very often, but maybe boiled up the things in the copper. You'd to make a fire underneath it. We used to play boats in the copper. And at Howwood we had a very big garden.

I'm not sure exactly when we moved from the two-room cottage to a council house, but maybe when I was about 12 or 13, in 1935–6. We moved then because of the size of our family – two parents and seven of us children or teenagers. The council house seemed wonderful because it had a living room, quite a big kitchen, three bedrooms, a bathroom and electric light – just a palace. I can't remember if there was a boiler for washing the clothes in. I think my mother just used a scrubbing board for the washing. And there was a garden: but I have to say my family were not great gardeners. I don't think my father grew vegetables in it. The garden at the two-room cottage had been just pretty wild. It had a rowan tree in it. And the drying green there had been up the back, and I remember my mum used to get bites on her legs when she hung out the clothes there. I remember, too, that for us to get the council house the two-room cottage had to be condemned, and my father was very indignant about that because it was a good solid cottage. He'd put in work on it himself.

* * *

When I was five I began school at Howwood Public School. There were seven classes but only five rooms. So there were two classes in some rooms – not with a partition: they just sat alongside one another. The head infant teacher, was terrifying, absolutely terrifying. I remember once getting a slap on the legs for dropping a stitch at knitting. Every year there was a school concert, a wonderful concert, which she organised. And every year my mother used to make us six girls a new dress. That was our best dress for the summer. She was a very handy person at make-do-and-mend. Oh, she had to. She made things out of her own sisters' cast-offs.

At Howwood School I was good at sums; it was only later that my arithmetic ability seemed to fade! But I enjoyed everything – writing essays and reading. I was a keen reader. At the end of Primary One I got the first prize: *Grimm's Fairy Tales*, on very thin paper, with very small print, and no pictures. Not the sort of book you would give a six-year-old now.[3] But I suddenly realised I could read it myself, and no longer needed to ask my big sister to read to me. My parents encouraged us to read.

But I don't remember much about a library at Howwood: maybe the library came to the school with books in boxes. But we always had books in the house. And I think we occasionally got comics. My big brother Charles got the *Hotspur*, and we all read it. It was difficult for my parents to afford comics regularly. But Charles got the *Hotspur* and passed it round the family.[4]

Then we played a lot. It was always a joy when the evenings started to get light and you suddenly realised you could go out after tea. We played in the garden at the two-room cottage. A game we played a lot was called Queenie. You have a ball, somebody's het. The aim is to hit anybody below the knee. If you managed to do that you could jump, dodge, run, or whatever. And if anybody was hit below the knee then he or she was het. Queenie was our favourite game. Then I collected scraps. But I was never interested in collecting foreign stamps.

My mum and dad believed in having holidays. So before the war we went to places like Millport on Cumbrae, and we went camping at Girvan on the Ayrshire coast and at Maidens, a fishing village also in Ayrshire. We used to go camping in our father's single-deck bus, and would take two tents with us: one for my brother Charles, and a bell tent for mother and the daughters. So as children we almost always got a holiday. Sometimes we'd go to a flat in Millport. At Maidens we had lovely holidays, because the same families went there every year. So you had these friends you saw in the summer every year. And my father taught us all to swim in the sea, and took us out fishing in a hired rowing boat. So I had a very happy childhood.

I went to Howwood Public School till I was 11, passed the Qualifying exam there, and then I went to Camphill Secondary School in Paisley. To be quite frank, I was always first! I enjoyed school, we all did. I got the bus from Howwood to Camphill Secondary: 14 miles there and back. At Camphill I loved science because I adored the science teacher. I had a great big crush on him. And I was fairly good at geometry, but began to lag in arithmetic. Algebra I was never awfully good at either. I also did French and Latin. I had the sort of memory that I could swot things up, get good marks in the exam – then forget it all. I didn't retain it, and I'm still the same – only worse!

My older sister Margaret and my brother Charles both took their Highers at Camphill when they were 16. I didn't, though I loved the Secondary school, I loved it. But I was 15 and halfway through the fourth year in 1938 when I left. The reason I left then was because the rector came round to say they needed a young person in the Renfrewshire Education Offices, starting as a telephonist on a PBX [Private Branch Exchange]. And I thought, 'My mother needs the money. I'll just volunteer for this.' So it was my idea to leave. My parents weren't shocked. I think I got 16s [80p] a week as pay, and my mother said, 'It's lovely to get that regularly.' My travelling expenses – a season ticket on the bus to and from Paisley, where the Education Offices were – would come off that. And I went to night school to learn shorthand and typing.

At the Education Offices I worked at the switchboard in a little room just like a little cubbyhole. It was an old-fashioned PBX. The phone rang and you said, 'Education Offices.' (My sister told me I used to say this even in my sleep.) Anyway, the callers told you who they wanted to speak to and you plugged them in. I remember thinking, even at the age of 15, as I sat in that little room feeling a little bit cast down about it, 'Here I am until I'm 65.' But I didn't come to have regrets fairly quickly about leaving school, not at all. Because even as a young girl my over-riding ambition was to marry and have a large family. That was what I wanted, rather than becoming a nurse or a doctor or a teacher. That was my ambition.

The hours of work when I first began were nine till five, and an hour off for lunch. And we worked Saturday mornings, which was usual then. As I say, my pay was 16 shillings [80p] a week – paid monthly though. I gave all my pay to my mum, and she would give me my bus fares and some pocket money – how much pocket money I can't really remember. And we got holidays.

I had been quite a delicate child, although I have been a healthy adult. But I remember the boss at the Renfrewshire Education Authority, who was quite a fearsome figure, calling me into his office and giving me a jar of cod liver oil and malt for my cough. He must have been concerned about me!

So I remained with the Authority until I joined up in the ATS. But after a time I moved from the switchboard and became a junior typist. And it was very interesting. There were four typists in this room, two older ones and then two juniors. I remember my senior typist sending me out to get a pennyworth of carrot and turnip for her to make soup at home: she kept house for her brother.

I was going to classes two nights a week in Paisley for typing and shorthand. I got on fine there. I think I got to about 80 to 100 words a minute in shorthand, but I find it hard to remember what my speed in typing was by the time I ceased attending the classes. But I also went for shorthand to a private teacher, a funny wee man who had a big class and read out at different speeds. But by the time I left Renfrewshire Education Authority to join up at 17½ in the ATS I was still really only a very mediocre typist.

* * *

My father had been in the army in the 1914–18 War. I think it would be the Army Service Corps he was in: he could drive. Later on in his life, after the 1939–45 War, he became mentally ill. My sister Anna was convinced that his illness was to do with him being gassed in World War I. He didn't speak to me about his experiences in that war. He used to sing the songs, *Keep The Home Fires Burning*, *Pack Up Your Troubles*, and all that. He had been in France, and I think he maybe had some horrors – they must all have had.

Oh, I remember the coming of the 1939–45 War. And I can remember my big sister Margaret saying, when Hitler marched into Poland on 1st September 1939, 'That means we will be at war.' And I remember the declaration of war by Mr Chamberlain clearly. But I had really no idea what it was all about, not a clue. I wasn't political at all. I'd never been a member of a political party. I can remember my brother and my father arguing about politics, and that upset me. I hated them to shout at one another. But I was very patriotic. And there were all these patriotic films like *In Which We Serve*.[5] Later on, when I was in the ATS, we had these ABCA [Army Bureau of Current Affairs] discussions groups, and I remember this delightful man explaining what Conservative, Labour and Liberal meant. And it was all just astounding to me. My parents were interested in political ideas. But before or at the beginning of the war I wasn't at that stage. With me, it was all patriotism. Margaret, my older sister, had volunteered to join up. She joined the ATS and was called up a week or so later, just before the outbreak of the war. So once the war broke out it made me think almost at once of volunteering, too. But of course in September 1939 I was only turned 16, and 18 was the age to join – though if you were going to a relative in the Forces they would take you at age 17½. So I volunteered as soon as I was 17½ in January 1941. But I failed my first medical because I had a sore on my leg. I think I must have had a fall or something, and they wouldn't take me till that healed up. So that delayed me a little.

And boyfriends did not want me to go into the ATS, as some people were of the opinion the ATS were Scarlet Women and leading loose lives. The ATS did have a certain reputation, whether justified or not. Boyfriends just did not want me to join. But 'I'm going to do my bit!'[6] It didn't occur to me to join the WRNS or the WAAF instead. It was specifically the ATS I wanted to join, because my sister Margaret was already in them.

So I got a medical again, but I can't remember where I got the medical, which was, oh, a fairly thorough one. Then I'd to report to Edinburgh. And that was a big adventure to me, to go to Edinburgh. I'd been there on school trips, but I hadn't been very often to Edinburgh. Anyway, it was a barracks I'd to go to. It wasn't Redford, Glencorse, Dreghorn, or Newbattle Abbey. A friend in the Education Offices who joined up some time after me went first to Glencorse. So Craigmillar was maybe just at the beginning in the war. Anyway, it was Craigmillar – a lot of buildings. I just got the bus there.[7]

Maybe it was just a big house they'd taken over. I can remember we had to do a lot of sort of cleaning chores at Craigmillar of these very old loos and baths, really big old-fashioned baths. Another of my clear memories of Craigmillar was of one of the young officers, who would be a very upper-class young lady, saying to me: 'Crosbie, be a darling and get me so-and-so.' It was this 'be a darling' that was so foreign to me. I can't remember how long I was at Craigmillar. But we did some square-bashing, and I loved that.[8] And we must have had some lectures, although I'm very hazy about it. But, oh, we were issued with uniform, and I can remember the items we were issued with. They were all big, and these thick lisle stockings, and really clumpy heavy flat-heeled shoes. I've never taken to high heels, and I still can't wear them. And we had skirts, a hat, tunic, knickers, vests, pyjamas, I think – everything. Then there were all the different trades in the ATS, and at Craigmillar you had to choose what you were going to do.[9] Of course, I chose shorthand and typing: that was my trade. Well, I wasn't awfully good at that. I'd only been a junior typist in the Renfrewshire Education Offices, and I seem to remember wasting a lot of paper there as I typed things over again.

I must have been in a room at Craigmillar with other girls, but it doesn't stick in my mind. I can't even remember how long I was at Craigmillar, whether it was two weeks or three weeks. As an introduction to the ATS it probably wouldn't be all that long.

Well, from Craigmillar I went to Strathleven House, Dumbarton, which is where my sister Margaret already was. I think Strathleven House is now an industrial estate. It was a big house, and we used to walk in the garden and I would think, 'This is the manner to which I would like to become accustomed!' It was so pleasant, with all this land and space to walk. Though I can't remember what Margaret did there, I think she worked on the ATS side. But I was secretary to the adjutant, a man. Strathleven House was a heavy anti-aircraft [ack-ack] regimental headquarters. But now and again I would be loaned out to a battery. I remember I was once at a battery headquarters at Helensburgh, across the Firth of Clyde from Greenock, and I was also for a while at Auchendennan House, near Balloch on Loch Lomondside.

In March 1941, on the night of the Clydebank Blitz, we – women and men – had gone in a truck on an outing from Strathleven House into Glasgow. I remember we had egg and chips, bread and butter, and tea, all for a shilling [5p], in a canteen. I think it would be an All-Services canteen. Then we went to an opera. The opera was one I haven't seen since then, and now I just can't remember the name of it. On the way back from Glasgow to Dumbarton that night we heard the enemy planes and the bombs going off. It was absolutely terrifying. Clydebank is half-way between Glasgow and Dumbarton, but now I'm not sure that we actually went through Clydebank as it was being bombed. I remember there was actually a bomb, though it didn't explode, in the grounds of Strathleven House. And what I can also remember is going home on leave. I used to get a bus from Dumbarton to Yoker that went through Old Kilpatrick and places. And, looking at the tenements, they were just sliced down the middle. It was terrible. I remember being sick at heart. Hundreds of people were killed in that Blitz and hundreds more seriously injured. And I remember clearly that journey home on leave. I went from Yoker to Renfrew, from Renfrew to Paisley, and Paisley to Howwood.[10]

At Strathleven House there were more army men than ATS. There were maybe about a dozen of us ATS. I wasn't there terribly long – months, but not many months. But by about the summer of 1941 the regiment was going to embark for service abroad, and we – including my sister Margaret – went down with it to Derby. That was a very traumatic time, because it was very hot, far hotter than I ever remember. And the camp was much rougher. But Margaret and I were actually in private billets there. We'd be at Derby for maybe a couple of months. Then from Derby we went to Glasgow, where I was still with Margaret. She had got married in Derby to Kenneth, a sort of public school boy from Birmingham whom she'd met in Edinburgh, where she was first stationed. We all thought Kenneth was so charming and witty. Margaret had told me she and Kenneth would like to get married before he went overseas. But they didn't know how to set about it. So when I was taking a letter the next day from the assistant adjutant, I said to him: 'Sir, can you tell me how to get married?' I think he thought I was proposing to him – he'd be so lucky! Anyway, he did the trick. He found out all about it, got a special licence, and Margaret and Kenneth were married then. Kenneth immediately went overseas, I think to Gibraltar.

When the regiment left, Margaret and I were both sent then from Derby to Glasgow, to the 12th Ack-Ack Division at Pollokshields in Glasgow. I wasn't in the same digs there as Margaret. Very soon after that Margaret and I were split up when she left that area. Margaret was very clever but she didn't ever become an officer. However, still in the ATS, she did go to Cambridge and she was involved in the first computers. Shortly after that, she left the ATS because she was pregnant and went home to Howwood. It must have been 1942 by that time, and she'd had that experience in Cambridge. That stood her in great stead, because after the war, from which her husband returned safely, she emigrated to Canada, got into computers there and earned lots of money. During her pregnancy and when she'd had the baby after leaving the ATS, Margaret ran the family shop again at Howwood. I don't know whether my mum and dad had kept it going till then or whether they'd opened it up again. But I know Margaret ran the shop for a wee while. It sold sweeties, cigarettes, biscuits and home bakeries.

I was stationed in Glasgow for some time – for exactly how long I find it hard to remember. The interesting thing that happened to me in Glasgow was that I had a new boyfriend who was very interested in music. I went to the opera and to concerts quite a lot with him, which was culturally rewarding.

Then the headquarters was going to leave Glasgow and go overseas. So we went down to Yarmouth, where they were to get ready to go abroad. But when I was away on leave an absolutely terrible thing happened at Yarmouth. There was something in the newspaper about ATS being killed in a German bombing raid. When I got back about three in the morning to Yarmouth after my leave, I found that the ATS billet, which was on the seafront and next door to Divisional headquarters, just wasn't there any more. The ATS paraded every morning at a quarter to nine, before everyone started work at nine. This German plane had come in under the radar, and dropped a bomb that just got the ATS billet and killed 26 of the girls. I would myself undoubtedly have been killed if I'd been there. I lost many of my friends among the 26. It was dreadful. It was a terrible grief. It was like an illness.[11]

And I can't remember now if it was before or after that that Charles, my brother, was posted missing. He was in the RAF, an observer, I think, on a Lancaster bomber, and he was lost over the Bay of Biscay. Charles would be then in his later twenties. He was the only son in our family, and he hadn't married. His loss was a terrible grief to my parents. They never got over it. Right to the end of their life they grieved for him. That he was posted missing gave them some hope that he was a prisoner of war. But that wasn't the case. It was in April, I think, that they had got the dreaded telegram. And under the date in a notebook of my mum's after she died I read: 'The old grief which still hurts.'[12]

I can't remember when I was made a lance corporal. But I remember I was afraid that one day I would have to shout commands such as 'Left Turn!'. So from Lowwood I took my four young sisters up into the countryside, and drilled them to march, halt, salute, and so on to the word of command!

One of the ATS girls killed by the German bomber at Yarmouth was Anna Macleod from Stornoway. It was actually Anna who encouraged me to become an officer. One day in Yarmouth we were running down the officers, as one does. And then Anna said to me, 'Maybe we should have a go. Come on, let's do it.' And we applied. But Anna was killed by the bomber before I'd even had my interview.[13] I didn't get an USBie – Unit Selection Board – first. I got only a WOSBie – War Office Selection Board. I can't remember where I would go for the WOSBie. But it was a two-day thing. You'd to do all sorts of quite demanding things, and do psychological tests and all that. I remember one of the interviewers, a much older lady, at the WOSBie asking me what would I do if I had ATS under me who were much, much older than me. I had no idea what she was wanting, but I said, 'Well, I think I would try and charm them over to my side.' She said, 'Of course, you're Scottish. So you would naturally respect somebody older than yourself.'

Wartime experience in the Services, I think, meant people were moved around so much it's difficult to remember some things. You were here, there and everywhere. In fact, it's a joke in my family that when anywhere is mentioned they say, 'Mum says she was once stationed there.' I was certainly in quite a lot of places with the ATS.

Anyway, I got through the WOSBie. I think I must fairly soon after that have gone to Windsor, where the officers' training course was based. It's hard to remember if we were in barracks there or huts. I was there eight weeks, I think. In the middle of the course numbers of people were returned to their units, and there was a kind of gloom about the place. But we had a show by Joyce Grenfell which cheered everybody up.[14]

I found the officers' training course at Windsor very interesting from the point of view of social nuances, mixing with rather higher social levels. I found it very advantageous to be Scottish, because they couldn't pigeonhole you as they did with English working class girls. Not that there were many of the latter there. But the others definitely couldn't quite place you. I couldn't say I encountered there a fair bit of snobbery, not really. One thing I learned was that sometimes you would think about some upper class twit, 'She must be a pain to be with.' Then later on for some reason, being on a course or something, you'd to share a room with that person and you'd find she was just human like yourself. So I firmly believe familiarity breeds respect, not contempt. You certainly had to mix with all sorts of people. Another thing I remember was a Catholic girl turning quite pink and saying she couldn't stand it if anybody ran down her church. There wasn't a feeling like that in Howwood, but I realised there must have been lots of places, notably including of course Northern Ireland and Glasgow, where there was.

So the OCTU, Officer Cadets Training Unit, was very interesting to me, the lectures and just everything about it. I remember I had to make a five-minute speech as part of the course. Once I had been down a coal mine and that's what I spoke about. The mine was somewhere around

Sauchie in Clackmannanshire. I had a boyfriend who was stationed there, and his parents, sister and I went to visit him. We were taken down a mine, to entertain us. But, I mean, it was horrific. The amount of headroom was only about 18 inches. It was dreadful, claustrophobic, absolutely terrible. I've never forgotten it. So that visit was the subject of my speech on the OCTU course.

The number of girls on the course when I was there would, I think, be 80 or 100. There wasn't a big proportion of the girls on it who were told just to go back to their units – a small percentage, I would say maybe about eight or 10, something like that. But it certainly cast a gloom on everybody.

So I got through the OCTU course, there was a big passing out parade at Windsor, and I became a commissioned officer as a 2nd lieutenant. I was only 20 – a very young 20 – then. From the course at Windsor I went to the 93rd Searchlight Regiment, which was something new for me. But I think I must have gone on a searchlight course. By this time I was engaged, and my fiancé was in Searchlight, and I think I must have had the opportunity of joining the 93rd Regiment. There was only one women's searchlight regiment and that was it – the 93rd. So my fiancé of course wasn't in it. It was a purely women's regiment, though they had male officers. The commanding officer was a man, and so were the battery commanders. Each battery had, I think, four troops. All troop commanders and their seconds in command – like me – were women.[15]

When we were at a battery headquarters at Hatfield [Hertfordshire], I remember being on a motorcycle driving course, where I shared a tent with another young woman. We had our meals in the officers' mess, but there wasn't a bedroom for us two. Her name was Veronica Ward. She was very interesting to me both socially and academically, because she was a graduate, which was unusual. She wasn't Scots. And she was a socialist. And, I mean, she was quite posh as well was Veronica. I couldn't tell you if she was a member of the Labour Party or not. But I remember she laughed and said to me, 'Och, Jean, all the best people are socialists.' So she had a big influence on me – another new experience for me. I do remember Veronica clearly because we were out all day on the motorbikes, then we had a bath and we had our dinner. Then we really lay in bed and read and talked. It was hot, sunny weather. And the motorcycling around Hatfield was delightful.

When I went back to my battery I was stationed in Harefield in Middlesex, not far from Pinner. All the searchlight sites were in sort of North London. One day when I was out on my motorbike it began making a terrible noise. A man on a push bike overtook me. Then I realised that because it was becoming dark I was so nervous that I was in far too high a gear for the speed I was going! Somebody once asked me what I did if the motorbike stalled. I said, 'I stand at the side of the road and take my helmet off so people can see I'm female, and I wait for some good Samaritan to come along.' The motorbikes we used were only 250, though I did once ride a Norton 500 – but only for five minutes!

Well, I had my 21st birthday in the Searchlight Regiment in July 1944. By that time, of course, the German V1 flying bombs and V2 rockets had started coming over. We were involved in trying to point our searchlights on them. We were around Harrow then, and, as I've said, there was a searchlight site at Pinner and Harefield and so on, all round that area. I was on duty night after night, really we were sort of nightshift workers with the searchlight battery. There was one time I was posted for a week's training to a male searchlight battery. Now I can't even remember where this was. But I remember the man who was looking after me was Johnny Kinsella. We'd to take post one night, and all was quiet at this point. So Johnny and I were singing over the inter-com thing, singing *Dream Angus* and songs like that to entertain the troops, in the middle of this serious post.

Once I'd become an officer I found some difficulties in relations with the Other Ranks, I certainly did. My biggest thing was that I felt I was a rotten officer. It took me ages to learn that if you said, 'Do this,' to somebody and they smiled at you and said, 'Yes, ma'am,' that didn't necessarily mean that they would do it. But I was mostly on the search-light site with Greta Scott, a lady several years older than me, who I'm still in touch with. Greta was at that time one of the few people I knew – one of two, I think – who was actually divorced. She's since remarried and is very elderly now of course. Greta was the troop officer and I was her assistant. We shared a Nissen hut. Oh, we got on very well together, and that again was a very, very educational experience for me. Greta, who lived in Derbyshire, was quite an upper class girl. She said to me, as she was seeing somebody out to their car, 'My mother always said, "Always see your guests to their carriage."' She was very humorous and I learned a lot from Greta. Though most officers were very much drawn from the upper classes I didn't feel kind of overwhelmed or out of my depth as an officer. And I don't remember any of them being nasty to me.

Another person who was quite an influence on me at Harefield was my driver Di Purdie. Di, just a private, a very nice girl, was maybe near my own social standing. After the war she went out to Australia, but I've seen her twice since then.

I think it must have been after VE Day in May 1945 that the Searchlight Regiment closed down. I was in London on VE Day.[16] We all went up to London that night. We were just in among the hordes of people in Trafalgar Square and Pall Mall. It was absolutely a night to remember. I and others were posted to a place in Kent, where there weren't the usual sort of searchlight things to do. So I was made education officer for the troop.

After that we all went into sort of admin, and I must have been with an ATS unit in Kidderminster in Worcestershire. I was there at Kidderminster when the July 1945 general election took place. I remember as the election results were coming in all these ATS officer women were saying, 'It's the end of England, it's the end of England.' And I thought, 'I can't be two-faced.' And I burst into tears and said, 'I have to tell you that I am a socialist.' And I was so upset over it that I had to go to bed! But none of those women officers turned nasty with me, not at all.[17]

So that's it. In January 1946 I was demobbed. I was delighted to be going home and going to get married. I'd been engaged by then for a couple of years. My fiancé was from Howwood, the same village as me. I'd known him since I'd worked beside him in the Renfrewshire Education Offices, bursaries department. I had kept a diary from the time I joined the ATS in 1941 until I got engaged, and then I was writing to him every day.

Looking back on my five years in the ATS I feel it was very enriching really, a tremendous experience that I wouldn't otherwise have had. I have no regrets about volunteering into the ATS. And then I did get married in June 1946, and I have my five children, which was what I'd always wanted to do. Incidentally, the essay my daughter Liz chose to write in her Highers was titled 'On Missing The War'. When she told me, I asked her, 'What on earth did you say, Liz?' She said, 'Well,

I noticed when people talk about the war they've a lot of very happy things they say.'

After we got married we were terribly hard up because my husband was a local government clerk. So after we had, I think, three children there was an advert in the newspaper for a part-time medical secretary to a gynaecologist. I'd been secretary to a professor of anatomy in Glasgow University, so I knew some medical jargon. Well, I worked for this gynaecologist for 13 years. Ultimately I was doing five half-days' work for her, and I saw her on Sunday. Unfortunately, my husband wasn't well, and he died in 1961.

Then in 1967 I went to Strathclyde University, graduated in 1971, went to Jordanhill College of Education, and then taught economics at Glasgow College of Technology. So I've had a good life.

Isobel Cumming

Ah aye wanted tae be a driver. Well, there wisnae much chance in civvy street o' daein' that. When the war broke out in 1939 ah wis 17½. Ma father had been in the army in the First War, and wis in the Home Guard in the Second War until, in March 1941, he volunteered intae the army. So wi' him already away ah think ah sent away myself then for the joinin' up papers. And ah volunteered intae the ATS in November 1941.

Ah'd been born on the 23rd o' April 1922 at Waukmill Cottage, Spitalhaugh, West Linton, Peeblesshire. Ah wis the oldest o' the family. There wis five years between ma sister Rena and me, and then a year and a half between Rena and ma brother Ian.

Ma father was jist a sawmill and forestry worker. He worked on estates most of his life. He'd done a formal apprenticeship as a sawmiller. Ah've still got references for him from Kilbride – ah'm not sure whether East or West Kilbride – and from Navar in Angus. So he served his time as a nurseryman as well. He was born at Kilmahog in Stirlingshire in 1894 or 1895, ah'm no' sure which; but he was 77 when he died in 1972. In the 1914–18 war he was a machine-gunner in the Seaforth Highlanders, and he had the Military Medal.[1] Ah would think he would come to West Linton at the end o' that war. Ma father – wi' ma mother, me and Rena, who wis jist a baby then – left West Linton in August 1927 and came tae work and live at Kailzie estate, two miles from Peebles. Ma father stayed there till 1949. He wis an under-forester there and worked in the sawmill.

Ma mother belonged Evanton in Ross and Cromarty and was brought up by an aunt. Ah think she would meet ma father jist before the 1914–18 War, when he was up workin' in Navar nurseries near Brechin. Ah remember her sayin' they were engaged when she wis seein' him off on a train durin' the war and he flung the engagement ring oot the window tae her! They were married in 1920. Ma mother was in domestic service as a table-maid at Blairvadock House, near Helensburgh, at the entrance tae the Gare Loch. And at West Linton, after she wis married, she wis often table-maid tae Sir James Ferguson. Ah think Sir James wis murdered much later on in Kenya at the time o' the Mau Mau.[2] She must have worked there tae after ah wis born, because I remember goin' tae the big hoose there. Ah never met ma grandparents on ma mother's side, ah dinnae ken anything much aboot them at a'. As ah've said, ma mother wis brought up by an aunt. Ma father's faither wis a watchmaker, but ah don't know where aboot.

Ma earliest memories are o' where ah grew up at Waukmill Cottage, West Linton. It wis a wee hoose, a little but and ben, jist a room and kitchen. It wis down by the River Lyne. It wis a tied house, but it wisnae actually tied to a farm: it would be tied to the big estate hoose. The cottage wis a' stone floors. It had a pantry, ah think, and there wis a box bed in the kitchen. There'd be no sink in the cottage, because ee used tae wash outside at a bath beside a well. Ye had tae fill the bath from the well. It wis one o' these steep-sided baths, and ah fell intae it one day. Ah wis standin' watchin' ma father, and of course he turned away, dryin' his face, and ah fell head first intae the bath! It wis a good job he turned roond and fund me, otherwise ah wouldnae be here.

The cottage wis lit wi' paraffin lamps. Ah dinnae remember the toilet at all, ah cannae remember where it wis: ah wis only five when ah left Waukmill Cottage. But, oh, it wouldnae be a flush toilet. But it wis an open fire that ma mother did the cookin' on. It wasn't a range. And we used tae ca' it punk – pancake bungle, because she wis always makin' pancakes. Ma mother had an oven at the side, and a girdle swee where she made her pancakes. And a big black kettle wis always on the fire. Ah cannae mind now if it wis a vegetable or a flower garden, but they had a garden in front o' the cottage.

Ah'd be five years old in the April before we came in August 1927 tae Kailzie. There wis a livin' room and a parlour there, and two bedrooms upstairs. There wis an alcove in the livin' room wi' an ordinary bed in it. Ma parents slept in this alcove in the livin' room. Rena as a baby wis there tae. Ah had a room tae myself upstairs. Ah cannae remember the other room bein' used at that time. Ah remember that when we were aulder Rena and I slept thegether in one o' the rooms for a while. There was quite a wide bit at the livin' room window. It had a cot in it and that's where Rena was at one time, maybe when ma brother Ian wis a baby. That Kailzie house had a flush toilet. Then about 1938 they renovated the houses, put the electric in, and gave us a bathroom at the same time. For cookin', there wis a range, a big black range, with an oven and a wee water tank at the side. But ma mother also had a little Primus stove in the kitchen.[3] We didnae actually have a kitchen at first, because the sink wis in the window. And there wis a long lobby goin' doon to the toilet. Then they built a bit further on for the bathroom. Before we had a bathroom we jist used the sink for baths. Ah remember once Rena, jist a wee soul, havin' a bath in front o' the fire, because it wis a Christmas party we were goin' tae. And Rena fell intae the bath wi' her party frock on. I got the blame o' pushin' her in, and got skelped for that! So that's the only time ah remember a bath in front o' the fire. Anyway, it wis quite a good house at Kailzie, and stone-built too.

Mrs Cree lived in the big house at Kailzie. She had lost her husband in 1926, the year before we came. She built a chapel – the William Cree Memorial – just opposite Kirkburn School nearby. Ma brother Ian wis the first child to be christened in the new chapel in 1928. So ma mother wis quite chuffed at that. The chapel's still there, and there's an old churchyard jist behind it where we used tae play from the school, and we werenae supposed tae. It wis the greatest place tae play hide and seek, behind the gravestones and behind the trees. Oh, we were aye gettin' rows in the churchyard.

Ah remember around that time a hail storm. Ah've a feelin' it wis August 1929. The hailstones were like golf balls, because ma mother had tae shut the shutters in case the windows got broken.[4]

* * *

Ah started school at Kirkburn School in August 1927 after their summer holidays. Ah'd be five in the April before that. The school wis between Kailzie and Cardrona. Ah used tae walk there, aboot a mile and a half. It'd take mair than 20 minutes, because oo played on the road: oo did not go straight tae the school! They were fun days. There wis six of us from Kailzie, all girls except one boy. Then there wis another lad from the farm doon the road, he went tae. There wis quite a gang o' us. Ah went wi' the butler's kids, because they were both aulder than me. Ah dinnae remember ma mother ever goin' tae the school wi' me.

Ah don't know how many children there would be at Kirkburn School when ah started, but ah ended up in a class on ma own, because o' ages, ye see. We were all steps and stairs. Ee didnae stay at Kirkburn till ee were 14. Ee went tae Peebles High School at the Qualifyin' exam when ee were aboot 11 or 12 years auld. Ah don't think any o' the children stayed on at Kirkburn School if they didn't pass the Qualifyin'. They had to move on. Kirkburn was a purely primary school. There must have been four or five different classes. The children came from Cardrona as well as Kailzie, and one or two from farms round about. But they were all in the one room: there wis only one teacher – a woman – and only one room in the school, and she had all these different classes. There werenae any partitions in the room, we were all together. I wid say there were aboot a dozen tae 14 children, definitely not as many as 20. Oh, it was a very small school. It wis a different style o' teachin' then a'thegither.

Ah did like the school and got on well there. Geography and spelling ah did like. It was quite a friendly place and, oh, she was a good teacher. But we were kind o' scared o' her, ye know. She wis strict. Oh, ah often think about the pointer! It was on ma knuckles, a pointer on ma knuckles, rather than a leather belt on the palm o' your hand. But she didnae do it often. She wid jist let ee know she wis boss.

So when ah wis 11 or 12 ah sat the Qualifyin' exam at Kirkburn. Ah remember the inspector comin' and givin' us the different things – the spellin' and things like that. Obviously, oo must have sat an exam. But ah dinnae remember writin' an exam, ah cannae remember much aboot the exams. But ah wis the only one in that Qualifyin' class. So then ah left Kirkburn and went off tae Peebles High School.

Ah didnae like the High School. Well, ach, ye didnae know anybody there, and it wis a big school compared wi' what we were in at Kirkburn. That put me off. Ah felt ah wis a sort o' country lassie. Ah never really fitted in. Ah did make friends wi' another two lassies, much the same as masel' – very quiet, ye know. One lived at Kings Meadows and one at Peebles. Then the subjects at the High School: the only one ah liked wis the French class. Ah got a prize for French. But ah never ever liked the High School.

What ah did like wis that ah cycled from Kailzie tae the High School. It wis, oh, a couple o' mile. It wisnae too far. It took about 15 minutes. I got a second-hand bike, a hand-doon, that had been one o' the farmers' daughter's. I wis chuffed wi' the bike, but ah had tae get big wooden blocks on the pedals, because ah couldnae reach them! Oh, ah did like a bike. It gave ee a sense o' liberation. Ee could cycle roond the roads and explore the countryside. Ye felt you'd achieved something. Ah did feel that.

So after ah began at the High School ah started cycling round about. Ah went jist on ma own: ah wis a bit of a loner anyway. Ah didnae cycle very far at first, probably jist doon tae Peebles or Cardrona. It wis only later on ah'd cycle as far as Innerleithen, aboot five miles from Peebles.

Ah wis only 12 when ah got the bike; ah didnae get much freedom then. Ah had tae work a lot in the house, helpin' ma mother. Ah did a lot. And ah wis sent for messages on the bike to the Co-operative in Peebles. They had a big counter in the shop. And ah wis so shy ah used tae stand in the corner till somebody noticed that ah'd stood for aboot an hoor, wi' ma mother's Store book in ma hand! Oh, ah did that for a long time before somebody suggested that ah should go straight to the other counter and ah would get served straight away because ah wis frae the country. And then the milk wis left along the Kings Meadows Road, behind some ferns. The man would leave it there and ah knew where to pick it up. Ah had the milk tae cairry an' a', ye see, on the way home frae the High School. So ah did that.

Well, ah wis taken off the School early. Ah had an exemption, because ma mother had a very bad ulcerated leg, and ah got off because o' that. Ah'd be 14 in April 1936, and ah wis taken off the school that year. Ah wis quite glad tae leave. Ah didn't like the High School at all. So ah stayed at home then for a while, oh, months, tae help ma mother. Then ah started work in the tweed mill in October 1936, when ah wis 14½.

* * *

As a girl ah didn't have ambitions tae be maybe a dressmaker, a shop assistant, or anythin'. Ah never got away wi' ambition in these days! But ah wanted tae be a driver. Ah don't know what gave me that idea, but ah wanted tae be a driver – a taxi driver. Ah didn't try tae get a job as a driver when ah left the school, no' at that time. Ye'd have tae be older, ye see, than ah wis then.

So ah started work in Ballantyne's March Street mill in Peebles on the 19th o' October 1936. Ah didnae see an advert for that job or apply for it. Ah didnae want tae gaun intae the mill. Ah think ah wis dragged tae the mill in tears! Ah think ma mother would enquire at the mill. She must have gone down there. The first ah knew o' it wis ah wis startin' in the mill. Oh, ah did not want tae work in the mill. But there ah wis, quite a shy lassie, lackin' in confidence, and suddenly ah found masel' sent oot tae work in the tweed mill.

March Street mill wis a more modern mill and a bigger mill than the other one in Peebles, Thorburn's Damside mill, which wis more old-fashioned. Ah started in March Street as an apprentice. And at first ah had tae go in ma school gym slip because ah hadnae a peenie! Ah come home that first day and ah said tae ma mother – ah wis in tears, 'Ah'll have tae get a peenie.' But it wis a long time afore ah got yin. And, oh, it wis terrible, oh, it wisnae half. Ah hated the mill, ah hated it.

Ah felt completely lost. Ah mean, it wis an entirely different world for me. Ma mother had never worked in a mill, nor ma father. Ah didnae know anybody that'd worked in a mill, no' really. None o' the lassies leavin' school were goin' intae the mill. There it was, ah wis myself again. Ah wis the only girl at Kailzie that wis startin' work then. Ah think the butler's lassie went intae an office. She wis older than me and left the school before me. So ah felt very lackin' in confidence, oh, it wis terrible.

But then you found at the mill that somebody sort o' took you in hand and kept an eye on you. You were taken tae see the manager. The first words he said tae me were: 'Can ye sweep a flair?' Ah wis quite indignant because, ah mean, ah wis yaised tae sweepin' the flair and that at home. Oh, ah wis quite indignant aboot that! And then of course ah wis no' very big. But the brush for sweepin' the flair had one o' these big long handles. And the brush wis aboot three feet wide, oh, a huge thing. But that wis ma first job in the mill, sweepin' the flair. That wis the normal job given tae a young girl startin', the sort o' job ee were given tae dae. Ah wis in the weavin' shed so, oh, ah wis doin' away tae that sweepin' for quite a while – weeks, ah think. And then ye were put on tae what they ca'ed the ingiein'.

Well, wi' the ingiein' there wis the web, like a tent, and ee sat inside it. The drawer wis on the outside, you were on the inside, and ye had a bundle o' threads and ye'd tae pass them through what they ca'ed the huddle. Ee passed them through and the drawer drew them through. If ye werenae quick enough Jimmy Broon, the bloke that ah had as the drawer, used tae gie iz a kick. Oh, tae me Jimmy wis an old man. He used tae put his cap on back tae front. Ah dinnae ken if this wis tae make it easier for him tae work. Oh, he wis a little man, and he wore little short baggy troosers and a tweed apron. And somebody said tae me what Jimmy was, ye see. Ah went hame tae ma mother and ah asked her: 'What's a Jenny Wullock?' Ah didnae ken what a Jenny Wullock was. And ma mother never told me yet. How ah found oot ah don't know.[5] And ah'd still tae work wi' this man. But Jimmy wis alert. He used tae gie me a kick noo and again under the table: ah wisnae gaun quick enough, ye see. Oh, you'd been shown what to do. You had tae sit beside somebody for a week or so showin' ye. But when ye got on by yersel' it wisnae . . . So ah worked tae Jimmy for quite a long time, oh, months. That didnae help ee tae settle in tae mill work, oh, no. But, och, ye gradually settled in once ye got tae know the other people. The other girls and women were quite helpful and friendly then. Well, ye went tae the canteen maybe wi' somebody and ye got used tae the mill, och, aye, ye got used tae it. There wis another apprentice ah went wi' there. She wis as big as what ah wis wee. They ca'ed us Laurel and Hardy! Aye, ye got laughs, ye really got laughs then.

After that, when ah wis aboot 16, ah wis tooken through from the weavin' shed tae the other bit, the warehoose. Well, no' actually the warehoose but the cleanin', darnin' place. Ah wis put on tae what they ca'ed the shavin' – the finishin' anyway. In the finishin' or shavin' there wis long tables where ye pulled the webs across and shaded them wi' pencils. That wis tae make sure the colours wis the same through-out. And ye looked for any knots or flaws. Ah got used tae that. Ah liked that job because ah think ah liked a creative side o' things. And that's when ah met Hilda Hope and we became friends a' our life. Ah wis sent on as apprentice tae Hilda when ah went on tae the shavin'. So we went aboot a lot thegither after that. Oh, Hilda wis aboot 12 years older than me.

We started work in the mornin' at eight o'clock till, ah think, half-past five. Ye had your lunch and ye got your breaks for tea in the mornin' and afternoon. There was a canteen. But I used to carry pieces, because I used tae be sent doon every day tae Bella's, an old friend of ma mother, in Peebles High Street for ma dinner. But I carried ma pieces wi' me, and Bella made me a cup o' tea. We a' went tae the canteen for the mornin' and afternoon 10 or 15-minute tea breaks. And we worked on Saturday mornins; ah think it would be tae the back o' 12 – eight till 12 or half-past, somethin' like that.

Ma wages when ah started as a girl o' 14 were seven shillins [35p] a week, wi' tuppence [1p] off for insurance. Ah gave ma wages tae ma mother. Ah didnae get any money back for pocket money. But she would give us money for the pictures. Ma mother bought ma claes for me. Mind you, ah didnae have many claes, no, never, ah didnae. Ma father didnae have a big wage. Ah ken what it was: 38 shillins [£1.90] a week. So the whole family income wis 45 shillins [£2.25] a week, that wis a'. Ma mother didn't work outside, she wis always at home. She had the three o' us, Rena, Ian, and me. But ah mind ah did get latterly, no' jist then, a shillin' [10p] a week tae put away for a bike, because ah had somebody in the mill wi' a friend that had a racer bike and she would sell me it for £2 10s 0d [£2.50]. Ah paid it up, a shillin' a week. And ah got it. Ee didnae get things easy. Anyway it wis a better bike. Ah wis chuffed tae bits. By that time ah must have been gaun on for 17. So ma parents were quite happy to let me cycle further roond the countryside. Ah used tae go quite far wi' it: Lyne station, Manor way, Drochil Castle, up the Glasgow road, and Dolphinton and Broughton and these bits – villages in Peeblesshire. There wisnae much traffic in those days. But ah never went as far as Edinburgh or even tae Innerleithen. Ah went masel'. Oh, ah liked the bike. It gave me a sense o' enjoyin' the countryside more. Ah've always been aware of the environment. Ma father and mother used tae take us bikin' when we were wee. Ma father took Rena on the back o' his bike, and ma mother Ian on her bike. Ah had ma ain little bike then. We used tae go tae Neidpath Castle. That's what started us off cyclin'.[6]

Ah don't remember ever joinin' a union in the mill, no, ah'm sure ah didnae. Ah wis never in anythin' like that. The management o' the mill were quite strict. Ah wis aye runnin' tae work at the mill at the last meenit. But the gateman wis very guid tae me. We had tae clock in. But the gateman, when he saw me comin', would put ma number in! It wis numbers. Oh, he knew fine ah wis at the last minute. But ah wisnae quartered so that ah suffered loss of wages for bein' late.[7] Ah wouldnae be that late. Ah mean, it would be a meenit or two minutes. But the gateman wis very good. So ah carried on workin' at March Street mill till after the war broke oot.

* * *

When we were children we were sent to the Sunday School and to the church, the William Cree Memorial. Ah think it wis the afternoon we went. And we got a little motto – a text, sort of Good Words. Ye had tae memorise it for the next Sunday. There wis one that ah still cannae understand tae this day: 'Sufficient unto the day is the evil thereof.'[8] Ah dinnae think ma parents were really regular church attenders. Ah don't remember ma fither and mother bein' much in the church at all. But on the estate they'd have tae go maybe now and again for appearances sake tae communion.

As a girl workin' in the mill ah had the bike, and ah went tae the pictures maybe two or three times a month. Ah, but ah had a boyfriend by that time, at 14, efter ah went intae the mill. He wis a young lad that worked in the mill. For two or three years ah wis goin' steady wi' him. So there ye are. Oh, ah wis a very shy girl. But ah got tae the pictures right enough, ah went tae the pictures, and got paid intae the pictures – a' unknown tae ma mother! Oh, ah wis afraid o' tellin' ma mother. Oh, it wis definitely unusual in these days for a girl o' 14 to have a steady boyfriend. Ah'd be ower young. Oh, ah wisnae able tae take ma boyfriend home tae Kailzie. So we had tae meet in different hooses, well, oo met in the street actually. Ah dinnae think anybody in Peebles ever told ma mother. Ah, well, ye see, she wis oot in the country. She didnae go tae Peebles much. So word never got back tae ma mother, no' that ah know of – well, no' until he started writin' tae me. She opened the letters, ye see. Well, ah didnae get many letters, but ah remember she opened one anyway. Oh, ah resented that, of course ah did. Ah don't know, but probably in that era that wis the practice, tae, wi' other mothers at Kailzie or the mothers o' ma friends. But, ah mean, ah wis still young. My boyfriend wis jist over a year older than me. Anyway, then he went away tae join the Royal Navy. He was in boys' service. He must have joined some time before the war broke out, maybe 1938, because he wis actually on HMS *Mohawk* at Rosyth in the Firth o' Forth when it wis bombed by the Germans. That's how ah remember October the 16th 1939. But he wisnae injured in the bombin'.[9]

Ah wis 17½ when the war broke out the previous month. Ah remember the declaration o' the war. Ah dinnae remember the comin' o' the war havin' much effect on the mill, except that we started makin' khaki. They must have been contracts for uniforms. Ah remember workin' on the khaki because there wis an awfy lot o' static electricity in it.

As ah've said, ma father wis in the army in the 1914–18 War and he wis in the Home Guard in the Second War. But then in March 1941, when he wis aboot 45 or 46, he volunteered intae the army, the Royal Scots. He went in as a PSI or something.[10] He wis trainin' the Home Guard men on weapons. He wis at Redford Barracks for a while. Well, there wis a big row about that, him volunteerin' intae the army, because he didnae have tae go, no wi' the estate, ye see. Ma mother must have felt it terrible. Rena and Ian were still at the school. Ian wis at one o' the schools in Peebles and it wis overcrowded because there were evacuees there. Ah think there were three sittin' to a desk. Well, Ian wis knocked off the end o' the seat and broke a rib. It punctured his lung. The first day the sirens were heard in Peebles – ah think it wis the same time HMS *Mohawk* wis bombed at Rosyth – Ian wis in hospital then. Though ah don't remember hearin' rows or shoutin' at home, there could have been disagreement between ma parents when ma father volunteered intae the army. It must ha' been dreadful for ma mother, when you think back aboot it. And of course, as ah say, ma fither went away from home. And the Kailzie House butler's girl went away tae the WAAFs. Everybody wis goin' away. Ah wis aboot the only yin left o' my age like. Mrs Cree that owned the estate had died on 19th October 1936 – the same day ah started work at the mill, and there wis new folk come intae a' the different houses. Ma father and the butler wis the only ones that wis kept on. The rest o' the workers were all given their notices. Even the head forester had got his books. There wis nine or ten girls in the Big Hoose – cook, housekeeper and others – and some o' them were kept on. And there wis aboot nine or ten gardeners and there wis none o' them kept on, none o' them at all. Some of the folk had been workin' for years at Kailzie, and must have been distressed at losin' their jobs. Mrs Cree's nephew, who was in the Black Watch, became the new owner o' the estate.[11] Well, they brought in another gardener and another head forester. Ma fither didnae get on awfy weel wi' the new head forester: ah think he wis kind o' runnin' and tellin' tales, ye know. And that's how, ah think, after the war began, ma faither would be up and away tae the army.

Ah don't think ah wis gettin' fed up wi' workin' at the mill. Ah still enjoyed the work. But ah still wanted tae be this driver. And that's what ah wanted tae be. Ah saw a chance o' becomin' a driver by joinin' the Forces. Maybe the uniform had somethin' tae do with it, ah don't know. Ah hadnae had discussions wi' ma mother about goin' intae the Forces, because ah knew there would be a row and she would forbid me tae go. She and ma father could have stopped me if they wanted tae. But in fact ah don't remember havin' a row over it wi' ma mother. Ah think that, after ma father left tae join the army in March 1941, ah sent away myself for the joinin'-up papers. Then the papers would come in and ma mother'd probably open them, because she opened ma letters and everything. But, as ah say, ah don't remember fa'in' oot wi' ma parents or anythin'. Ah think they jist accepted ah wis goin' tae go.

It was for the WAAFs that I applied. And ah had tae go tae Galashiels for a medical. But ah didnae pass the eye test. So ah thought, 'Well, that's it.' Ah hadnae known there wis any weakness o' ma eyes, and they never said ah was colour-blind. Ah never had any difficulty wi' colours. Anyway, ah think ah must ha' been disappointed at no' gettin' intae the WAAFs. What had given me the notion tae apply tae the WAAFs wis, well, the ATS hadnae a very guid name had it? Oh, no, the ATS wis the lowest o' the Services. They jist got that name, ye know. Ah think it must have been a sort o' morals thing, that the ATS girls had a low reputation. There wis a feelin' they were maybe a bit 'common', and had a reputation o' bein' a bit easy maybe wi' their morals. Whereas WAAFs and WRNS were a wee bit better.[12] But ah had heard that ee couldnae get intae the WRNS unless ye had either a relative already in the navy or somebody that knew somebody in the WRNS, because they were upper class. So ah never thought aboot applying tae the WRNS. But when ah wis rejected by the WAAFs ah then applied to the ATS. Ah must have been determined to go intae the Services! And tae learn tae drive! So ah must have swallowed ma feelins aboot the ATS. Ah wanted tae be a driver. And there wisnae much chance in civvy street o' daein' that. I mean, the mill would have vans and lorries, but the drivers would be men. And ah hadnae the money tae go and do anything aboot learnin' tae drive. You couldnae afford tae pay out o' your ain pocket for that. Ah mean, ye had enough maybe tae go tae the pictures wi', and that wis it. Lack o' cash meant quite a lot. Ye didnae have it.

Well, tae get intae the ATS ah must have had tae go for a medical. Ah think it wis the Drill Hall in Peebles where ah got the medical. Oh, there wis nothing said about ma eyes then. And ah got a letter sayin' ah wis accepted. It wis Newbattle Abbey at Dalkeith ye'd tae go tae first.[13] And again ah dinnae remember havin' a row then wi' ma mother about goin' tae the ATS. There wisnae much closeness between ma mother and I, ye see. Ah think ah wis closer tae ma father. He seemed tae understand things better. Well, would ma father maybe have talked her doon? He wis home at weekends, no' every weekend, but he was home.

So it wis November 1941 ah volunteered intae the ATS. Ah wis 19. Ah thought if ah volunteered ah would maybe get the job – drivin' – ah wanted.[14] So ah went up on the bus from Peebles tae Edinburgh then on tae Newbattle Abbey. We were a' collected together wi' oor cases and things, and a motley crew we were. Ah remember walkin' down the drive at the Abbey. Ah can remember the hut where ah stayed in there – Hut 8, definitely Hut 8. There wis a stove in it in the middle o' the floor, wi' a chimney up. Ah don't think they were Nissen huts, they were wooden huts, fine huts. There'd maybe be a dozen beds in the hut. Ah cannae remember if they were double beds – bunk beds – or no', but ah think they were bunk beds. Aye, ah'm sure they were bunk beds. Because later, when we went tae Hereford, we got single beds and we thought this was great. At Newbattle ah think ah wis in a top bunk.

Of course, this wis a very new experience for me. Ah'd led jist an ordinary life. So, oh, ah wis homesick, aye, ah wis homesick for twae or three days. Ah didnae know anybody else there at all, not a soul. There were no other girls there from Peebles or from the mill. Ah wis on ma own again, on ma own again. But ye jist sailed through it a'. Ah think it wis sixish when we got up in the mornin'. You'd tae turn oot whether you liked it or no'. Ah wisnae in the habit o' gettin' up as early as that. Ah didnae like gettin' up early in the mornin'. At the mill I was always runnin' at the last minute. But, och, ye got accustomed in time tae the early rise. Ye jist had tae do it, oh, ye had tae do it, and that wis it.

On the whole the food at Newbattle Abbey wisnae too bad. Ah wis dreadin' that ah would be put into the cookhouse. Ah didnae want the cookhouse. To be a cook: that ah didnae want. As ah say, ah'd volunteered intae the ATS because ah thought ah'd maybe get the job ah wanted – drivin'. They did consider that – if ee volunteered. Ah had told them ah wis keen tae become a driver. Later on, in ma paybook it said, 'Refused Ack-Ack'. Ah did have a test for joinin' Ack-Ack. But ah never knew whether they meant they had refused me Ack-Ack or that I had refused Ack-Ack. But I certainly had refused Ack-Ack! Ah didnae want that. Ah wanted tae be a driver![15]

At Newbattle we were issued wi' uniforms and everything. Ye didnae get measured for your uniform. They'd have a look at ee, then jist bunged it at ye and said, 'Try that on.' But the uniform did fit me, it wis a' right. Ye jist got one uniform – a jacket and skirt, and a greatcoat, your tie and three shirts, and a cap. Ah hated the caps. Och, ah dinnae ken why: ah had a wee face, ah think. Then two pairs o' brown shoes; and ye got three sets of bloomers and a'thing. Ah remember goin' up the drive at the Abbey and trippin' over a tree root or somethin' that made a hole aboot that size in ma stockin' knee. And ah asked for a new pair o' stockins. But, oh, they couldnae give me them. Ah had tae sit and darn that muckle hole. It wis aboot the size o' the palm o' ma hand. And ah had tae go aboot wi' this damned stockin' on. Oh, no, it wisnae easy days. Ah remember we got oor inoculations there. And there wis only two o' us could turn oot for breakfast the next day: somebody else and masel'.

Ah wis at Newbattle Abbey three weeks. I don't remember any of the other girls there at all, no' by first names or anything. We went aboot thegether and that, but ye werenae very . . . Ye didnae get very close tae them in three weeks. None o' the girls in ma hut were married that ah can remember. The girls there came from all walks of life. And, oh, ah don't think they jist came from the Edinburgh-Lothians-Border area. Ah'd felt very homesick masel', but ah remember some o' the other girls in ma hut weepin' wi' homesickness. Ah think oo would a' feel much aboot the same. Then ah remember the stove in the middle o' oor hut went oot. The girls didnae ken how tae light it. Ah wis the only one that did. So ah went oot and gethered some sticks and lit the stove. And, oh, ah wis hailed as a hero. So ah wis a' right efter that!

We were never allowed intae the big house, Newbattle Abbey, itsel'.
Was it no' jist officers' quarters? We were never allowed there. Our huts
were on the left. As soon as you got in the gates you turned tae the left.
Then there were other huts across the road – King's Lines. Oo were
separate. Ah don't know if the King's Lines ATS girls would come in
at the same time as us. Maybe one intake went intae our huts, and the
next went intae King's Lines. Ah don't know. But ah remember when,
after oor three weeks were up, a new intake wis comin' in and us aulder
yins were sent oot tae meet them and take them round and that. It wis
in November in a pourin' wet time. And it gradually got darker and
darker, and, oh, ah wis oot and trudgin' aboot, up and doon the drive.

The intake that were shown round by us were nearly a' Irish girls,
well, the ones I had: 'You take that half-dozen, you take that half-
dozen.' And by Jove they were rough. Ah don't know whether it wis
Northern Ireland or no'; ah wouldnae think they'd be there from the
other part o' Ireland. But what they were already callin' the corporals
and so forth – and they were only in one day! Oh, swearing; they were
rough. Wi' us, och, ah think the relationship at Newbattle wi the
NCOs wis quite friendly. There wasnae a lot o' shoutin' and bawlin'
and swearin' by them at us, oh, no' really. You were treated as a
human bein'. The men, ah think, were different. Though ah dinnae
remember seein' any men at Newbattle Abbey. There wis no men at
all. Ah think it wis all women officers. But we were treated as volunteers and shown a bit o' respect by the NCOs. Ee jist took it that that
wis their job and we were there and they were the boss. But wi' the
Irish girls, ah think the weather had a lot tae dae wi' it: and mud wis
up tae our ankles. Ah wasted a pair o' shoes. Ah couldnae get them
renewed and they never were the same. Bein' brought up in the country ah wouldnae take it so badly, ah don't think, as some o' the other
girls. And then, ah mean, some o' them when they arrived were
wearin' high heels and what-not.

We got drill, marchin', square-bashin'. Ah liked that very much,
because ah think ah'm a bit regimented in ma outlook. Ah think you
took a pride in it. You got it every day for half an hour or an hour, more
or less. Ah did like square-bashin'. We must have had a parade ground
among the huts somewhere. Then we used tae get route marches to
Dalkeith. Ah mind o' goin' through Dalkeith singin'! We didn't get any
PT – physical training, or instruction or training on weapons, nothing

like that. Ah cannae remember any lectures, ah dinnae even mind o' the canteen there, though oo must have had a canteen. And ah cannae remember bein' out that camp at all, except for the route marches. Some things are a blank really. If it's a thing ye werenae interested in ah think ye would jist blank it oot. Well, after three weeks at Newbattle Abbey ah wis sent to Hereford.

* * *

Ah went by train tae Hereford. Ah cannae remember any o' the other girls at Newbattle Abbey goin' wi' me, but ah suppose some o' them would. Aye, there must have been a few o' us goin' tae Hereford because we had tae change trains – wis it at Crewe? Well, ah didnae ken anythin' about trains or anythin' else. Ah jist tagged on and follaed the rest o' them. And there wis a vehicle meetin' us when we arrived at Hereford. That took us out to Bradbury Lines as they called it, jist on the outskirts o' Hereford town. Bradbury Lines wis all huts. They ca'ed them spider blocks. They were a' intersectioned: one led intae another. There were sort o' wee corridors, then a room, and another wee corridor. They were a' interconnected. And the huts were bigger than at Newbattle. There might have been a couple o' dozen girls in ma hut.

Ah remember that's where ah got ma hair cut. Before that ma hair wis shoulder length. And ah used tae put rollers in. So ah wis seeck o' jumpin' oot and in the bed, every time the lights went oot, puttin' rollers in and losin' them tae drop on the flair, and that kind o' thing! Ah said, 'Aw, tae hang wi' this', got rid o' the rollers, went intae the town, and got ma hair cut – quite short: ah had the Eton Crop![16]

The girls in ma hut were mainly young girls like masel', late teens, early twenties. But ah palled up wi' a woman – well, ah call her a woman, she'd be no' much older than me – and we were very friendly. Evelyn Wigginton they called her. She came from somewhere down Cheshire way, ah think. But Evelyn wis married, or had been married. Her husband wis no longer living with her. And she had a wee girl. Ah don't know if it was Evelyn's parents or no' that wis lookin' after her wee girl. Because Evelyn had the wee girl she must have volunteered intae the ATS. Anyway, ah got friendly with her early on at Hereford. We palled up together. We were in the same hut. She wis quiet, too. Ah can see her yet. She wis a wee blonde woman. Ah don't know what Evelyn had done for a livin'. Ah don't think we discussed her past. Well, near the end o' ma time at Hereford Evelyn got a letter one day. Ah remember her gettin' it. And, good heavens, she fainted at ma feet. The letter wis something tae do wi' this child o' hers. Ah don't know whether it wis a case o' custody. Well, Evelyn wis sent away home. She got compassionate leave or somethin'. And by this time ah wis tae be drafted away from Hereford. Ah didn't have Evelyn's home address so ah could write tae her, and she didnae have ma address. So ah never saw her again.

Well, ah wis at Hereford a'thegether 12 weeks, ah think. That's where we were trainin' tae drive. We were doin' that nearly all day. They had a lot o' driver instructors there. We got a lot o' marchin', parade work. But mostly we were out in the mornin' on the vehicles. In fact, we were oot all day. First, we went round the barrack square. We did that for quite a while before ee were taken on tae the road. Ee stood in a line, and the instructors all stood by their vehicles. Ee were allocated to an instructor. Usually you got a different vehicle. Sometimes it wis a lorry, sometimes it wis a car. It depended on jist the luck o' the draw, ah suppose. So you didn't pass all the time driving nothing but lorries or nothing but cars. Ye got quite a selection. They gave ye a written thing every time ye went out: passed so-and-so, or that you needed to have extra tuition. Ah still had ma record o' that till a few years ago, and ah don't know what happened tae it.

They were all different types o' lorry. There wis a three ton lorry, and a 15 cwt one. The Guy wis the worst tae drive. It wis a lorry but it had different gears tae the others. Ah liked the Bedford. The Bedford was a straightforward one. The Guy wis a divil. Ah cannae remember if it wis bigger than the Bedford or no', but it wisnae sae easy tae drive. Ah cannae remember if it jist had three gears. There wis somethin' different aboot it. Ah didnae like it. Then there wis the Fordson – 15 cwt, ah think.

So ye got up intae the cab o' the lorry or ye got intae the car, and an instructor sat beside ee. There wis no women instructors; they were all men. Relations between the instructors and the learners were quite friendly. Ah never had any bother at all. Ah don't know how they put up wi' us at times. The instructor didnae have a second steering wheel, there wis nothin' like that, it wis jist ordinary. Ye went round and round the barrack square for ages. Ah think ah managed that a' right. Ah never crashed the lorry or car! Ah quite enjoyed it, ah really did. That's what ah wanted tae do, what ah'd joined the ATS for! Learnin' tae drive probably helped tae develop ma confidence. So ah wis beginnin' tae settle doon in the army.

And we got time off at Hereford. Ah cannae remember if it wis jist at any old time or no'. Ye would jist have certain times when ye were off. Ye could go to the pictures. Ah don't remember any sport there – runnin', hockey, netball, swimmin': ah would have minded aboot swimmin' Ah cannae remember any PT, or a gym. If there wis a gym ah wis never in it. But, oh, you were up early in the mornin'. Ah remember gettin' up at five o'clock tae get a hot bath. Somebody wid go in, fill a bath, and shout, 'Bath's ready!' Ye know, it wis sort o' one bath between all the girls in the hut. There might have been two, but this wis all. So ye had tae get up early if ye wanted hot water. Ah don't think everybody could have a hot bath in the mornin'. Some o' the girls would maybe take a bath at night. But ah liked mine in the mornin'- so tae make sure ye got it ye had tae get up aboot five o'clock. Reveille would be sixish. It wis early, it wis really early.

Ah cannae remember when we had the marching and the parades. But we got quite a lot o' them. So at Hereford it wis a mixture o' learnin' tae drive and marchin'. We didnae get more uniform at Hereford – except ye had trousers. Ah cannae remember havin' trousers at Newbattle Abbey, but we certainly had them at Hereford. Ye wore them rither than a skirt when ye were drivin'. And the food at Bradbury Lines wis no' bad, no' bad. Though it wisnae like home cookin'. But ye made do. Ah remember their steam puddins. They werenae like steam puddins at a'! They were more like dough-balls. Ye used tae call them depth-charges! They were cut intae squares. But they were solid, really solid. But ah don't remember bein' awful hungry at Hereford; we were reasonably well-fed.

The only time we saw the men at the camp wis when we were drivin'. Ah dinnae remember if the camp wis only ATS. The men instructors must ha' had quarters. Ah think they had their quarters in the camp itsel'. But they didnae mix wi' the ATS. Oh, there wis quite strict segregation. The girls' quarters were entirely private; men were not allowed in them or anywhere near them. There wis a men's camp further intae the town, maybe even far away in the outskirts. Ah do remember some o' the girls went tae a dance, ah think it wis RAF. I didnae go masel'. And ah don't remember seein' any ATS Military Policewomen.

Well, after bein' oot a' day on learnin' tae drive, and marching and parades, we finished at five o'clock, then we were fairly free. The only time ah remember doin' duties after a day's work wis on Auld Year's Night in 1941. Ah think the head ones in the camp thought all Scots people there would go mad on Auld Year's Night. So a' o' us Scots people there were put on to fatigues. Half a dozen, or whatever there were, o' us Scots were put on tae peelin' tatties. I resented that very much. No' that ah wanted tae go wild on Auld Year's Night. But why should they pick on us? That's what I thought. But of course that was the reason. It was very pointed. That's the only time ah remember peelin' tatties in the ATS. Ah'll no' forget it!

Ah can't easily remember what the pay was when ah went intae the ATS. It runs in ma mind it wis seven shillings a week, something like that.[17] Ah cannae even remember goin' for a pay at Hereford. It wasn't until later, when ah wis at Edinburgh, that ah remember pay parades. And ah don't think ah sent ma pay, or most o' it, home tae ma mother. No, ah think ah kept it! But maybe ah had signed something tae give ma mother an allowance. I don't know, ah cannae mind. Ah hadn't fallen out wi' ma mother. And ah went home on leave. But ah didn't get leave from Hereford: ah got tonsillitis. Ah should ha' had sick leave then, but me bein' so far from home they didnae send iz.

But ah remember that, ah can remember the tonsillitis well, being put intae this wee place. This was the sick bay. It wis like a cell. Ah wis sent in there. There wis one bed in it and a table, and the floor wis jist concrete. Ye hadnae slippers or anything wi' ye for your feet. There wis a corridor wi' like one, two, three, four, or so many cubicles, and there was a sink at the end of it. Nobody came near ye. Ye got one pill sent in. Somebody jist shoved it in on to your table in this wee cell. They didnae come near ye for fear o' infection. And somebody came wi a plate o' food, and put it on the floor . It wis like bein' in a prison. Ah cannae remember how long ah wis in there. But, by Jove, it felt like ages. Ye just lay there. Ye had nothing tae read. Somebody in the next cell or cubicle used tae shout across. In fact, ye used tae shout across tae each other. Ye never saw who it was, jist, 'What are ee in for?', and, ken, a' this. But the medical folk never gave ye any attention. Ah cannae remember a doctor comin'. Ye'd tae go oot wi' your bare feet and wash your plate at this sink along the corridor. Ye never saw anybody.

Ah knew fine it was tonsillitis ah had. Ah used tae take it every year, ye see. Ah had it every year when ah wis a teenager, though no' very much since then. It wis pretty uncomfortable, wi' temperatures . . . But ah think them in charge o' the sick bay thought it wis something more than tonsillitis – diphtheria. Anyway, ah must ha' been in the sick bay ten days or a fortnight. The laughable bit was that it wid be by then gettin' on for Christmas, 1941. And ma mother had sent me a clootie dumplin' – which shows she and I hadnae fa'en oot. After ah got oot the sick bay this parcel wi' the clootie dumplin' wis waitin' for me. Ah opened it up, and cut slices off the dumplin' tae gie tae some o' the girls. Naebody wid have a bit. They thought ah wis infectious. Ah think they jist thought, 'Ah'm no' eatin' that, ah'm no' eatin that.' Ah could-nae share it at a'. So ah had tae eat a' the clootie dumplin' masel'![18]

Well, ah carried on at Bradbury Lines at Hereford tae the end o' the 16-week drivers' training course. Ah passed the course. And at the end o' it we got tests like primary school tests, ye know, fittin' triangles intae the right bits. And if ye passed wi' a certain amount o' marks ye got sent on tae become a car driver. If ye didnae have the necessary marks ye were put on tae lorry convoys. Well, ah wis dyin' tae come on tae convoys. Ah thought it wis mair excitin'. And, ye see, in convoys ye were more or less in a group again. Ah preferred tae be wi' other girls. And if anythin' happened, well, ee'd help each other. When ah wis a lassie ah'd been very shy. But by the time ah'd learned tae drive ah'd come tae prefer bein' wi' the other girls. However, ah had passed the tests wi' a mark of 76, which ah thought wis no' bad, and ah wis put on tae drivin' officers in staff cars. That meant ah'd be mair on ma own again. Before ah left Hereford ah wis disappointed that, because ah'd had tae catch up wi' the course and the practical tests, ah couldnae go on the passin'-oot parade.

* * *

From Hereford ah wis posted tae Edinburgh. There wis no' jist me, there were quite a number o' us came up by train then tae Edinburgh. The other girls had no' really been in the same hut as me at Bradbury

Lines, but in the same squad. Oh, ah knew some o' them. Ah wis quite glad tae get some o' them ah knew, rather than jist come up wi' a strange bunch.

We were posted tae Rothesay Terrace, at the West End in Edinburgh, tae begin wi', and billeted there. That was a big hoose. Ah shared a big room, wi' the beds and things, and a big bow window. You were given a big wood box tae put a' your belongins, your cutlery and everything, in. It stayed under your bed. Ye had tae be tidy and a' that. There'd be aboot six o' us a'thegither in the room, in single beds. After a time, for some reason we were shifted across the road in Rothesay Terrace.

When we arrived at Rothesay Terrace we were sent intae the garage nearby at Belford, opposite Belford Church. And ye were allotted tae somebody. Ye had tae clean and maintain your own car and a' that. Though ah wis a staff car driver ah jist drove a little canvas-topped utility van. Then ah progressed tae a Ford Prefect, a small car. Ah wasnae driver for one particular officer. You were just on call, whaever wanted ye. There wis a kind o' pool o' drivers. There wis a drivers' room, which ah hated. It wis a room where we sat and waited for a call. But ah used tae be fund under ma car doon at the petrol pumps. Ah preferred daein' practical work and didnae like the drivers' room. Maybe twice a day ah'd be called on tae drive an officer. Ah remember once goin' oot tae Craigiehall, army headquarters in Scotland, jist outside Edinburgh in West Lothian. The brigadier's car, a big Humber, had broken doon. Ah must have been the only one there at the garage they could send. Ah went oot in this wee car and, oh, the brigadier wis very indignant. And no place tae put his flag! Another time ah wis sent tae St Andrews in Fife, tae one o' the gun sites. Ye had tae go by the ferries, of course: there wis nae Road Bridge then. Ah went wi' the Ford Prefect. And the officer wis a captain, an awfy nice bloke. We went up tae the gun site. It must have been late, because it wis dark. Ye couldnae see much at a'. But ah remember seein' the searchlights. They were a' masked. The captain must have noticed ah wis gettin' tired, and he said he would drive. Well, ye're no' supposed tae let somebody else drive in your car. But ah let him. It wis three o'clock in the mornin' when we got back intae the garage in Edinburgh, after he'd been roond the gun sites. And ah had tae report for duty next mornin' at seven o'clock, jist the same.

The driving job wis a bit borin', jist hangin' aboot, waitin' for a call, when ye were only called oot aboot twice a day. Ah drove mainly within Edinburgh and its outskirts. And, ah mean, ah wisnae a good mixer. Some o' the lassies were a bit hoity-toity. They werenae my sort. That's why I disappeared away doon tae the open place down by the petrol pumps at the garage, down by the Water o' Leith. There wis a big wide place doon there where ye took your car if ye wanted tae do maintenance. There wis a pit, but the pit wis in the garage. I got away by myself to learn more about the engines and that. Ah liked workin' wi' the nuts and bolts. And ye got intae a habit o' cleanin' the car. It wis somethin' tae dae really, and ah took a pride in it. No' that there wis any inspections o' the vehicles from time tae time, no' really.

Most o' the officers ah wis drivin' wis below field rank – no' as high as major. The only exception wis the brigadier. The rest were maybe, och, lieutenants and the captain. The lower the rank they were the worse they were. Och, aye, ah didnae like them at a'. Ah don't think ah ever drove any ATS officers. Ah think it wis nearly a' men. And then ah had a big shot at drivin' an ambulance. They took iz out in this ambulance. Well, they were big, big ambulances in thae days. And if ye passed this test ye were goin' tae be sent tae Wick or tae Corpach near Fort William. Ah thought, 'Ah'm no' wantin' tae go away up there. Ah'm quite enjoyin' masel' in Edinburgh now', ee ken. And ah wis near home at Peebles. So ah decided ah wisnae wantin' tae pass this ambulance drivin' test. Ah pleaded that ah wis very nervous on this, ah wisnae, ye know, lookin.' So ah played the daft lassie, and ah never got posted away on that.

However, there wis this ATS Sergeant Montgomery that took iz out in the ambulance. Ah'll never forget her. She wis on ma back nearly a' the time. Every time ah passed this wee office door she seemed tae have somethin' for me. She wis harassin' me. She jist seemed tae get hold o' a name and that wis it, ye know. Of course, ah wis awfy quiet – awfy quiet until ah wis really roosed. Ah demanded tae know why ma name wis always on the roster. If ah wisnae gettin' the garage floors tae sweep ah wis gettin' somethin' else tae do, ye know. So ah complained aboot it, and it did stop.

As ah've said, ah never got leave from Hereford, because o' ma tonsillitis. But we must have had leave from Edinburgh when we came up from Hereford. But ah cannae remember it. It wis possible for me tae get home wi' a weekend pass maybe, because Peebles is no' far from Edinburgh. Ah do remember a wee sergeant – she was a little lass – took iz out drivin' one day from Edinburgh. It wis a Sunday. We were oot gatherin' snowdrops! And ah mentioned ah lived at Peebles. The wee sergeant said, 'Oh, it's 20 mile, that's no' far.' Well, there wis five o' us in this Austin car, ah think it was, and we a' descended on ma mother. And this wis highly illegal. And, oh, good heavens, ma mother made us tea or something, as she wid do. It's a wonder we werenae catched. Ah mean, we must ha' been away a long time, the whole afternoon probably, and if somebody had been wantin' that car . . . Ah don't know how we got away wi' that.

Then ah wis posted tae Newcastle. Ah wis sent from Edinburgh doon there wi' a truck, one o' these little utility vans. Ah don't know why. But ah wis tae be attached tae this unit, ah think the one wi' the bow and arrow shoulder flash. It wis the artillery anyway. But ah wis there aboot seven days when, och, ah got posted back again tae Edinburgh. Ah had tae take three officers back up wi' me in this little covered-in utility van. It wisnae comfortable, jist two seats in the front and two at the back. Ah remember gettin' a row frae one o' the officers for goin' over 40 mile an hour comin' up the road. Ah wis anxious tae get back tae Edinburgh, ye see. It wis the filthiest van ah think ah'd ever seen. So ah wis back tae the Belford petrol pumps in Edinburgh again.

But ah wisnae sent back tae Rothesay Terrace, it wis Palmerston Place nearby ah wis sent to then. It wis a house no' quite opposite St Mary's Cathedral. So down in the garage five o' us lassies were put on to buildin' a chassis. Ah still have a photiegraph o' that. That reminds me aboot the pits at the garage. When ah started there first, after ah came up from Hereford, ah wis right green. The garage pits were covered round wi' these sleepers. And of course when you were in a pit underneath your car you had your lamp and you were workin' away. Then of course ye drove your car off. And once what did ah do? Ah forgot tae put the sleepers back over the pit. And yin o' the men came along and fell doon the pit. Oh, ah run away and hid in the boilerhoose! He wasnae injured, but he suffered shock. If he'd got a hold o' me he'd ha' murdered iz. So ah hid in the boilerhoose for ever so long afore ah could come oot! When ah think aboot it now – terrible. It wis an accident but, ye know . . . Oh, God, ah wis feared for that man efter that. Oh, he knew it wis me. But ah wid never ha' done it again. Ye learn through your mistakes.

Mostly at Edinburgh you had your evenings tae yourself, though sometimes ye were on duty. Ah cannae mind if it wis fire duty or what. But if you were off at nights, well, ah had an aunt and uncle, ma fither's brother, in Edinburgh. They stayed jist roond the corner in Stafford Street. So ah visited them, and sometimes got ma tea there. Oh, they were kind tae me. And ma fither wis in Edinburgh as well. He wis down at Eton Terrace at the Dean Bridge. Well, ah used tae go oot wi' him and maybe have a cup o' tea or somethin'. So, ah mean, ah wisnae actually away frae hame. Ma fither wis a what they ca'ed PSI, trainin' instructors tae a' the big factories, like the chocolate works. He went round a' these, showin' them, the Home Guard, guns: he wis a firearms instructor. Then he wis posted doon tae the Borders and went round a' the bits in the Borders instructing the Home Guard about weapons. Oh, he enjoyed that.

Ah didn't get tae know any householders in Edinburgh, no' really. Ye know, ye heard o' some people, from wantin' tae be helpful durin' the war, that took in ATS girls. Ah didnae know any people like that. But ah remember bein' in a café – ah think it wis ca'ed Harwell's – in Colinton village in Edinburgh wi' the wee ATS sergeant that took us in the car tae ma mother's at Peebles. We had our cup o' tea or coffee, and there wis two ladies sittin' at another table and they paid for what we'd had.

Then ah mind o' gaun tae the pictures in Edinburgh. We got paid seven shillins [35p] or somethin' a week, so we wouldnae have much money. And ye didnae get more pay when ye passed your drivin' test. The only thing ee got wis ye had a band roond your hat, and ye could put it up on top if you were a driver! So maybe four or five o' us would go oot tae the pictures, something like that. But ah never went tae the theatre or tae the public library or an evening class, or developed an interest in knitting or sewing, and I never went dancing. No, ah never did anything like that. And what ah did hate was Current Affairs. Ah hated that, because ah didnae ken enough aboot what wis goin' on. It was a regular weekly thing, a sort o' discussion, Sometimes you were picked oot. It was called ABCA: Army Bureau of Current Affairs. Well, ah wisnae clever enough for that kind o' stuff. Ah dinnae mind even o' readin' a newspaper in the army, and followin' the war news. So ah didnae develop new interests in any o' these sorts o' things. Ah wis still a country lassie!

But then ah used tae take the bus oot tae some terminus like Colinton or Corstorphine and walk from there. Usually ah went just masel', but sometimes wi' one o' the other girls. But ah walked a lot on ma own. Ah never ta'en a tram along Princes Street, the main street in Edinburgh. Ah walked a lot in Princes Street: we were very near the west end o' it. Ah wis able tae explore Edinburgh, discover it. Ah liked lookin' at the buildins, the architeture, because ye had nothing like that where we were at Peebles. Ah mean, this was an adventure. Ah used tae walk away up the Mound and all over. The city wis full o' Services people tae at that time. And there wis no' so much traffic then, only necessary traffic wis on the roads.

Ah didnae go tae any Services clubs. The only thing ah went to wis the Church of Scotland canteen in Randolph Crescent, where ye could get pie and beans quite cheap: they catered for Services folk. And there wis one at St John's Episcopal Church at the West End, ah mind o' gaun in there. But ah dinnae mind o' gaun tae any other ones. So though, as ah've said, ah did feel a bit homesick at first when ah went away tae join the ATS at Newbattle Abbey, ah didnae feel homesick or lonely when ah wis in Edinburgh. But ah liked tae be on ma own. Ah couldnae get enough time tae masel'. There wis too many folk around me. Ah never felt that ah needed company, ah never have done. Ah didnae make a particular friend in Edinburgh like ah had wi' Evelyn Wigginton at Hereford. Though among the girls in Rothesay Terrace we had guid laughs, oh, we had guid laughs.

One episode though in Edinburgh – aboot the meal – wis maybe no' sae funny. One day there wisnae enough food sent up for oor lunch. Well, ye were a' sittin' on forms at the long table, and ah happened tae be at the end o' the table. When the lunch came up it wis jist like a wee bit meat swimmin' in a lot o' gravy. And ye had mashed tatties or something or other. They werenae really tatties, they were POM or somethin' like that.[19] Of course, everybody wis complainin' aboot it. So here there happened tae be a brass hat, one o' the bigwigs wi' a rid band roond his hat – a staff officer, maybe a colonel – came round that day. Ye a' stood tae attention when he come in. And he asked us, 'Any complaints?' 'No, sir.' So ah thought, 'Hell, everybody's been complainin'. What are they sayin' "No, sir," for?' So, when the bigwig asked me, what did I say? 'Yes, sir. A complaint.' 'Oh?' And the wee corporal in charge o' the kitchens, Cpl Cairney, who wis Irish, her face hit the flair! The bigwig asked what wis wrong, and ah said, 'Well, there wisn't enough food on the plates.' 'Oh?' So later ah wis dragged up in front o' an officer, wi' an escort on either side o' me. God, did I no' get a severe dressin' doon about that! But they did admit the complaints wis justified. And the next day we got a guid meal. But ah never sat at the end o' a table again, ah made shair o' that, no way! Ah wisnae confined tae barracks. But ye're no' supposed tae answer back! And, ah mean, why did the bigwig ask if there were any complaints? And I was angry at the rest o' the folk that had said there wis no complaints. They were definitely afraid tae speak. Of course, ah wis green! What ah did wisnae so much courage as stupid!

Once ah came back tae Edinburgh from Newcastle ah wis attached tae the Royal Army Service Corps and could wear the RASC badge above ma pocket. Once you'd passed your driving test ye were called Driver, but ye got called Private as well. Ah wis never promoted tae lance corporal: ah wisnae in the ATS long enough! But ah remember they gave us interviews for OCTU, Officers Cadet Training. We all got interviews, and they tried tae speak ye intae it. But the ones I could see frae where I was that were goin' for this were sittin' behind a desk pushin' pens. Ah didnae want that. Och, no, ah jist wanted tae be a driver. Ah wisnae wantin' tae gaun and sit and push a pen. Ah said no, that ah didn't have any interest in that side o' it at all. Ah enjoyed the drivin'. That had been ma ambition as a girl, and that was still what ah wanted tae do. That wis why ah volunteered intae the ATS when ah did, because ah didnae want tae be called up. If ye volunteered ye got a choice, ye got a choice.

At one point ah volunteered tae go abroad. Ah wis thinkin' aboot the Middle East. Ah wis quite keen tae go, and of course ah put ma name doon for it. But, bein' under 21, ye had tae have your parents' permission. And of course ma mother widnae sign. Ma faither might have signed, but they wouldnae agree on it. So . . .

There wis a padre attached to our unit. He was the minister of the Belford Church. A nice man he was. For church services we went up tae the Dean Orphanage. It wis a church parade. Ye had tae parade, ye more or less had to go every Sunday. Ye marched up in your best uniform, right roond a big bend from the Belford garage and up, and the Orphanage wis on the right-hand side. It wisnae jist us on the church parade. There wis more from other places. Oh, there'd be others.

Well, ah must have been aboot 15 months a'thegither in Edinburgh. Ah'd come from Hereford about March or April 1942. Then in February 1943 ah got married. Ma husband wis an Edinburgh lad. And ah wis pregnant by the summer o' 1943. So ah left the ATS then. In your paybook you get 'Family Affairs'. Ah left because of Family Affairs.

Ah'd been in the ATS aboot a year and a half. Ah think ah wis quite glad tae be oot o' it. Ah think ah'd had enough o' it by then. Ah don't think it wis a' cracked up tae what ah had expected. Ye see, ye went intae a thing. Bein' older now ye wid realise what ye were gaun intae. But when you're young you dinnae. It was an adventure. Ah didnae feel it had changed ma life, didnae change ma sort o' outlook on life or anythin' like that, no' any dramatic changes anyway. Maybe if ye'd been away on active service it might have done, but no' plitterin' aboot the way ah was. But ah didnae think it did iz any harm. Ah never regretted volunteerin' for the ATS. But ah didnae drive after ah came oot o' it. Well, ye couldnae afford a car, and ye couldnae afford tae keep your licence on. So ah never had a job as a driver after the war and ah never tried tae get a car, though later on ah did get masel' a wee motorbike.

Isobel Cumming (Mrs Isobel Thomson) died on 26 May 2013.

Esther Cowper

I volunteered into the ATS. But I knew that otherwise I would be conscripted. I volunteered also because I wanted to get a particular job in the War Office, which I did.

I was born at 6 Chalmers Cottages, Linlithgow Bridge, West Lothian, on 1st September 1918. Chalmers Cottages belonged to the paper mill, and were designed by Lorimer, a well-known architect.[1] The cottages are still there. Well, I was born when my dad was in Italy on military service in the 1914–18 War. He'd got home leave in November 1917: I was the result of that leave!

In peacetime my dad was a wages clerk and sort of general factotum in the office of the Avon Paper Mill. At that time there were two paper mills at Linlithgow – as there were in Penicuik.[2] And Penicuik was where all my people belonged. My father and mother came to Linlithgow Bridge from Penicuik just after they'd got married in July 1910. Both of them had worked there in Esk Mill, and had met there. They'd both been born and brought up in Penicuik. My dad had left school and went to work at 12 years old. That was common in these days. When he and my mother came to Linlithgow Bridge as a young married couple, Willie Aitken, a local chap who later built up a huge great big empire in transport and so on, but who at that time was a horse and cart coal delivery man, said to my mother, 'Aye, you're new here, hen?' And my mother said, 'Yes.' 'Well,' said Willie, 'ah'll gie ye your first bag o' coal for a present.'

My dad was born on the 18th of September 1879, and he died on the 1st of May 1949. I'm not really sure if he was a volunteer or a conscript in the '14-'18 War. But I think he must have gone away to the war about maybe the end of 1915 or beginning of 1916. I think he would be a volunteer because of the religious beliefs he had and the strong moral sense that you had to do your bit for your country. He was in the Service Corps, the RASC. I'm not sure if he actually served in France. But he was certainly in Italy. He wasn't wounded in the war, though his brother was: he had quite a bad leg wound and came back.

My mother, maiden name Meikle, was born on the 20th of February 1885, and died on the 3rd of September 1966. My mother was only four years old when her father, William Meikle, was killed in the Mauricewood coal pit disaster at Penicuik.[3]

Grandfather Meikle came, I think, from the mining country somewhere round about the Lasswade-Bonnyrigg area in Midlothian. He was 44 years old when he died in the Mauricewood disaster in 1889. Two of his sons, William jnr, aged 14, and Walter, aged 12, died with him in the disaster. So did my grandfather's brother Thomas, aged 41. Including my mother, my grandfather Meikle left six dependent children under the age of 11, the youngest of them a month-old baby. His brother Thomas left five children under the age of 14.

I was very close to my granny Meikle. Oh, she was a fantastic woman. There was practically nothing she couldnae do. She was strikingly good-looking, and a very, very intelligent person. I don't know what she'd done for a living before she married grandfather Meikle. I suspect she may have gone into service or was employed as a nanny. She was the only girl in a family of seven children. Her mother, my great-grandmother, had come up from the Isle of Wight. Whether they were originally Scottish and had lived down there for a while for whatever reason, I don't know, but she and her husband and children came up here. When grandfather Meikle was killed at Mauricewood, oh, granny just soldiered on. When some lady said to her it was miraculous that she hadn't become embittered, and 'How can you still believe in God?' Granny Meikle says, 'Aye, lassie, He's ta'en a lot o' ma faimly away. But He left me wi' six bairns and a job tae dae.' And she did it. She kept them all on at school, long past where most folk were. My mother got Latin and French and a wee bit, a tiny wee bit, of German. And she could play the organ and the piano. And my grandmother just made sure her children got whatever was to be got from the situation.

Well, I never knew either of my grandfathers. James Cowper – pronounced Cooper – my father's father, was killed on the railway at

Penicuik. He was a plater. Unfortunately, an engine – a rogue engine or whatever – struck him, and he had to have his leg amputated. Gangrene set in – very often the result of that kind of accident. He was a Penicuik man, though I think the Cowpers originally came from Fife. Grandfather Cowper would only be, I think, in his middle thirties when he died. He left a family of four boys and two girls. My dad was the second son.

But I remember granny Cowper fine. She lived in a wee place at Penicuik called Oak Leaf, but the building is no longer standing. I used to go and stay for the summer holidays with granny Meikle at Penicuik, and I used to go down regularly to see granny Cowper. Oh, she was a very warm, welcoming nice person, and a beautiful knitter. She had a very hard life bringing up the family on her own – and nae financial support at all. But I don't remember granny Cowper ever working. Well, John, the eldest of her four boys, would be married before my dad, probably in 1908 or 1909. As I've said, my dad, granny's second son, went to work at the age of 12. The third son was Jimmy, who didnae marry until the middle of the '14-'18 War. Andrew, the youngest son, never married at all, so he was the mainstay of the family for granny. One of the sisters, Nellie, died in childbirth, and the baby died as well. All granny Cowper's family were university material, but none of them had the slightest hope of getting near a university.

I had two elder brothers. James was born in June 1911, and William, middle name Meikle after our maternal grandfather, was born in January 1913.

My earliest memory of where we lived was of No. 6 Chalmers Cottages at Linlithgow Bridge. It was just two rooms there, a very large living room, and a kitchen not much smaller. And at that time there was no toilet. There was a shunky, a dry toilet.[4] Ah remember ma dad taking me down there on his shoulder. Eventually, och, I was still only quite a wee lassie when the mill put outside toilets in, but in the wee courtyard. Only our family and the immediate upstairs neighbours shared this outdoor toilet. As for baths, they were taken in front of the fire in a great big tin bath. Oh, I'm no' so shair aboot whether I got the bath first then my brothers. Knowing my mother, everything was for the boys. I think it was in order of age – or of troublesomeness, because I had a mop of curly hair! Then the lighting there was paraffin lamps. Oh, and they were beautiful. My mother had a kind of silvery one. As soon as it was just getting to the darkening, she would trim the wicks and make sure that the receptacles were filled. Eventually we graduated to a Tilley lamp. For cooking, my mother had an oil-filled stove, a paraffin stove. But there also was a fire, with wee things like an iron grid, and you swung it round over the heat. And the stock-pot and soup pot of course were never off it. And she had an oven and she baked in that. The sleeping arrangements at Chalmers Cottages were, well, there was a bed recess that was curtained off in the kitchen. And there was a recess as well in the big room which the two boys had. I had a single bed in the kitchen. So I was more or less in beside my parents.

We graduated to a range when, about 1930 and I would be about 12, we moved from that house at Chalmers Cottages to one in the main street in Linlithgow Bridge. It was just called Lovell's Buildings. It was a flat and it had five rooms. It was in a self-contained place. There was a flush toilet there – a big improvement. Though in these days you'd nae toilet paper like ye have now. It was bits o' the newspaper tied up in a bundle wi' a hole speared at the top end and hung up! And there was a washhouse and a great big tin bath stayed there. So when it came to bath time in that house my dad just lit the boiler and we could all bath down in that washhouse place. We didnae need to bring the bath up and have a sort of laundry performance in the living room. The two boys shared a room, and I got a wee bedroom, oh, a minuscule wee bedroom, to myself. My mum and dad had a bedroom, too, of course. In the kitchen there was a range, which I had to blacklead. The range had a wee boiler on one side, with a wee brass tap, and that always had hot water for the dishes. On its other side the range had a good oven. So if my mum was baking she used to put on what she called a quick fire. Oh, she was a rare baker there, too, and, och, she found it much more easy to bake on the range. And, of course, we ate in the kitchen. Oh, no, you did not eat in the parlour! Then there must have been paraffin lamps as well when we went to Lovell's Buildings first. I can't remember when we got electricity, but, oh, it was later on. The house belonged, I think, to a farm. Both those houses were tied houses. The Chalmers Cottages one belonged to Loch Mill, the other paper mill at Linlithgow. But I don't think the rules of tied houses would ever have been rigorously applied as long as you paid your rent. But certainly we never had a council house until very much later.

As children we were very well fed. My mother was a first-class manager of money and also she was an excellent cook. Oh, I can mind her soups yet. You just don't get food like that now. And my dad had a fair-sized garden at both our houses. He was not a natural gardener, but he did his best. We always had tatties and leeks and lettuce, but not carrots: I don't think it was good soil for carrots. So come the summer we had always lots of salads. So we ate quite well, and, oh, I was never hungry as a child. My mother dealt with the same butcher from the time she married in 1910 until she died in 1966. And Jimmy the butcher would aye put in a bone for soup, or something. Oh, we ate probably a lot better than an awful lot of people in Linlithgow Bridge because of my mother's natural sense of making the most of things. And, luckily, my dad kept his job all his life and was never unemployed.

My dad did, however, have a very sensitive stomach. I remember him coming in from work, and my mother would say: 'A rare pot of kail on. Could you manage a wee drop?' 'No,' he says, 'if I as much as take one teaspoonful I'll suffer for it all day.' I remember the digestive or tea biscuits, and Maclean's Powder mixed up in milk: he had to take a lot of milk. My dad lived on that very, very light diet, with rabbit, which of course you could get in a country area like ours nae bother. So he could always get a rabbit, chicken, eggs, and things like that.

* * *

Oh, I loved the school. I couldnae wait to get there. I kept bombarding my mother: 'Am I no' at the right age now?' She said, 'No, you're just four-and-a-half. You've to wait till you're five.' So I started at the local primary school at the age of five years and two days. Oh, I loved it. Well, I loved mental arithmetic. We had ten minutes of mental arithmetic every morning, and I just about jumped out of my seat. My hand was up and down like a yo-yo. And I loved spelling. And we got drawing, music, singing. Mostly they were English songs, but occasionally we got a Scots one – *Charlie is my Darling* or something or other, which we belted forth with great gusto. I just loved school full-stop, everything pertaining to it.

Mind you, there were some awful teachers. Some of them were slightly sadistic, to say the least! Oh, you got belted. And one thing that in retrospect gars me greet is that Scots was dinned out of us. We spoke two languages. We were literally bilingual. We spoke braid Scots in the playground. But as soon as you went through the door into the school you reverted into English – and woe betide you if ye didnae! You probably got one of the belt. I remember getting the belt. In these days in the primary school you never got lines. You couldnae write, apart from anything else. You couldnae have written lines.

I remember one teacher called Grace Ross, who was a frustrated spinster if ever there was. Women teachers in these days until, I think, up to the Second World War couldn't marry – well, they could marry but if they did they lost their jobs as married women. This Grace Ross was a very attractive-looking woman. But, oh, she was a little fiend! I remember one day she tied my hands at my back with my gym girdle, not for the heinous crime of talking (of which I'm sure I did quite a bit). This punishment was for fiddling with my gym girdle. Nowadays she'd have been up in court on a charge. Well, she forgot to take this girdle shackle off. Everybody was out of the classroom. I went home at lunchtime, and here am I sort of straggling out the classroom with my hands tied behind my back. And of course there were red raw weals on my wrists. My father was livid. He should have taken it up. He was normally such a mild-mannered man. It took something awfy, awfy drastic to make my father livid or react that way. But anyway I said, 'Don't, dad. She'll just take it out on me. I'll get it all the worse.' I don't remember anybody else ever being punished by Miss Ross in that way. It was just in her nature. As I say, she was frustrated. Oh, with the laddies it would just have been either one or two of the belt straight away. That was quite commonplace in these days.

Well, I sat the Quali exam. I began at school in 1923. So it must have been about 1928, I'd be in P5 [Primary 5], as it's called now. And there was a 'flu epidemic. A lot of the teachers in Linlithgow Primary got 'flu, and one of them was ours. We had a very go-ahead, forward-looking chap called Andrew Dea as headmaster. The previous headmaster, old Corky Forbes (I don't know why he got called Corky) would never allow a pupil to sit the Quali before she was 12. Mr Dea, however, took eight of us – the top eight in the class – and put us in this Quali class. The rest were just dispersed round the school. And we had a very nice teacher called Mary Bennie. She must, I suppose, as good teachers do, have seen the potential in us eight. She stayed on one night or two nights a week to give us fractions and decimals, which of course we'd never had. When Mr Dea came in one day and asked her how our wee bunch of eight were getting on, Miss Bennie says, 'They're doing great.' Mr Dea says, 'Right. Just let them sit the Quali this year.' So I sat the Quali when I was 10, passed it, and in September 1929, when I was newly aged 11, I went to Linlithgow Academy.

I loved the Academy, too. There was a great crowd, an awful nice crowd, in the class. Mind you, from the maturation point of view, I would have been very, very much better staying on at the primary and sitting the Quali at the right time, because I was small, slight, and much too young, I think, and juvenile in my outlook. But I don't think that dawned on me then actually. Anyway, I loved all the subjects at the Academy. I was particularly good at French and Latin. We didn't do German at all, which was a pity. So I took French, Latin, English, art, maths, and science – general science, working with Bunsen burners. We had a very good maths teacher, Jimmy Dawson. I liked maths.

The rector at Linlithgow Academy was Willie Milne, Alex Salmond's grandfather.[5] Willie, who didnae belong to Linlithgow, was a captain in some regiment in the First World War. Those who did know him said he was very brutalised by his experiences. He was all right as long as he hadn't been drinking. But he used to nip down to the *Star & Garter*, which was the pub-hotel just across from the school, for a wee fly one at playtimes. We had Willie on a Tuesday and a Thursday, after the break, for two periods of Latin. And he used to shout and roar at us. I can remember his voice still. Though I loved Latin, if I made a wee mistake at all we all got it: he shouted at us. I don't suppose Willie Milne really meant it. And I don't think he was much of a belter.

We did have one or two belters. We had a maths teacher who was a belter. But he gave you the option: write the catechism ten times or whatever, or six of the best of the belt.[6] Most of us just queued up, you know: 'Hope he misses.' I would take the belt any time. But I loved all the subjects at school.

So I stayed on at the Academy till my 6th year. My parents wanted me to stay on. In my 5th year I passed Higher English and French, and Lower art and maths. In these days you had to pass a group of subjects. It had to be four in a group. The minimum was two Highers and two Lowers. By that time my Latin had slipped back a bit. As I say, we were all, I think, a wee bit cowed by Willie Milne, a bit petrified. If you know somebody's cross at you you don't perform well. I dropped the Latin at

Mr Milne's request. That was a pity when I was so interested in the subject. But I passed Higher maths in the 6th year. So, just under age 16, I left the Academy in the summer of 1934, with three Highers (English, French, and maths), and one Lower (art).

* * *

As a girl, I think my principal activity was Guides. I was a Brownie and then I flew up to the Guides. There was quite a group of us. Then, oh, I certainly walked a lot, too. I mean, if you know how Linlithgow's placed: there's the Palace and the kirk, St Michael's. But you could walk round the loch. And there's a wee hill – Cock-o'-Roy, Coq du Roi, or something – and of course we thought it was a mountain. It was huge – all of 200 feet.[7] And you would get to the top and see all the view from there – quite a ploy. There was also the Union Canal. We used to go along the canal and fish for tiddlers and so on. Oh, we liked stravaiging.[8] We were never inside in the summertime. Your parents had tae come and howk ye oot from wherever ye happened to be.

At that stage I wasn't so much a reader of books. Our house wasn't full of books at that time, and I didn't join the public library – I don't remember when I did join it. But the habit of reading must have come much later. I'm wondering if there was a library in Linlithgow Academy. I don't remember either there or at the primary school wooden book boxes coming in from the county library. I wasn't what would have been called an avid reader from an early age. I did have my school books to get through, and you had a lot of homework to do. In the summertime you came home, washed, and had your meal, and then got your school homework done. That was the priority. Mother wouldn't let us out to play until our homework was done.

I read the *Rainbow*, a girls' comic. I got it regularly: Monday was *Rainbow* day.[9] Oh, it was mair than a rainbow, it was a shaft of light! I don't think it was delivered to our house. I think we collected it from a wee shoppie in Linlithgow. I don't remember exchanging my *Rainbow* with my friends' comics. My brothers of course just skived off and did boy things. I think by that time they probably had bikes. I didn't get a bike till after I started work.

As a girl I was a regular Sunday School attender. And I went as well to the main Church of Scotland service. So it was twice on a Sunday.

And ma faither was a twicer at the Church o' Scotland. My father's family were, oh, strong. If they werenae in their pew on a Sunday the minister was roond the next day. Ma mother's family were Plymouth Brethren.[10] But she left the Brethren and . . . I was going to say jined the Sisters! Not quite that: she joined the Church of Scotland, and very often she came with me unless she wasnae feeling too good: you had a mile to walk to Linlithgow Bridge. It wasnae a particularly bonny kirk. Mother liked to go to the evening services. She'd often say to me, 'Oh, come on, come on with me.' So, as I say, including Sunday School, I went at least twice on a Sunday, sometimes three times. My grandmother Meikle, my mother's mother, never joined the Church of Scotland. She went with my aunt, the oldest girl in the family – Mary Anne, called Lilly, on the train from Penicuik to Edinburgh on Sunday nights to what they called Meetings. My mother thought it was far better for the family to be brought up in one church. But her sister Liz remained a Plymouth Brethren and didn't join her husband in the Church of Scotland. Oh, a Sunday was devoted to religion. And in granny Meikle's house, by goodness, you didnae dare sing or do anything on a Sunday. She wis very strict about sabbath observance. I remember once whistling on a Sunday. Oh, she nearly went berserk. On a Sunday! It wis a' right on a Saturday. I never could see the distinction. But anyhow they were all very strict.

I always had a holiday as a girl, that's one thing. We went over to the Clyde coast or very often over to Fife. I remember once going to Leven. I was walking along the beach with my dad when a fellow came hurrying up to him. 'Wullie Cowper?' Ma dad says, 'Aye.' 'Jimmy Pringle.' They'd served together in Italy and met all these years later. I was just a school lassie . It must have been late 1920s, early 1930s.

I didn't have any particular ambitions about work. My mother wanted me to be a nurse. And I trod very, very much in my mother's footsteps. She'd been herself a frustrated children's nurse, because granny Meikle didnae like the lassies gettin' oot the hoose in case they got into bad company. So this nursing strain was certainly there. But leaving school as I did at 16 you couldn't get into nursing until you were 18. And my father used to say to my mother, 'Oh, don't let Esther go in for nursin', because,' he says, wi' him bein' in hospital himself then, 'I see the seamy side of it. They're just drudges for the first two or three years.' Lots of jobs were barred from you because of your age. I suppose I could have got into university at 16 or 17. So I think there was probably a good lot of discussion between my parents of what tae dae wi' this lassie. They probably decided that a clerical career or something like that would be quite suitable. So after I left school I went to Skerry's College in Edinburgh for I think it was just a six-month course.[11]

While I was at Skerry's I sat the Civil Service exam for sorting clerks and telegraphists. I was fourth in Edinburgh in the exam and sixth in Great Britain. But I didnae get a job. My dad, as I say, was a very calm, mild-mannered kind of man. So he didn't take the matter up until he happened to meet somebody who'd been in the same classes as me and had been much further down the exam results than myself, but who told him, 'Oh, I got a job ages ago.' So my dad then took it up and they said I'd been passed over on residential grounds because I couldn't get in from Linlithgow Bridge to Edinburgh. In fact, I'd got into Skerry's on the bus: it passed our door at Linlithgow Bridge. And there was a bus at half-past six in the morning so I could easily have got into Edinburgh by eight o'clock. How they came up with this cock-and-bull yarn I have no idea. Anyhow, as a compensatory gesture they offered me a job as a part-time telephonist in the local telephone exchange in Linlithgow.

I worked there for about a year. I'm no' really sure now if I worked there alternate days or a half-day at a time, but I think it would be a half-day – mornings only. Most business folk would phone in the morning. I can't remember either how many hours per week I worked. I would imagine probably about 20, say, from nine till one, five half-days a week. I must have got Saturday and Sunday off – well, maybe not every Saturday. But I can't remember. And I haven't a clue what my wages there were – a pound a week or a couple of quid or something.

The work was quite interesting. It was the old PBX switchboard. A wee light would go on, and you had to plug into that hole. Of course, you had your headphones on. You'd say, 'Number, please?' Then, 'Just one moment, please. I'll connect you.' And the call would go through. Och, I quite enjoyed that job.

While I was there one or two of my friends with whom I kept in touch, mainly again through the Guides, had got jobs in ICI [Imperial Chemical Industries] at Grangemouth. They said, 'Oh, Esther, you should apply. It's a great firm.' You know, great conditions and you got a good lunch just for pennies, I suppose, in the club, and so on. My friends told me when a vacancy at ICI was coming up, and to watch for it in the *Linlithgowshire Gazette*.[12] So I duly sent in an application for the vacancy. I met one of my friends two or three days later, and she said the job had been filled. She said, 'Did you not apply for it?' I said, 'Yes, I did.' 'Well,' she says, 'I'm in the mail department and definitely no application came in from you.' So that was taken up with the head of the section. And I was offered the next job that came along, which was in the costing department.

That job was extremely interesting. My hours were nine till five, and Saturday morning nine till 12.30pm – standard, regular office hours then. I would imagine my wages when I first began at ICI would be somewhere about £2.50 or £3.00 a week. But out of that of course you would pay for your lunches, though they were subsidised. And you paid your bus fares. I got the bus from Linlithgow Bridge into Falkirk, changed at Callendar Riggs in Falkirk, and got the bus to Grangemouth. The bus journey took about quarter of an hour to Falkirk, and about ten minutes from there to Grangemouth. The buses from Linlithgow Bridge were only every half-hour, so I think we left there about the back of 8am: half-past eight would have been too late. The buses from Falkirk to Grangemouth were frequent: An awful lot of people worked in the dyes department of ICI there.

I did ledger work, keeping ledgers of all material coming in to the factory, and on the other side of the ledger of course. And the same thing going out. It was all costed. But the out-column was all made into colours. I had calidon and solidon and various names like that, and various different colours. The colour range of course was huge, because we exported pretty well all over the world. ICI was really a first-class firm. Oh, hundreds worked there for it at Grangemouth, 17 of them in our department. I don't think any processes would be automated at that time. We're talking about men doing physical work or mixing the dyes and so on. It was ICI Scottish Dyes & Gases Ltd.

Looking back on my job at ICI, it was a great department and very enjoyable. There was 12 boys and five girls in it, with one of whom I'm still in touch. She was a comptometer operator. We've remained friends all these years. I think I was the only actual clerkess. Another thing that happened there was I had a very serious relationship with a chap I worked beside. However, he was called up and went off to the war. He came back from Dunkirk in 1940 and was somewhere down in England, met this Hungarian lassie, and, oh, it was a whirl-wind romance. Well, he and I weren't engaged so I wasn't in fact jilted. But after that experience my enthusiasm for going to the dyes waned somewhat. My bike would hardly turn in at the dye works gates! I'd got a bike about 1937 or '38, when I was 19, and cycled to and from work. I'd saved up after I'd joined Scottish Dyes and I'd got this second-hand bike, which I called Almost – because it was almost the bike I would have got if I had had mair money! Anyway, I cycled down the Salmon Inn Brae. I saved money on bus fares, and cycling was good exercise. And it didn't take much longer than the bus, on which gey often you'd to stand. So, och, cycling gave you a certain amount of freedom. And I was extremely strong. We were a very strong, healthy, fit family – except for my dad. So I worked at ICI for roughly six or six and a half years, from some time in the earlier part of 1936 until I joined the ATS in May 1942.

* * *

I actually did apply to the Women's Royal Naval Service. I think I liked the uniform. But they weren't interested at the time. For some reason, I didn't think of applying to the Women's Auxiliary Air Force. Maybe I never saw myself as a kind of air person. I think it was just having heard about this great career in the ATS from this lassie who used to come down to the ICI office and see us at times. Everybody did that if they were home on leave, came down in their uniform. And we got on the talk about things. She told me the kind of job she was doing. It sounded so fascinating! She was on secret ciphers in the War Office. So I volunteered into the ATS on the 15th of May 1942. But I knew that I would be conscripted. I volunteered because I wanted to get into a particular job, which I did – secret ciphers in the War Office.

I don't remember how I went about volunteering, whether there was a depot in Linlithgow, or whether you just answered an advertisement. And I'm not really sure where I went for a medical. There couldn't have been any set-up in Linlithgow. The number of lassies joining the army in Linlithgow wouldn't have warranted it. It would mean Edinburgh again on the bus, I think. I don't remember having a medical or an interview. I think these things all took place actually when you turned up for basic training.

So I was sent first to Glencorse Barracks, the Royal Scots depot near Penicuik in Midlothian, where the Regulars were, though there may have been other regiments there too. But Glencorse was the first contact I had with the army.[13] Well, we were all allocated to a hut. That was the first thing of course. And I think the next thing would be taking all our civvy stuff and so on across to our hut. There was 24 of us to a hut. And one corporal had a cubby hole, a wee totty room, at the top end of the hut. They were wooden huts, not Nissen huts. Probably it would be at the very beginning of the war they'd been put up. Then I think medicals must have come pretty quickly, because if anything was wanting – if they found you had flat feet or some grievous impediment (no pun intended) like that – they would have got shot of you.

I didn't know anyone when I first joined, and I can't remember a great deal about any of them. I remember the corporal but I can't remember her name. She was quite nice, well, one of the more respected, more decent NCOs. Some of them were of the you-know-what school! They were a bit regimental, given to shouting. Especially so was the drill sergeant, a man, a Regular and, gosh, absolutely beautifully turned out. But he used to bark his orders.

We were fitted out at Glencorse with uniforms. Oh, that was really hilarious. We were all marched into this great big, well, I suppose it would be an interior drill hall thing. RASC personnel stood at the back of great big long tables. There were piles of skirts, piles of vests, piles of shirts, ties, boots, you name it: the whole caboodle. And the RASC personnel just kept flinging things out from these piles: 'Right. Have you got so-and-so? No? Well, here ye are then, here ye are.' Och, they maybe made a slight attempt to give you things that fitted, like they wouldnae give a woman wi' a 46-inch chest the same size of shirt as they'd given me. But it was not by any means tailored to your exact measurements or requirements: it wisnae a case of going to the fitting room. It wasnae scientific. It was like an awful lot o' things that went on in the army. And we were told, 'Take them back to your hut and swop around until you get something that is reasonably wearable.' That was what we did. So we turned out the next morning in somewhat ill-fitting uniforms! But gradually you could get things exchanged. It was just to get us started and out of the RASC's hair.

I've no idea what sort of heating there would be in our hut. But I think there was a stove wi' a funnel up through the roof. If your clothes got wet you certainly were able to get them dried. And I think the food at Glencorse was reasonable. It was still a serving Regular soldiers' base. So presumably we in the ATS got the same food as them but in smaller quantities.

While I was there I missed my mum and dad a lot of course, and my brothers. But I didn't really feel homesick. Some of the other girls would never have been away from home. I think a few of them were kind of weepy wi' homesickness. But to me it was an adventure. And I don't remember any of the girls giving up in that initial period. If there was a bed suddenly empty in the hut, I don't think we'd be told why. It would be, 'Oh, she's not been well', or something. The army was pretty good at covering things up.

Then you got intelligence tests. Having done Higher maths at the school, an awful lot of the intelligence tests were quite easy, because you could see from what angles and so on . . . It was a multi-intelligence test – linguistic, arithmetical, and all sorts of things like that.

Basic training at Glencorse was three weeks. But I was posted to London on the Thursday, I think, of the third week, which was about the first week in June – as soon as that. And I'd just come out of the gas training. You had to undergo gas training. So we – all the intake of ATS – were in this large room. I don't know how many hutsworth there were there. And you got mustard gas put on your skin, and you'd to breathe the tear gas. You had that in your eyes, and you'd to breathe all this stuff in. It was then the duty corporal came in and said to me, 'Cowper, you're wanted in the Company office.' With eyes streaming and skin burning, Cowper duly trotted along to the Company office, to be told I was to be on a train at seven o'clock that night to go to London. Though I quite wanted to go to London (I'd never seen the place), it was rather unfortunate in a way. Mum and dad had come through for a week to my granny's in Penicuik. However, the army authorities very graciously allowed them to come with me in the army utility car or van, a wee canvas-covered jeepy-type thing. So my parents got into it with me. I was the only ATS going: I had been singled out, offered higher service! I was going to the job in London I had actually wanted.

So we went down from Glencorse to the Waverley station in Edinburgh and I got the train to London. And I was that green that when I got to King's Cross it never occurred to me to get a taxi. I had a long sausage-type kitbag and also the one that tied at the top. So I lugged the two of these on to the Tube to Knightsbridge, and then I had about half a mile to walk with them to the billet, which was somewhere near Knightsbridge. Actually, I wasn't put into the War Office at that time. I was in an ack-ack unit which did low-grade cipher, which was less technical. It was just an office – somewhere near Hyde Park – dealing with cipher messages. You got messages coming in in code, and you had to decode them. And then you had to encode messages going out. The messages were RAF messages. I can't remember the details about it, but it would probably be about raids and flights by our bombers going out, and German bombers coming in. We were just trained on the job. I think the corporal in the office just explained how the codes worked. Of course, the codes were changed every day, though the basic principle doesnae change. The office was a civilian building which had been taken over, requisitioned, by the army. Almost all the buildings in that area had been requisitioned. We more or less worked office hours. I don't think we worked shifts or through the night. And I don't think we suffered air raids there. There might have been the odd raid, but by the time I got to London in June 1942 the big bombings by the Germans were finished. Once Hitler invaded Russia in June 1941 – the biggest mistake he could have made – the blitz on Britain had been scaled down. I definitely don't remember passing nights in an air raid shelter at that time. The V1 buzz-bombs and the V2 rockets came later in my army career.

The only person I remember in the office near Hyde Park was the corporal. Her name was Rose. She was Jewish, very, very dark-haired. She was quite good fun, quite nice, and quite nice to work with. But I was only there less than a year, I think, when I was posted to the War Office. I can't remember if I'd applied. Some folk would have been perfectly happy with the job near Hyde Park, because there really wasn't a great deal to it. There was a lot of free time. But you couldnae go out and sort of wander round the Park or do things like that. But you could sit and do a crossword.

The billets there near Knightsbridge were terraced houses. The system in London was that the army took over properties – the town houses – of the rich, most of whom skived off to the countryside. And the houses were all the same as you get in any city – big, with several floors. So we were lodged in one of those terraced houses. I shared a room with three or four other girls. The rooms were quite spacious.

And it would be a corner each for your personal possessions. We all got on reasonably well. We used to have some good discussions. I don't remember the girls there so well as when I went later to the War Office billets and got to know people there better. The food at the billets near Knightsbridge must have been quite good; I've got no memories of it either way. I suppose it would be some days edible and some days less than edible. Then every three months you got seven days' leave. It would need to have been a pretty big emergency, I think, before they stopped that. Because, certainly in the War Office, it was almost mandatory to take your leave. You could juggle around with it a wee bit, say your fiancé was coming back from service overseas or whatever. But they insisted on your having to keep your health.

When I came to work at the War Office in 1943 I was billeted in a town house of some lord or other in Cadogan Gardens, quite near Sloane Square. We were the original Sloane girls! Four of us shared this 20 feet square room. I remember the other three girls extremely well, and we got on well. We were a disparate bunch. Lyn, a schoolteacher in civvy street, was a Geordie. Sheila was from Edinburgh. Marie was from somewhere in Surrey. And we used to have great arguments, very often political. My politics are Scottish nationalist. And right fae the time I was at my primary school they used tae say about me: 'See her? She's got tartan blood.' My brother Bill was a nationalist as well. We knew Billy Wolfe very well.[14] My other brother Jim wasnae politically thingmied at all. Our discussions in our Cadogan Gardens billet usually finished up with Sheila, who I think was probably a bit Left (Lefter even than the Nats), and Marie, who was very Conservative, going on at each other. And finally Marie would say to Sheila, 'All right, Sheila. How right you are. How right you *always* are!' So it was stimulating company but, och, we all got on together and didn't fall out over matters of political principle. Lyn, the Geordie lassie, got married on St Valentine's Day in 1944. Later, her husband, a strikingly handsome chap who was flying with a Canadian squadron, was shot down and went missing.

After being in the army a few weeks I got one stripe – and became a lance corporal. That was soon after I left Glencorse, and it was because you passed this original cipher test. And then I got another stripe – corporal. Well, it didnae depend on your ability as a drill NCO or anything like that. If you could do the job you got the rank that went with it – otherwise I would still have been a private! So I was a corporal when I went to the War Office. Then I sat another exam and I became a sergeant. Some time maybe in autumn 1943, I think, it was. Oh, my father was fair chuffed!

I suppose my pay improved with each promotion. I never thought about that. I remember our very first pay was 11 shillings [55p] a week. That's what I joined up for, 11 shillings a week.[15] When I was posted to London I went to Harrod's and bought a box of Elizabeth Arden face powder! It took the whole 11 shillings. We were a' daft at that time. I'd never done anything so rash before, nor after. So it was 55p a week, with bed and board of somewhat dubious quality. By the time I left the army – I was an SQMS [Staff Quarter Master Sergeant] by then – I think I got £2 3s 0d [£2.15]. As an SQMS you got your cloth badges on your forearm. And if you were going out in your best uniform you got brass badges. Well, I think I was a sergeant for maybe more than a year, so it would be maybe late in 1944 when I became an SQMS. We were all either sergeants or sergeant majors in the War Office. But the details and dates would be in my army paybook. Your promotions were put into your paybook, as were all your inoculations, any crimes you committed, and anything else like that that might be of interest.

Oh, the work at the War Office was so fascinating! I think it's pretty common knowledge what the work was, from the programmes about the Enigma. Those were the machines that we worked on. Anyhow, there were three teams. As I say, nobody was under the rank of sergeant. There was officers of varying ranks, mainly captains or lieutenants. There was an awful nice wee lassie lieutenant I remember. Of the three teams one did a day shift. That was 9am till 5pm. The other two teams worked alternate nights. So we did a 16-hour shift every second night. Tell that to the trade unions! It was heavy going, but the work was so fascinating. On night shift we were allowed an hour off in the evening, from 7pm to 8pm or from 8pm to 9pm, or thereabouts. And you got a chit for a shilling [5p], and you could take this chit to any one of five canteens. There was a canteen in the War Office. So if it was bucketing with rain you didnae need to go out. There was another one up Charing Cross Road, which was the New Zealand Club. There was one in St Martin-in-the-Fields in Trafalgar Square. I can't remember where the others were. But you got your shilling chit. I think actually it was valid in Lyons Corner Houses. And if you were lucky you could get sausages and mash or gravy. And now and again you got about an inch of ice cream. In these days ice cream came in a great big long shape like a sausage. And you were terribly lucky if you got a wee bit of chocolate sauce as well, and a cup of tea. So that was what your shilling got you.

Then back to work. And we got two hours off for supposedly sleep or a rest between, I think, 1am and 3am, or 3am and 5am. At one o'clock food came in from our billet, which at Cadogan Gardens was quite near. Mostly the food was sandwiches and things like that, and they came in steel boxes because the whole War Office basement place where we were was overrun by rats. We were two floors below ground because of the highly sensitive nature of the work. If the machines and our work had been on the ground floor and a bomb had fallen, all the papers would have been all over the place. But, as I say, the place was rat-infested – and bluebottle infested too. So if you did manage to get a five-minute break sometime (which was very, very unusual) we used to roll up newspapers and swot the bluebottles. We had a Bluebottle-swotting League. Don't ask me how I fared.

But, as I say, the work was extremely interesting. A lot of it was for Winston Churchill, and Mountbatten, who was down on SEAC, South East Asia Command, and, oh, various other people of high rank or nae rank.[16] The work was graded by urgency and also by secrecy. There were, I think, five grades. The top grade was Most Immediate and Most Secret. So if you got a Most Immediate message coming in, and it was also Most Secret, the officer would just say, 'Cowper, skip what you're doing and take this one over, please.' It had to be dealt with immediately, pronto, presto. The messages came in actually by teleprinter, and they were in groups of five letters.

When it came nearer to the end of the war, I asked if I could take my two-hour rest period from seven to nine. At the rest period you went up a floor, and there there were bunks in three tiers and you could lie and read or try to sleep. The work was so exciting that you couldn't get unwound. When I asked to change the time of my rest period, oh, my goodness, you would have thought I'd dropped a blooming bomb on the place. It was 'Unheard Of '. However, they considered it and let me do that. So I got off at seven o'clock instead of nine. It was quite nice.

But the job I liked best of all was called DUDS. Occasionally we got an awful lot of what d'you call it? – toing and froing from

Washington in the States. DUDS were incoming messages which wouldn't play out. You know what Enigma machines were like. You took the top off, swung it back and there were several drums – four or five – and each drum had about five or six different cylinders in it. At 0001hours every morning the new coding for that day was set up. Everybody had to put their machine on to that. But you finished the messages. Any messages going out would be sent on that day's coding. Now if you got a message coming in which was a DUD, you'd to put yourself into the position of the person who had enciphered it. She might have used the previous day's coding. She might just have transposed the first two letters of the first group of letters. There was ever so many things that she – it was all 'shes', I think – might have done. And it was very costly both in time and expense to have things re-set. So one of us used to do it. And that was great. You just thought, 'Now what would that lassie over in Washington maybe have done?' And if you fiddled about with it you very often got the DUD out. That was really quite a trial. But I used to enjoy doing that. Some folk hated DUDS. But there was just this wee table set aside and there was an in-tray. Of course, everything being prioritised, the things which had no priority at all, and which an operator usually only got down to doing later, were casualty lists. Once you were either dead or missing you werenae of much importance to the army. I suppose it's logical enough. But that was the way it went.

So the messages came from all over the world, everywhere we, the British armed forces, had a base. Likewise going out, messages went to any of these places. It was fascinating. Of course we had to sign the Official Secrets Act. I got engaged in February 1944. (Incidentally, I could have gone to Washington at the end of the war: there was a sort of exchange going on, and one or two of my friends went there. But I missed out on that when I got engaged.) My fiancé was Jimmy Craig, a cipher instructor. But we knew each other for months before we realised we did the same job. He just didn't talk about it. He never talked about it anywhere. You may remember the wartime cartoon with this wee Humpty-dumpty person and the slogan, 'Walls Have Ears'?

I hadn't met Jimmy Craig at the War Office but at the Royal Scottish Corporation Hall, just off Fleet Street. He was an instructor, but not in the War Office. I don't remember any men at all in our section at the War Office in Whitehall, two floors below the building. There might have been higher up the echelon. But certainly there were no men operators.

I mentioned there the Royal Scottish Corporation Hall. If you were off duty on a Friday night, and sometimes on a Saturday, all the mad Scots gathered there. I've seen as many as 12 or 15 pipers up on the stage, and four or five hundred of us mad things birling around the floor in Scottish country dancing. There was no ballroom dancing, only Scottish country.

When we went on day duty – as I say, you did two weeks on nights, and a week on days – we used to get out at Charing Cross Tube station, and go padding along behind all the top brass, you know – field marshals and all them. I used to have the greatest desire to creep up behind one of them and shout, 'Left, right, left, right, left.' But I never did it, because I would have been cashiered and out of the army pronto!

* * *

My fiancé, Jimmy Craig, who became my husband, was a journalist. Before he joined the army he had worked for a commercial paper called *Freight*, which dealt with every cargo coming into London docks, the prices it gained at auction, and also the outgoing cargoes and where they were destined. *Freight* was, however, taken over by Reuters, the news agency.[17] Jimmy wisnae an investigative journalist: he was such a quiet, shy person. At the end of the war in Europe, when I was due for demob in October 1945, Jimmy and I both signed on for an extra year. Jimmy could have got a job with Reuters but he didn't want to go back there: 'I'm not going to go back there and be an office boy.' And then newsprint was still quite scarce. But anyhow he couldn't find a job at all after the war ended. Mainly because, I think, he always wanted to start at the top. He wouldnae even draw unemployment benefit. Part of it was my fault, because I always had savings behind me, and I just subsidised him. So after the war Jimmy went back over to Germany.

After signing on for another year from October 1945 I got myself, still as an SQMS, posted to Germany. That was bungled and botched as well. I had two lots, I think, of embarkation leave. I was asked as the senior rank to take a squad of ATS girls with me. So I had to report to a colonel in Minden, one of the four wee towns that made up the British headquarters. The colonel was dragged out of his bed at eight or nine on a Sunday morning. He very gruffly asked me who I was and where I'd come from, and 'Where's your husband stationed?' I said, 'He's in Cologne.' He said, 'I don't approve of husbands and wives being stationed near to each other. I think I'll send you to Berlin.' And he did,

So I arrived in Berlin and reported to this colonel who was in a division called PW and DP – Prisoners of War and Displaced Persons. He said to me, 'I really can't think what you're going to do here, sergeant major, because I don't keep any files. I keep everything in my head.' He was quite an intelligent chap. And very often on Thursday he would say, 'Oh, I think you could go down to Cologne for the weekend.' And he allowed me to bring my knitting into the office, so I think my husband benefited from a sweater.

In Berlin you weren't allowed to go out in the evening unescorted by an armed soldier, because of the threat from the Russians. What they were going tae dae tae us I don't know. But anyhow they used to come on the train when it left the British zone in Berlin and came through the Russian zone outside the city, and they were very civil and very polite. They knew that most ATS were so poor they couldnae afford to buy any smuggled goods.

Then I was moved from Berlin to a wee house in Herford, another of the four wee towns including Minden that made up the British head-quarters. So I was there until Jimmy, my husband, and I were demobbed in October 1946 – well, we weren't officially demobbed until the end of December 1946, because you were entitled to so much demob leave. All the men demobbed got a suit, a hat and an overcoat, something like that. But I don't think the girls got anything. Certainly I can't remember getting any clothing. You could never have got the ATS to agree on that, and probably none of us would want the stuff anyway. We did, however, get a monetary thingmy – a gratuity – and so did the men.

Once demobbed I went back to work at ICI. As I've said, Jimmy found it very difficult to get work, so he went back to Germany in March 1947 to work as a civilian in the occupation administration. Margaret, our first child, was born in September that year. But because of my Rhesus-negative blood and they had no facilities in Germany for exchanging blood had it become necessary, it would be about January 1948 before I could go to Germany. It was a long time to be on my own. It didn't do our marriage any good. I'd been living at home with my parents. Housing was very difficult. That was what made many, many marriages founder after the war: having to live with his folk or your folk. Anyway, I remained in Germany with Jimmy from early in 1948 till June 1950. By then our son James was three months old. We did try after that to settle down in London, in a wee flat that Jimmy's mother had had in Stockwell, quite near Clapham Junction. Then we came back up to Scotland. And Jimmy got a plumb job: he became foreign correspondent for *Picture Post* in Munich.[18] But he blew it. He never went anywhere there by car, by bus, by train, or anything. No, he always went by taxi. And he didn't send in enough copy to the paper. So after a year the firm said, 'This is where we part, James.' It was a pity, because Jimmy was a good journalist. But we struggled on for a year, again on my savings. Then eventually I came back home with the two children. If I hadn't there would have been either a murder or a suicide, or both. It was a horrible part of my life. However, I never died a winter yet.

Well, looking back now on my ATS service, I enjoyed the work enormously. I profited greatly, I think, from the company of other people of different backgrounds, different views. I don't think I would join up again and join an army. I know this sounds really bad. But it was England's war. It still is. Scotland's hardly ever mentioned in any of these [radio or television] programmes. That's just how I felt about things latterly, but not at the time. We were all imbued with zeal to do your bit for your country. Yet, really, my sense of Scottish patriotism, nationalism, was magnified by my experiences in the war. An awful lot of people down there in the south of England had no idea of any life north of Watford. And the salient point is – they didn't want to know. No interest. 'Oh, Scotland, it's a nice country to go to on your holidays.' Hardly anybody that I met in the ATS had ever been to Scotland. So I think my sense of nationalism was certainly increased. Certainly, my puggy was up on many an occasion!

Esther Cowper (Mrs Esther Craig, then Mrs Esther Ogg) died on 20 January 2017.

May Kerr

Ah decided just before ah left school in 1937, 'Ah'll go and work in a shop.' Some o' the shops and that used to put into the school that they had a vacancy. So Nettie Murray from Melville Grange in Midlothian and me, the pair o' us went and got jobs in Pennycook's, the grocers and bakers, in Nicolson Street, Edinburgh. Pennycook's had a cellar on the opposite side of the street, and we used tae keep all our big cheeses there. And there you were, a lassie of 14 or 15, staggering to the shop across the tram lines wi' one o' these big heavy Canadian cheeses! And they had a' yon cloth – sacking or backing, whatever it was – over them. Ah used tae look for holes in the cloth in case the mice got doon among them. Ah wis terrified o' mice, and there wis quite a few mice at Pennycook's, oh, aye, there wis always mice there. In fact, ah think one o' the things that sort o' set me off to the ATS in 1942 was when the rats started. And Pennycook's got ma Uncle Davie Laurenson – he worked for the government as a rat catcher – in to the shop. That was it, and ah left!

I was born in St Leonard's Street, Edinburgh, on the 26th o' June 1923. George Kerr, ma father, known to many folk as Geordie Kerr, had lived as a boy at Greenside, just off Leith Street. He was a man wi' many jobs. Even at the school he had the job o' ringin' the handbell at the playtimes. But one day he rang the bell, laid it down, and ran away up Calton Hill. He was sent to the Industrial School on, ah think, a diet o' bread and water; but he got home every night.[1] When he was 16 he'd joined the army – the Royal Scots Fusiliers, ah think it was.[2] But he hated the army so much that his mother had to buy him out. In the 1914–18 War he worked at Rosyth naval dockyard. He spoke about how after the battle of Jutland in 1916 he and his workmates had to hose down the bloodstains from warships returnin' to Rosyth. After the dockyard closed down in the 1920s he was often unemployed. Ah remember he worked as a gardener for a while, jist for anybody and everybody, up at the big houses in the Grange. And ah know at one time he was a grave-digger up at the Grange cemetery. Then his friend Johnny Arnot – we called him Uncle Johnny, that was the stoker at Holyrood Laundry, got ma father in there.[3] He drove the boss's wee Austin Seven or Morris car to begin with. Then he got to drive the laundry lorry, deliverin' the washin' and pickin' up the dirty washin'. But at the beginnin' o' the war in 1939 they took the lorry away – requisitioned it, as they called it. By then ma father certainly had a bunion wi' pressin' his foot on the lorry pedals, and thon used tae be awful. He used tae cut a big hole in his new boots: he couldnae bear the pain. But when the laundry lorry was requisitioned that wis him unemployed again. And ah remember he was havin' his afternoon nap yon first air raid we got in October 1939.[4] Rosyth dockyard had been opened up again before then. Ah wis home for ma lunch, but ah'm outside there sayin', 'What's a' that?' And it wis ack-ack shells in the sky. But ma father wis havin' his nap! Well, it wasnae long after that, about Christmas 1939, that he got started tae work again at Rosyth dockyard. He was a driller there, drilled holes. And he worked at Rosyth till he retired about 1960.

Ma mother, Robina Laurenson, known usually as Ruby, had worked in laundries before she married ma father at the end o' the 1914–18 War. Her father had been a joiner, and it seems her grandfather Laurenson, a fisherman, had come from Shetland to live in Leith.

Ah had an older brother, Jack, born in October 1920, nearly three years older than me, and a younger sister, Margaret, born in July 1928, five years younger than me. After he left school at 14, Jack got a job wi' Alexander's, the motor company, at Tollcross.[5] When they went for their apprenticeships in these days they stoked the fires and did the odd jobs till they got tae age 16. Then Jack began his apprenticeship as a woodworkin' machinist wi' Alexander's. And he wisnae that long at that when he lost the top o' his left thumb. He must only have been about 17 at the time. Ah remember him comin' home on his bike, swathed in bandages. He'd cycled from the Infirmary. And he'd never get a penny compensation. He was off his work, but never got paid or anything else. The apprenticeship wis tae go on for five years. They were 21 when their time was out. But before then Jack lost his job at Alexander's because he ate his lunchtime piece at the wrong time! They stopped for the break, say, 12 tae half-past 12. But they were obviously starvin' before then. So Jack must have started eatin' his sandwiches at five minutes tae 12, and – 'Oot!' It wis terrible, eh? Folk now wouldnae believe what they'd tae put up wi' in these days. Anyway, after Alexander's, ma father taught Jack tae drive, he got his licence, and got a wee job drivin' a van. Then in May 1940 he volunteered intae the RAF.

My parents lived first in West Nicolson Street, near Surgeons Hall. Jack was born there. Then they moved to St Leonard's Street, opposite the Nelson Hall. Though ah wis born there, ah can't remember anything about our place in St Leonard's Street, because we must have left there about 1926 when I was about three year old. We moved from there to No. 4 St Patrick Square, where ma sister Margaret wis born in 1928. The only thing ah can remember about our place in St Patrick Square was that it was a garret, wi' this coom ceiling. And, oh, another thing there that's stuck in my mind is that Jack and I, in this bitterly cold winter, filled our tin mugs wi' water and put them on the window ledge overnight. They were solid ice in the mornin'. Then in 1929, in May, I think, we went from St Patrick Square to live at 5 Clearburn Gardens in Prestonfield, new corporation or council houses, down off the Dalkeith Road. I can remember going to Prestonfield; I'd be almost six by then and already at school.

The house we got in Prestonfield was really ma Granny Laurenson's, ma mother's mother. Ah don't know what had happened to Granny Laurenson's leg but she walked wi' a stick all the years I can remember her. She had lived in Simon Square before we went to Prestonfield, and that was a slum clearance, as it was called. They'd probably only have given her a one-bedroomed house. But I think ma mother must have agreed to go with her to live at Prestonfield. So we got there the two bedrooms – but two bedrooms for three children, our two parents, and an elderly person. So Granny Laurenson lived with us, and she would be the tenant of the Prestonfield house. Granny Laurenson was on the parish.[6] No' that they bothered aboot whether you were disabled or anything in these days. But ma parents must have said they would take over the tenancy of the house.

As ah say, when we moved to Prestonfield in 1929 ah wis already at school. I started in Preston Street School, at the top o' Dalkeith Road. I must have started there when we were livin' in St Patrick Square. But even after we moved to live in Prestonfield I carried on at Preston Street School for a couple of years. And I used to take there a wee lass Marion MacNeil, just that wee bit younger than me. The MacNeils lived in the four-in-the-block further along. There wasnae much between Marion and her younger brother, so then ah took him as well up to Preston Street School when he started there. But, what a shame, he later died of TB. He would then be only seven, eight, or nine.

Then I moved to Prestonfield Primary School the day it opened in the summer of 1931, when I was eight years old. I was there for four years. Well, there was two laddies and myself in our class, and the three o' us must have always had the top marks. I remember gettin' these papers and takin' them to ma mother, because they were for sittin' for the bursary. Ah said, 'Ah'm no' sittin' the bursary.' And the two laddies didnae want tae go in for it either. The school sent for our mothers, and ma mother said she'd get me up to the headmaster at Prestonfield School, a Mr Gray. And he said, 'Ah think you should sit the bursary. You've got a very good chance.' If you passed, you went to James Gillespie's Girls School or maybe to one o' the other senior secondary corporation schools, like Boroughmuir, though it had fee-payin'. At Prestonfield we had Mr Wilson as our class teacher – an exceptionally nice man. But I have to say he was a bit o' a dead loss as far as teachin' actually went. He should have schooled us in some things for the bursary exam, but we had absolutely nothing, no papers or anything, from the previous years to go through.

So when we got the question papers in the bursary exam it wis English. Well, ah wouldnae have said it *wis* English. So ah got oot o' that school and went home. But ma mother wasnae in. That didnae make it any better! Ah wis sittin' in tears on the doorstep waitin' for her. And ah wisnae goin' back to that blinkin' school the next mornin'. In fact, she jist aboot had to drag me there! There wisnae any o' the three o' us – the two laddies and me – got through. We'd had no prepa-ration whatsoever. Ah mean, some o' the questions we didnae know what they were talkin' aboot. Ah didnae even know anything about Gillespie's. Ah wasnae weepin' on the doorstep because ah felt awfy disappointed. Ah think it wis probably jist the sense o' humiliation that made me cry. The fact that ah'd gone through the class and was always up within the top three, then tae get this exam and ye cannae even decipher the questions – ah think it was jist pure frustration and humiliation. And the fact that ma mother wasnae in when ah got home! So that was a dead loss.

But we got through the Qualifyin' exam all right. Then I went to James Clark's junior secondary school. I wasnae interested in a commercial course at the secondary school – shorthand and typin' and that. Possibly the thought o' workin' in an office just put me off. Ah don't think that as a girl then ah had ambitions. So I went to the domestic science course. And, ye see, ma mother and father never ever spoke about anything. Ah think everybody round about ye at Prestonfield they a' worked at Nelson the printers at the top o' Dalkeith Road, Millar's sweet factory in Causewayside, and thae places. And that was the ambitions – as long as ye got a bloomin' job! That wis the main thing in these days.[7] And, as ah've said, ah suppose ah decided when it came to leavin' school, 'Ah'll go and work in a shop.' Probably that seemed to give ye a bit more freedom, moving about in a shop rather than sittin' down in an office. And maybe it was more somethin' that ah'd been used to – goin' all the messages as well! Ah did a' the messages for Mrs Fraser and other neighbours. And ah had delivered milk for, och, a month or two, but ah'd never had any sort of regular milk or newspaper delivery job: ah wis too busy goin' the neighbours' messages! But aboot ambitions and jobs, ma parents never put me under any pressure at all. They never ever talked aboot what ye wanted tae do, as long as ye got a job. And, let's face it, at that time in the 1930s there were so few jobs goin' you were lucky that you got one.

So ah actually started in Pennycook's, the grocers and bakers, in Nicolson Street jist before ah left James Clark's School in the summer of 1937: ah wis goin' in part-time. They said, 'Jist come in.' Ah think ah went in on a Saturday, and after school on Tuesdays and Thursdays for the last few weeks at the school. It wis jist to get your hand in. And Pennycook's had promised me a full-time job once I left the school. So I was just turned 14 when I started work full-time in Pennycook's.

The wages wis 12 shillins [60p] a week, and they paid very well – but when ye thought about the hours ye worked! Officially, ye started at half-past eight in the mornin' till half-past six. That wis on Monday, Tuesday and Thursday. On a Wednesday ye worked till one o'clock – then ye got the half-day off. Ah think it wis till eight o'clock on a Friday, and till seven o'clock on a Saturday. They were the hours the shop wis open. But then it wis the hours that you spent *afterwards* as well, when the shop wis closed, between testin' eggs, makin' up butter, cleanin' up, and all sorts o' things like that. Oh! I mean, especially on a Friday, ye were lucky if ye were away at nine or ten o'clock at night. And ye never got out on a Saturday for your lunch. Mind you, it was very nice, because Pennycook's had the bakers as well as the grocer. Well, they used to say tae us, 'What do you want for your lunch?' The boss's sister worked in at the back, at the bakers. So we used tae take through from the grocers a nice slice of gammon and a lovely big egg, and we'd get something out o' the bakers – rolls and things. So you had a nice lunch on a Saturday. And you didn't have to pay for that. But if you happened to be in the middle o' eatin' it and the folk were queuein' away along the street outside, ye had tae leave your piece and ye stuck it in the oven! So there was no set time for your lunch break. They'd jist say, 'Aye, we're a bit quieter the now. Jist go away now.' And somebody else would come back. But durin' the week you got an hour and a half for your lunch. So I used tae walk home tae Prestonfield and walk back to the shop again. That was almost a mile and a half each way. That wis quite a long break for your lunch, but then considerin' how long we were in the shop at night . . . Maybe on a Monday it wisnae sae bad: ye got away maybe at seven o'clock. But Tuesday was the day ye used tae get a lot o' the butter made up. For that they had a machine o' sorts, a long thing that they could set tae cut the halves: ye know, the wire, ye brought it down on the butter. And then ye wrapped it. That took a long time. So you were doin' that and baggin' sugar. Ye got nothin' brought in ready for sale. Practically everything had tae be parcelled up in the shop, put into bags, wrapped up, tied up, and so on. Ye didnae have time to do that when the shop was so busy. So on a Tuesday you were very often there till about eight o'clock. And even on the Wednesday half-day you didnae get away home then, because some customers were still in the shop at one o'clock, and though you brought the door thing down then you still had all this sweepin' up. Like in the pubs, it wis sawdust on the floor. And all the stuff was tae be put away, the money tae be counted, etc. It wis long hours, oh, aye.

As ah say, ah used to walk up and down between Prestonfield and Pennycook's twice a day, except jist once on Wednesdays and Saturdays.

Ah never took the bus, except in the dark or the wet. In these days there wis awfy queues for the buses because, needless to say, nobody had cars. You could walk along from Pennycook's to Surgeons Hall and stand there for ages waitin' for a bus.

Ah found the wages gradually went up. They didnae have any set time for that, but if somebody happened to leave and they were short o' workers . . . Ah think ma wages went up maybe after about a year, from 12 shillins [60p] to 14 shillins [70p], and then probably to 16 shillins [80p]. Ah wis on 22 shillins [£1.10] a week when ah left Pennycook's in 1942, when ah wis 19, to go into the ATS. Ah think when ah started at Pennycook's ma mother and me maybe came tae an agreement, and she got 10 bob [50p] and ah got two bob [10p]. Mind you, ye wouldnae get the whole wage then o' 12 shillings [60p], because ye paid – was it 4d [2p]? – for an insurance stamp. Anyway, ah gave all ma wages to ma mother and ah got two bob [10p] or half a crown [12½p]. And, well, what did you spend it on? The pictures.

Then we also got a Christmas bonus – 10 shillings [50p]! Pennycook's closed on Christmas Day and New Year's Day. But they used tae have a Christmas minodge [ménage], where folk used to put in 6d [2½p] a week. So in the shop we used tae spend hours and hours after it shut at night, makin' up these parcels o' stuff for the ménage folk. Oh, the hours the shop wis open over Christmas and New Year. Ah mean, it was nothing to come out the shop about half-past nine, ten o'clock even, at night on Hogmanay. And a' that for a 10 shillin' [50p] bonus!

Then if there wis a Monday public holiday, ye got that. But the shop wis then open all day on the Wednesday. So ye lost your Wednesday half-day. However, after you'd been workin' at Pennycook's for a year ye got 10 days' paid holidays. That was quite generous, because most other people got only one week's holiday a year, and it wisnae always paid holiday.

Mr Pennycook – ah think his first name wis William – wis the owner o' the shop and he worked in it the first couple of years I was there. He and his wife had one o' these big houses down at Duddingston Park, up Milton Road. Their son was James. And I was one of the waitresses when their daughter got married. By then Mr Pennycook was dead: was that just at the beginning of the war? Anyway we, the girls from the shop, were the waitresses at his daughter's wedding. And they had the whole top o' the house. It was like a big ballroom. That's where all the tables and that were laid out. Oh, it was a big house. And Mr Pennycook must have had a very good nature, because not only had he had his wife living there but his wife's two sisters as well. One of the sisters worked in the back shop – the bakery; the other one worked in the house. Mr Pennycook had had the shop a good number o' years when ah started there in 1937. He was well-known. And, oh, it wisnae half a busy shop. He was famed for his bacon and butter and everything, good quality and cut price sort o' thing. But he died quite a young man. He went into hospital not that long after ah started in the shop. Nobody told ye then what was wrong wi' him. But ah think it was gall-stones or something. Ah think he maybe came out the hospital, but he wisnae out that long and he wis away in again. He wis an old man tae me, but ah think he wis only in his fifties when he died.

There were quite a few women and girls worked in the shop. Mind you, there was a big turnover of girls because o' the long hours they had tae work. When ah started there Mary Hislop, an older woman, was the manageress. Ah mean, she looked old to me, but then she was maybe about 40 or so. Ah think she'd been in wi' the bricks there. Then there was Mary Sime. She wis about 22 then. She lived down near Portobello. Nettie Murray, the same age as me, like me had been at James Clark's School, and started work in the shop the same day as me. Then a lot o' the girls at Pennycook's came from mining villages or small towns around Edinburgh like Bonnyrigg and Dalkeith/Eskbank or, as Cathy Nugent did, from Rosewell. Nina Hay came from Newcraighall, and a girl Peaston from Loanhead worked in the shop for about a year. But she wasnae well, was off her work, and she died o' TB. She wis only about 21. But, oh, what a bonny girl she was too, very, very fair. Oh, TB wis a terrible thing in these days. And then Anna Hart – it sounds ridiculous – came all the way from Cleland near Motherwell, ah think by train. Anna wouldn't get a lift to work in a car, because in these days nobody had cars. The only person ah knew that had a car before the war was James Pennycook, the shopowner's son. So there were usually two or three girls worked in the bakery, and there'd be half a dozen anyway in the grocers. And nobody worked part-time in these days, they were all full-time workers. Well, ah started in the grocers but after a wee while I ended up in the bakers, then ah went back tae the grocers again. There wis a passageway between the bakery and the grocers. Both shops had windows on to Nicolson Street.

As for a trade union at Pennycook's, oh, naebody had heard o' one! Ah wis never asked tae join a union. Nobody ever mentioned it. Ah didnae know of any o' the other girls bein' in a union. Ah think you had tae be in the Co-op and places like that, tae be in a union. Ah wis never inclined tae look for another job myself. Ah never applied for another job. Probably ah didnae because ah could walk back and forward from home to Pennycook's, and it seemed to be a bit better paid there than some other shops. In most of the shops, ah would say, a girl's wage wis 10 shillins [50p] to start with, whereas ah had 12 shillins [60p]. Before ah'd left school I remember going to the Silk Shop to look for a job. Ah didnae get it – probably because ah lived at Prestonfield, a slum clearance. But the wage at the Silk Shop wis tae be six shillins [30p] a week. And later on when Ella, ma brother Jack's wife, started tailorin' in R.W. Forsyth's in Princes Street, ah think her wage wis only five shillins [30p] a week.

Ah've mentioned that at Pennycook's we got 10 days' paid holiday. Before ah began at school, or maybe about that time, ah remember ma parents talkin' about when ma brother Jack was a wee boy and ah wis a wee girl, us all goin' up to Milnathort in Kinross-shire for a week's holiday. Ah suppose it wis jist as we used to do at times: you paid somebody. They called it attendance. And you got a room and they did your cookin' for ye sort o' thing. But after that ah don't think ma mother and father ever had a holiday. Once ah wis taken away wi' the Arnots, close friends o' ma parents, for a week to somewhere in Perthshire – Glen Lyon or somewhere. And ah had a birthday there. But whether it was ma fifth or ma sixth birthday – 1928 or 1929 – ah'm not sure.

Then in 1937 I went on holiday for a week wi' my Aunty Mary and her three boys to Kinghorn in Fife. Again it was attendance. Ah remember it was in a modern house. Then in July or August 1939, this time wi' ma younger sister Margaret, ah went again wi' Aunty Mary and ma cousins to Kinghorn. But we had this wee poky place to ourselves, and that was what was so depressing about it. Aunty Mary had booked the place for a fortnight, but I had only the ten days' holiday. And there was a lot o' rain that time as well, and a lot o' sea mist. And it really was such a depressin' wee place. We a' had the feelin' that something awful was about to happen. And there were big guns practisin' – boom, boom, boom – maybe along the coast from Kinghorn or on Inchkeith island in the Firth of Forth. They shook the place. When ma ten days were up and things werenae gettin' any better, what between the rain, the mist, and the big guns booming, it wis jist so dreary. So Aunty Mary said tae me, 'Ah think ah'll jist come back wi' you.' And comin' back in the train to Edinburgh it wis these wee blue lights and the train a' blacked out! Of course, by then the outbreak of war wis comin' nearer.

Apart from these few holidays, as a girl ah really hadnae been anywhere. Ah think we were down on the bus once or twice at Peebles. And the Sunday School picnic used tae take us tae Dysart in Fife. But ah'd certainly never been over the Border or anywhere near the Border. Ah'd never been away on ma own anywhere, any time ah went it would be wi' company, ma parents or ma Aunty Mary, or ma closest friend Cathy Arnot. Cathy had an aunty at Dunbar and we used tae have a day down there or to Gullane. Once, ah think it would be early in the war, ma friend Nettie Murray, who had an aunty near Gladsmuir in East Lothian, and me did stay there overnight because we couldnae get a bus back home. But that was all. We hadnae got any money either, let's face it. But, no, ye really never went anywhere. Ye didnae know anything o' the world. So when ye got posted somewhere in the ATS and ye'd never heard o' the place, ye said, 'Where in the name are we goin'? Timbuctoo?'

At home, as ah've said, ah went tae the pictures. When ah started workin' at 14 at Pennycook's in 1937 the trouble wis workin' there so late. At James Clark's School they had this club on Friday nights for former pupils like me. So not long after ah started at Pennycook's ah asked if it would be possible for me to get away from the shop at the back o' seven on a Friday night. But, oh, no, no, that wisnae on at all. So really ye didnae get anywhere. So mainly it was the pictures or the dancing, sometimes through the week after work or on the Wednesday half-day. The dancing was at the Silver Slipper at Morningside and then the Palais de Danse at Tollcross – but I suppose really it wis more durin' the war that ah went to the Palais: ah wis only 16 when the war started. But these were the popular things then, the pictures and the dancing. That's what it was. Ah don't remember anybody goin' playin' badminton or anything like that: we didnae have time or the energy! And we hadnae television to go home and watch.

* * *

Ah remember the declaration o' war by Mr Chamberlain. Ah wasnae workin' at Pennycook's that day, because it wis a Sunday. But ah remember walkin' up the Dalkeith Road on the previous Friday after hearin' the Germans had invaded Poland. Ah opened up the shop, and when Mary Hislop, the manageress, come in ah said, 'Did ye hear?' No. she hadnae heard. She jist says, 'Oh, well.' Everybody wis expectin' by then that war wis comin', and of course all the lights were goin' out and everything.

In May 1940, jist before the evacuation from Dunkirk, Jack, ma brother, volunteered intae the Air Force. He thought he was goin' tae get intae air crew. Of course they all went tae Blackpool first – it wis like us in the ATS all goin' first tae Newbattle Abbey. But of course things were in such a state that Jack ended up across at Driffield aerodrome in Yorkshire, near Hull. Jack wis a great writer, always writin' tae ma mother. It's a shame we didnae keep any o' these letters that came from him. Because he'd gone right through the Battle o' Britain. They were in action a' the time more or less when they were at Driffield.[8] He came back on leave a nervous wreck. Ah remember him sittin' at the back o' a chair in our house one night. Ma father never used tae come in from Rosyth for his dinner till about 11pm, especially if there wis air raids and the train couldnae get across the Forth Bridge. We'd a' had our tea, and ma mother was boilin' potatoes for ma father comin' in. Then Jack nearly went through the roof. It wis the noise o' the potatoes boilin': Jack thought it was the guns rippin' across the aerodrome. His nerves were a' shattered.

As ah've said, one o' the things that sort of set me off to volunteer into the ATS in 1942 wis the mice, but especially the rats, in Pennycook's shop. Conscription for girls and women o' 19 upwards had come in in December 1941, and you all had to register. By then ah wis 18½. You had to go round to the old Labour Exchange at Tollcross to register. Ah can't remember when they actually called you. But they were takin' people. Nina Hay that worked in Pennycook's and lived at Newcraighall, she was that bit older than me, maybe 21. And she went off to work in munitions in Birmingham or somewhere. So I suppose that you got it into your head, 'Well, there's no way that ah want tae go and work in a munitions factory.' Ah couldn't even have thought about it. And ah think it was as much that as anything, apart from a' your pals goin' as well. Everybody wis goin'. Nettie Murray had already gone from

Pennycook's to work at R. & T. Gibson's, the big grocer in Frederick Street, but then she went to the WAAFs away down at Cardington in Bedfordshire. And then maybe there wis a wee bit of a carrot if you joined the ATS, for, as ah'd never before been away anywhere on ma own, it meant you were only to go out to Newbattle Abbey in Midlothian for three weeks tae begin' wi'. Ah don't think ah even gave too much thought at all tae goin' intae the WAAFs or the WRNS. Ah jist decided ah'd go into the ATS. And then at that time ye didnae know anything about any o' these things that, later on, ye heard were said about the ATS havin' a kind o' reputation as fast young women. And workin' in Pennycook's shop where ah was amongst a' these women they would never do anything like that, ye know! But ah suppose ah wis takin' a step in the dark really when ah volunteered intae the ATS.

Ah don't think that ah'd ever said anything to ma mother about joinin' the ATS. So ah think it was on ma half-day on the Wednesday ah went down to a recruitin' place in George Street – the Music Hall, at the Assembly Rooms, filled in the papers there, and then went back and told ma mother and father, sort o' thing. Ah think ah went to George Street for a medical as well, and a wee sort o' test thing – an intelligence test. And then ah think ye got a message tellin' ye to report at a certain time to Newbattle Abbey. Ma Aunty Mary took me oot and bought me a case tae carry ma stuff in. Ma mother went down to St Andrew Square bus place wi' me, and ah got on a bus and went out to Newbattle. It wis an adventure. Oh, I had no idea where Newbattle Abbey was.

Ah think we reported first to the Abbey itself. And then we were marched up the drive and through the gates again, and we were put in King's Lines, across the road from the Abbey. It's all houses that are built on King's Lines now. Ah think the only time ah wis in about the Abbey itsel' was that day that ah arrived, sort o' thing. And ah think you had another medical in there, in the Abbey buildin' itsel', if ah remember right. It wis huts we were in. How many huts there were – ah've not a clue. It's so long ago. Ah think they were single beds. We were there, well, jist a day short o' three weeks, ah think.

Probably it was seven o'clock we had to get up at in the mornins, and probably lights out at ten o'clock or something like that. Most of the day we were doing physical exercise, physical training, and marching. And some lectures o' some sort. And maybe we did go into the main part – the Abbey itself, for lectures. There wis certainly a heck of a lot o' physical jerks. And when anybody since then has said about joinin' any Keep Fit classes – no thanks, no thanks! It put me off for life! Maybe many of the girls wouldn't be as fit as young women nowadays. Well, in ma own case, ah wis always walkin' up and down to ma work at Pennycook's and on ma feet all day long, so ah suppose ah wis as fit as most o' them. But ma recollection is that we were kept busy all day long.

And, by Jove, we had a sergeant that, when ye were no sooner finishin' a' this physical jerks than, 'Right! Get Out! Get Out!' And of course what used tae get us wis ye'd never been used wi' a back stud and a front stud in your collar, and a tie. And, of course, tryin' tae get these things done, ye were a' fingers and thumbs! And the sergeant, she's bawlin' her head off, ye know: 'Hurry up! Hurry up!' Oh, it wis part o' the scheme tae keep us on the move a' the time – and ah'll say they did! You were rushed into the gym, off wi' everything – more or less anyway. What did ye keep on? (They didnae have T-shirts in these days.) It must have been your pants – these big elastic pants! We didnae have special clothin' for the gym. And ye wouldnae keep your shirt on, because that's what really bothered me. You'd have a vest. Anyway, as ah say, ye were no' sooner finishin' a' this physical jerks than the sergeant's bawlin', 'Right! Get Out! Get Out!'

Then they used tae have ye marchin' route marches. We used tae be able to march oot the top o' King's Lines somewhere and – don't ask me how – we came back round again. It might have been only a couple o' miles. But ah feel it would probably be quite a march for us poor wee souls!

Another experience wis when we got our first inoculations. Ye were-nae allowed out at all. The inoculation absolutely laid you out. It didnae half. And that reminds me about the beds in our King's Lines hut: ah'm sure ah wis lyin' then on a single bed, ah wisnae lyin' on a bunk.

And, oh, we were always starvin'. Ah think the food wis, oh, all right, quite good quality, and a reasonable amount. It wis jist that all the fresh air made us hungry! And when we were allowed out the first thing we did wis get up tae that railway station at Eskbank, jist up the road, and get the train in tae Edinburgh. Twice, ah think, ma mother and father met me at the Waverley station there and they found some-where that wis sellin' somethin' ye could eat. There wisnae much available: they were all rationed by that time.

Then we got our uniforms at Newbattle. Ah think it fitted a' right. Ah mean, they more or less measured ye, ah think. We didnae have sizes like 12s and 14s! No, ah suppose it was 32, 34, 36 in these days. Ye tried your shoes on and your jacket. Ah think they were all quite reasonably fittin'. But ah remember much later on, when ah wis comin' home on leave and wis standin' all the way from York to Edinburgh in the middle o' the night, that ah'd got a new pair o' shoes jist before then. Ah hadnae worn them very much. Ah wis at the chiropodist two or three days later. Ah could hardly walk. Ah could hardly bear wearin' thae shoes. They didnae measure your feet. They were lovely shoes, beautiful leather shoes. But ah had very narrow feet and these were wide-fittin'. So since then ah've had a bunion and it wis probably the ATS shoes that started it. Ah'd never had any trouble wi' ma feet until then.

In the King's Lines ah think it wis all women – ATS – if ah remember right. Our sergeant wis a woman. But from what ah remember there were troops – men – down at the Abbey itself. But the women were always kept separate from men. Of the other girls in ma hut in King's Lines ah kept in touch wi' Isa Upton that lived near Portobello in Edinburgh, and we remained lifelong friends. Isa, who was older than me, had worked in her brother's newsagent shop at Craigentinny until she was conscripted into the ATS. She kept in touch with a few of the other girls in our hut; one o' them later emigrated tae Canada. But the other ones we kept in touch wi', well, it fizzled out even durin' the war. There was one girl ah remember from Burntisland, but ah don't remember any at Newbattle from the west o' Scotland.

It must ha' been jist no' long before ye were finishing the three weeks' trainin' at Newbattle and goin' tae get posted when, ah remember, ye a' had tae go through the gas business. They had sort o' hut things up the very top. The gas business really depressed ye. Ah mean, ye got all sorts o' stories about it. But you had to whip off your mask as ye went through this thing. Would that have been mustard gas? Ah know it jist choked ye, absolutely choked ye. Well, whatever gas it was ye just had tae hold your nose and rush through as quickly as you could. It wis jist tae give you the idea that, if that's what you smelt, you got your gas mask on! So it was very encouraging! Ye felt a bit depressed – no' that ah'm a type that gets depressed. But ah think it sort o' put a . . .

* * *

Well, after Newbattle, Isa Upton and I were both posted down to Mansfield in Nottinghamshire. Ah can't remember clearly the journey by train down to Mansfield. Ah can't remember if we got on the train at the Waverley station in Edinburgh or at Eskbank station, up the road from Newbattle Abbey. It was the St Pancras train that went right down. But going down on the same train was quite a lot of other ATS from Newbattle that were going down to Chilwell at Nottingham, which was a big Ordnance store depot. And ah think we changed the train at one place and then changed again to get to Mansfield in the east Midlands. We definitely changed trains, but whether we changed at Nottingham and then to somewhere else and then to Mansfield, ah don't know. But, ah mean, it took the whole day. Ah'm sure it must have been about six or seven o'clock at night when we got there. And whether anybody met us at the station at Mansfield or what, ah jist havenae a clue. Ah suppose they must have given us rations – subsistence – to eat on the train, because there was nothing on the trains. Ye couldnae buy anything on the trains. So ah would think we must have been given sandwiches by the ATS – or they would need to have lifted us off it, we were so hungry! Ah suppose we really had a feeling we were travellin' intae the unknown. As ah've said, ah'd never been over the Border before, never been further south than Galashiels. Anyway, as ah say, ah can't remember whether anybody met us at Mansfield but, you know, they did use tae meet folk off the train. Somebody must have done that, because we wouldnae know how to get to our billet. And we had our kit – all our worldly possessions – in one bag. That's why they used tae have army lorries or a utility van that came. So ah assume that we were probably taken first to the company office, which had only one officer. And then we were taken to our billet in Leyton Avenue.

Our billet in Leyton Avenue was in houses that were obviously requisitioned. Isa Upton and I were in No. 15 Leyton Avenue, which went round in a sort of crescent. Then there was a sort o' wee lane thing went jist round to the back o' the houses where they took the coal and everything. Our billet wis on the end, and it wis on three floors. Another girl, Joyce, joined us there. She'd come up from London. Well, at No. 15 ye came in the front door and there wis your sittin' room. You went through, and there wis the kitchen. And then there wis what you'd probably call the back sittin' room: it looked out to the back. So the three beds for us were in there. They were all single beds, There wasnae any bunks in these houses in Leyton Avenue at all.

There wis a lot o' shoe factories and hosiery factories round that part o' Mansfield. So the army men were in an old shoe factory in St John Street, jist off more or less the main street of Mansfield. The men slept in the upper part. Down below wis the cookhouse. So we had tae trail down there to the cookhouse for all our meals. It wis maybe about a ten-minute walk for us ATS girls to get there. But we made an arrangement with the men that at the weekend we would collect bread and milk on Saturdays at lunchtime. And we also used tae get some o' those sausages from the butcher. They hadnae much meat in them, but they filled a hole. And somebody would maybe have been home on leave and would bring something back for us to eat. So we cooked for ourselves at the weekends – well, we existed anyway. We used tae fry these sausages. But ye couldnae buy eggs or anything.

The ATS office in Mansfield wis in one o' these requisitioned houses near Leyton Avenue. Isa Upton and I both ended up workin' in the office. Isa was on statistics: ah'd never heard o' statistics before! And I was on – what did they use to call it? It was progress chasing. I don't know if they had a job like that in civvy street.[9]

The unit had taken over half of the Mansfield and District bus garage. And when we arrived in Mansfield it was the Ordnance Corps. But then it was changed to REME [Royal Electrical & Mechanical Engineers] just about a couple o' months later. So we all changed our badges over. We had an ATS badge in our hat, and we had the REME badge on our tunic. On the top o' our sleeve we had the North Midland District flash, which was the green apple. And ah feel we might have had something for Northern Command on the top o' our other sleeve.

Then, oh, ah think everybody, when they left Edinburgh, felt homesick. In fact, ah have a vague recollection that Isa Upton and I were only in Mansfield two or three days and we put in a request to be removed up to Scottish Command! As ah've mentioned, ah'd never before been over the Border, never been further afield in that direction than maybe Galashiels. Whereas Mansfield wis right in the centre o' England. Ah suppose at that time there wisnae too many of us had been across the Borders. But ah certainly remember feelin' quite homesick. Oh, we – Isa and me – were desperate tae come back again tae Scotland. Ah wrote home regularly, once a week at least, because they didnae have phones at home in these days, or at least ma parents didnae. Ah think ye corresponded wi' all your old aunties (they werenae old at that time of course) and everybody else. Ye did correspond a lot. And ye got letters at Mansfield back again from family and friends and so on. Some o' them were theirsels in the Forces. Well, the likes o' ma cousin Ellen Spence, that wis in the WAAFs. Ellen and I corresponded quite a bit. Not so much her sister Nan, that wis in the ATS, and me. If ah remember right Ellen wis then at a bomber station in Norfolk, and later she come up tae Drem aerodrome in East Lothian. Well, ah'd joined the ATS in August 1942 and I was in Mansfield by the September. And ah remember ah must have been soundin' terribly homesick then, because ma father sent the money and ah came up home for a weekend. Ah think Isa Upton did as well. The pair o' us were really homesick. Funnily enough, ah think we settled down after that. Although we had both put in for a posting straight back tae Scotland, nobody paid any attention tae us. And ah don't think we even followed it up. We never gave it another thought. But ah think probably part o' our problem wis that you left the beautiful city of Edinburgh wi' a' these lovely build-ings, and what did you end up in? Mansfield – wi' a' these red brick colliery houses, jist different altogether. Well, a lot of it was mine company housing. And where we were in Mansfield it wis still red brick, though they were nothing tae do with the pits. But they were all red, even the shops and that were red brick.

In our billet in Leyton Avenue there wis only the three of us down-stairs – Isa Upton, Joyce from London, and me. Then there wis this big room upstairs that ah think five ATS girls slept in. And there wis a single room that the corporal in charge o' the billet slept in. We had an open coal fire in our bedroom – if you could get the coal for it. Well, they used to allot us some coal, because that wis the only way you got your hot water. We all had to have a bath, so there was a bathroom and a separate toilet there. There wis also a toilet outside the back door. So, oh, the billet was fine. But there wis only the army furniture jist, so it wis very bare. However, ye didnae have any possessions, so it didnae matter. So in the whole billet in Leyton Avenue there wis usually about a dozen ATS. And we all got on very well.

We all worked at different jobs. Isa Upton and I were in the office, with two civilian women and a chief clerk. He was a sergeant, a Regular soldier. Ye see a' these things in the paper now that folk take them up? Well, ah think somebody could ha' taken him up, oh, jist for harassment. Ah don't know that ye could call it sexual harassment. They werenae so much into the sex in these days as they seem tae be nowadays! He was just a bully. His name wis Sergeant Johnston. We hadnae got a National Health Service then: so he had a' his front top teeth missing, and that – like fangs – made him look even worse. Ah don't know how long he'd been in that office when ah got there, but, oh, the folk . . . Anybody outside the office couldnae stand him. He was a very nasty, unpleasant person. He wis one o' the sort that snarled. And anybody that did anything wrong, ye know, oh! Oh, he wis a nasty man, he really was. When he got moved we were a' very pleased. That wis when we started gettin' different ones in that lived maybe within about 50 miles o' the office. They were on a home posting after bein' abroad for three years. We got quite a lot o' them, but they were young blokes. They'd seen action in the war maybe. They were always very pleasant. You could work wi' them no bother. They were all REME men, as Sgt Johnston wis. Of course, the chief clerk was always a sergeant. But we had quite a selection o' them.

Ah mentioned earlier how some folk seemed tae think ATS girls were fast young women. One o' these blokes in our place at Mansfield that had been abroad and were brought back – I can see him now in my mind's eye, but ah can't remember his name – a big bloke that wis made postman for our place, the workshops and that, he says tae me one day, 'Ye know, what a nice crowd there is here.' Mind you, there wisnae that many of us ATS there. It was mostly males, wi' it bein' a bus garage that we were usin'. And he says, 'Ye know,' he says, 'ah wis amazed to find such nice girls in the ATS here. Where ah've come from what a name they had!' He'd come from Egypt or somewhere. He says, 'Really, if you associated wi' them at all you had a bad name.'

Anyway, in the stores in the workshops there wis about four ATS girls. Three o' them came frae Dundee area, and one from Newcastle. Well, they could jist about understand each other's accents! Then there wis a girl from Liverpool, and she wis in the electric shop. And another one, ah think, wis in the motor cycle shop. And we had quite a few driver-mechanics. One of them, a tall lassie, came from Motherwell. But we had one girl, she wis jist a driver though, that used tae drive the wee utility van around. Her name was Gerda Weiss. And her family had fled here from the Nazis before the war, probably about 1937–8. Gerda and her family were German Jews. Gerda's brothers must have been naturalised, but her mother and father weren't, and they were interned at the beginning of the war. When her brothers went into the British army her parents were released. Then Gerda herself went into the ATS. She wis a very nice girl.

One o' the things that struck me, especially in ma early months in the ATS, wis that ah wis meetin' wi' girls from all different parts o' Britain, some o' them – maybe from Newcastle, Liverpool, Bournemouth – wi' accents that were strange tae me. But we got on all right wi' one another. Of course, at Mansfield folk were movin' out at different times, and we did get a wee bit of a turnover, a fresh face now and again. But some were there all the time. But, as ah say, in the main everybody seemed to get on wi' one another. And of course they were all out at their work durin' the day; and at night, well, there always had tae be some on duty. You had your duty for the fire-watching, for instance. You could expect to be fire-watchin' maybe once a week or so. And then, well, you were out tae some nights at the pictures and at dances.

Then, ah think, we got seven days' home leave every three months – so about a month each year. And ye sort of stuck your day off on to it, and possibly travellin' time as well. So probably it was seven days at a time stretched up to about nine days. Ye got four passes a year, ah think, for the train journey. Ah think ma first leave – about the time the pair o' us, Isa Upton and me, were feelin' so homesick – would be in November 1942. On one o' ma leaves Joyce from London, the other ATS girl that shared our room at Leyton Avenue, came up with me to Edinburgh and had a week's holiday with me at Prestonfield.

At Mansfield the local people were very good. Even if ye wandered into Woolworths and they heard your voice and your accent and saw your uniform . . . They were very, very good, sympathetic and friendly. In fact, about the first week Isa and me were in Mansfield we met and got friendly with the Parkins, an older couple that lived up the road, not far away from our bus garage workshops. The Parkins were very, very good to us. I used to be invited up to their house more or less every Sunday. To begin wi', Isa went too; but she dropped off later on. And even people that the Parkins knew would invite us for our tea. Then at Christmas, if we werenae away home on leave, the Parkins would invite us out to Sutton-in-Ashfield, an old hosiery town where their family lived, two or three miles away from Mansfield. The Parkins all came off mining stock around that area. Mr Parkin himself was the secretary of the Mansfield & District Co-op. So we did very well wi' the Parkins, they really were very good tae us. They're all dead now, but ah kept in touch wi' them till they passed away.

* * *

Well, ah wis jist about three years at Mansfield, from September 1942 till maybe the end o' September 1945 when ah wis posted tae York. After the war in Europe finished in May 1945 they were closin' things up and the REME workshops closed down. When ah'd volunteered into the ATS in 1942 ah think it was for the duration o' the war. Then everybody got a demob number. But ah didn't come out the ATS on ma demob number, because ah got married at the end o' December 1945 and then ah wis able to give them notice and leave! Before that, so long as the war wis on, you couldn't leave the ATS unless you were expectin' a baby. So ah actually left the army on the 7th o' February 1946. If ah'd waited till ma demob number had come up it might have been the end o' April or the beginning' o' May that year. So once the war ended, but not before it ended, a married ATS girl like me could apply tae leave the Forces. Ah must have just written in, and it took about six weeks to get through. From York ah came back up to Redford Barracks in Edinburgh to be demobbed. Then you had so many weeks' paid leave. After that ah went down to Hull, where Benny Buchanan, ma husband, was stationed in REME.

In the ATS we didnae really get anything when we were demobbed. You could keep your uniform. And it shows how everybody then wis in such a state wi' clothin' coupons. The daughter o' a friend o' the Parkins down in Mansfield was in the Girl Guides, and she got the tunic o' ma uniform. Ah assume they dyed it for her. And ma mother ended up wearin' ma uniform skirt for her cleanin' up! Ah think ah wore the ATS pyjamas myself. Ah don't know what happened tae the shoes – maybe ah wore them. We were all in dire straits wi' clothin' bein' rationed.

Ah'd met Benny Buchanan, a REME electrician, at Christmas 1943 at Mansfield. He'd come there from Newcastle, where they were over-established – more folk than were needed. He wis trainin' wi' the

15th Scottish Division in a mobile workshop, gettin' ready for the Second Front that began on D-Day in June 1944, when he was posted from Newcastle first to York then to Mansfield. He wis only at Mansfield three or four months then he wis sent away to Irvine in Ayrshire, on a course for water-proofing. But we kept in touch with each other by letter – the post was better in these days! At the end o' the war in Europe Benny wis posted tae Hull.

So it wis in February or March 1946 ah joined Benny at Hull. The army marriage allowance then was about 19s 6d [97½p] a week. Benny's army pay wis about £2 3s 2d [£2.16] or something. So that wis our total weekly income. And findin' a job for myself wis not easy. Ah must have been down in Hull about a month before ah found one: in Needler's confectionery factory, four floors up where they made the toffee! When ma mother heard, she said, 'You'll never stick that.' But it wis amazin'. When ye know ye're only goin' tae be there a short time ah think ye can stick it. So ah got on all right. Ah wouldnae have been any good if they'd put me in the chocolate place, because the heat would ha' killed me! But in the toffee place ah used tae take the misshapes and then weigh them. It was a job and gave us some money.

Finding somewhere tae live in Hull wasnae easy either. But when Benny had first arrived in Hull he and some o' the lads had met this Mr and Mrs Dannet, who used tae take them back tae their house for a cup o' tea. So of course when I arrived and started goin' over to the Dannets they asked me to stay at their house, and ah used tae sleep wi' the young daughter that wis still at school. The Dannet's other daughter wis married and had a spare room in her place, and that was what Benny and me ended up wi'. But we didn't stay there long because she had two children, her husband had just come out the army – and she herself was absolutely lazy. All the time ah wisnae workin' ah wis scrubbin' her floors! And they were all scrubbed because there wasnae any carpet. Ah cannae even think there wis electricity. There certainly wis no bathroom, and the toilet wis a flush toilet, but it wis oot the back. Ah came in from ma work one night and found she wis pregnant again, her brother's wife wis also pregnant and they had fell out wi' the mother, and the brother and his wife had moved in as well and were havin' the baby at home. So ah let it be known at Needler's that ah certainly didnae feel like becomin' a midwife! So Benny and I ended up instead in a terraced villa wi' three bedrooms. We had the wee bedrooms. So we were there for probably about ten months anyway. Benny got an out-pass and was allowed out o' his camp to be wi' me in this villa. As he hadnae gone intae the army until February 1943 he wis still in the army till he wis demobbed in May 1947.

Well, ah wis in Hull for 14 or 15 months, and then Benny, when he got demobbed, and I came up to Edinburgh. It wis very difficult for Benny to find a job as an electrician or garage mechanic. We were gettin' desperate because two months passed and he'd run right out of all his demob leave. He had only three days left to claim back, as he wis entitled to do, his pre-war job in Manchester where he had grown up. Luckily, ma Aunty Mary knew one of the bosses in the SMT [Scottish Motor Traction] bus company in Edinburgh, and Benny got a job there. So from then we remained in Edinburgh.

Well, looking back now ah've no regrets about volunteerin' into the ATS. I would say the experience had quite a lot o' influence on me. It certainly did broaden the mind! Well, ah'd worked only wi' women in Pennycook's shop in Edinburgh. So the ATS wis quite an education in itself, meetin' different people from all over Britain – and of course meetin' Benny, ma husband. Ah never came to feel ah'd have been happier volunteerin' for the WAAFs or the WRNS. No, ah wis quite happy in the ATS. But ah wouldnae like tae have thought ah wis goin' tae be on any o' these gun or searchlight sites, ye know, where they were out a' night mannin' things or gettin' bombed. Well, even the WAAFs, a lot o' them on these air bases were bombed tae blazes and quite a few were killed. And ah suppose even the ones in the WAAFs that were on the barrage balloons were exposed. At Mansfield ah suppose factories – the Metal Box Company and all these places – were makin' components for various things. But it wis mostly hosiery and shoes they were makin' in that area, and ah don't think they were ever bombed. Ah suppose most o' the German bombin' had finished anyway before ah got to Mansfield in 1942.

May Kerr (Mrs May Buchanan) died on 13 November 2017.

Williamina MacNab

Well, Dorothy Edwards and I from Dewar's Whisky cellar office in Perth both wanted in to the ATS. I was 17 and I'd been maybe 18 months at the most in Dewar's. I would have liked to have stayed there, but they were calling up our age group. And at that time they were putting the girls on to the railway as carriage cleaners. If you were called up that's where you were going. So we jumped the gun and just went, volunteered, and joined up.

I was born in Perth on the 28th of March 1926, just before the General Strike.[1] My father was a shoe repairer, a bootmaker, a cobbler. Well, he was trained to do bootmaking but he never actually worked at that. So he was a shoe repairer. That was the only job he ever had. My dad was an orphan and he was brought up at the Fechney, a big house on the Glasgow Road at Perth, a home for orphans – just for boys. And they weren't ill-treated but they weren't coddled, oh, a very Spartan regime. I can remember him saying they got porridge every morning for breakfast. One morning they got treacle on it, the next morning milk. And ah think the other meals were a bit skimpy. The boys were taught a trade: that's where he learned the shoe repairing. But they were sent out to do message boys' jobs, too – ah think that may have been for private shops.

Ma father was actually illegitimate. His mother – ah think her name was MacNab – hadn't wanted him. She was a maidservant and worked in one of the houses he went to to deliver messages. His mother knew who he was. And he had been told by somebody who his mother was, so he did actually know that. Oh, it was awfully sad. And he had a sister, but she was brought up by an old lady they called Granny Dewar.

Whether she had any connection ah never . . . People didn't talk much about things. And of course ma father never knew who his father was. And let's face it: in those days it was often the master of the house where the maids were! Ma father took his mother's name – MacNab.

He was a fine-looking man. He died about 1960. He hadn't had a lot of retirement so he must have been then about 67 or 68. So he was born maybe about 1892 or '93. He was in the Royal Scots in the 1914–18 War, and he was a Military Medallist. Ah think he'd volunteered. But he never spoke about the war. But he was all through the war and was badly wounded. Well, he had a shell went through the back of his neck, and he had shrapnel that travelled in his leg and all through his body. At one time it started to come out at the back of his neck, and his hair – I can remember this – his hair all fell out. He had black, curly hair. But then it all grew in again. But our own doctor, who was a surgeon, said to him: 'Now, Wullie, you can go to the military hospital in Edinburgh. And I'll [support your claim] if you want to claim for a pension. But,' he says, 'I'm telling you now they'll X-ray you, and the shrapnel will be there. But by the time they operate it'll be some place else. You'll end up with no legs.' So ma father never had a war pension, never had a war pension. There were still bits o' shrapnel in his body all his life. And though he didn't speak about the war, ah know he was always in France and Flanders, and had been at Ypres, the Somme, Arras, Passchendaele . . . In 1916, halfway through the war, he was home on leave, and that's when he and ma mother got engaged. Ma mother said her engagement ring was bought with blood money. They were married when he come back at the end of the war.

Ma mother was born, a wee bit younger than ma dad, in 1896. When she left school she went to work in J. & P. Coats's thread mill in Dunkeld Road in Perth.[2] But she didn't like it, and after a short time went into domestic service in some of the big houses in the Glasgow Road. At one time she was a sort of nanny and took the baby out. But she did housework as well. And then in the 1914–18 War she was in a munitions factory in Annan, Dumfriesshire. She must have volunteered. I've a photograph of her then, though I don't know where it is now, and she looks like an Indian squaw in it, because they weren't allowed hairpins or anything, nothing with metal. And it was just a sort of loose khaki outfit, trousers and a top. In the photo she had nothing on her head, but she had beautiful black hair. It was all in a pigtail so, as I say, she looked like a squaw. I think she was in Annan maybe about two years. Because in 1916, when she got engaged to daddy, she was still in Perth. But she liked the munitions work; there was a lot, I suppose, of companionship of other girls, whereas in domestic service it could be quite a lonely job. And ma mother, ah think, maybe felt, especially after becoming engaged and ma dad going back to the war, that it was patriotic to go and volunteer to work in munitions.

In the early 1920s, well, my dad was unemployed. There was no work. Ma mother by then had had two children who died in infancy. Then my sister May was born in 1923. Daddy was at home, looking for work. Finding it was difficult. Well, people were unemployed, so they couldn't afford to have their shoes repaired. It was as simple as that. And my dad was a piece worker. If there was no work there was no money for him. You'd to go to the parish – oh, absolutely a humiliation. Ma dad never went to the parish. Ma mother was too pridefae. She sold a lot of her good blankets, and knitted lovely baby shawls for the ladies of the Episcopal cathedral: she sort of knew them through the Child Welfare. She was a lovely knitter. So they had asked her if she would knit shawls for babies. She used to sit up half the night knitting. I think she got 7s 6d [37½p] for each shawl. And, oh, each shawl was more than two or three days' work. Though my sister May was just a baby, maybe about six or eight months old, my mother got the chance of working as a servant-cook for somebody titled – ah can't remember who they were – but within the Perthshire area. So she lived in there with May, and daddy stayed at home, looking for work. He eventually got a job with a cobbler at Bridge of Earn, 4½ miles from Perth. He walked there, with his bad leg, and walked back home each day – for very little money. But again he was earning. Except for his wounded leg, which made him limp, he was fit enough. That was the only work on offer, so he took it. But I don't think he was there very long. Anyway, my mother was able then to come home with my sister May, and my dad found work with MacLaggan the bootmaker, a family business in Perth. Eventually he worked for Norwell's, a big shoe business with two shops in Perth High Street, and a shoe repair shop in the Skinnergate with about five cobblers in it. Again it was piece work: no work, no pay, no flat rate or anything. Norwell's was my dad's main job and he was with them for years. But what a hard life he had.

My dad was a very quiet man. He didn't push himself. Ma mother was, oh, a very determined woman. She was the eldest in a biggish family. She had to do a lot because there wasn't much age between them, and they lived in more or less a room and kitchen. Ma mother had one brother, Michael, and four sisters: Kate, Ina, Nora, and Eva. And there was one or two others that had died. And my granny Rae, my mother's mother, unfortunately went away from home and left a six-month old baby. Well, in those days before the 1914–18 War my granny hadn't much time between her babies, and my grandfather Rae was away from home a lot. So I think things got on top of her. I think she knew she wasn't coping. I remember my mother saying, well, if you were nursing your baby, a bottle of stout did you good. It didn't do granny Rae a lot of good. So when she went away my mother, as the oldest child, was left to look after the family. Grandfather Rae had money, enough for those days. So the children weren't neglected. But it was hard on my mum. As she got older my mother tried and tried to find where granny had gone. But they never knew where she went until – I don't know how many years later – my mother got a letter from a convent somewhere in England, saying granny had died there. She'd gone to the nuns and she would be too ashamed to come back home. Granny Rae was an Irish Catholic. Her family had come over from Ireland during the Potato Famine.[3] Granny, a Murphy from County Mayo, was a fine, tall, nice-looking woman, and mum said she was a great cook and needlewoman.

My grandfather Rae must have belonged to Perth, but my mother was actually born in Dundee. My grandfather worked with horses. He used to break them in, but he also travelled with them in the hold of the ship to Canada and America when my mother was just a child. He worked for a horse exporter, so he was often away from home. When he came home after my grandmother left, he saw to everything. As I've said, he had money, not a lot, but enough for those days. Eventually he worked in Perth for an undertaker who had horse-drawn carriages. My grandfather drove one of those at funerals. He had a lum hat. Then he worked at stables in Princes Street in Perth, after the undertaker went over to cars, as he saw the future was the motor vehicle. But my granddad wouldn't see it: he remained a horse man.

* * *

The house that I first remember we lived in was in the Watergate, near the river Tay and the Sheriff Court, and between South Street and George Street. When James I of Scotland was king the Watergate was where all the nobility attending the king's court stayed. So they were very old buildings, and by our time they were all divided into very small houses, just rooms and kitchens. There was the Front Land and the Back Land. We were in No. 72. It's no longer there – demolished quite a few years ago. The old house where King James used to stay was still there when I was a child, but it became past repairing and was demolished.

In the Watergate house we had to come down two stairs. There was, as I've said, the Front Land as we called it. You went in the close, and there'd be about eight families there. Then you went further through to the Back Land, and there was two households on the ground floor, and then about eight, eight as well there. There was wooden stairs there, and they were white-scrubbed. I never thought about it then, but now when you think about it wooden stairs would have been dangerous in the event of a fire. But we were quite lucky, because everybody was awfully clean, and the stairs were white-scrubbed.

The door from the stair opened right on to the kitchen, and there was the coal bunker and the sink. And my mother had a white-scrubbed table and a white-scrubbed dresser. The window looked right over Tay Street, that ran alongside the river. Then there was a biggish room that my mum and dad had. And there was a wee room with only a single bed. My sister May and I slept in the wee room. When my brother Duncan was born about four years after me and the youngest in our family, he had to begin with, I think, a wee bed in the same room as my mum and dad. Duncan was asthmatic. When he got older, mum and dad slept in the kitchen, May and I slept in the big room, and Duncan had the wee room. That was a usual sort of arrangement in those days in such circumstances, depending on the number of children and whether there were boys and girls. The baby normally slept with the parents till there was a new baby and then joined the older children – or the baby slept in the drawer of a dresser or something.

The form of lighting in our Watergate house was gas. There was just cold running water. There was no range; all my mum's cooking was done on the open fire. But eventually she got a gas cooker. She may not have had that when I was very young. She was determined to get things. She used to have flat irons for doing the ironing, but she saved her pennies and scrimped and eventually got a gas iron. She was determined to get out of the sort of poverty line. There was no toilet inside the house. You came back down those stairs to further down the back, where there was two flush toilets. They served the eight families there. So there were four families all sharing either one or the other of the two toilets. We were lucky, as I say, because they were all very clean people. You had to be clean, otherwise you just sank under.

And then of course on washing days they went to the public wash-house in Canal Street, a short distance away from the Watergate and just along from the Sheriff Court. My mother had a wee pram that she pushed the washing along in. Then she'd bring it home, and we had a pulley with ropes out the window and she dried a lot of washing there. Oh, it was a hard life for my mum, everything was hard for her.

When I was a wee girl and my dad was working in Norwell's shoe repair shop in the Skinnergate, he came home for his dinner at midday. So we used to run through from the Watergate by the kirk and run along with him, to get a ha'penny for sweeties. But he, like my mum, had a hard life, too.

When I was growing up as a girl in Perth we had very plain fare. My parents didn't have a lot of money. But my mother was a very good cook and, oh, we were never hungry, though we didn't get anything fancy. She always made good soup. Oh, no cakes of course. Well, that was not quite true. My dad's sister Grace worked in the bakehouse at Kennoway's, that was another famous family shop in Perth, on the corner of St John Street. Aunty Grace would come over to us in the Watergate and say to my mother, 'I've brought some cakes, Mary.' And it was a real treat. In those days we could go round to the baker after closing time or early the following morning and get what we called auld tea breid – stuff left over. Sometimes it was cakes, sometimes buns. There was nothing wrong with them and you'd get them cheap. You got quite a lot for a penny. And, oh, broken biscuits. All the grocers sold broken biscuits because in those days they didn't have them in packets, they were all loose and some got broken. But other than that my mother could never afford to buy chocolate biscuits or anything fancy.

We didn't get a lot of fruit. The lady who stayed in the next close to us happened to be a midwife. Well, it was all home births in those days, and my mother used to go and help her if she was needed. The lady's daughter Daisy, who was grown up compared to us, worked in a fruit shop, and Daisy used to bring us what, I suppose, would be bruised fruit. But there was nothing wrong with it. So we did get some fruit. Then we got porridge in the mornings, and we always had fresh soup, and plenty vegetables. We'd no garden in those days at Watergate. My dad wasn't interested in gardening, having been brought up in the way he had been, and he had his wounded leg anyway. So he never had an allotment either. Two of our neighbours, Mr Winton and Mr Farmer, who lived behind us at Watergate, had an allotment on Moncreiffe Island, further down the river Tay from us. So maybe my mum got vegetables from them. But we went to the shop, too, for vegetables. Mum would be ready to make soup and she'd say, 'Now you go round to the FDL [Fruit Dealers Ltd] and get a pennyworth between carrot, turnip and leek.' The FDL was where our neighbour Daisy worked, and a pennyworth was enough to make a pot of soup. And mum would have probably a marrow bone or something to make stock.

Monday was washing day, the day mum went to the washhouse. So it was soup and pudding for dinner that day. We didn't get an awful lot of meat – again we couldn't afford it. We did have fish. The fish man, Auld Sandy, used to come round with a two-wheeled fish barrow. Fish was cheap in those days. And mum always made clootie dumplings: good on cold winter days. We never had birthday cakes: it wasnae the thing in those days. Then at Christmas we each had a long black school stocking that was filled, though by today's standards it would be very, very poor. However, we always got an orange and an apple, and maybe a sixpence [2½p]. And we always had presents. So that was a lot for us. There was not much in the way of toys or games. Well, we would get a book. Aunty Grace always managed to give us something. I particularly remember one year I got a doll, with a china head and eyes that shut and opened, and the joints all moved. Oh, that was something! And ma mum knitted clothes for it. But we used to run along to Joe Anderson's, the big toy shop in St John Street, and gaze in the window. They made all the wonderful toys – train sets, dollies and prams. We'd come home and tell ma mother. I'd say, 'Can we get that, mum?' 'Oh, yes. You'll get two, one for through the week, and one for Sunday.' And we believed her. But we were quite happy. There was a lot of children that lived in our building in the Watergate, and nobody there had a lot, nobody had any more than we had, and some had less. Some of them weren't as well fed as we were.

Then we'd two dresses in the summer, two print dresses: one on, one in the wash. And they were washed and dried over the fire. You'd no spare clothes. But we were always clean and well cared for. And we'd have gym dresses; my mother had to pay it up, of course. There was no big shops in Perth really. But at this one – I suppose you could call it an account in a way – but, I mean, she had to budget for this. We got our gym dresses and our school things. But she knitted our jumpers and that, of course. We were always well clad – not a lot of clothes, but we had what was necessary. And we got our shoes, and my dad had a last of his own and mended our shoes himself.

* * *

Well, we lived in the Watergate till I was about nine, so it would be about 1935 that we moved. By then new council houses were being built, and we moved to one in Tulloch Road, off Crieff Road, and about 1½ miles from the Watergate. Well, my mother had haunted the city factor. She was determined. There was three other ladies in Watergate who were all very similar to my mother and desperate to get a decent home. My dad used to say, 'Look, Mary. If you're goin' to get one o' these houses they'll tell you.' 'Well,' she says, 'I don't care what you say.' And she was down at the city factor's office every day. I think they were tired looking at her! She and the other three Watergate ladies said, 'We just want one o' these four in a block.' And they each got one. It was really nice because it kept the four neighbours together in Tulloch Road.

The new council house in Tulloch Road, oh, it was wonderful, you've no idea. They were very nice houses, lovely wood, and much better built than many they build now. And, oh, here was a bathroom with hot water and a real bath! In the Watergate we used to go to the public baths for a bath. Well, we went there to the swimming, too; but you could have a slipper bath there.[4] So in our new house there was hot and cold water, and that was wonderful. Electric light and, what mum had already at the Watergate, a gas cooker. There was a living room, and a lovely big kitchen with a gas boiler in it. And we had two bedrooms, of about the same size. I don't know why my mum couldn't have had a three-bedroomed house, though. She had us two girls and a boy, Duncan. At his age then – he was still very young – he counted as a half. But it may have been because there'd be a bigger rent if we'd had three bedrooms. My sister May and I, as we got bigger, had the one bedroom, and Duncan the other one. So mum and dad ended up sleeping on a bed-settee in the living room.

My mother had been saving towards this move, and she managed to buy a dining room suite, a sideboard, and a bedroom suite for the front bedroom. Oh, having lived in big houses as a domestic servant she knew what she wanted. Then there was also a drying green that two families shared; the other two in the block of four shared another green. And each had a plot for vegetables. The three other men in the block all liked gardening and kept lovely gardens. They also kept the grass in the two drying greens. And we had a lovely window that looked out to what had been part of a farm. There was sheep and that there then; later on there was a hotel built.

From Tulloch Road you could get a bus into the town. The corporation buses started then – the town owned the buses at that time. Maybe five minutes' walk from our house there was two shops: a baker that had opened up because of this housing scheme, and a Post Office-newsagent. Of course, living in the Watergate or the centre of the town, you could just run out to shops, even late at night. The shops were all round you, and the food there was cheaper because there was more competition than further out where we now were. But my mother was quite happy having this new house, and she didn't complain that the local shops' prices were maybe a bit higher.

From Tulloch Road to our school in the High Street was also much further for my sister May and me than it had been from the Watergate, when we'd been able to run through the Vennel, which took only a few minutes. Also we had now to take our brother Duncan to the school. That was a damn nuisance. In fact, we had to trail him everywhere. I had started school at St John's, the Catholic school, which was in the High Street in those days, where British Home Stores was later. There was no Catholic secondary school in Perth then. If you were the clever clogs you went to Lawside Academy, a Catholic secondary, in Dundee. Well, there was quite a few went there from Perth: those that were better off could afford it. In Stormont Street there was a Catholic convent in a huge ground. The nuns were moved, the convent was sort of knocked down and, while I was still at school, they built a new

Catholic school with big playgrounds. The boys' side was in Barossa Street, the girls' side in Stormont Street. The nuns, only four by that time, lived in a house next to the church in Melville Street. I would maybe be about 12 when the new school was built. Nowadays up at North Muirton we have a Catholic secondary school, St Columba's, and there's still of course Lawside Academy in Dundee. Anyway, I went to the new school in Stormont Street not long, I think, after we moved to our new house in Tulloch Road.

I didn't like school. I was a very quiet person, a slow learner. I needed time, and if you weren't bright at school, a wee bit slow in the uptake, you were, och, sort of passed over. Oh, there was a kind of intellectual snobbery about it. But there was a little bit of it if you didn't have the right name or the right . . . It certainly was there, unfortunately. Most of the teachers, I would say, weren't really qualified, but they were Catholics. I would say there was a lot of favouritism. As a youngster I felt discriminated against, very much so. That didn't help me to learn. I wasn't stupid. I was just a wee bit slow. I was never brilliant at school, but I got prizes for various things.

They were the type of teachers who made you stand up to answer a question, or come out to the blackboard to do it. Well, I was shy. It was a terrible ordeal. Some of the teachers were all right, but I couldn't cope with that sort of thing, and then it makes you look stupid, doesn't it? As I recall, most of the teachers were quite – well, they weren't really elderly, but they were old in a way. Most of them were unmarried. I felt they didn't understand children really.

In the old school in the High Street the girls and the boys were separate. So we girls were in one classroom which had a big partition that could open up. The boys were in the room on the other side of the partition. I remember particularly this teacher. I can picture her yet. She was tall, had ginger hair in what we called the earphones. And she was grumpy. I don't know why she was so nasty to me. I'd never done anything naughty. But one day I couldn't do this sum on the blackboard. Of course, I was terrified. Anyway, she threw open this partition and said to Mr Lafferty, the boys' teacher there: 'Just look at this girl. She can't do this.' Now how do you learn anything that way? I learned more after I left school.

I never was very good at arithmetic, yet after leaving school I did clerical work always. I liked and was quite good at English and at writing essays and, oh, always enjoyed reading. My parents encouraged me. I joined the Free Library at seven years old. I was never out of the library. As a girl I read, oh, anything. Well, I didn't like sloppy romantic books. I liked adventure books and various things that I could really get into. As a girl I never got comics: there was no money at home for comics. But some of my chums had comics, and they would pass them round. We had one neighbour – they moved to Tulloch Road when we did, and it would be when we were there – who had relatives in America that used to send them these big American comics. My particular chum was the youngest of a big family and she had four older sisters who were all working, and they would buy her things that we shared, so you got a look at them.

Anyway, I sat the Qualifying exam when I was 11 year old. I must have passed it. But then I wasn't bright enough to go on to Lawside Academy in Dundee. And, oh, there was no money at home so there was no way my parents would have been able to afford to send me there. I think the boys and girls who went from Perth to Lawside Academy, about 20 miles away, must have travelled by train. It was only half an hour in the train. They maybe got a scholars' ticket. But most of them who did go were from people who had a bit of money: Italian business people that had the chip shops and ice cream shops. Anyway, I left school at 14. I had enjoyed most of it. But I was frightened at the teachers. It was as simple as that. The teachers inhibited me.

As I've said, my mother's mother, Granny Rae, was an Irish Catholic whose family had come over from County Mayo in Ireland during the great Irish Famine, and my mother herself was of course a Catholic. I don't know what my father had been, but he turned a Catholic. He became a Catholic convert because my parents wouldn't have been married in the church otherwise. They didn't marry you in those days unless you turned. So he had turned just before he got married. I don't think he was born a Catholic, because my aunt, his sister, wasn't a Catholic. My father wouldn't feel particularly strongly, so he just went my mother's way. And then he didn't care much. I don't think he went much to mass until my sister May was old enough to go to school. And then I wouldn't say he was a devout Catholic. But he started to go because he didn't want us children asking, 'Why don't you go to church?' He was very good that way. He was a very good-living man actually.

Again, to come back to this at the Catholic school. Originally, our church didn't have Brownies or anything. But two or three of us just did our own thing and we joined the Guides at the Episcopal cathedral. We were in the Guides for quite a long time, and our church had to conform. My mother was quite happy about us joining the Guides. She liked you doing anything like that. She was all for it. The Guides were interesting, you learned quite a lot from them. But then I wasn't interested in sport, we didn't get sport at school. There were no playing fields there. So we only got gym indoors. And I never had a bike, and I couldn't ride a bike because I'd never had a chance to do so.

Dancing was an interest for me, once I was away from school and a bit older. There was a lot of dancehalls, but there were no bars, no drinks – they were just dancehalls. It was a main interest for young people at that time. And we had some good musicians that came. We thoroughly enjoyed that, and we used to go out to Luncarty, a village four miles north of Perth, because it was mostly country dancing there. Of course, we didn't come away from it in time to get the last bus: we walked back from Luncarty. There was a crowd of us. We were quite happy. Oh, I liked dancing. It was great to be young.

* * *

As far as I can remember, as a girl I wanted to be a hairdresser. But that was out because you had to pay to be an apprentice hairdresser. No money – so that was a no-no. I mean, there wasnae any fuss about it. But that's what I would have liked to have done. So I just had to forget about that. So when I left school in 1940 when I was 14, well, there was any amount of work at that time, with the war on. When you left school you could just walk into any job, and I thought this particular one was on. I can't remember where I saw it, maybe in the *Perthshire Advertiser.*[5] But in those days you didn't go to the Employment Exchange. Anyway, I went to MacGregor, the printers and bookbinders, in the Skinnergate. I thought I would like to learn to be a bookbinder. It sounded interesting. The pay was six shillings [30p] a week. Oh, the hours would be eight or half-past eight in the morning till five or something. I mean, you didn't get short hours in those days. But I only stayed there a week. It shows how ignorant I was about being an apprentice. I discovered I was expected to clean the toilet. And it was all men at MacGregor's, except for one lady. So I just didn't go back. When I went home at the end of the week I said to my mother, 'I'm not going back. I'm not cleaning the lavatory for the men.' My mother supported me. She didn't bother and didn't harass me about getting another job.

Well, I got another job – in the public washhouse, the steamie, as they call it in Glasgow. I must have known somebody that worked there, so I thought, 'Oh, that might be all right.' So I went there, and that was working in the calender room, where the big rollers are, and you put all the sheets. That was an education in itself, because in those days a lot of the local women, older women, took in washing for boarding houses and that, and it was all done in the washhouse. Oh, I never heard so much bad language in all my life! But that job was quite interesting. So it went on for a while. It was all right. It was a cheerful job and everybody was quite happy. And I was used to the washhouse because of going there with my mother. I can't remember what the pay was, but it must have been more than six shillings [30p] a week. The hours were seven in the morning till maybe 4pm or 5pm. It was an early start because if, on the night before, you weren't in time before the calender closed, you could have a penny bundle. You bought a penny ticket, your name was put on it, and your bundle was all put on a big table. You had to be there for 7am to get your bundle put through the calender. Of course, from our house in Tulloch Road I walked about a mile in all weathers to the washhouse in Canal Street: there was no buses as early as 7am. I got up about 6am every morning. Then I'd walk home again at night, or maybe got a bus: the fare was only a penny-ha'penny [less than 1p]. The pay might have been 10 or 12 shillings [50p or 60p] a week. We probably got an hour for our lunch, and I probably took a sandwich with me for lunchtime. Anyway, the washhouse had a little office, a booking office, and eventually I got into that to do clerical work. There was only one other person in the office, Miss Todd. She had been in there, I think, with the bricks, but she was a very nice lady. There was also an older washhouse in Mill Street, next to the Skinnergate. They had there the big old wooden tubs, and also slipper baths for men and women, with separate bathrooms and separate entrances. I used to have to go to the Mill Street washhouse at the odd time, maybe to see the money over there. After a while I think I must have wanted more pay or something better. I can't remember, it's all so very long ago. But I decided

I wanted to move on. And Laing, a high-quality, licensed private grocer – oh, a very posh shop – were looking for another clerkess, and I thought, 'I'll apply for that.' So I got in there.

Laing's was in St John Street, the next street to the Watergate. There was three other girls in Laing's little office. It was shop hours there, probably a half-past eight start – so I would get a bus there – and probably a six o'clock finish, and an hour's lunch break. I probably took a sandwich with me from home. Evelyn, one of the girls, and I used to go up the stair to the stockroom at lunchtime. The stockroom was where all the big bags of all sorts of things were kept for the grocers. We went up there in a lift. Laing's didn't offer us anything for our sandwich, oh, no lump of cheese or chocolate biscuit. We were into the rationing by then. I can't remember what the pay was that I got at Laing's, but it was a bit more than at the washhouse.

There was a lot of titled people round about, people like Lady Margaret Drummond Hay.[6] All the upper crust shopped in those shops. They sometimes came in themselves, or they just phoned their orders. Some were people who lived up Kinnoull Hill. Well, they must have been well enough off. It was all big houses. The message boy used to have to cycle up Kinnoull Hill with his order book and take their order. If it was a big order the van took it up. Otherwise the poor message boy had to cycle up there. And that was horrible, it was dreadful. But, oh, they didn't pay their bills, they didn't pay their bills. They waited. And they would say they were waiting 'Till the interest came into the bank.' That's when they paid their bills – *if* they paid them. Lady Margaret Drummond Hay was the worst. I don't know if she had any cash. But she had plenty of property and suchlike – or just the name of having them maybe. But she ran up tremendous bills. And she wasn't the only one. But they were bowed and scraped to, bowed and scraped to, and welcomed the whole time. Oh, it was a new world to me, absolutely different from living in the Watergate! When we lived there and I was a little girl mum used to send us round to Laing's for maybe a bit of cold meat or something that wasn't terribly expensive. So I knew the shop when I was a little girl.

But I quite liked working in Laing's office. There was three other girls there and they, the head clerkess and that, were very good. Old Mr Butters was a sleeping partner of Laing's. But the other partner sat at a desk up behind the counter. He was very much the old type of boss – kept glancing round the staff to make sure we were working. When he was out of sight we used to get one of the girls at the provision counter to pass us in a bit cheese or butter. One of us would keep watch for the partner, see he was out of sight, then we could get this bit cheese or butter on our roll: when the cat's away! Of course, it was rationed. But he did allow you to have a cup of tea, though you had to hide it between your ledgers: you hadn't to be seen drinking a cup of tea. Oh, he was an old-fashioned man! He gave me a row for putting lipstick on in the office, and made me rub it off. And I wish you'd seen his own daughter. She was a very pretty girl. But she had a lot of make-up on. I wasn't allowed any. He made me look in the mirror. I thought I looked all right! It was only lipstick. He wasn't too bad about the clothes we wore; anyway we were reasonably dressed. All the grocery staff had their white coats, aprons, and so on. The men had aprons as long as their white coats. The number of workers at Laing's was, well, we had two van drivers and two message boys. One of the van drivers worked as a storeman as well. Harry Fotheringham was the head grocer, there was about four female assistants, and there was four of us at the desks in the office. So there'd be a round dozen.

Laing's had a big lot of customers. But it was definitely up-market – county customers. I had to do their order books and accounts and that. I quite liked that. It was interesting. I hadn't been trained in clerical work but I learned as I went along. And I went then to night school to study book-keeping. It helped me along. I could have gone also for shorthand and typing, but I thought I'd just try the book-keeping. That was two evenings a week. But the blackout was on, and the buses stopped at nine o'clock. We told the book-keeping teacher we had to go for the last bus because we were not allowed to walk home. But in fact we went to the dancing! There was a band and you met up, with our dance shoes stuck inside our book-keeping books! Oh, how devilish!

By this time – about 1942 – my sister May, having worked on the bottling in Dewar's Whisky bond, was promoted into the cellar office. There were only three of them in the cellar office. May was married in August 1941, her husband got embarkation leave and was sent away to North Africa with the Forces. He was non-combatant – in the Dental Corps. Then May herself was called up after conscription was introduced for women at the end of 1941. There was no choice of which

Service for May that I remember. She went right into the ATS. She had been still living with our parents at home; she didn't at that time have a home of her own or any children. So of course I thought maybe I could get May's job at Dewar's Whisky. So she spoke for me and I got in there.

My pay at Dewar's was 15 shillings [75p] a week, paid by cheque. So I must have been better paid in Dewar's than I had been in Laing's. So each change of job I'd had since leaving the school gave me a little more pay. By the time I began at Dewar's I'd be about 16. Well, I was there – maybe for a year or at the most 18 months – till I went when I was 17 into the ATS. I would have liked to have stayed at Dewar's office, but they were calling up our age group. In the office there were four of us the same age. There was only Dorothy Edwards and I in the cellar office, but there were two others our age in the main office. They were shorthand typists, and we two were clerical. So Dorothy and I decided that they would probably take us. And at that time they were putting the girls on to the railway as carriage cleaners. If you were called up that's where you were going. So we jumped the gun and just went, volunteered, and joined up before they could put us in. Dorothy and I didn't wait to be conscripted, because volunteering gave us some choice. And it was specifically the ATS we wanted. If I remember, when we went and volunteered that was what was on offer at that time in 1943. I'd be 17 and a bit.

Well, then I went home and told my mother. There'd been no discussion with her beforehand. Oh, she wouldn't have let me go. She was a very formidable lady. But we didn't have any row about it. I'd already joined up, so, I mean . . . I suppose she was quite pleased for me in a way, because she had plenty spunk too. She went away in the 1914–18 War to work in munitions. So you could say I'd done a similar thing. But having said that, she was a very possessive lady, and that was her two daughters away to the ATS, and she's left with a young son that was asthmatic and still at school. Anyway, I went away quite happily to the ATS.

Dorothy Edwards and I had to report to Newbattle Abbey at Dalkeith. We went there together. The two of us got on a train at Perth just on our own. There may have been other girls on it also going to the ATS at Newbattle. But I don't remember. I'd never before been far afield from Perth. I'd never really been away even on holiday. Oh, my parents would never be able to afford it. We went as a family on the local holiday on a midsummer Saturday to visit my aunt in Dundee. My dad went to Forthill at Broughty Ferry for the cricket. Then, just before the two of us volunteered into the ATS, Dorothy and I went for the weekend to Edinburgh. She had friends there. We went dancing and met two Air Force lads. Oh, the excitement! It was a lovely big ballroom with a revolving stage. I think it was called the Palais de Danse. So that was the furthest I'd been, except that as children my sister May and I spent some of our school summer holidays with an aunt at St Andrews. Mum and dad didn't come, my dad had no paid holidays at all. Granddad took us through and stayed with us. My aunt – a young aunt – took us moonlight bathing. My grandfather was horrified: 'Takin' these girls out at midnight!' It was great. But that was our holidays, or to my other aunt in Dundee, and once to Edinburgh.

So Dorothy and I got to Edinburgh and then went out to Dalkeith. There must have been transport of some kind at Dalkeith to take us to Newbattle Abbey. I don't remember. But I do remember arriving there. I didn't know what to expect. The first meal was macaroni and cheese. I didn't like it, but I've loved it ever since then. Then we quite enjoyed getting the uniforms on. Well, the uniform wasn't exactly attractive. The shirts and everything was khaki, and the plain ties. Everything was all squashed, too. Then I had a lot of hair and it was up, and I had to have it up off my collar. They didn't force you to cut your hair. Eventually, when I was down south, I got it cut because it was an awful nuisance. Before that I'd had to get it up in a tight roll. That was the fashion, in a roll. But it was so thick and curly. And it was lovely, because when you had your forage cap on it all sat up and it was really nice.

The shoes, well, eventually they were comfortable. But I never wore shoes like that – flat walking shoes. And thick stockings, lisle stockings, and thick knickers – they came down to here! You got two pairs of white woollen knickers. And you got these celanese, as they were called, like a thick silky material. They were what you would call bloomers, because they were elastic round the knees. They came down to there, and your skirt – it wasn't a long skirt – was only to your knee. But when you were doing your marching on the square these damn things kept slipping down. The underwear wasn't to be admired. But then that was all you got. If you were lucky you had your own with you, and you could wear it whenever you were off duty. You weren't allowed to wear civilian clothes when you were going out the camp, but you could wear civilian underwear. Later on we bought Van Heusen collars – officers' collars – and an officer's tie. And we had a dress cap which was rather nice, a forage cap, like the ones the soldiers wore, in the Royal Signals colours. That was for walking out, it was smarter. It didn't cover your head but it was more attractive. Appearance was everything. I mean, if it came on rain who cared about getting wet? And we had, I think, an overcoat, and the khaki shoulder bag, a sling bag, like they wear now but it was a satchel. And you carried your bits and pieces in there.

I was at Newbattle Abbey for a fortnight or three weeks, it wouldn't be more than a month anyway. There was no tents there. It must have been huts and, well, double bunks, because it was double bunks in most places. But I don't recall how many in the hut. I honestly don't remember about that or about heating in them. And then you got a certain amount of drilling and, och, the basics, till they sorted you out and decided where you were going. I wanted to get into transport, to be a driver, to do things I hadn't done before. I'd been in the ambulance service – voluntary. I used to do that. It wasn't the St Andrew's or St John's, it was just the ambulance service.

Newbattle was the beginning of a new world, absolutely. You met quite a lot of girls there, but you didn't have time to get friendly with anyone. It was all new. You were doing this and doing that, learning things, and being drilled. You were kept busy. You were tired at night. And then all this about how to make your bed, and everything had to be spit and polish. If you didn't fold your blankets and make your bed right you didn't get your breakfast. It had to be right done, and stand by your bed in the morning. You had to be up and your bed made. The sergeant in charge of the hut had a look. Everything had to be just so. I was a tidy person anyway, so it didn't bother me. And I don't really remember feeling homesick at Newbattle. I had my friend Dorothy Edwards there in the same hut, though then we were posted away to separate places. And of course I didn't get to become a driver.

Well, I was put into the Royal Signals and sent down to Old Dalby in Leicestershire. There was a huge Ordnance camp there and a unit of the Royal Signals attached to it. As I've said, I'd never really been far away from home before. And of course from Newbattle Abbey I was sent down south on a troop train. I hadn't a clue. I had my big kit bag. The train was full of soldiers. I was only 17, and they were young lads, too. Some of them were coming back off leave. The train was packed. But they were very, very helpful. I had to come off, if I remember, at Grantham and change there to a local train for Old Dalby. It would be about midnight when I arrived at Old Dalby railway station. There were several soldiers also getting off there. 'Where are you going, dear?' And I said, 'Well, I've to report to Signals.' 'Come on.' And they took my kit and everything and walked me up into the Signals to report. They were awful good. That made all the difference. But at Signals nobody was expecting me. So there wasn't a bed for me and I got somebody else's bed for the night: they were on shifts.

Well, I was put on to working at the switchboard. Well, they had to show you what to do. It was the old type of switchboard. I'd never worked a switchboard before and I kept getting all the lines mixed. You were supposed just to pick it up, which you did. You just had to learn as you went. But all the time I was at Old Dalby I worked the switchboard. I didn't move to any other job.

The officer was a woman, a clergyman's daughter. She was as daft as a brush. She used to go away on weekend leave, and she would sign all these travel warrants in case you wanted to go off! She was a real . . . She'd been privately educated, a real upper crust, oh, she was. I think she was a conscript. Oh, no Regular would have carried on like that, no way. She was just one of the girls, you know.

At Old Dalby we had a big American camp near us. And we had a small fire service and our small Signals unit. And the Yanks used to run dances in their own camp. They'd send over the truck for us. Somebody would be left to man the switchboard, and the rest of us would be over there for the dance. And there was chocolate and all sorts of food. As I say, I was young. But there were some of the girls in my own hut who were Londoners and a bit worldly-wise compared with me. One or two of them got friendly with some of the officers, and they used to take them over in their plane for the weekend to Paris once Paris was liberated in 1944. I was quite amazed at this sort of behaviour. It was all foreign to me. It was an entirely different world from what I'd been accustomed to in Perth. And a mixture of girls from all walks of life. I mean, I'd had a certain amount of freedom – going to dances at home. But some of them had never been away from home – and they just went gyte, as we say. Just young lassies, and they couldnae cope.

I was homesick at Old Dalby. Well, I was that much further away from home than at Newbattle Abbey, and I was only 17 and I'd never been away before. I remember one day a pipe band played in the square at the camp, and I thought, 'Oh,' you know. But there was one or two Scots girls and I made a friend of one, Rita. She came from Stonehaven. We kept up after that, and later I was at her wedding in Stonehaven. Rita was in the same hut as me at Old Dalby. But there was a mixture of girls there, some from Yorkshire, a Welsh one, several from London. The Londoners weren't friendly. I've always found Londoners tend to be like that: 'You're from the sticks', you know. But this Londoner who'd been a hairdresser she was very friendly. She cut my hair. Anyway, most of the girls were friendly, and we all got on quite well. The stove was in the middle of our hut there. We used to buy a big tin of Carnation milk, cocoa, and doughnuts in the NAAFI, then make cocoa in a pan on the stove.[7]

Your pay wasnae much of course: 13 shillings [65p] a week. But then I was getting my keep in the army. You had to leave your mother something, it wasn't much. I can't remember how much – something like five shillings [25p]. But then she didn't need much. At that time I smoked and you got your cigarettes cheap in the NAAFI. And when we ran out before the end of the week we used to share stuff – daft, when you look back. Some of the girls might have been a bit better off or got food parcels from home. My mum would make a dumpling and would send me it. Oh, we didn't go hungry, because the NAAFI was quite good and it was cheap. The cookhouse food was quite good. But, och, when I was 17 and 18, I mean, your appetite's vast. You'll eat anything and you can digest anything.

At all stages in the ATS the officers in charge of us were women. The men's and women's Forces were kept quite separate. We were a separate unit in the Signals. There were no men officers there. We had one officer that I think may have been a Regular. But she was out of the top drawer. She had this horrible little dog. He had long hair. He wasnae a Peke but something similar, with a pointed nose. And she used to say to it, 'Now the girls will bring you some scraps.' And she made us bring scraps from the dining room. They had a pail there that they put scraps into. So you had to take some scraps for this damned dog. I used to get annoyed about it. We all got annoyed. But what could you do? She was a major or something. She was a besom.

Oh, we got leaves home. We used to come on the train to Grantham and then on to Edinburgh. And mostly we stood all the way. But you got rolls and sausages. There was a canteen at Edinburgh. They kept it for the troops. I had to wait for a connection from there to Perth. I don't remember any of the Servicemen rising when they saw an ATS girl coming on the train, to give her a seat. You maybe sometimes hunked down in the corridor on your kitbag. But during the war the trains were overcrowded. Oh, they were just like sardines. It wasnae as if the train started from Grantham. If you started from King's Cross you might have been lucky. Going back from leave the trains werenae so bad, because you were starting off from Perth. But it was fine to get home, and my parents were delighted to see me.

As well as going on home leave, I got out the camp sometimes because I made friends with other girls there. One was Mary, who had an aunt in Old Dalby. The aunt and uncle were both doctors. They had a lovely home, and Mary and I were invited to it and we stayed over-night. Oh, it was a lovely bedroom, and they had an orchard and stored their apples in the bedrooms. Oh, it was a different world from the one I'd been accustomed to. Then I made friends with Dickie, another Yorkshire girl. Dickenson was her name, but we called her Dickie. I went with her to her home for a weekend. I couldn't go to my own home for a weekend because of the distance from Old Dalby. Dickie's father was the local butcher, and, oh, we had the Sunday roast. I was very fortunate to get into two homes like that. So I was broadening my experience, meeting people from all walks of life I'd never have met at home or in Perth.

I don't recall any girls in my hut or in the unit who had lost relatives in the war. I think some of the Londoners may have. But, as I say, they tended to keep to themselves. They felt they were sort of closer. They didn't ignore us completely, but they weren't just as friendly as the Yorkshire or Welsh girls. The girls in my hut were of varying ages. I'd be the youngest maybe. Rita from Stonehaven was a couple of years older than me, and Peggy, the sergeant, was a bit older. I think she was married and that her husband was in the Services – which didn't hinder her having American boyfriends! It was quite an eye-opener in lots of ways. You see, everybody lived for the day really. You didn't know what might happen. That's why so many of the soldiers coming home got married. It was an entirely different world then. You just had a different outlook. And every pair of hands was needed in the war. It gave women a new lease of life.

Well, then I was fairly quiet and didn't make friends very easily. I wasn't very outgoing. I didn't get involved, like so many of them did, with the boyfriends and the soldiers – the American soldiers especially. I always had my mother at the back of me! Well, the consequences could be serious if you just went with the crowd. But I was too frightened at what mum would have said. I think mostly girls that had never been away from home – well, a lot of them – I mean, it could have spoiled their lives, and I dare say it did. Because an awful lot of the men were already married. Or were even led astray by girls who were more worldly-wise. But I wasn't aware of any girls that had to leave the ATS, not in my unit. But I did hear about it happening. They were dismissed, well, they couldn't stay. It was a disgrace going home, it was a terrible disgrace then.

Well, just before the war ended in Europe in May 1945 my mother was ill. She decided she was ill. Well, she was asthmatic. She tended to need somebody. Actually, she wasn't worried. But I think she wanted one of us – my sister May or me – at home. And of course May was married, so my mum had no control over her. So I just had to go home. She didn't actually ask me, but it was a sort of emotional blackmail. That's what she wanted. I was demobbed on compassionate grounds. So it would just be a couple of years really I was in the ATS. I went in in the summer of 1943, and I was out maybe March, April 1945.

Looking back on it now, I thought being in the ATS was really worthwhile for all sorts of reasons. It was just a different world, and you could see how other people lived. And it could have been a good career, if I'd been allowed to stay on. I've always said I might have seriously considered remaining in the ATS after the war as a Regular. I just liked the way of life, the order. You did certain things at certain times, I quite liked that. It was so different from any job I'd done before then. And there was the comradeship of the other girls. And then you did feel you were making some sort of contribution towards the war effort. You did feel that, because all the boys I'd been friendly with at home they were all away. Some of them were prisoners. Some of them never came back. All my friends, we all wrote to all the boys that were away, you know. But, oh, no, no, no, I never had any regrets about joining the ATS.

Williamina MacNab (Mrs Williamina Dow) died on 6 March 2009.

Margaret McLeod (far left) and two colleagues in their ATS uniforms. (Courtesy of Mrs Jean Simpson)

RAF station, Digby, Lincolnshire, in the 1938–45 War. Agnes (Nessie) Lawrie is centre front.
(Courtesy of Nessie Lawrie)

Right.
Christina Chisholm (later Morrison) at the front of
her childhood home, Innes Street, Inverness, June
1939. (Courtesy of Mrs Marion O'Hara)

Opposite.
Christina Chisholm (later Morrison), front row far
left, with colleagues at Cameron Barracks,
Inverness, June 1939. (Courtesy of Mrs Marion
O'Hara)

Below.
ATS Headquarters staff at Craigmillar Park, c. 1942.
Nancy Cowe is somewhere in the rear row.
(Courtesy of the late Mrs Nancy Dickson (née
Nancy Cowe))

Right.
Jean Crosbie (later Mrs Jean Smith) aged 20, newly commissioned in 1944 as a 2nd lieutenant in the ATS. (Courtesy of Mrs Jean Smith)

Below.
Isobel Cumming (later Mrs Thomson) in her ATS uniform, with her father who, as Corporal J.J. Cumming, Seaforth Highlanders, had won the Military Medal in the 1914–18 War (Courtesy of Robin and Muriel Bald)

Esther Cowper (later Mrs Craig, then Mrs Ogg) in her ATS uniform. (Courtesy of Mrs Margaret Strand)

May Kerr (later Mrs May Buchanan) in her ATS uniform. (Courtesy of David Buchanan)

Williamina MacNab (later Mrs Williamina Dow) in her ATS uniform. (Courtesy of Roy and Ann Dow)

Isa Dougan (later Mrs Isa Inglis) in her WAAF uniform. (Courtesy of Mrs Inglis's daughter Sheila)

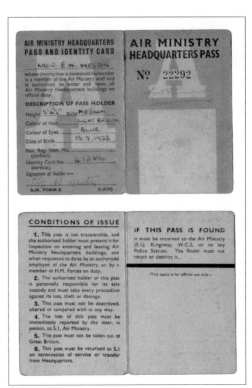

Left. Elizabeth Weston (later Mrs Elizabeth Herriot) in her WAAF uniform. Right. The Air Ministry Headquarters pass belonging to Leading Air Craft Woman E.W. Weston. (Courtesy of Ron and Alan Herriot)

Agnes (or Nessie) Lawrie (far left, front row) at Digby RAF station, Lincolnshire, in the 1939–45 War. (Courtesy of Nessie Lawrie)

Above.
Christina Millaney (later Mrs Christina Morrison) in her WRNS uniform. (Courtesy of Mrs Morrison's family)

Left.
Jean Robertson (later Mrs Rooney) in WAAF uniform. (Courtesy of Steve Rooney)

Below.
Margaret Campbell (later Mrs Harris), WRNS, far right, in her WRNS commissioned officer's uniform, taken at Greenock in the 1940s. (Courtesy of Mrs Jess Wilson)

Timber Corps Girls standing at ease. Alexina McGlinn (later Mrs Alexina Bolger) is in the rear row, third from the left, looking straight ahead while the woman on her left looks straight at the camera. (Courtesy of Maureen Rooney)

More than half a century after the war, Agnes (Nessie) Lawrie lays flowers at the graves of RAF airmen in Scopwick cemetery, Lincolnshire. (Courtesy of Nessie Lawrie)

Ann Baird

Ah got home leave in August 1944 at the end o' the six weeks' ATS trainin' at Newbattle Abbey. And then ah wis posted tae London, south-east Dulwich; and it wis awaiting tae go overseas. Ah wis quite happy at the thought o' goin' overseas.

Ah wis born in Glasgow on the 19th o' June 1925. Ah had three brothers, ah wis the youngest o' the family. Ma dad was actually born in Edinburgh, but his mother and father took him and the family when they were small tae Glasgow, and he grew up in Glasgow. Ma mother wis born in Motherwell. But they met in Glasgow. Ma dad wis a boilermaker in the shipyards at Govan and Scotstoun – Alexander Stephen's and Yarrow and Co., ah think. He wis born on the 15th of September 1886 and died in January 1959. He didn't work at anything else, and he retired from the shipyard when he wis 67.

Ma mother before she married wis a domestic servant in Glasgow. As far as ah know she worked up in the big houses in Peel Street in Partick. But she didn't work again after she got married. She wis born on the 5th of November 1891, and she died in 1976.

As ah've said, ah had three brothers. The eldest was David, then Daniel, then Andrew. David was approximately ten years older than me. And then there were roughly two, three or four years between each o' the rest o' us. David was a clever lad. In fact, then they were round asking about television, and of course he would have had tae go tae college or something. And ma mum and dad didnae have the money tae send him there. So of course he ended up in the shipyards as well. He wis a plater. Daniel didnae like the shipyards, so he wis intae the fruit. The man used tae come round wi' the horse and cart and the fruit. So when Daniel left school the man asked him if he would like tae come wi' him. So he done that. Then of course the war came. David wis exempt because he wis in the shipyards. He wis married when he wis 21, and he had a wife and two children. But Daniel wis called up just after the war broke out. And he wis away tae the war when he wis only about 19. He wis in the 51st Highland Division. He was at Dunkirk in 1940. He got back safely. But he wis never the same after it. He never spoke about it, it wis too painful. And then ma brother Andrew, when he left school he wis in the shipyards as well, as a plater.

Ma earliest memory is when I was two years old, sittin' on the bunker in our house in Hosier Street, Partick. Across the road was an old lady called Woods. But ah couldnae say Woods, so ah called her Granny Doods. Ah can see her yet sittin' at her window, and ah waved across tae her. We lived in Hosier Street in a two-storey tenement. Our house wis jist a room and kitchen. As a baby ah slept wi' ma mum and dad in the kitchen. Ma three brothers were in the room. Ah think it wis gas lightin' we had in Hosier Street. There wis no bath or shower. It wis an outside toilet, and ah think it wis shared wi' another family: ah think there wis only the two families on that landing. For the cookin', it wis jist a range, wi' a wee oven and a swee, and a tap for a wee water tank at the side.

The next place we went tae, when ah wis between four and five, wis Rosevale Street in Partick. It wis the same as in Hosier Street, a room and kitchen; but ma mum had an extra bed there. So that ah wis in the room with the boys. It was a bed recess and an iron or a brass bed, ah think, in those days. It wis gas lightin' there as well. And ma mum had a gas cooker there, and ah'll tell you why ah remember that. Ah started school at Rosevale Street School, jist up the road. And ah wis very good at the three Rs: readin', writin', and arithmetic. And this day, because ah had the best writing, the teacher gave me an egg as a prize. She said, 'Ye'll have tae go home and get a bowl or something.' Ma mum always went tae the mothers' meeting. So ah knew ma mum wasn't in. We were on the ground floor o' the tenement. So ah climbed through the window and ah fried the egg. Ah wis five years old! And in these days ye had tae be very careful, for ma mum had some bad times. Ma dad was unemployed at times in the 1930s, maybe for months and months. And of course what did she get then for tae keep six of us? Not a lot. It wis hard times. So when ma mother came in

from her meeting she said, 'Who's fried an egg?' Ah says, 'It . . . '
'You?!' Ah remember her lookin' at me, five year old, fryin' an egg.'
She says, 'Ye might have burned yerself tae death.' But, oh, I was fair
away wi' maself, because ah'd done that, cleaned it all up after me, ate
the egg and enjoyed it! So that's how ah remember ma mum had a gas
cooker in Rosevale Street. And then we had our own toilet there. That
wis a boon tae. There was a back green at Rosevale Street and at
Hosier Street. Ma mother could hang her washin' out there, and you
could play in the back green. And there wis the washhouse, shared by
the tenement. Each family had certain days for washing. Oh, it wis a
big day for women, the washing. Ma mum used tae be up at six in the
mornin', and she wis still workin' away at it at six at night. All by
hand, too. Oh, it wis hard work in those days. Of course, for the
women that wis comin' for their turn the next day they would fill the
boiler and get it a' ready for them. That wis what they done. Oh, there
wis quite a lot o' neighbourliness. And if ma dad wis working, ma
mother always gave to other people.

Later on, by the time ah left school at 14, near the beginnin' o' the
war, we were livin' in Scotstoun, jist along the Clyde a bit from
Partick.

As ah've said, ah'd started at Rosevale Street School, jist up the
road from our room and kitchen there. Ah loved the primary school.
But as ah got older ah didn't like the secondary. Ah wisnae that clever.
Ah liked tae draw, and loved to write and read – loved readin', ah wis
a keen reader. It wis mostly comics. Ah cannae mind the names o'
them. Wis it *Comic Mix* or somethin'?[1] It wis a wee girls' comic, sort
o' jist in black and white. I got it every week, ma mum would buy it
and bring it in for me. The lads used tae get the *Hotspur*, ah think it
wis, and the *Rover*.[2] So when ah started at the school ah could read.
Ah didnae join the public library till later on. But, oh, ah loved the
primary school.

Ah remember sittin' the Qualifyin' exam. Oh, ah passed it. Then ah
went on tae Victoria Drive Secondary, and then there was the Higher.
Ah didn't have tae leave school when ah wis 14. But by then ah wis
dyin' tae leave. If ma mum and dad could have afforded it, ah could
have stayed on. But ah wisnae keen on maths. Ah liked geography and
history and English. Ah didn't take French or German, or shorthand
and typing. But ah wasnae really interested in stayin' on at school and

maybe trying tae get Highers. Ma parents left it tae me tae decide and didn't put pressure on me tae stay or tae leave. Ah made up ma own mind. So ah left at 14.

As a girl ma interests were – well, as ah've said, ah wis a keen reader. Then there was an older girl stayed a wee bit further along the street, and she used tae go to the tap dancin'. So she used tae take maybe three or four o' us and we would all be doin' the tap dancin'. But ah never went to proper classes for tap dancin', because, ah mean, it was money in those days and ma mother couldnae afford it. But ah used tae love dancin'. And, when ah wis a bit older ah jist went tae the public dancin' wi' ma pal. Ah picked up ballroom dancin' myself. It wis very popular then. Ah loved it, ah loved dancin'. We never went to any particular dance-hall. It wis mostly in Partick, jist the wee local ones I used tae go tae really. Ah didnae go intae any dance-halls in Glasgow itsel', I was never in them. Ah didnae do much country dancin', though ah enjoyed eightsome reels and that, ah could do that. But, oh, ah loved ballroom dancin'. And then, oh, ah loved tae sing, ah still love tae sing. Ah wis in a choir at the Sunday School and at the church as well. Our church wis called The Mission. Ma parents were both members o' it, and ah wis brought up in it. It wis something like the Seamen's Mission. It wasnae the Church o' Scotland or the Free Church. Then, as ah got older, ma regular attendance at The Mission dropped off. Ma mum wanted me to go. But ah went then only occasionally, and with this other girl. Ma father wasnae so much a keen churchgoer as ma mother. Ma mother wis a great Christian, a great Christian. Ma dad wid go tae The Mission tae please her. But he wasnae such a Christian as ma mother.

Apart from the church and the Sunday School, ah wis never in a choir. Ah jist used tae always sing away tae myself! Then we used tae go tae the pictures, as they ca'ed them then, maybe once a week, every Saturday or that. And at an odd time we'd go tae the theatre. It wis 6d [2½p] tae get in, and you were away at the top o' the place. When ah wis young, and before ah went tae the ATS in the war, ah didnae go tae evening classes for dress-makin', cookin' or that. Then as ah got older before the war, as a reader it wis women's magazines ah read, the *Red Letter* and *The Secrets*. Ah think it wis the *Women's Own* that wis on then, and the *Family Friend* – no' the *People's Friend*.[3] Ah used tae get two or three o' the women's magazines every week. So in those days it wis these magazines rather than books ah enjoyed readin'. And then before the war ah always got holidays wi' ma parents. We went to Millport, Rothesay, Dunoon, Largs, Ardrossan, and tae Stewarton where ma Uncle Jimmy stayed. But ah wis never away on holiday on ma own before the war, except once when ah went on the train with a friend down to ma grandfather's at Barrow-in-Furness in Lancashire. Another interest ah had as a girl was ah sometimes went cyclin'. Ma brother Andrew – the one next to me – had a tandem, and ah used tae go cyclin' wi' him. So, wi' cyclin' and dancin', ah suppose ah wis really quite fit. Then when ah wis 17 ah joined the Girls Trainin' Corps.[4] It wis mostly drill ah learned in that: how to march and swing your arms, salute, turn left and right. So ah knew the basics and that helped me when ah joined the ATS. But when ah wis at school or after ah left it ah cannae really say ah had any particular ambitions, maybe tae become a nurse or a teacher or anythin' like that.

* * *

When ah left school in 1939 ah didnae have any qualifications or certificates. Ma first job wis in a well-known biscuit factory in Anderston. Ah think ah got the job through adverts in the paper, and ah remember goin' for an interview for it. Ah think ma mum had tae come with me. But ah got the job nae bother. So I was packing biscuits in tins. Ah think the hours wis eight o'clock tae half-past five, wi' an hour break for your lunch. It wis eight till 12 on a Saturday. So it wis 46½ hours a week. It wis quite a long day for a girl o' 14. Ah didnae go home at lunchtime, because the factory in Anderston wis maybe about five or six miles from where by then we stayed in Scotstoun. Ah took something wi' me tae eat, though there wis a canteen there and ah could get something in it. The wage wis eight shillings [40p] a week. Ah handed all ma wage tae ma mum, and ah got a shillin' [5p] for ma pocket. Well, ah hated that biscuit factory job. Ah said tae ma mum, ah says, 'It's horrible.' So ah only stayed there three weeks.

From there ah went tae work at Pirie's Dairies in Anniesland. It wis a dairy and a shop. It wasnae too far from where ah lived. The tram took me along tae it. In the shop ah served at the counter. It wis jist a wee shop. Ah think the hours there wis much the same as at the biscuit factory: eight till 5.30, and an hour break for lunch. You worked all day on a Saturday and got a half-day on a Tuesday. Ah think the wage would be about 12s 6d [62½p] a week, a wee bit more than ah'd had in the biscuit factory. There wis just two of us – another girl and me – worked in the shop. Barr & Stroud, the scientific instruments makers, wis jist down a wee bit from the dairy and they were on war work.[5] So there were big queues o' workers, men and women, from there used tae come along at dinner time to the dairy and, oh, were standin' waitin' for pies or rolls and wee half-pints o' milk. And some days the other girl would be away for her lunch so I wis left on my own in the shop. Ah wis only 14 or 15. And even when there wis no customers in the shop you were kept busy makin' up butter, because there wis big slabs o' butter and o' cheese as well. There wis a wire thing tae cut them wi'. The dairy sold butter, cheese, eggs, milk – everything. The other girl wis a good bit older than me, in fact a mature woman. We got on fine together and got friendly. Ah used tae bring her down to ma mum's, and ma mum would make us a nice tea and everything. And this woman had the same feeling as me that we were run off our feet in the shop. She would complain tae myself. But she wouldnae complain tae Mr Pirie, the boss. He didn't serve in the shop, he worked wi' his cows, round the back o' the shop. Looking back now, ah feel Pirie's Dairies were puttin' it on to me. Ah said tae ma mum, 'Ah'm no' happy here either.' And ma mum and dad said, 'Well, ye're no' goin' tae do that.' So ah left Pirie's Dairies. Ah think ah wis there for nearly a year, till the middle o' 1940.

Ah moved then tae Byres Road to a local baker's shop. Mr John Fleming jist had that one shop. Ah loved the work there. Ah think the job wis advertised in the paper. Ah went and applied for it, got an interview, and got the job. The hours wis from eight till six, wi' an hour off at lunchtime. Ah went home for lunch, it wisnae too far away from the shop. Ah used tae walk. But sometimes ah used tae go down on tae Dumbarton Road and get a bus or a tram along. It didnae take me long. The wages when ah first started wi' Mr Fleming wis, ah think, about 18s 6d [92½p], something like that. So it wis quite a considerable increase on ma wages at Pirie's Dairies. Ah think it wis quite a good wage for a girl o' ma age at that time. But then ah had ma bus fares and everythin' off it. And again ah gave all ma wages tae ma mum, and this time she gave me a half-crown [12½p] back.

As well as Mr Fleming, his daughter May, that wis in her twenties, and his niece Matty, that wis in her forties, worked in the baker's. Mr

Fleming did the baking himself along with his son and another man, and a woman, Emma. In these days a woman baker wis unusual. It maybe wisnae because o' the war. Ah think she'd been there for a number o' years before the war. She wis an old spinster. Mr Fleming had originally been a shipyard worker, and he knew ma dad well. Ah don't know whether he'd got a bit money or whatever and bought the shop. But, oh, it wis a busy shop. Because durin' the war ye only got so much flour to make cookies and bread and cakes and that. Ye got them at an odd time when ye got the flour. It was really quite a difficult time. But there wisnae any bread rationin' till after the end o' the war. Though we didn't get any bakeries from the shop home with us as part of our wages, or at a reduced price, ah used tae get what they called tea bread: ye got eight for 6d [2½p]. Ah got that every day. So we had wir Paris buns, cream cookies, and things like that. We used tae get cream cookies in a' the time, and Paris buns wi' sugar on the top.

When ah worked in Pirie's dairy and then in Fleming's the bakers, ah never joined a union. Never heard o' a union, there wasn't any. Well, ah worked in the bakery till 1944 when ah wis 19 and then ah joined the ATS. Mr Fleming, as my employer, had applied for a deferment for me, tae keep me in the shop. So ah'd been deferred for about six month. But then ah had tae go.

Ah got a thorough medical. That wis jist up from the Western Infirmary and near Kelvin Hall. Ah got through that ok – A1. About two or three weeks after that ah got a letter tae report tae Newbattle Abbey at Dalkeith, the ATS camp for Scotland. Ah wis quite happy, ah wasnae upset at leavin' home, though possibly ma mum was, but she didnae show it. So from Glasgow Queen Street station ah went on ma own by train tae Edinburgh Waverley station. Ah met up there wi' other girls goin' by train tae Eskbank station at Dalkeith for Newbattle Abbey. It wis a big step for me as a girl o' 19, because ah hadnae really been away from home on ma own before, except that once when ah went tae ma grandfather's at Barrow-in-Furness. At Eskbank station ye were met by an officer, and you just walked down, carryin' ma case, tae Newbattle Abbey, less than a mile away.

At the Abbey it wis huts, jist wooden huts. In the hut where ah wis there'd be about 18 to 20 other girls. There wis about 10 beds on one side o' the hut, and 10 on the other. They were jist single beds. Ah think the girls in ma hut came mostly from the west o' Scotland.

Ah can't remember any from Edinburgh or Aberdeen or Dundee or Fife. Ah always remember the two that wis opposite me in the hut, because when we were doin' the drill and had to right turn, they were turnin' left! At drill ah had an advantage because ah'd been about a year in the Girls Trainin' Corps when ah wis 17. Another thing ah remember about these two girls wis that they slept together. They were in adjoinin' beds until the lights went out. Then they moved into the one bed. Ah think it wis because they felt cold or they felt lonely maybe. They were best friends. They'd joined up together, ah think they'd know each other before. They both come from Ayrshire. But bein' two in one bed would be frowned on by the army authorities in these days. They never got caught. But, ah mean, they were two very nice girls right enough. In fact, they were comics. And ah think they were the type that maybe went tae each other's house and stayed at the weekend, and things like that. Ah didn't myself have any friends that went wi' me tae join the ATS or that ah found at Newbattle. Everybody there wis a stranger tae me. But ah didn't feel out o' ma depth or homesick. And the girls were all quite friendly. We were a' in the same boat and all about the same age, 19. But ah remember one or two older than that right enough. Ah don't think any o' them were married. Anyway, it was fine, no problems. And there wis no shouting or swearing at us by the NCOs, so ah didnae feel frightened. The food wis very good and there wis enough of it. Ah cannae remember ma mum sending me a food parcel or anythin' like that from home when I wis at Newbattle. And ah don't remember any o' the girls bein' really homesick or upset about bein' away from home and finding it wis a different life at Newbattle Abbey. But, oh, if you were in trouble and you wanted tae speak tae the sergeant, the corporal, or the officer, you could speak to them. There wis a sergeant and a corporal in charge of our hut, and there'd be an officer above them. Ah wrote home maself at least once a week, and ma mum wrote tae me; she wis always a good writer.

The basic trainin' at Newbattle Abbey wis six weeks, mostly drill a' the time and a bit o' physical training (PT). Ah think we did the PT inside. Ah think ah remember wall bars, and climbing up ropes, and ah felt back at school again! Of course, through dancin' and cyclin' before ah went intae the ATS ah kept fit, and I'd never been ill. Some o' the other girls complained about sair feet, things like that. We had shoes, jist flat-heeled, lacin' shoes. They were uncomfortable until you got used tae them. Then we used tae go on route marches, maybe a couple o' miles or something, not too far. Maybe we'd go tae Dalkeith and back again, or tae Gorebridge or Newtongrange, jist tae get us a' fit and that. We didnae do runnin', jist marchin'. And ye never had weapons, we never had any. But of course we were issued wi' uniforms, and got them sorted out and a' the rest o' it. So at the end o' the six weeks ye felt sort o' more confident.

As well as the ATS huts at Newbattle Abbey, on the other side o' the road there wis men's huts. They were well away from the women. The men and women were kept well apart, and ah don't really remember seein' many o' the men goin' about in the women's hutment section. And the women didn't go over to the men's. Ah don't think you were allowed tae mix with them. Ah don't remember any rules about that. But ah don't remember any sort o' mixin'. And ah don't remember that the girls and the men got taegether at dances in the camp at Newbattle. We used tae go tae dances at Dalkeith, and there were cinemas there, too. So we used tae go tae the pictures. And then it's the first time ah wis ever in pubs. Ah wouldnae have been before: ma father wis teetotal; we never had anything, never had any connection with pubs. There wis a crowd of us all went in Dalkeith intae a lounge, ah jist went in tae. But ah don't think ah had anything tae drink. It would probably be a lemonade. Ah felt a bit nervous about goin' intae a pub. Girls tended no' tae go intae pubs in these days. And then ah wis never a smoker, never started in the ATS.

* * *

Well, as ah've said, ah got home leave in August 1944 at the end o' the six weeks' trainin' at Newbattle Abbey. And then ah wis posted tae south-east Dulwich in London, tae await postin' overseas. Ah wis quite happy at the thought o' goin' overseas. We didn't know where we were goin', it wis all kept hush-hush. And while we were at Dulwich ah don't think we did very much really, just a wee bit o' square-bashin', that was all. We weren't given courses in office work, clerical work, typing – nothing like that. We jist sort of waited until we were sent somewhere overseas.

It wis January 1945 when we got word that we were tae go and embark from, ah think, it was Southampton. But we weren't told where we were going beyond that. It wis like a guessin' game, ye know. It could be anywhere. So about a dozen of us ATS went by train from south-east Dulwich to Southampton. Whenever we got to wherever we were going to overseas it was to be mostly on clerical work. Ah had no experience o' clerical work, but ah managed it. And, as ah say, we hadn't had any trainin' in clerical work and that sort o' thing at Newbattle Abbey or at Dulwich.

Ah can't remember the name o' the ship we went on at Southampton, but it wis a big, big ship. It might have been a merchant navy ship, a transport ship, not a Royal Navy one. But we had naval escorts. There wis different groups on board our ship. As well as our group of 12 ATS from Dulwich there were other ATS – maybe 50 or 100 althegither. And there wis a lot o' the lads that had been home on leave and were goin' back overseas again. All the soldiers were underneath, on the lower decks, o' the ship; the ATS girls were up on the top deck. They were quite strictly separated. On our deck four o' us shared a cabin. It wis bunks, not hammocks, we slept in. Well, we sailed through the Bay o' Biscay. The sea wis gey rough – it wis January. But I ate normally, ah wisnae up nor down. Most o' the girls were seasick, but ah wisnae. And ah slept well at night. I was very fortunate.

The ship didn't stop at Gibraltar, but a lot o' Spanish came out in wee boats, trying tae sell us things. But, as ah say, the ship never stopped. But ah remember seein' the great big rock o' Gibraltar. Then on the voyage there wis one or two alerts through the night – air raids, or it could have been submarines. We weren't told if it wis airplanes or submarines. Ah jist cannae remember what we did when alerts sounded. We had life jackets right enough. And we had that drill and were taken up on deck. But there wis no attack on the ship.

Ah didn't like the sea, and yet on the ship ah wis never up nor down. Afterwards ma mother used tae say, 'Ah never knew how you ever went on a boat or a ship.' Because when ah wis younger and we were on holiday, ma dad would take us out on the water in a wee rowin' boat, and ah wis terrified. But on that ship through the Bay o' Biscay and the Mediterranean ah never thought about it. Ah had come through the Clydebank blitz in 1941, and ah wis frightened then, because it wis bad. We werenae in the shelter on those nights, we and all ma mother's neighbours were in our house in Scotstoun, on the ground floor. Ah wis 15 then and workin' in Fleming's bakery. Glasgow wis badly bombed as well as Clydebank. It wis terrible, dreadful. One of ma friends ah'd been at school with, she got killed then in Scotstoun. Ye see, we were on the outskirts o' Clydebank. Ma dad said it wis the big ship that wis in for repair at Yarrow's yard in Scotstoun that saved us. They had big guns and they were firin' tae keep the German planes away. Oh, it wis an awfy experience, it wis terrible right enough. Ah canna forget that. But ah thank God that jist our windows were broken.[6] But there wis nothin' like that on our ship in January 1945. So I was very fortunate then: ah wisnae frightened or seasick, and ah slept well. One o' the lads on the ship played the piano, and he heard me and two or three o' the girls singin' on the deck. So we had a concert on board, and ah wis singin' a solo there.

Well, after 11 days at sea through the Bay o' Biscay and the Mediterranean, we landed at Naples.[7] It wis a hotel, ah think, that we were put intae. We were there for a time, and then we went up to Rome. We were there for a while, then from Rome we went to Rimini. We stayed there for some weeks. It wis when we were there, and had already been in Italy four months, we got word that the war in Europe had ended – VE Day. It wis one o' the sergeants that came and told us. We hadnae known till then. Oh, ah wis happy that the war had finished. Ah mean, all ma youth had been taken up wi' the war. Then from Rimini we went tae Padua. And after a time there ah went tae Venice. So there I wis, a young girl from Partick and Scotstoun, away across at what seemed tae me the other side o' the world.

In all these places we stopped in for a time – Naples, Rome, Rimini, Padua – we were really no' doing anything, jist sort o' sittin' about. It wis all big hotels that they took over where we stayed. Oh, they were good billets. And Italians cooked the food. Oh, it wis completely different overseas than what it wis at home: the discipline wis more relaxed. You were practically left jist tae find your way through the day. Ye didnae have a lot o' drills, marchin' up and down, or anythin' like that. Ye got the chance tae get out and round about, and with the other ATS girls explore on foot Rome and these other places. Ah liked it, and ah loved the Italian people. Ah always found them very friendly. When we got there there wis still fightin' goin' on in northern Italy. Ah remember at Padua we used tae hear the snipers in the city. There wis wee pockets o' Germans still around then.

Ah had ma 20th birthday, in June 1945, when ah got tae Venice. All the Italian girls that helped wi' the cookin' gave me a beautiful card.

The girls were sort o' domestic servants, and some o' them were in the offices as well, helpin'. There wis a big canteen. Ah didn't actually work in the canteen, but ah used tae help out there. If they were needing the likes o' maybe tea or sugar, ah would have tae see that they got it. Ah wis sort o' catering and things like that, a kind o' catering assistant. Ah did enjoy doin' that. And ma experience in Fleming's bakery at home helped me. We usually worked from eight in the mornin' till two in the afternoon, quite short hours. The rest o' the day wis your own. You could wander about Venice then. Oh, it was a great experience, me 20 and bein' able tae wander about in Venice. The furthest ah'd been at home wis Millport, Dunoon, Barrow-in-Furness.

All the dozen ATS girls that'd come wi' me from Dulwich had all went to different places in Italy. Ah think ah wis on ma own in Venice. We were separated, and they'd been dispersed at Rome, Rimini and Padua. We were all under the Eighth Army, and in Venice it wis part of an army headquarters that ah wis attached to.

Ah kept in touch all the time with home. Ma mother wrote tae me every week, at least every week ah got a letter from her. Sometimes if they were held up ah'd maybe get two or three at the one time. But ah did start tae feel a wee bit homesick when ah wis in Venice, toward the end o' ma time there. By then ah'd been away from home in Glasgow six or seven months. And, ah mean, in these days it seemed a long time.

But there wis still unrest then wi' the Yugoslavs about the border wi' Italy. So after bein' in Venice about three months ah moved in September 1945 from there tae Trieste.[8] Ah went wi' one or two other ATS girls. At Trieste ah did the same kind o' work as in Venice, catering, and a wee bit clerical work. We were billeted in a hotel at first, and then we were moved intae flats. But an Italian woman did all the cookin' and cleanin'. The flats werenae so nice as the hotel. In the hotel there wis jist two o' us in a room – that wis a luxury; in the flats it wis three in a room. But ah got on well wi' the other girls. And, ah mean, ah would never have got tae these places before the war. Ah picked up a bit o' Italian, so ah could make a conversation. And, oh, many Italians could speak some English of course.

Trieste was where ah met ma husband, Bob Hastie. He belonged Edinburgh. Ah met him at the dancin' of course. He was at Trieste in the artillery. Bob was a Territorial and he'd been in the war since the beginning. He wis with the Eighth Army all the way through: North Africa, El Alamein, Sicily, then up through Italy. He couldnae get leave, even when his brother, who had rheumatoid arthritis, died in 1944. So Bob had been away from home for a number o' years. When ah first met him ah thought he wis Clark Gable, the film star![9] And, of course, he stuck tae me like glue after that! It wisnae love at first sight. It wis jist he grew on me. We met in December 1945 and we got married in May 1946. Bob wis demobbed in March '46, and ah wis comin' home on leave. So we decided. And ah wrote tae his mum and dad, and he wrote tae mine, askin' permission and that. So it wis all right. Ah hadnae met his family, ah jist wrote letters to them. So ah'm from the west o' Scotland and Bob wis from the east, and we met in the north o' Italy. That wis the experience o' so many in our generation. But it turned out well.

So when ah'd been married ah wis able tae come out the ATS. Ah had tae go down tae Dulwich, the headquarters, and got demobbed there in June 1946. So ah'd been in the ATS about two years. Oh, ah still think about these years. Oh, exciting, aye, I enjoyed it. Ah never had any regrets.

Bob, ma husband, as ah've said, belonged tae Edinburgh, but when he wis a wee boy he came tae live in Musselburgh and always remained there. Before the war he'd worked in Brunton's wire mill in Musselburgh. After the war he worked in Inveresk paper mill there. But he wis only there about six weeks and he took tuberculosis. We were jist married, and then he wis sent away tae the sanatorium at Bridge of Earn in Perthshire and was there for ten months. He had half his lung taken away.

Well, what ah did was ah got myself a job as a nanny in Musselburgh. This woman had a child and was pregnant, and she lived facin' Linkfield at Musselburgh race course. She asked me tae come, ah lived in there, and she gave me every Saturday off. Before that ah wis livin' wi' Bob in a room in his mother's house, because o' the terrible housin' shortage. But Bob's mum stopped speakin' tae me when Bob fell ill. Of course ah understood she had already lost her other son, Bob's brother, and maybe she thought she wis goin' tae lose Bob tae. But ah never really understood why she stopped speakin' tae me. It wis terrible for me. Ah jist used tae sit and cry every day. Ah thought, 'Now ah've got tae either go home tae ma mum or get a job here in

Musselburgh.' So ah decided, 'Ah'll stay in Musselburgh', because ah heard that if you didnae stay there you wouldnae get a house. Ah could have got a house in Glasgow, because Bob had priority, bein' ill wi' tuberculosis.

Hail, rain or snow, ah went to visit Bob every Saturday at the Bridge of Earn sanatorium. Ah normally went in the bus. But in the winter o' 1946–7 the snow wis away up tae here. But if ah couldnae get through in the bus ah got a train. It wis a long journey. But ah wis the only one that went tae visit Bob. He used tae watch for me comin'. Ah wis the only one that came up this road every week. Even his parents and his sister never went tae see him, not once in ten months. But after, when Bob got better and come home, his mum offered tae let us stay in her room again until we got a prefab in Musselburgh. We didnae have tae stay in the room very long before we got a prefab, the first house o' our own. That wis in 1947. Then of course ah fell pregnant wi' ma first son. We wis in the prefab for nearly 12 years, then we got one that wis in a four-in-the-block in Musselburgh.

Ah would maybe say that at first when ah got married ah missed not livin' in Glasgow. But then ma mum and dad used tae come for a holiday at our prefab. Ma dad wis retired then, and they used tae come through often. Well, eventually ah had three boys. And Bob, once he got fit again, wis with the council parks department. But in the wintertime it wis gey bad for him. He wis off an awfy lot wi' his chest. Oh, TB wis an awfy scourge in these days. Well, they said that Bob got it when in the army they were lyin' in tents in the water and mud. Ah used tae say tae Bob sometimes when we were in Trieste and could look down from the buildin' we were in and could all see our boyfriends comin' up the road, 'Bob, ye don't look awfy great.' He'd say, 'Ah've no' been feelin' awfy well.' But then it seemed tae lift again, ye know. But, oh, that wis definitely the beginnin' o' his TB.

So there were women and girls in the ATS and other Services that, like me, were sent abroad. Not an awful lot, ah would say.[10] And tae be sent tae Italy wis quite somethin'. Since the war ah've been tae Spain and Majorca, but ah've never been back tae Italy. Ah've often thought about it, but we jist never seem tae have gone back. It wasn't because there were unhappy memories – far from it. The Italians were all very nice. And when ah left tae go home and get married the ones that knew me were all cryin' and everythin', and they clubbed together and bought me a nightdress and underwear and everythin' a' tae match. Ah often say that ah could write a book.

Ann Baird (Mrs Ann Hastie) died in 2017.

Isa Dougan

I don't know why it suddenly came into my head. But one day in August 1941 I asked the time off from Thomson & Norris, which was then Reed Packaging, near Turnhouse aerodrome at Edinburgh (they didn't know where I was going). And I went down to the Assembly Rooms in George Street, volunteered into the Women's Auxiliary Air Force, and got my medical. And they gave me a microphone and told me to call S for Sugar, as though I was talking to a plane. Then they said to me to go home and they would send me word, and when I got word I should report with a parent to wherever I was told. I don't think I told my mother about it until a letter came saying I had to report with my father to the Caledonian Station, West Princes Street, Edinburgh, at nine o'clock in the morning or something. And when I went to the Caley Station I was told I was to get the train down from there to Wolverhampton, and that I was going to a place called Bridgnorth in Shropshire. So my father put me on the train at the Caley. But I remember my mother having hysterics because she didn't know where I was going, plus the fact she was losing the monthly bonus I was bringing home from the office of Thomson & Norris!

Well, I was born in Edinburgh on the 9th of July 1922. My father, Ross Dougan, began work as an engine cleaner on the old North British Railway and he ended up as running foreman at Haymarket depot in Edinburgh. He drove the royal train quite a few times, and he held the record for speed. So I'm rather proud of my father. He was the kind of man that, if you were one minute late, you were signed off for a shift. If a train was to go at six o'clock it went at six o'clock. And you could be his best friend, but that was it. He was a very strict disciplinarian.

But when your shift was over, he was away playing bowls with you and all the others. He was too young to be in the Forces in the 1914–18 War.

My father was born in Stranraer and all his relatives are still there. I never knew my grandfather Dougan and never heard of him ever being mentioned. My father had half-brothers or adopted brothers.

My mother came originally from Aberdeen. She told me she was born in Crown Place there. She was the youngest one of nine children. The others all died in infancy. I don't think they ever reached the age even of 10 or 12. My mother used to say she was very surprised because she survived. I don't know how she and her mother came down to Edinburgh. My mother became a shop assistant there. She had two children, my sister Molly, two years older than I, and myself.

My granny – my mother's mother – was a wonderful lady. She'd had about nine brothers and she was the only girl. So she stayed at home and had to look after them all. There wasn't one of her brothers that was under six feet tall. And my granny was like me – five feet chuttle [sic]. But she used to rule them with a rod of iron. And there wasn't a man in the world that she wouldn't take on. Before and during the war I often used to think I should send her out to Germany: she would be fine for dealing with Adolf Hitler. Originally granny's people, as far as I can gather, were seamen from South Shields in Durham, and must have come up to Scotland. Granny must have stayed for a time in Aberdeen, as that was where my mother was born. But granny didn't have a very happy marriage. Her husband was very cruel to her.

Granny owned her own house or flat in Edinburgh, right at the top of a tenement in Elm Row, part of Leith Walk; and she and my parents and my sister Molly and I lived there until about 1935–6, when I was 13 or 14. Granny had never had any schooling. She couldn't read at all, and she couldn't write. But she had her own bank account and signed it with a cross. Where finance was concerned she was great. You couldn't do my granny out of a ha'penny. She managed her money and brought up a family, my mother's family, like us. She used to say to me when I was a girl, 'Isa, go down and get me a quarter o' ham out of Low's.' We had Low's shop and Cochrane's around us in Elm Row. So I'd go down and when I came back she'd say, 'Why haven't you got this amount of change?' I'd say, 'Because it was 4¼ ounces.' On went her coat: 'Come with me.' And I used to get trailed by the hand down to Low's and right in there, and she'd say: 'When I send my granddaughter here for a quarter, that means four ounces. It does not mean 4¼ ounces. Four ounces I want and four ounces is what I'll get.' And she'd say all this in a loud voice in front of all the other customers! Oh, I died of shame. Of course, that's the oldest trick in the game: send a wee soul for a message – half a pound o' this – and the wee soul comes back with three-quarters o' a pound. But no' wi' my granny, oh, no' wi' her. And they used tae say, 'She should bring her granny!' Oh, she knew exactly what she wanted.

Well, my granny had very much to do with my sister Molly and me as we grew up. We used to say, 'We've not got our blouse or our knickers. She's washed them again!' I mean, if you took a thing off, granny washed it – everything. Then I had long hair and she used to make me stand on this wee stool while she brushed my hair. And all the time she brushed she used to sing: 'Dirty was his name, Dirty was his colour, and Dirty was the kiss that I gied the miller.' As she'd lost all her own children except for my mother, she doted on Molly and me. When Molly and I took scarlet fever at the same time my mother wouldn't send us to hospital. So in those days it was quarantine. The two of us were in the one room. And granny nursed us in there. Nobody was allowed into the house when we were in that room. Molly and I are so close now, but in those days when we were young she and I always fought. And I remember my father tying our legs together in the bed, to try and stop us kicking each other.

Every single day from Monday to Saturday granny went to the pictures. There were cinemas all round about us in or near Elm Row: the Salon, the Eastway, the Capitol, the Alhambra, the Picture Drome in Easter Road, though granny never bothered about the Playhouse. My granny's one weakness was sweets. She had a quarter of sweets in her pocket every day when she went to the pictures. Oh, she ate them in the cinema. So it was a very great blow to her when sweet rationing came in during the war. Granny, a great worker, was up at six o'clock in the morning, working away. But every afternoon you knew where to find her: she was at the pictures. I never myself went to the pictures with her.

One thing granny couldn't stand was a man taking a liberty. I can still see in my mind's eye my granny one day at the sink in Elm Row. In those days she spoiled my mother by scrubbing my father's dungarees. She was scrubbing away when this day the husband of a woman relative came in. He was very fond of drink. He put his arm round my granny's waist, though she had told him repeatedly not to come near her and not to touch her. Well, I don't know what happened that day, but she just turned round wi' her fist and knocked him flat out – flat out for the count! That's the kind of woman she was. She would face anything. Of course in those days sex and all that was a thing you didn't talk about. I mean, even when Molly and I were both quite well up in age we were put out the room if the older folk got on about things like that. If somebody not married was expecting a baby we got put out the room then, too!

Granny probably died a bit sooner than she should, because she was coming up from the Provi [Leith Provident Co-operative Society], crossing the road at Pilrig, and there were steps and a sort of fountain thing. She tripped on the step, broke her nose, and that brought on a shock. Granny died about 1947, aged about 78.

* * *

So granny's house in Elm Row is the one I remember earliest. We had a kitchen there, a bathroom – we were lucky we had both; and we had a bedroom and a parlour, and we had running hot and cold water. And the windows at the top all faced to the front. We never had gas lighting there, and I've never been in a house that had. At Elm Row we had electric lighting. Then I remember having the wireless in Elm Row when I was quite wee, and getting sent down with an accumulator to get it charged up. The sleeping arrangements at Elm Row were, well, there was a double bed in the kitchen, and a double bed in the bedroom. So to begin with my parents were in the kitchen, and I was there too when I was wee. God knows how I got any sleep. And my sister Molly and my granny were in the bedroom. The parlour was used at first as a parlour, but then we had to get a bed put in the parlour because we were growing up. Then Molly got the bedroom, and I got moved in beside my granny in the parlour. We were fortunate because granny's house in Elm Row was rather larger than many other people had at that time – and we had a smaller family. And my father as an engine driver was relatively better off than many other working men. He had a steady job and he was never out of work. We were lucky. Molly and I of course were spoiled as far as toys and things went, because we were the only two grandchildren of my granny. So I think on the whole we were comfortable.

Then my parents and Molly and I moved from granny's house in Elm Row to McDonald Road, further down Leith Walk and running at right angles from it. We moved there, as I've said, about 1935–6, when I was 13 or 14. My granny didn't want to come and live in McDonald Road, so she remained at Elm Row. But she came down more or less every day to see us at McDonald Road. She was never left on her own.

Our house in McDonald Road was bigger than granny's at Elm Row. We had a nice big living room, which had a bed in it, and a bedroom which had a double bed in it. And there was a bed closet off the kitchen, with a double bed in it. And we had this great big parlour, oh, a lovely big front room. As well as the kitchen we had a separate place that in those days we called a scullery. Oh, we had everything: electric light, hot and cold running water, and a lovely big window. The house was on the second flat. And you had your two sinks and your cooker – no fridges in those days. And there was a lovely big walk-in cupboard, a bathroom, and a good-sized hall. The only thing the bathroom didn't have was a washhand basin. But they had got a thing made that sat on the bath and had a basin in it.

I can't remember the sleeping arrangements at the McDonald Road house as clearly as those at granny's at Elm Row. But I remember dad was on three shifts, and because his shifts were different he often slept in the bed closet, while my mother slept in the kitchen. I remember my mother used to swear she never had a wink of sleep when dad was on night shift, never. She heard him coming in every time. And I remember Molly went away for a while to stay with granny at Elm Row; so I had the bedroom to myself then. So McDonald Road was where we were, right up until I was married in 1945. Incidentally, Jackie, my future husband, who used to carry my school books for me when I lived in Elm Row and who himself lived further down off Leith Walk at Balfour Street, used to cycle by McDonald Road on his bike when I was at the secondary school. And as he passed he used to ring the door bell. And I remember my mother saying, 'If he rings that bell one more day I'm going down to wring his neck!'

Molly and I both started school at Leith Walk Primary in Brunswick Road, quite near Elm Row; and then from there we went to Bellevue Secondary School, later renamed Drummond Community High

School. Bellevue was quite near McDonald Road. I was interested in athletics and in games. And I was quite good intellectually. I never had any problems at school. I liked history, always history. I don't know whether that was because the dates were easy to remember so that you were always sure of high marks. I also liked geography – getting told about other places than where you lived. And I loved sport, oh, high jumping, running, netball. It was hockey or tennis when I went to secondary school. Years later there was a 'Where are they now?' photo and story in the *Edinburgh Evening News* about our school champions with their cups and shields, and there was me with my long hair. Even when I went on the Pilrig Church Sunday School picnic I came back with prizes.

When it came to the Qualifying exam at Leith Walk Primary I never had any bother and passed the exam. You could go then to Bellevue Secondary or to Broughton Senior Secondary, which was just at the end of McDonald Road. But, you see, we thought Broughton was awfy toffee-nosed.[1] So I wanted to go to Bellevue because most of my friends in those days were Bellevue. My father and mother decided I would go to Bellevue: I mean, they knew where I wanted to go. For me there was another bonus, because Bellevue had tennis courts right in its playground. And Bellevue offered a commercial course. For the life of me I cannae remember, but I don't think senior secondary schools like Broughton offered then a commercial course, or at least not from your first year there. I was qualified to go to Broughton, got the marks, but just didnae want to go. So I signed up for commercial at Bellevue – that would probably be the reason I went there.

I don't remember my parents ever passing any comment on what my sister Molly and I wanted to be or didn't want to be. Molly too had passed the Qualifying exam, also went to Bellevue and then went to work in a painter's shop as a clerkess. I got French at Bellevue, but of course I also got shorthand and typing. I think my parents would be looking ahead and maybe thinking, 'Oh, she'll get a job easier.' I think I wanted to work in an office, and shorthand and typing work was what I took up when I left Bellevue when I was 15 in the summer of 1937. I'd got up to 110 words a minute in shorthand and about 40 in typewriting. I did have fanciful ideas I'd like to be a vet. But my mother had very rigid ideas that the younger daughter – me, shouldn't do anything that the older daughter – Molly, didn't want to do. I don't know what

Molly wanted to do, because we werenae that close. But, as I've said, she became a clerkess in an office.

I've often tried to think this out, and Molly and I have talked about it, whether because we were a two-girl family it was my father I was closest to, and my mother was closest to Molly. And I think my mother used to put on a bit of bias, because it was always a case of, 'If your elder sister hasn't got a boyfriend you do not have a boyfriend. If your elder sister doesn't want to go dancing, you don't go dancing.' That made me rebellious. Molly and I used to get sent to the pictures every Saturday afternoon – we never went with granny – and we arranged that one of us would go upstairs and the other would go down. We wouldn't sit together. And I had more than a few friends at school and round about. I always seemed to have plenty to do in those days, and I was always getting a row for going away and jumping from the bike to join a group. Well, when you think about it, it was a gang. I remember even at Elm Row the police coming to our door one day. In those days the bobby knew all the children, they knew everything. And it was just because one of the boys had had an air-gun. And I of course, daredevil, had to have a go with it. Somebody had seen me shooting the air-gun and told the police. When the bobby came up it was my father he saw, and, oh, I remember getting told, 'Never again. You are going to grow up to be a lady. You will not handle guns.'

Anyway, as I say, I left Bellevue Secondary School aged 15 in 1937 with, I think it would be, a Lower Leaving Certificate. By that time I was ready to go out and face another challenge: I was quite keen to start work. I was quite competent in what I was doing and was keen to go on. So I wanted to find work as a junior shorthand typist. My first job was with Munrospun down at Restalrig.[2] I saw a vacancy for a junior shorthand typist there advertised in the newspaper, I wrote after it, and got it. I can't remember what my wage there was when I first began. Would it be somewhere about 15 shillings [75p] a week? My mother anyway was quite pleased. I gave all my wages to her and she gave me something for myself. I was about eight months at the most there, just till I got sort of used to the routine, and then I must have been filled with big ideas. Because when I looked through *The Scotsman*[3] one day there was a job advertised to be trained as an assistant secretary with the firm Thomson & Norris, which was then Reed Packaging. So I went away out there to their place at the edge of Edinburgh on the Glasgow Road, again got a shorthand and typing test, and got the job. I liked working there too, and made good friends there. The pay was more than at Munrospun: it would be £1 a week or maybe 21 shillings [£1.05], and I got rises. More than that, I got a bonus every month. Again I just handed over all my pay to my mother, though I got an increase in what she gave me back, because I had increased money. I can't remember how much she gave me back. I remained at Thomson & Norris/Reed Packaging for about three or three-and-a-half years till I volunteered in 1941 into the WAAF.

After leaving school I didn't play in a hockey team or take part in sports generally. One of my main spare-time interests was dancing. Oh, I loved dancing. I just went to some of the local dance-halls. We weren't allowed to go to some of the places, Fairley's in Leith Street was one of them.[4] But I never told my mother half of the places I went to anyway. But, oh, I loved the Palais de Danse in Fountainbridge. Then latterly, about the beginning of the war, the Cavendish came in at Tollcross. Then I always liked Stranraer, where my father belonged and where I had one aunt in particular I liked to visit. So all the holidays I remember were always down in Stranraer. We got two weeks' holiday from work each year, and I always got Christmas Day and New Year's Day off. Then in those last years before the war I joined the League of Health and Beauty, and went down with our outfit of black pants and a white vest to Meadowbank to do gymnastics and Keep Fit.[5] When I had been at school there was a display in the Waverley Market in Princes Street, and I was one of the team chosen there. Another interest I'd long had was reading newspapers from beginning to end. I've always been a keen reader. At home we got the dailies, maybe the *Daily Record* or the *Daily Express*. I can't remember getting a Sunday one, but we got one called the *Gazette*. I don't think it was the *Railway Gazette*, and I wonder if it had anything to do with Stranraer.[6] Then once the war started I took up first-aid and used to attend classes in Leith Walk School. There Mrs MacKenzie, a hospital matron, gave us all the basics. I don't think I would have gone to the class had it not been for the war: I realised I had to do something.

* * *

I was very happy working at Thomson & Norris/Reed Packaging and I was coming on fine there. They were satisfied with me, and I was to be trained to go on to be secretary to Mr Barclay, a director. But of course by this time war had broken out. I remember the day war broke out in September 1939. There wis bells chimin', and there wis this solemn announcement that we were at war. That was it. I think it just suddenly hit you, the word 'war'. Jackie Inglis, my future husband, had already joined the Territorial Army when he was only 16. The rest of my friends volunteered into the Services after the war broke out. I think Jackie – I'd known him since I was at school – joined the TA even before war broke out, because he had a very unhappy home, and also I think the tanks fascinated him. I think that's what it was.

The outbreak of the war may have begun to make me think of volunteering. But I think it really sort of started to hit you when your own friends – not the girls – started to volunteer and go away. Mike MacKinnon went away to the navy, and he went down in the *Royal Oak* when it was sunk, just at the end of 1939.[7] He was just young. Bill Francis joined the Air Force, but he was killed, between 1943 and 1944, as a bomber pilot. Then Dougie Steel, who wasn't one of our group but I had been introduced to him and I'd been out with him a few times, Dougie was on the first bombing raid over Germany, when they dropped leaflets asking the Germans to surrender. We never knew what happened to Dougie. But years later Jackie and I went to the RAF Memorial at Runnymede in Surrey, and Dougie's name is there. Then Freddie Kinnear, one of Jackie's friends that I also knew, he got blown up by a landmine down near Land's End, I think it was.[8] So their going away to the Forces by so many of our friends could have influenced me. The war really filled my mind: shall we say that the future was all war? Anyway, I was the first girl in our group of friends who joined up and I was the only one that went to the Air Force. One of my girl friends, Isa MacKinlay, joined the Women's Royal Naval Service after I joined the WAAF. Molly, my sister, joined the Land Army, but I can't remember now if that was before or after I went away. I think it must have been just round about the same time as me.[9]

So I'd been thinking about volunteering, but I don't know why it suddenly came into my head. And, as I've said, without saying where I was going I got time off from my job at Thomson & Norris/Reed Packaging, went to the Assembly Rooms in George Street, got a medical there and some sort of knowledge and microphone test, was given some instructions and told more would be sent me. Actually, when I was younger I wanted to go to the WRNS, but when I'd mentioned it I was at that time too young. I really don't know why I joined the WAAF. I'd no specific reason, I wasn't interested in flying, and I didn't know any other girls at all who were in the WAAF. I think I just liked the idea of the Air Force. Anyway, I was one of the ones that they called The Four Years, when you signed on for only four years.

Well, my father duly took me down to the Caley station and put me on the train for Wolverhampton en route for Bridgnorth in Shropshire. I seemed to be the only girl at the Caley station who was going there. I saw three other girls at the Caley, but they were in the ATS. Of course, there must have been other girls in other parts of the train, but in the carriage where I was there wasn't. And also of course any of us going to join the WAAF or other women's Services would be wearing civilian clothes.

When I arrived at Bridgnorth I was picked up and taken to the camp. But it was dark, and the blackout was on. I couldn't see anything. I remember we were given something to eat. And that almost made me take the first train home, because it was fish – and I don't like fish. We weren't put in tin huts, we were in like barrack blocks. You weren't allowed off the base until you had done your training. You answered all your questions, and you got issued with your uniforms. I got most of my uniform. I got a skirt, a tunic, a blouse, a shirt, and a hat. I was lucky. Some of the recruits before me had got just a raincoat. We got just one set until they got more supplies. Then we got stockings and blackout knickers – all black, and vests. We sent all our civvy clothes home. We had to get up at five o'clock in the morning, to go in and share the ablutions. There must have been about eight washhand basins. And I remember it was a cold place, and I don't think there was hot water. After a time you had to take the gas test, run through mustard gas in a room in a hut. So we were quite glad to get away from Bridgnorth camp. It was pretty grim. So after five weeks there we were allowed home on leave.

Then I was posted to Morecambe. I was billeted there with a Mrs Pickles. She had one of these boarding houses that had rooms and rooms and rooms. We were up at half-past six in the mornings, and we had to get out on the promenade at half-past seven doing gymnastics. Mrs Pickles did all the cooking for us – if you could call it cooking. I think we got something – a packed lunch – when we were away at lunchtime, but you got your breakfast there and your meal at night. And we got our injections at Morecambe. That's when you started to feel sorry for yourself. I had a bad reaction in my arm – but I wasn't the only one. So there were a lot of us feeling kind of sorry for ourselves. You never got to lie in your bed. I don't think you could have lain around anyway in Mrs Pickles's house. You had to get out of your bed and march about. And you had all the people watching you doing this. I mean, you used to get told that you were anything but a lady.

I remember one of my relatives who was going to be aircrew was at Blackpool, at the other end of Morecambe Bay. But I wasn't allowed to go and see him, and he wasn't allowed to come to me. Morecambe seemed to be specifically the WAAF training ground, and it was out of bounds to the RAF men; Blackpool, as an RAF training place, was out of bounds to WAAFs. So we both wrote letters stating that we were relatives and wanted to meet. Well, he came to Morecambe to see me then.

Then quite a laugh for me was the business of getting our pay. I can't begin to tell you how many names I got instead of Dougan when it came to pay days. If it hadn't been for the last three numbers on my paybook I wouldn't have got paid at all! I never seemed to find myself among Scots girls, who, unlike English folk, wouldn't have had difficulty with my name.

Well, at Morecambe we got trained in marching, and were put through the various tests they did. Then we got our postings in our trades. So after six weeks at Morecambe I got posted to Yatesbury RAF station in Wiltshire.

Yatesbury was a proper RAF station, oh, a very posh station. You weren't allowed to walk across the parade ground. And somehow we were all convinced that they had invisible eyes watching us, even when it was dark. If you dared step on to it there was a volley from somebody: 'Get off the parade ground!' You had to go away round everywhere.

At Yatesbury you got tests for your eyesight, and you started your training for the job or trade you were to do in the WAAF. When I'd volunteered at Edinburgh I'd said yes to undergoing training for a new trade that was coming up. So that was arranged right from the outset. But it was all very hush-hush. We had a guard on where we were going down to do our training. So I knew I was going to be RDF – Radio Direction Finding. One of the tests that stuck in my mind was this thing that was going round and round, and there was as many different aircraft in the thing, and you had to say how many there were. You weren't to identify the aircraft, but you had to identify the number of them. It was so quick when it was going round and it was in various colours. But I didn't pass the tests. So that was the end of my attempt to work at RDF. I was so disappointed. But I decided I'd just go back to the trade that I'd been used to – shorthand and typing. So I was at Yatesbury a few months, I think, then I was sent to Gloucester to re-muster.

I was at Gloucester maybe about a month or five weeks. Documents and various things all had to get sorted out there. Anyway, I was re-mustered to work in administration as clerk GD – general duty, not as a clerk-shorthand writer. It meant I could be posted anywhere to do any clerical work. And that's when I got posted to Drem in East Lothian. At Drem I was in the admin section, typing out various things. Sometimes it might be an airman who'd been killed, and all his belongings had to be listed. I had to type out everything. That was quite a sad business.

When I arrived by train at the wee station at Drem I got taken down to the airfield. You could see the conglomeration of huts and the admin block, the offices. But there was nothing spectacular about it that I can remember. The airfield covered quite a large area, and of course the WAAFs were in one part of it. The cookhouse was away up the top at the other part.

Drem didn't feel to me to be exactly like the Air Force, because I could easily get home to Edinburgh from there. Up to then I'd been away at Bridgnorth, Morecambe, Yatesbury, and Gloucester. I hadn't asked to be sent to Drem. Whether being posted there was a sweetener because I'd signed on for four years, I don't know. But, as I say, Drem didn't feel like being on a proper RAF aerodrome, because we could walk up the road and get a train into Edinburgh – which we did. We got home most weekends. One matter that arose as a result (I'm not ashamed about it) was that once when they came round for kit inspection one of my undergarments was missing. Actually it was on my granny at home. Well, she was cold.

So were the huts at Drem, very cold. It was unbelievable. There was quite a few of us in my hut there. And outside there was a bin that they put the coal in for the fire in the hut. But you didn't all get coal at the same time, which meant you raided the bin of whoever had some. Well, our billet was so cold that we started putting the beds together, and sharing your blankets that way, which was all right. We must have got about three bed biscuits – sort of mattresses – each. Now it was at Drem that I met Lizbeth Weston from Newtongrange in Midlothian. Lizbeth and I seemed to hit it off together right away. Whereas I was in admin Lizbeth was in signals. Anyway, in our hut Lizbeth and I were together in this blanket-sharing. Well, I took ill once in the night. One of the girls had gone and reported it, and was told I should stay where I was till a medical officer could come to see me. Well, there was then a mad scramble. Everybody in our hut had to get their beds and put them back into single separated order. It was strictly forbidden to move them together as we'd done to keep warm. So I got taken away and put in sick quarters. But, oh, Lizbeth always helped me. We had to polish the side of your floor very, very much. Lizbeth was good at that, she was big and strong. When I was sick one night it was right over the bed where she'd just polished the floor. It might have strained our friendship very much, but she just laughed.

At Drem, wherever Dougan and Weston were we were always in trouble together. As I've said, the cookhouse was away at the top of the other part of the airfield from where we WAAFs were billeted. It was forbidden to take a shortcut from our billets to the cookhouse. In fact, there was a wire fence to prevent that. However, this winter morning it was very, very foggy. So Lizbeth and I decided to take a chance and reach the cookhouse more quickly. Well, we were creeping through this wire fence when a voice said: 'I might have guessed it: Dougan and Weston again!' This was the flight sergeant, waiting to catch anyone taking the shortcut. It was a woman flight sergeant; some of them were as bad as the men.

I remember a Blood Transfusion group came to Drem and they wanted volunteers to give blood. I volunteered, but they ended up having to take a pump to get the blood out of me, and I was told, 'In future, don't volunteer. You're more likely to be a recipient!' Because home in Edinburgh was so near I didn't feel homesick at Drem. But for all that I was so near home, I didn't get home for Christmas 1942. Lizbeth, too, was with me. The Christmas dinner at Drem that day was served by the officers. And it was a good meal, and it was good company. The previous Christmas, when I was at Yatesbury, was the first one that ah'd been away from home. The officers who served the dinner at Drem were men. If there was a woman officer at Drem I certainly didn't have very much to do with her. Anyway, it had been more or less arranged that the English WAAFs would get home at Christmas 1942, Lizbeth and me and the other Scots girls got Hogmanay.

Though German bombers had come up the Firth of Forth earlier in the war and Drem was only about four miles from the Forth, we didn't see any action at all in the 18 months or so I was there.[10] But I did experience bombing when I was on a weekend leave once in London. Though I can't remember the date – it was, I think, in 1942, when I was at Gloucester the first time – it was called the Great Fire. As I've said, I loved dancing, and that weekend I was actually dancing to Joe Loss's Band in Hammersmith Palais.[11] The Germans had been bombing London pretty badly at the time. Anyway, all the incendiaries were coming down. I was at the Palais with a girl friend, and we were dancing of course. I've tried to remember how it all came about. But I know that it was a tap on the shoulder. We were told all Service people were to go off the dance floor and go to the air raid shelters. My girl friend and I went outside but we got separated. And there I was, with the guns going and these incendiaries coming down. An ARP [Air Raid Precautions] guy came and said, 'You'll have to go into the shelter. You'll have to go into the shelter.' And he said something about a subway. I'm a bit claustrophobic, and I started saying, 'I'm not going there.' I didn't know what to do. But there was a family passing by and the woman said to the ARP man, 'We'll take her to our shelter.' So I spent the night with that family and other people in their shelter. We talked, they gave me a drink. A man down at the end of the shelter kept playing his mouth organ periodically; the children amused themselves; some of the women were knitting. Outside, all hell must have been breaking loose. When I came out the shelter the first thing that struck me was, oh, the smell – the smell of burning; and there was a pall of smoke. But my girl friend and I both managed to get back to where we were staying for the weekend. We were certainly quite glad to leave London and go back to our billets at Gloucester.

Well, as I've said, Lizbeth Weston was in signals at Drem. She was allowed to have someone to stay with her when she was on night duty, and that someone was me. When she went that morning to get the signals, she said: 'Oh, you'll never guess who's been posted!' I said, 'Me?' 'Yes,' she said. And the pair of us very nearly burst into tears. We'd got on very well together. Lizbeth was great.

I was then posted back to Gloucester. I felt terrible. I hated Gloucester. I went down there by train. In fact, they had to stop the train from Edinburgh at Drem to put me on it and take me down. I was on my own; I always seemed to be on my own on trains taking me from one posting to another. I'd moved from Edinburgh to Bridgnorth, Bridgnorth to Morecambe, Morecambe to Yatesbury, Yatesbury to Gloucester, Gloucester to Drem, and now Drem back to Gloucester again. Well, I passed six months at the very most that second time at Gloucester. It was certainly monotonous there. But round about Gloucester were camps of GIs [American servicemen], and they used to ask for WAAFs to go to their dances. And the covered wagon would come for us, and there would be a sergeant and a flight sergeant or two. They counted you as you went into the wagon. Then you went off to the dance. Well, we liked to go to the American dances, because we got half a chicken, and we had peanut butter and jelly sandwiches. And if you smoked there were plenty of cigarettes there. So it was good, and of course it was warm. The Americans made a fuss of us because they thought the WAAFs were terrific. This big guy from Texas kept telling me his mother 'would love a little Scottish daughter'. When we came out of there we were counted again as we got back into the truck. I remember once that one WAAF was a bit late in coming. We didn't leave till she arrived. When we got back to our camp we were counted again to make sure that we were all . . . that we hadnae nipped out again and gone back into the dance. So those dances were good and made being at Gloucester bearable. But I didn't keep well. I felt in Gloucester that I couldn't breathe right. I felt it was too low-lying. I just wisnae getting it. And I was ill quite a bit and was in sick bay. I think they got fed up popping me in and out of sick quarters. So eventually they said to me would I like a posting, and would I like to go back to Scotland? 'Oh,' I said, 'I would love it.' 'Well, name three aerodromes and we'll see if we can get a posting for you.' So I named Turnhouse at Edinburgh, Leuchars in Fife, and West Freugh near Stranraer. After a time they came to me and said, 'You're posted up to Scotland.' I said, 'Wonderful! Where?' They said, 'You're going to Tiree.' 'Tiree? Where in heaven's name is Tiree?!' I'd never heard of it.

They tried to reassure me: 'Now it's all right. Tiree is only a couple of hours away from Oban.' But they never told me the main thing about Tiree. From Gloucester by train to Oban proved to be some journey. The worst part of it, funnily enough, was when I came to Scotland, because I had to change trains at Stirling, and the train north from there stopped at all the wee stations. But I soon found the train seemed to have very few toilets. So if I needed the toilet I got out at one of those wee stations, went, and then got into a carriage at the front, and stayed there till I got to the next station. So invariably I was running this way and that way during the journey. When we arrived at Oban it was late. So they took me to a hotel right on the sea front at Oban and asked a WAAF to look after me. I got something to eat, got a bed, and was told I had to be down at the pier at six o'clock in the morning. I duly got an early breakfast, then this WAAF girl said to me, 'When you reach Tiree tell Jessie Dawson I was asking for her.' When I got to the pier I said to them, 'Where is Tiree?' 'Oh, it's an island.' Oh, God, an island! I looked at this boat. I don't like boats. I don't like the sea. When we got on this boat it was MacBrayne's, but it was a cattle boat.[12] I found there were aircrew aboard but I was the only WAAF. Then on came the cattle and the sheep, all on deck. Being of the female species, if I wanted the loo I had to hunt up the mate and see if I could use his toilet. And also I found the old captain wasn't at all happy about having Service people aboard. His main concern was the cattle and sheep.

By the time we got from Oban to Tobermory on Mull I was beginning to feel a bit queasy. The passage to Tobermory wasn't actually smooth, but it wasn't as rough as it was when we got further out. The aircrew guys on board were very good and told me, 'You'll be all right. You'll get a cup o' tea at Tobermory.' There was nothing, no refreshments, on the boat itself. When we got to Tobermory I could have wept. We couldn't get right into the pier, because there was another boat already there. So they put a plank across from our boat to the pier and they said to me, 'You'll be all right. Just hold on to the jacket of the fellow in front of you.' The one behind me gripped my jacket. And that's the way we got ashore. I got a nice cup of tea from the WVS [Women's Voluntary Service] woman there. And I very nearly asked her, 'Do you want another helper?'

Then back on board again – by the same method: holding on to each other as we crossed the plank. Well, it wasnae all that bad. But it was far too far for me, because, as I say, I don't like the sea and I don't like boats. Well, of course, soon after leaving Tobermory we were out on to the Atlantic. And we were fairly getting it, because she was a flat-bottomed boat and she was going this way and that way, rolling and pitching. Without exaggeration, I think the hankies of everybody on board were somewhere in the Atlantic with my insides, because I was over the side of the boat being sick all the time. Oh! It wis terrible. And it seemed a long voyage, certainly a long time to be seasick.

Then we came to the island of Coll. Again you got your eyes opened there, because the boat didn't go into Coll. It lay off, the locals rowed out to it, a cow was lowered into their rowing boat, and they took it back that way. Well, Coll is close to Tiree. So we got to Tiree. But I don't really remember landing at Tiree. I suppose I did land that first time, but I had to get helped. There was always an RAF ambulance came down from the airfield and waited there when anybody came off the boat. They knew what to expect. Then I got wheeched away in the ambulance to sick quarters. So for a couple of days I lay like a dog in sick quarters.

But things settled down and I went and sort of signed in. I asked, 'Is there a Jessie Dawson here?' They said, 'Why? Do you know her?' I explained the reason, and they said, 'Oh, well, we'll see if there's a billet in her hut for you.' In Yatesbury I'd been billeted in married quarters. On Tiree it was a Nissen hut, not wooden but corrugated, and right down near the beach. In the hut there was Jessie Dawson, a clerk GD [General Duties], Mac, a WAAF hairdresser, Marie, who was in the equipment section, and Kit, who was in catering. Mac's name was Laurie Mackie, but we called her Mac. They were great. So the five of us were together in this Nissen hut. It had a stove in the middle. And there was a wee toilet there.

It would be the autumn of 1943, I reckon maybe about September, I arrived on Tiree. I didn't really realise what was in front of me. But, believe me, you have never known what a gale's like unless you are on an island in the Atlantic – and then you know. It was RAF Coastal Command on Tiree, and it was Halifax bombers there. The number of WAAFs on the station would be about three dozen. Well, we five were Hut D5. There would only be at the very most six or seven WAAF billets, with five WAAFs in each hut. And there would be about 100 or 120 RAF men. The airmen were all away at the other end of the aerodrome. As well as aircrew and ground staff, there was the medical section, the hospital, with their two doctors, a dentist, and their order-lies. So there'd be a total on the station of about 150 RAF men and WAAF. I can't remember how many planes there were on the base.

I think our planes, as part of Coastal Command, would be out a lot on patrol on the Atlantic. I never heard of any German U-boats coming in close to Tiree. And it wasn't, I think, from us on Tiree that our bombers were going to bomb Germany. It was from down in England they were going. So I don't remember any of our planes at Tiree coming back badly damaged or not coming back at all. But there was a terrible tragedy there one day. Two Halifax bombers were involved in it. One was coming in to land, the other one was taking off. They hit nose to nose. Both crews – 16 men altogether – were burned to death. We just all heard the crash. And there was no hope of survivors. It was dreadful. And the smell. One of our WAAFs had married one of the aircrew. And she was actually expecting a baby. There was a funeral service in one of the big hangars used for planes. And that was a very, very hard time. And of course you knew all or most of the men killed in the crash.

When I'd arrived on Tiree I thought I was going to work in the admin section beside Jessie Dawson. But it turned out they wanted me to work in sick quarters, because they had a squadron whose senior medical officer was Squadron Leader Colin Brander, a great big fellow, who was a South African. He was in about his thirties. And there was also Flight Lieutenant Magner, who came from southern Ireland, and was very Irish, and there was Sergeant Walker and others. So I was the typist there. Well, I really enjoyed it. It was great. Sqn Ldr Brander mustn't have liked my name, because he christened me Gloria. Why, I've no idea. I used to think to myself, 'What a nerve!' But I never got called anything but Gloria all the time I was there. He'd be sitting for sick quarters – sick parade, you know. I would be in the office, and there would be this yell, because he never just spoke: 'GLORIA!', for me to come down the corridor. And I'd go along, thinking to myself, 'They'll all be thinking a nice willowy blonde will be coming through the door, but it's only me,' you know, wee Tutti Frutti. Oh, Sqn Ldr Brander was great. He was a very good medical officer. But there was one thing he could never remember. Occasionally, there was an emergency – we called it a mayday signal – when a plane was coming back in from a patrol. We had what was called a perimeter and we had an outside perimeter. One was named Oxford and one was Cambridge. So this beautiful sweet yell used to come down from him: 'GLORIA! WHAT THE HELL IS OXFORD?' And I remember that sometimes Sqn Ldr Brander used to be called out to treat civilians on Tiree, if there wasn't any medical person there available. And Flt Lt Magner had got the Oak Leaf for actually going out and trying to save somebody in an aircraft that had crashed.[13]

So I liked the work on Tiree. But it was still a bother to go up to the cookhouse in the morning for breakfast. However, Henry, who was the cook for sick quarters, used to say to me, 'Now never mind. I'll have your breakfast ready here when you come up.' So I had a wee extra ten minutes. But coming into the winter the gales set in. And the message came over the tannoy: 'All WAAFs to stay put', until two RAF men came down to us with food. Well, on Tiree, which was 11 miles long and three miles broad, there wasnae a tree. There just wasn't. And the grass was that stringy. But the island had beautiful golden sandy beaches. Somebody called it The Riviera of the North.

We were plagued, however, with earwigs. They were said to come from the beaches. Our huts were very close to the beach. Earwigs must have been endemic on Tiree. They used to drop from the ceiling. They were in your blankets. You used to be cutting them from inside your pyjamas. Everything around was sprayed, everything was done to get rid of them. But we still got them coming in. Some of the WAAFs were in a bit of a state perhaps about them, and at the beginning you could hear an odd scream or two if they discovered them. The earwigs were-nae very pleasant but, oh, you gradually got used to them, and you got over them.

As well as being very windy on Tiree, oh, it was cold in the winter. In our hut Mac, the WAAF hairdresser, would go and ask for a shov-elful of hot coal from the fellow who stoked the boilers for the fires and also for her work, as she needed constant hot water. And she would put the shovelful in our hut stove. So Mac kept the hut stove going, which helped all five of us in it to get on very well together and it was a happy atmosphere.

Looking back now I smile when I think how the islanders had previously had the run of Tiree for their cattle. Before the war they had never been bothered with bombers coming down on to runways. When their cattle were wandering on to our runways our wing commander got rather annoyed. He told the farmers or crofters that if they didn't watch them their cattle would be impounded and taken away from them. So he had a corral built and he impounded the cattle concerned. And it was the RAF Regiment that used to guard the corral.[14] The WAAFs used to always call them Cowboy Joe when they were passing by. I don't think the men liked it when the girls sang the popular song of the day with that title.

As time went on, a recreation hall was built for the WAAFs and RAF men on Tiree. It was to be opened with a dance. We had had dancin' before this, but this was a proper hall we were getting. And the islanders were being invited to come and join the celebration. The Queen Bee – our WAAF officer – had a little quiet word in our shell-like ears not to refuse any invitations from the islanders if they wanted to come and dance. Well, it was all right in the first half of the evening, because it was our own Air Force band that was playing. We were enjoying the ball, it was great. But then the islanders announced that for the second half they would provide the music. And that was the bagpipes. I'll tell you this: it was many a long day before ever again I would dance Strip the Willow, 'cause my feet never touched the ground. The reason for that was that the islanders were big and I was wee. And when they were swinging me round my feet I was airborne! And I wouldnae like tae tell you what the queue for the ladies' toilet was like. But, oh, it was great. These were great nights we had on Tiree.

When I was posted to Tiree I was supposed to be there for only 10 months. But toward the end of that posting I volunteered to stay for another 10 months. They asked me if I was sure. And I said yes, because I was happy up there. So I actually stayed for two postings, 20 months altogether, on the island. In all that time I had, I think, three home leaves. But they weren't as regular as they would have been on the mainland. The weather conditions had a lot to do with that. I remember one occasion when I was to be going on leave, freezing on the pier on Tiree while waiting for MacBrayne's boat to come in. The waves, however, were also coming in, and you'd all to fly for your life because you feared they were going to crash down on you. The boat hit the pier and took off again. It tried a second time, but again failed to berth. So it just went away then. One time, I think, it was seven or eight months before I actually got home.

On two occasions, I think, I went by sea and once by air. Sqn Ldr Brander got so tired of me always getting put in sick bay each time I arrived on Tiree, that on one occasion when I was going on leave he came and asked me if I would agree to fly. I was quite brave, and said yes. So they took me down to the airfield next morning. And it was a Halifax bomber. I got taken up through the belly of the plane and put on a Mae West.[15] I was in Prestwick in about an hour and 15 minutes – terrific when you think of the time and troubles the sea journey involved. One point about that flight to Prestwick was that, whereas we WAAFs wore trousers on Tiree, which made sense, the minute we landed at Prestwick I had to be taken to the ladies' room to change back into my skirt. Otherwise RAF police would have charged me for being improperly dressed. Oh, very strict, very strict. You weren't allowed in the WAAF to wear trousers unless you were on an island.

Mention of the sick bay reminds me that when I was on Tiree I got dysentery. I don't know what the cause of the dysentery was. But it was thought it was something to do with meat. The camp meals were very good. There was a medical orderly who brought them to the patients.

Then in sick quarters, where I worked, Luigi, an Italian prisoner of war, also worked. There were no British army personnel on Tiree, but we had Italian and German prisoners of war there. Luigi was a nice wee quiet fellow. He had to do the fires and polish the floors and everything. He used to put my fire on first, so it was nice and warm working there. In return, as I used to save apples I got, I would give Luigi an apple. He and I got talking, and he showed me this locket containing a photo of a lovely lady and three infants. By this time Luigi was able to speak broken English, so I asked him: 'Their mama, your wife?' He said no, but that he was the father of the three childen. He added: 'If three bambini still when I go home I marry her. If four – no.'

Before I left Tiree we got an RAF cinema, and islanders used also to come to it. As I've said Sqn Ldr Brander was sometimes called out as a medical officer to treat islanders who were unwell. He took me with him once when there had been a death. I think an RAF man, not belonging to us, had married an island girl but had fallen to his death on the rocks. So his burial was to take place. Colin Brander took me with him to see how the widow was doing. The mourners were all sitting with their shawls on their heads and doing a sort of Gaelic chant. It didn't stop unless you left the room. If you left the room it quietened down but started again when you came back in. It was a wake. So I think relations between the islanders and the RAF were very good eventually. Because they realised that they really got the benefit of a lot of the services that we could give them – medical services, and they maybe got helped by our engineers with practical things. I don't really know if the islanders then still had paraffin lamps or whether they might have had generators.

Well, after the war ended, I got married in October 1945 to Jackie Inglis. We had known each other in Edinburgh since before the war, when we were still children or young teenagers. My girlfriend at school was Jackie's cousin. Jackie was away, oh, all through the war. Because he was a dental technician he was transferred from the tanks to the Dental Corps. He was with them in North Africa and Italy. He had to build up again the faces of badly wounded soldiers. When Jackie came home from Italy to marry me in 1945 he hadn't been home for four years. So he had 28 days' leave then; I had seven days. But I sent a telegram to the RAF or WAAF authorities, saying I was getting married, and they gave me another seven days' leave. Once I was married I was posted down to RAF Benson in Oxfordshire. I never went back to Tiree, where by then my tour of duty was up. They sent all my things down from there to Benson. Jackie went with me down to Benson, but they wouldn't let him in and he had to stand outside the gates. So we booked into a hotel for bed and breakfast. Then Jackie got four more days' leave, and so did I. After that, Jackie went back overseas to his unit for nine or ten months, and then he finally came home. I was at Benson for only a couple of months or so and then I got demobbed in January 1946.

It was only at the end of 1945 or the beginning of 1946 – after the war had finished – that you were able to resign from the WAAF. Jackie had already told me to resign and go out and try and get a house for us. Before then the only reason you could get out of the WAAF was if you were pregnant. And that did happen, oh, it did happen. When girls in that situation got to a certain stage they got automatically discharged. I don't remember any case like that on Tiree. But down in Gloucester, when I was waiting to be sent up to Drem, there was two WAAFs in there waiting to be discharged that were pregnant but not married. I've never heard of any girl in that situation being humiliated by having her name put up on the board, and on Tiree there was never anything like that. The two WAAFs at Gloucester were the only ones I ever saw that were being discharged, never in any of the other stations where I served.

Looking back on my four and a half years in the WAAF, from August 1941 until January 1946, I think, being very old-fashioned, it taught me the meaning of friendship and it made me more independent. I've a lot to thank the WAAF for, because it was a case of sink or swim. You knew nobody at first and you had to make your own way. And when you were down in England you got very much involved in the war, you know, the bombing. And also I think it taught us tolerance, because you had to live and mix with people that in everyday life in peacetime maybe you wouldn't have looked at twice.

Not one of the Servicewomen or Servicemen at the stations I was on did anything that I ever had any occasion to be distressed by. There wasn't anything like that. I found – maybe more so, being on an island as Tiree was – they were all very helpful and nice. It was like a big family, although of course there was rules and regulations. And I think during the war that's what counted, being there for someone and some-one being there for you.

I never suffered from homesickness. The trouble with me was I've always had a very enquiring mind, anxious to learn. I think that's what my life in the WAAF was, a learning experience. I moved around a lot – at eight or nine different stations, meeting different people from different parts of the country. Well, in our hut on Tiree Jessie Dawson was from Glasgow, Kit was from Sunderland, Mac from Edinburgh, Marie East Kilbride.

What used sometimes to make me a bit angry was the attitude, not to me personally, of some people – maybe civilians travelling on the trains – when you could almost see going through the heads: 'Oh, WAAF – Services, one of those, one of those,' you know, and they looked at you.

Then there are so many tales about Services girls going off the rails. Maybe that did happen, but not to the extent it was publicised. I heard the ATS in the early part of the war had a bad reputation.[16] Anyway, I never had any cause to regret volunteering into the WAAF. My friend who was a flight mechanic and I have both said we would go through it again. I found companionship and friendship that's lasted me ever since.

Isa Dougan (Mrs Isabella Inglis) died on 3 September 2009.

Nessie Lawrie

Oh, my wartime in the Women's Auxiliary Air Force – that was the happiest four and a half years in my life.

I was born on the 12th of November 1920 in the North Wynd, Dalkeith. My dad was a miner, and apart from that he had a part-time job Friday, Saturday, and Sunday in a fish and chip shop. He was the nicest wee man you could ever meet. Everybody liked my daddy. Andrew was his name, but he couldn't say his name at first of course. He called himself Bunny, so he was known as Bunny Lawrie all his life. He was born in Dalkeith on the 26th of January 1895. He went into the coal pits as soon as he left school, and he was a miner all his working life. He worked in the Woolmet and the Smeaton colliery and, I think, in Polton at Bonnyrigg. I remember before the war the miners worked an 11-day fortnight; so my dad didnae work on each alternate Saturday. He was 72 when he died in June 1967.

My grandfather David Lawrie belonged to Edinburgh but he came out to work in Dalkeith in the Cross Keys Hotel, which in these days was *the* hotel in Dalkeith. The Duke of Buccleuch used to come up from Dalkeith Palace to the hotel in his horse-drawn carriage, book a room for the night, and gamble. Grandfather Lawrie, who began, I think, as a barman, must have prospered, because he went with his sons to horse races at Lanark and elsewhere. He was in the throes of taking over an hotel himself when he collapsed and died. I remember once when I came home on leave from the WAAF, Mr Bee, a plumber in Dalkeith, said to me: 'If your grandfather had kept all the tips he got he would have been a rich man.' It seems grandfather used to buy all his friends drinks. I don't really remember grandfather Lawrie: I was only three when he died. All I can remember about him is going through Robertson's Close in Dalkeith, where there was an outside stair, and my mother said to me, 'Oh, there's your grandfather on the top of the stairs there.' And I saw this stout man with a white, white shirt that was gleaming.

My granny Lawrie was born in the south of England, but her father came up to Edinburgh and opened the Waterloo Hotel there. But he lost it through a crooked lawyer, and that was when they moved out to Dalkeith, where my grandparents met. Granny Lawrie died in 1953, when she was in her 90th year.

I had no brothers, but I had my sister Ella, 12 years younger than me. When Ella was born I felt pushed into the background by my other granny and her family, who lived at Newtongrange, a couple or so miles from Dalkeith. But granny Lawrie and my aunties on my dad's side never made any difference to me. I used to go to them a lot. I got on well with Ella, and when we were older we used to go out dancing and everywhere.

I lived until I was 15 or 16 in the North Wynd, Dalkeith. There had been a church and a manse there, but they'd been made into flats or houses. Across from there was a building, a slaughterhouse, where they used to kill cattle. Well, there were a lot of rats and they used to drink the blood from the slaughtered cattle. Eventually, when I was two years old, we moved up to live near the top of the North Wynd. And that house is still standing. So I grew up with animals all round me. Near us lived Mr Aitken, who had a coal business and kept two horses who used to look out through a broken window. Then the wee brother of one of my friends who lived next door to us was knocked down by a sheep coming up the North Wynd. And I was terrified when I saw all these cattle going to the slaughterhouse.

The house where I grew up was just one big room with a bed recess, and a little boxroom with a double bed, a chair, and my daddy's bicycle when he cycled to the mines. I was in the little boxroom, in the double bed. Then after my sister Ella was born she and I were in the boxroom. I remember once when my mother's eldest brother, who normally stayed with his uncles and aunts at Lugton, a village or suburb of Dalkeith, fell out with them. So he came down to us and he got my double bed. So I had to sleep at the bottom of my mother and dad's bed. Oh, overcrowding was common in those days. And I remember the woman next door to us had four of a family but she had only one room. But they were happy times in North Wynd, and everybody was friendly. Never ever did you go out and in one another's houses. But if anything was needed – neighbours were there.

In that house in the North Wynd we had gas lighting. Then on the top of the stair we had a sink that was shared between two families. That's where we used to get water: there was no sink within the house. So every day ma mother had to go out on to the landing with a kettle or pot and fill them up for my daddy coming in for his bath. I remember the big pot – a black one like that that she made the soup in. And she would boil the water in that for my daddy's bath. It took several boilings to fill the bath. While my daddy, back home each day from the coal pit, was being bathed by my mother, I used to have to go out on to the landing, or the stairhied, as we used to call it in these days. Our bath was a tin bath, just put in front of the fire. But eventually, before the war, across at the Woolmet coalpit where he was then workin', they got pithead baths installed. So that made it easier. Then I remember as a wee girl I used to stand at the top of the North Wynd with Agnes Letton, who lived in a house in the High Street that looked down the North Wynd. Agnes would watch for her dad, also a miner, coming off the bus, and I would watch for my dad coming on his bike. When I saw him I ran down and got a hurl up to our house on the crossbar of his bike. Sadly, Agnes Letton's dad was killed at the Lady Victoria colliery at Newtongrange when he was quite young.

My mother did her cooking on a range. And we had an oven that was heated with the fire. She didn't have a wee water tank at the side of the range, and she didn't have a gas cooker or a gas ring. Oh, what a life women had then! As for the washing, well, ma granny – ma mother's mother – lived at Newtongrange, in the last house in Ninth Street. She had nine of a family. Ma mother was the second eldest. So she used to go up to Newtongrange with her washing and help my granny with hers. Granny had five beds, and that was a lot of washing. When my mother went to Newtongrange with the washing on a Tuesday it was put in the bottom of a pram. And durin' school holidays I had to walk with the pram to Newtongrange and, pushing the pram up where the cowp and redd or pit waste was, the sweat was pouring down me. But as a wee girl I only did it about three times, because I think my granny Lawrie put her foot down.

At the North Wynd we had a toilet at the bottom of the stair, and four families shared it. It was a flush toilet. It had a wooden seat. And when I was only 11 year old my mother made me scrub the top of it – and you'd to scrub! The families that used that toilet took it in turn to clean it. So I only had to scrub it once every four weeks. But every other week I scrubbed down the stair and the landing.

As I say, I lived in the North Wynd until I was 15 or 16 then, in 1936, we moved to a council house in Newmills Terrace in the Woodburn area of Dalkeith. We were the first tenants in that house.

* * *

I never ever got away for a holiday with my daddy and my mother when I was a wee girl. My dad had only one week's holiday, in July. And it wasnae paid holiday, it was idle time. I spent all my summer holidays at my granny's in Newtongrange: seven weeks in the summer, a fortnight at Christmas and at Easter. I played there with the girl next door to my granny's. My Newtongrange granny's two cousins put up the first three caravans at Port Seton in East Lothian. They looked right over on to the sea there. It was really beautiful. Uncle Bill had a beautiful caravan, with even a baby organ in it. My granny and grandfather didn't take me with them to Port Seton. They got a taxi down and went on their own. I used to stand at the top of the North Wynd, the taxi would stop, and my grandfather would give me 6d [2½p]. That was a lot of money in these days. It was only a ha'penny [0.5p] for a macaroon bar, and a ha'penny for a Highland Cream Toffee. So you could get a lot with 6d. But my mother would take me down to Port Seton on a Sunday and a Tuesday during the summer holidays. We took the bus from Dalkeith into Edinburgh and then the tram from there to Port Seton. We always had a meal down there. On a Tuesday the fishwife used to come with her creel on her back to my granny. But from the age of 12, when my sister Ella was born, I was, as I've said, pushed into the background by my Newtongrange grandmother and her family. I didn't get back to Newtongrange for my holidays. I had to stay at home and take Ella out in her pram.

I had started at Dalkeith High School primary at the age of five in 1925. I quite liked school – well, I mean, you have to go and that's it. But I liked geography, maths, and art. I was always first in these three subjects. I was quite good at drawing and painting. I hated history – but I love it now. In my class at primary there would be about 30 or 40 pupils. Dalkeith had the Burgh and the Catholic school as well. So at the High School primary the classes weren't as big as I believe they were in these days in some other primary schools. So I passed the Qualifying exam when I was 11 or 12, and carried on at the High School, because primary and secondary were both there. In the secondary we got domestic science, history, arithmetic, geography, science, art, and of course English. We got sewing but not shorthand and typing – that would have been the commercial course. I wasn't interested in taking languages. I quite liked the secondary and got on not bad. Anyway, I left school at Christmas 1934 when I was 14.

When ah wis at school ah'd taught myself to dance. In the North Wynd there was only one lady had a wireless. And I could hear it. When there was nobody in our house ah used tae dance round the table by myself. But ah didn't go to the dancing until ah wis 18. Well, ma parents didnae have the money for that anyway. And then – ah wis so busy doing things in the house – as a young girl ah wis never out, except ah maybe got to the pictures once or twice a week, and that was it. Before the war, the dancing in Dalkeith was in the Masonic Hall and the Corn Exchange. The Corn Exchange was a big place, two partitions divided it, and the ballroom was at the back. At the front you could get a cup of tea and things like that. But, oh, ah loved dancing.

And as a young girl ah went to the Brownies in the Corn Exchange. Ah wis a Pixie in the Brownies, like head o' the pack. And ah went to Sunday School every Sunday from I was three years of age. When ma sister Ella was three ah took her as well. Ma parents weren't churchgoers, though ma dad – he had a bad chest and everything – always went to communion. As a girl ah didn't have a bike, and I wasn't a reader. Ma mother would say, 'Put the book down', and she would give me some work to do in the house. And at night ma mother would come through and say, 'Put that light out. You're wastin' electricity. And get that book down.' So you know what ah did? Ah got a torch for readin' under the blankets. Well, ma mother must have been in ma drawer and seen the torch. She come in this night and says, 'You've got a torch underneath these bedclothes. Get it out and get to sleep.' So I couldnae read at home. So I didn't start to read until ah left the house and got ma own house in, I think, 1968, long after the war. And I didn't join the library until I retired about 1980.

As a girl at school I wanted to become a hairdresser. Bunty Dunn, a girl I used to play with, and whose father had a bus that used to run between Dalkeith and Portobello (that's how we got to Portobello beach for the day) knew I wanted to be a hairdresser. Her father had got her a hairdresser's shop when she was 14. So one night early in 1935 when I had just left school, Bunty said to me: 'Oh, Nessie, my mum says you can come and work in our shop.' So I went home and said to my mother, 'I've got a job. I'm going to be a hairdresser in Bunty's shop, and I'm getting 2s 6d [12½p] a week.' In these days you had to pay to learn to be a hairdresser. But my mother wouldnae let me go: she wanted more money. I was heartbroken.

Well, I didn't have a job for two or three months. Then my granny Lawrie sent me to domestic service in Edinburgh. Oh, gee! I didn't want to go. I still wanted to get a job as a hairdresser, but my mother wouldn't let me. So granny Lawrie got this young girl to take me into a place, a guest house in Palmerston Place, at the west end in Edinburgh. And they gave me a job there as both kitchen maid and scullery maid. I lived in, and had a wee tiny room in the area at the back of the house. There was just space in it for a bed and a wee sideboard thing. But I got home on a Tuesday afternoon and every other Sunday. There wis 14 resident guests. There was three other girls worked there. Two were housemaids and the other one did the dining room. They all had a room to the front in the area. The woman in charge was like a lady cook. She was a woman on her own. She had her meals upstairs, where she had a suite of rooms. I can't remember her name. The four of us servants had our meals downstairs. The 14 permanent guests also had their meals upstairs. They all had their own room, no sharing. Oh, it was a posh boarding house.

Well, I was up at half past five in the morning and started work at six o'clock. I had to light this huge range in the kitchen. So I was working from six o'clock in the morning. The four of us girls were supposed to sit down and get 20 minutes for our breakfast. But there was no wee break after that for a cup o' tea. However, I did manage to eat my breakfast and my lunch and my supper at night. Then for me it was on until 10 o'clock some nights. I had all these dishes to wash after breakfast, lunch, and the main meal at night. Every morning, once I'd

washed the breakfast dishes, I started to do the vegetables for lunch.
That wis a big job, for they a' came back for their lunch. The residents
had a three-course meal in the evening about 7 o'clock. And I also had
some sweeping up, mopping up, and dusting to do at night before I
finished. I was just at it all the time. Sally Jamieson, one of the housemaids, about two years older than me, used to help me sometimes with
the dishes.

One of the boarders was a Mr Faust – or a name like that. He'd
maybe be then in his forties or fifties. He had a club for men and
women in Princes Street, just along from Palmerston Place. It was one
of these clubs where men could pick up women. And one night Mr
Faust took the three other guest house girls – I was too young – along
to his club. Oh, it had a certain reputation! That wee policeman
Merrilees once dressed up as a woman with a pram and sat across the
street from the club, watching what was going on. The club had four
lovely windows and, even years later, every time I passed there I'd look
up at the windows and think of that club![1]

I remember one night Sally Jamieson helped me do the dishes so as
we could go together to the cinema. And as I had almost no money she
lent me 6d [2½p]. I'll explain in a minute why ah never repaid that 6d
to Sally. If I had said to my mother that I had borrowed 6d, ma mother
would have leathered me, she really would.

Well, as a young lassie of 14 ah didn't have much leisure. After a
hard day's work at the guest house, from six in the mornin' till 10 at
night, ah sort of dropped exhausted intae bed. Of course, ah got a half
day off on a Tuesday from about one o'clock, and got home after lunchtime. Ah went home then every week. But I had to be back at the guest
house by 10 o'clock that night. Oh, I wasn't happy in that job. But I
think with the other girls being there I never ever cried. I was there for
six weeks.

I can't remember what the pay was but, oh, it wasn't very much – a
few shillings a week, I think. Of course I had all my food there and
lived in, so I didn't get much pay. At the end of the first week the
woman in charge said to me, 'Now I won't give you your week's wages.
You'll get them with your month's wages at the end of the full month.'
So I was paid monthly. Toward the end of the full month my mother
told me to hand in my notice. So on the Sunday I gave a week's notice.
'Right,' the woman in charge says to me, 'I'll give you all your wages

when you leave.' However, when I went home on my half day on the Tuesday and told my mother, she said: 'Well, you tell her you want all your wages now, because I need the money.' My mother also told me that I was to run away from the job at Palmerston Place the next morning. Anyway, I duly got my wages. So that night I packed my case, got up in the morning at five o'clock, went outside to the toilet, come back, got dressed, lifted my case, tiptoed through the door, up the area steps, tiptoed along Palmerston Place, then took to my heels and got a bus along to Waverley Bridge, where in these days buses for Dalkeith started. While I was waiting there for the bus two policemen came along. I thought, 'Oh, they've come to take me back.' But they just looked at me, smiled, and turned the corner. When the bus arrived and the conductor came for my fare, he asked me: 'Where have you been so early this mornin'? Up Arthur's Seat, washin' your face in the May dew?' So it was on the 1st of May 1935 that I ran away from the Palmerston Place guest house.[2] I must have started there some time in the March. And to this day it's in my mind that I owe that 6d to Sally Jamieson, because it was the night before I ran away that she and I went to the cinema.

Well, I was unemployed for a couple of months. It was still hairdressing that I wanted to do. But then in July 1935 I got a job in the Dalkeith Hosiery. And I loved the hosiery, I loved it. Mr Dunnett owned the hosiery. It was at the bottom of Dalkeith High Street, on the road to Musselburgh. The painted white building there now used to be the offices, and the hosiery itself was behind that, and that was another part of it behind what is now a garage. It was a hosiery mill that made ladies' sweaters and cardigans, but nothing for men. It was quite a small mill, with about 20 workers. It wis almost all women workers. There was one man that was the mechanic for mending the machines. And Mr Dunnett, the owner of the hosiery, was in the office all the time. He was a nice man. He used to smoke cigars in the office and the cigar ends were rolling about the floor! The most recent worker employed had to sweep up Mr Dunnett's office. I had to do that job when I started. Then Mr Cook from Edinburgh was the manager under Mr Dunnett.

When I started I got 10 shillings [50p] a week, and I got a shilling [5p] of that as my pocket money. Oh, that was a big improvement on what I'd got at the Palmerston Place guest house. You started at the hosiery at eight o'clock, with an hour for your lunch from 12.30 to 1.30, and we finished at five o'clock. We had a 10 minutes' break in the morning and the afternoon, but it usually lasted about 15 or 20 minutes! The work was Monday to Friday, then 8am till 12 o'clock on Saturday. The year after I began at the hosiery we moved house from the North Wynd to the council house in Newmills Terrace in Woodburn. Anyway, I could walk home from the hosiery at lunchtime in 10 minutes. Two of my friends at the hosiery mill used to walk to it from home at Newtongrange and walk back there at night – six miles a day. They couldn't get home for their lunch, they had it in the hosiery. There was a wee place for that there, and they used to bring sandwiches with them.

At my lunchtime every day I'd come home to Newmills Terrace from the hosiery and do all my mother's housework and everything. There was three jobs she used to give me to do: either clean the outside of the two windows, bedroom and sitting room, or do the vestibule, scrub the step at the door, and scrub the two steps at the front. They used to shine! On a Thursday I did the two bedrooms, the bathroom, and the lobby. And on a Friday, when my mother did the washing, I had to do the living room and scrub the kitchenette and all that! I did all her work for her. My mother wasn't disabled in any way. It was just that she saw me as the elder daughter as her assistant.

Then the Playhouse Cinema in Dalkeith opened in December 1938, with Deanna Durbin in the film *One Hundred Men and a Girl*.[3] My friend Winnie, that later joined the WRNS, worked in the Playhouse. Winnie came to me and says, 'Nessie, would you like a job in the Playhouse in the evenings and on Saturday afternoons? You'd get 12s 6d a week.' My mother said, 'The very thing. And you can start a bank book.' By this time my wage at the hosiery was 28s 6d [c. £1.42] a week. Three weeks later you know what my mother did? She gave me 2s 6d [12½p] pocket money, and she says, 'With the 12s 6d from the picture house you can keep yourself.' So from then, when I was turned 19, my mother never so much as bought me a handkie. And I had 15s [75p] a week to live on. Certainly, I didn't have to pay at the pictures: I saw them at the Playhouse for nothing! But for clothes and all the bits and pieces and going to the dancing – oh, I enjoyed dancing and was a ballroom dancer – and things like that . . . Of course, my mother provided my food for the 26s [£1.30] I gave her from my hosiery wages.

Anyway, when I finished at the hosiery at five o'clock I used to hurry home, have my meal, and be back down at the Playhouse picture house for a quarter to six. Oh, I managed it! But there was one thing that helped: my mother always had my meal ready on the table. So I had 25 minutes to eat it, do the dishes – sometimes my dad used to do them – and walk down in 10 minutes to the Playhouse. So I worked part-time as an usherette at the Playhouse from Christmas 1939 until I joined the WAAF almost two years later. But I didn't have an easy time as a girl. My mother was a wee bit hard on me.

Well, I worked at the hosiery for six years. I did everything. I did invisible mending, overlock – joining seams and the arms, putting V-necks on everything, and I was a cutter, sewing machinist, button hole machinist, overlooker, and examiner. In fact, I turned down two offers of forewomen's jobs. Then, after the war came, a lot of the girls in the hosiery were called up, and because of war conditions and the lack of demand the mill closed altogether.

* * *

Ah remember the declaration of the war. It was a Sunday morning and we all went outside. And when we turned round, ma wee sister Ella, she was only six, was standing with her gas mask on. And there was a plane going over, and the lodger with Mrs Purves across the road shouts, 'That's a German plane! Get in out o' there!' 'Don't be stupid,' ah says, 'they can't come from Germany in 10 minutes.' But he had the women a' frightened.[4]

Later on, when the first German plane was brought down, ma mother wis at our back door. She saw searchlights crossin' and recrossin' and then they shone on the plane. Ah wis in ma bedroom wi' Ella and ah could hear a neighbour outside shoutin', 'Come on! Shoot the b******! Shoot the b******!' Ella says, 'Oh, don't leave me, sister. Ah'm terrified.' So ah didn't see the plane brought down, but ma mother did.[5]

Ah'd been taken by surprise when the war came. But, ah mean, ah wasn't a political person, and we didn't have television then. If you'd had television and was lookin' at things you're lookin' at now . . . Oh, we had the wireless but, as ah say, ah wis taken by surprise by the outbreak o' the war.

Anyway, ah joined up in the WAAFs on the 28th of August 1941. I was 20, then 21 in the November. I asked to go into the WAAFs. I liked the uniform! I liked blue. It wasn't that ah'd been in the Girls Air

Training Corps or had any relatives in the RAF.[6] No, it was the uniform, I thought it was the nicest. The WRNS had nice hats, but I preferred the WAAFs.

Of course, we had to go to the buroo – the Labour Exchange – here in Dalkeith first, to register. After that we went into the Assembly Rooms in George Street, Edinburgh. We got a medical there, and they asked all your details and things like that. When we came out the Assembly Rooms, Maisie Davidson, another Dalkeith girl, and me went into the bakers down Hanover Street and brought home strawberry tarts!

So there wis four of us left Dalkeith in August 1941 to join the WAAFs at Bridgnorth in Shropshire. I knew the other three girls, one of them wis Maisie. We went down by train from the Waverley station in Edinburgh, via Carlisle and Preston, then changed at Wolverhampton for Bridgnorth. Bridgnorth was just where they took the WAAFs for giving out their uniforms and issues from the store, and being taught how tae march and everything – square-bashin'. Ah wis at Bridgnorth three weeks.

It was quite a big camp, with maybe about 300 or 400 girls there. There was lots of billets and a big square. I was in a long wooden hut that had a stove in the middle. There was about 30 girls in each hut, in single beds – no double bunks. It wis a new experience for me. I'd never lived in a dormitory with other girls before. But I quite liked it, I really did. We had inoculations there, and were told to keep our arms goin'. But this girl didn't do that. She ended up in bed and was as white as a ghost. I went to the corporal in charge of our hut and told her about this girl. She ended up in hospital, but I don't know what happened to her after that.

But to begin with, ah wis really homesick at Bridgnorth. One night when we were goin' to the camp cinema ah said tae Maisie, that had come from Dalkeith with me, 'Oh, Maisie, ah'm goin' hame. Ah'm goin' tae jump that dyke.' One of the girls, an English girl, says, 'What's a dyke?' 'A wall, of course,' said Maisie. But, ah mean, ah wis only 20 and ah'd never been away from home before.

At the end of the three weeks at Bridgnorth you got told the work or trade you were to be doin' in the WAAF. And of course wi' me bein' a machinist, I was to be an aero fabric worker. Well, then it came to our postings. We were all assembled in this room and they called out our names and gave us our postings. My name was called out with another three girls. One of them, Greta, was very good-looking, with fair hair. Another one, Agnes, had dark hair in an Eton crop. Well, if you went into the Services and you had you-know-what in your hair, they cut it into an Eton crop. Ah whispered to Greta, 'That girl must have something in her head: she's got the Eton crop.' 'That's my sister,' said Greta. Oh, I nearly died! But Greta and I became great friends, and I was Greta's bridesmaid when she got married to a Canadian in 1943, and we've kept in touch since. Anyway, I was posted tae Digby RAF station near Sleaford in Lincolnshire.

Of the three girls that had come to Bridgnorth from Dalkeith with me, Maisie Davidson and Jessie Hercus both went into the parachute-balloon things. But the other girl, ah don't know what she did and now ah can't remember her name or where she went. But Maisie, Jessie and I travelled together from Bridgnorth up to Birmingham station. Ah had ma kit bag and everything. Maisie wis on the other platform and ah'm callin' over tae her, 'Remember, Maisie, and write tae me. Don't forget.' It wis awful. Ah wis half-cryin'. We'd been in the WAAF only three weeks and already ah wis losin' ma three friends from Dalkeith. Ah never really saw any o' them again durin' the war. But when ah got to Digby ah wis put into ma billet and I was fine after that.

The billets at Digby, oh, they had been married quarters. There wis several houses right along once you went through the main gate. I was in the last house. It wis right across from the guardroom. In our house there was a small room upstairs with two WAAFs in it. Then there was a room to the front with three of us in it: myself, Nan, and Dorothy. Downstairs there was another three girls. The kitchen, the bath, and the toilet were also downstairs. So these were really very agreeable quarters. We certainly had more privacy there than at Bridgnorth, where 30 girls had shared each hut. And at Digby we were all so friendly and, ah mean, the laughs we got.

There wis four of us WAAFs worked in the fabric-working shop at Digby: Greta, her sister Agnes and I, and another girl who must have come not from Bridgnorth but from another camp near Cheltenham. But after about nine months Agnes was posted away from Digby. The fabric-working shop was actually inside the engine shop, where they brought in the engines to be repaired. So we four WAAFs were in a wee section there of our own, with a canvas screen separating us from the others. It was Spitfire fighters that we worked on mostly. Part of the Spitfire's rudder was a frame covered with fabric. Then wi' the ailerons at the back of the wings, you had to put your fabric on and sew it, using a special stitch. It was a very strong fabric – pure unbleached Irish linen. It was really a metal frame that was covered with fabric. And then we put on three coats of red dope, which tightened the fabric like a drum. Then we put on a camouflage dope, using a spray gun. So we had to wear a mask and also drink a pint of milk each day. Then we also made wind-sockets and covers for the guns. So we did lots of different tasks. It was really interesting. Ah thoroughly enjoyed it. And of course, having worked in Dalkeith Hosiery, I had experience – with sewing machines as well. So ah felt the RAF had paid attention to ma experience in work before ah joined it. So that was the work ah did in the WAAF at Digby, right to the end of the war.

We were paid every fortnight: 2s 6d [12½p] a day (17s 6d [87½p] per week). And you got your food and your uniform. I made an allotment – 7s [35p] – to my mother. So ah had 10s 6d [52½p] to myself, and ah found that wis adequate. And if ah had been killed ma mother would have got a pension. Then ah didn't smoke, ah haven't ever smoked. And ah didn't drink. Though we'd boyfriends and we'd go down to the village pub, I used to get a wee drop beer in a half-pint glass filled with lemonade, just to give it a wee bit colour. It wasn't even a shandy. And it lasted me all night. So ah didn't spend an awful lot o' ma money. Then because o' sweet rationin' we were only allowed two Mars bars or something like that. So there wis nothin' much you could spend your money on till you got a leave.

A' the four and a half years ah wis in the WAAF ah wrote home every day for maybe three years, then after that it wis maybe twice or thrice a week. Ma friend Lily, a tailoress in the WAAF and in civvy street, and whose bridesmaid ah was jist after the war, used tae say tae me, 'That money you're spendin' on stamps you should be puttin' in the bank.' But, oh, I mean, by the time you paid your bus fare and went to the cinema and things like that, ye could only go once a fortnight to Lincoln, which wis far bigger but further away than Sleaford.

I was never bored at Digby. And there was a companionship. Everyone was close to each other. Dancing and the cinema were main interests. As I say, we used to go to Lincoln to dancin' and the cinema.

But Lincoln was 14 miles away. Sleaford was nearer to Digby, only about six miles from it. But there wasn't very much in Sleaford.

There were dances at RAF Digby itself. And that wis why I refused to accept corporal's stripes! Four of us were called into the flight sergeant's office. And the flight lieutenant was there. They asked us questions about our work, and ah wis the one that wis offered ma tapes. But I refused them, because I was a ballroom dancer. Now WAAFs who were drivers, cooks, plotters, in signals, and whatnot – they were all on shift work. So they didn't work in the section office where you booked people in and out of the camp. That meant the few WAAF corporals at Digby – there were about 10 – were on bookin' in and out duty about every 10 days. As an ordinary Leading Aircraftwoman (LACW) ah wis on duty once every six months. So ah thought, 'Ah'm not acceptin' promotion tae corporal and missin' ma dancin' for that.' So ah wouldn't take promotion.

At Digby RAF station the army had a hut that was for pay accounts – payin' all the Royal Artillery crews on the guns around Lincolnshire. The commandin' officer's chauffeuse was an ATS girl who was a beautiful ballroom dancer. One night she came across tae me and says, 'Ah'm havin' a formation dance team for the camp concert, and ah want you to be in it.' Ah told her ah wasnae good enough for that, but she insisted ah was. Well, it wis lovely doin' that formation dancin' wi' the eight couples. Oh, ah really enjoyed it. And years later, after the war, ah saw that same ATS girl doin' ballroom dancin' on the television. She must by then have made a name for herself.

The Royal Canadian Air Force Salvation Army was on the camp at Digby, and they gave us a free cinema show on a Wednesday and a Sunday in the camp cinema. Ah remember one night we were standing in the queue for the camp cinema, and somebody shouted: 'There's a German plane! Hit the ground!' But the plane dropped its bombs outside the camp, and fortunately they didn't explode. But standing there in the queue for the cinema ah could see when ah looked up that the plane's bomb doors were open.

Another time at Digby, when I was going back to my billet, one of my WAAF friends, who worked as a plotter, called to me. 'Oh,' she says, 'you've got to come back. There's 54 Flying Fortresses landing here in about three quarters of an hour.' 'But they can't possibly land here,' I says, 'we haven't got a runway.' It was all grass at Digby, because we only had Spitfire and Hurricane fighter planes there.[7] 'Well,' she says, 'they've got to land here, because the whole of England is fogbound, apart from one station in Yorkshire and the Liberator bombers are goin' there.' So ah went back. Group Captain Ernie MacNab, our commanding officer, was standing up at the flying control, and I was standin' a few feet behind him. Everybody wis watchin' these huge Flyin' Fortresses comin' in. With no runway for them some ended up on their sides. So our people put up a red light to let the next planes know to take another circle until they could all land safely. Those planes were all shot up, wi' bullet holes and everything in them, you've no idea. They were comin' back from a raid somewhere. By the time they landed at Digby we could see fog reachin' the trees round the camp. Within an hour Digby too wis fogbound. And it wis like that for three days. But 48 o' the 54 planes landed: six o' them must have been lost in their raid. All those American airmen went away to Lincoln, we hardly saw any of them in our camp.

There were various nationalities among the aircrew men at Digby. There were Canadians that came over after I had arrived. They were really nice. Among them – he was at Digby when I was there, though I didnae know him myself – was John Gillespie Magee. He was actually an American, wi' an American father but an English mother that were both missionaries in China. He was born in Shanghai in 1922. When he was 12 he came to England and went to Rugby School, where he won an award for his published poetry. He went to America and was accepted for Yale University. When the war broke out but the United States remained neutral, John Gillespie Magee wanted to join the RAF. The Americans refused him a visa, so he went to Canada, and joined the Royal Canadian Air Force. Well, ah wasn't very long at Digby when John Gillespie Magee was killed. He collided in the clouds with another plane. He's buried at the little village of Scopwick. When he was killed they found a poem in his belongings. Ma friend Ellen Irvine in Corby sent me a copy of the poem, which she'd got out of an RAF magazine. The last line of the poem was: 'I put out my hand and touched the face of God.' When I read that poem I was sittin' cryin'.[8]

I remember one of the Canadians that always wore a Stewart tartan scarf. Fighter pilots were allowed to have their top tunic button undone. Bomber Command didnae do that, but Fighter Command, as at Digby, did. So this Canadian always wore his Stewart tartan scarf. One day, as they were coming from Colby Grange satellite station to Digby, his plane went into a tree and he was killed. So he was another one I knew.

At Digby we also had a few New Zealanders. One of our WAAF girls went out with one of them. But the New Zealanders were attached to the Fleet Air Arm, so they were only with us for a short while.

Then there was like a squadron, or a pair of squadrons, of Belgians at Digby. They were pilots. Two of those Belgian boys were killed as well. They're also buried at Scopwick village cemetery.

I didn't know a lot of the aircrew at Digby. I mean, they kept to themselves sort of thing. But there was a Polish boy, a pilot, I knew. He'd been at the dance one Saturday but he wasn't there at the next one. He was gone. It was really sad.

Aircrew had to be at least sergeants or flight sergeants. They got their half-wing on their tunic. It was a full wing if you were a pilot. If you were an engineer or something it was a half-wing. But it was more the other ranks airmen, the mechanics and so on, I came into contact wi'.

In Scopwick there was the old cemetery and then they must have built a new bit for the airmen who died. There was three rows of airmen. And up in a corner of the cemetery two Germans are buried. They were killed one night when Ellen Irvine and I were walkin' down the driveway to go to a dance in our camp at Digby. Ah says, 'Ellen, there's a raid goin' on.' Then we saw a plane burst into flames, and it landed slap-bang in the middle of Colby Grange aerodrome, our satellite or sort of partner airfield, a few miles away. The next mornin' this very handsome and monied Canadian – he was nicer-lookin' than Robert Taylor, the film star[9] – came in and said to me, 'Jeez, Scottie, ah could have had a smashin' pair of flyin' boots last night. But the German's 'chute didn't open and his legs went up through his body.' Oh, it was really awful. The day the two Germans killed were buried ah wis on a day off, but ah just happened to go over to the window. When ah looked out ah saw the van with the two coffins draped in the swastika flag: they got a military funeral.

Some of the WAAF girls at Digby became engaged to RAF men there. One girl with a RAF boyfriend was Molly, an awfully nice girl, very quiet. Ah had been goin' with a fellow from Falkirk, but then he was posted away from Digby. However, he came to Digby for the week-end and brought a friend with him. So ah asked Molly to make a foursome, as her own boyfriend was flying that day. The four of us went to Sleaford, had a meal, and we were walking out of Sleaford on the main road when we heard a crash. 'Nessie,' Molly says tae me, 'that's Jim.' I says, 'No, it isn't. It's all right.' When we got back to Digby camp the first thing Molly was told was that Jim, her boyfriend, had crashed and was killed. She'd had that premonition. She wasn't engaged to Jim, but I think she would have married him. What a nice girl Molly was. It was really sad.

None of the WAAFs at Digby were killed. And we had only two nights when we were in the air raid shelter. Our camp was so well camouflaged that even our own pilots used to navigate by the local farms, to get back to the camp. Oh, we were lucky. But I've read of other WAAFs. One of our girls, Daphne, was Welsh and had red hair. She was posted from Digby away down south somewhere. Years later I was reading in this book about the WAAF that said two WAAFs were coming back one night to their camp when the sirens went just as they got to the gate. Their camp had special air raid shelters for women only. There were beds for them in these shelters. One girl – and by her description it couldn't have been anybody else but Daphne – was in a bottom bed and her friend was in the one on top. The shelter was bombed. The girl on top died from her head injuries. And Daphne was squashed to bits. Oh, what a feeling ah had when ah read that. But that's what happened to Daphne.

* * *

We got leave from Digby camp: seven days' leave four times a year. And in between our leaves we had a 48-hour pass. We could add the pass on to our seven days, which gave us nine days. So it wasn't bad, and I was able to get home to Dalkeith four times a year. There was only once going home we couldn't get a seat on the train. Eight of us left the camp, and when we got to Grantham four of us got into one place. I was the last to get on the train, and this Geordie he's pushin' ma case and closin' the door. The train was jam-packed. So four of us had to go further down the train to look for a seat. Well, we were right at the toilet door. When we got to York four people came out the toilet. So the four of us went into it. Already inside there was this elderly person, a right sergeant-major type, sittin' on the toilet. There were two airmen standin' there, and ah gave them ma big case to sit on, and they gave me their wee case. And there wis two other men sittin' in the toilet, one a Canadian. Well, the nine o' us sat like that all the way tae Edinburgh. And not one other person came to get into the toilet. Well, it wis wartime and the trains were packed.

Another time I remember Ellen Irvine, my friend that came from Corby, was coming with me to spend our leave at my mother's house in Dalkeith. She and her boyfriend Jock from Edinburgh sat on her case in the corridor, and a fellow from Dundee and I sat on my case there all night. The trains were packed to the hilt.

Well, one night in May 1945 I was last in bed in our WAAF billet at Digby. Then ah heard this bangin' and ah wis seein' lights outside. When ah looked out there were red and green lights, and white lights that lit up the place for planes landin'. Then ah heard an accordion, then shouting. So I went outside in my WAAF-issue pyjamas to see what was happening. Mr Black, the station warrant officer, and a Canadian Air Force policeman were standing at the camp gate. I said to them, 'What's happened? What's wrong?' One of them said, 'The war's over, Scottie!' And just as he said that, one o' these white Verey lights went up. And here's me standin' in ma pyjamas! One of the WAAFs and I put on our WAAF trousers and sweaters and went up to flying control. Everybody wis singin' and dancin', and all these lights were goin' up. It was great! The sergeants' mess had a dance that night. This fellow from the RAF Regiment in the camp was a beautiful pianist and played for us. It wis jist a night tae remember! Super!

Honestly you've no idea how close people were to each other durin' the war. Neighbours were all concerned about each other. But after the war finished that wis all gone. No, people weren't so close after the war. But ah kept in touch with six WAAF girls and one Canadian.

So from ma time in the WAAF ah've remembered people ah wouldnae have seen or met or heard o' if it hadnae been for the war: Canadians, Americans, New Zealanders, Belgians, a Polish boy, and Germans. Another man ah saw at Digby the night before ah wis demobbed after the war had ended was a man from Dalkeith. A boyfriend and I were at the pictures that night, and sittin' in the back row wis Lambeth Walk. That wis his nickname. Ah think it wis because o' the way he walked. His name wis really Jock Dalgleish. He'd been a policeman in Dalkeith before the war. Well, the next thing ah heard was that Lambeth Walk had become pilot tae the king o' Jordan.[10]

As well as ma contact in the WAAF wi' people from other countries, ah would never have been to Lincolnshire, Bridgnorth, Digby, or anywhere else in England that I got tae or passed through durin' the war. Oh, ah loved every minute ah wis in the WAAF. The four and a half years ah wis a WAAF were the happiest in ma life. Ah've never had any regrets. In fact, ah wish ah'd joined up again.

I wis demobbed in January 1946, and in February 1946 ah started tae work again. But I felt a bit restless when ah first came home. Ah missed the company in the WAAF. And then when ah came home ah wis doin' the washin', ah wis doin' the ironin', ah wis doin' the garden – ma dad wasn't able. Ah wis doin' all the housework. Ah wanted tae go to the night classes and take book-keeping, because ah loved counting. It was ma best subject. But ah jist hadnae time tae go. Ah wis so busy doing things in the house ah wis never out, except maybe ah got to the pictures once or twice a week, and to the dancin' on a Friday night. And ah couldnae even go back to ma old job at Dalkeith Hosiery because it had closed down durin' the war.

Nessie Lawrie died on 17 August 2017.

Elizabeth Weston

Ah've never seen so many women and men – mothers and fathers – crying as what was on that platform at the Waverley station in Edinburgh. Well, we were only young girls, 19 or 20 years old . . . .When the train set off they left a' these folk on the station platform cryin' – mothers greetin' and dads wiping their tears away. They knew that we were goin' down tae Gloucester tae join the Women's Auxiliary Air Force. It wis October 1942, the same month as the battle o' El Alamein in North Africa.[1]

Ah wis born on the 13th of July 1923, at The Square, Newtongrange, in Midlothian. Ma father wis a contractor there in the Lady Victoria pit. He and another man shared a contract. And they were responsible, I suppose, for fighting for wages for the men in their section, as they called it. Because I remember ma dad comin' home at times, and ma mother would say, 'You're early the day, Henry?' 'Aye, ah've got tae go up that stair and see Mungo.' He would say it was something about men working in water, and he'd tae fight for an extra penny [½p] on their pay.[2] Ma father wis born in Rosewell. But he must have come tae Newtongrange as a youngster before he started work. I don't remember ma dad speakin' a lot about when they were wee. He didn't speak a lot about his boyhood at all. But he wis a great family man and his involvement was with his own family.

Ma grandfather Weston was a blacksmith. He went out to the Sandwich Islands to work on a plantation there.[3] But he took something like malaria and died a young man. He was buried out there. When ma grandfather died ma grandmother Weston was left with five children. There wis ma uncle Dave and ma dad, ma auntie Mary, ma auntie Mag, and ma uncle George that wis born out there and wis jist an infant. Then ma granny and the children had tae be brought home. But of course they had no money. So it was the freemasons that brought her home. Ma grandfather must have been a freemason, and they were responsible for getting her and the children on a sailing ship. Ma dad wis jist a wee boy. He said it took six or seven weeks on the sailing ship to bring them to somewhere in England, then a train home from there. Ah remember ma granny Weston well, and goin' on a Sunday wi' ma dad across tae Sixth Street in Newtongrange tae see her. When she came back wi' her children she hadn't a job: they lived on the parish. Ah wis about seven when ma granny died.

Ma mother wis born in Newtongrange. She lost her mother when she was only 12. Of course, big families in those days. So there were five or six o' them. Ma uncle George wis only a wee boy when his mother died. But ma aunt Elizabeth, ma mother's sister, she married and took her wee brother George and brought him up. Ma mother herself was only 17, goin' on 18, when she married ma dad, and he wis only a year older. Ma mother started her married life by taking in her two brothers who were unmarried. One of them, ma uncle Stephen, never married and was with ma mother all her married life. Ah've no recollection o' ma grandfather on ma mother's side. As far as ah know he wis jist a miner. They were all miners at Newtongrange.

Before she was married, I'm sure ma mother worked in the carpet factory at Eskbank, and walked there from Newtongrange. Then in these days women didnae work after they were married.

Well, ma mother actually had 10 children. She lost her first-born, George, when he was about 18 month old. He died with pneumonia. Then she had Alex, David, Stephen, Wullie, and Henry, then there was Katie, Jean, myself, and 10 years after me, Janet. When Janet wis born Alex would be 24, Katie 21. So there wis a generation really between Alex and Janet. That wasn't uncommon in those days, when you got big families like ours. So when Janet came along ma brothers were a' grown up. But they were late married. And David, ma second oldest brother, died when he was 36 with Weil's disease. They had rat poisoning in the Lady Victoria pit where David worked.[4] He was a great person, and the last person that should have got rat poisoning. He was so particular about himself. When Janet wis jist a wee girl David used to put her up on his shoulders and march her up and down the lobby playin' his mouth organ while she sang, till she fell asleep on his head.

When Janet wis born ma mother couldnae have coped without Katie, ma oldest sister. Katie, who was then 20, never got the chance to work outside our home. She wis ma mother's assistant. That's what happened in big families in those days, the oldest girl was kept at home to help mother. Katie was a lovely sewer. When she left school at 14 the sewing teacher got Katie an apprenticeship with a tailoress in Edinburgh. She came home that day, full o' the joys. She said tae ma mum, 'Ah'm goin' tae train tae be a tailoress.' 'Oh, well,' says mum, 'wait and see what your dad says.' When ma dad came home from his work, 'Oh,' he says, 'ye can't do that, love. Your mum needs you in the house.' And that was it. Katie just accepted it. Mind, they were good to her and made up in other ways. They got a piano and Katie got piano lessons, she got a gold watch on her birthday, and ma mother bought her a beautiful cabinet sewing machine. But Katie never got the chance to go out and work. In those days that was very common, oh, that happened regularly.

Jean, on the other hand, after Qualifying at Newtongrange Primary School at the age of 11, went on to Dalkeith High School, took the commercial course, and got her groundin' in typin' and shorthand. When she left school ma mother and father put her to a wee private commercial college in Edinburgh, and paid for a year's tuition there for Jean, where she got shorthand, typing and book-keeping. There again ma mother had tae keep her and pay her bus fares. Ah'm dashed sure it wis a lot o' expense. But Jean got that opportunity. Then she started work with Wardie's, a wholesale warehouse in Leith. Durin' the war Jean used tae get bashed tins o' fruit and things, cheap. Well, she worked there a few years, then she became secretary to James Hood, the owner o' the Lothian Coal Company. When he got older she sometimes had tae go out tae his house and take his letters. When Hood died he left Jean £100 – that wis something in those days. That's where Jean worked until she married.[5]

With ma mother havin' a big family, her hardest work was makin' food. Ma brothers were a' workin' connected to the pit, and they a' came in home at different times. They weren't a' miners. David wis a miner and so wis Stephen. But Alex, ma oldest brother, wis an apprentice engineer to start with. He ended up as the chief engineer at the Lady Victoria pit, then he landed in the National Coal Board offices in Edinburgh. He really worked his way up in the Coal Board.[6] Then Wullie, ma fourth brother, wis a joiner at the pit. Henry, the youngest o' ma brothers, was always very artistic in drawing, and he got into the drawing office at the pit after he did a year in the engineerin' shop. Then Henry won a bursary to train as a heatin' engineer at Heriot Watt College in Edinburgh. The bursary paid for his tuition. But ma mum and dad had to keep him for the two or three years he was there, includin' his travellin' fares from Newtongrange. Henry did really well for himself.

* * *

Ah wis born in one o' the big houses – upstairs and downstairs – in The Square at Newtongrange. Ah can't remember its street number. It wis the men in the pit like contractors, no' jist the ordinary five-eights, that lived there; you were a wee bit . . . , you know. And my dad had one o' the bigger houses, because he had a family. We left The Square when ah wis four, and we came to a brand new house in Ninth Street. They were two in a block – semi-detached; and ah wis there until ma sister Katie wis married from there in 1940. After the wedding we moved to 29 Reed Place in Newtongrange. It had four bedrooms.

In our house in The Square there was a living room, kitchen, and a room downstairs, two bedrooms upstairs, and a boxroom. It was gas lighting. And it had a range: that's where I got ma face burned when I was three. I dinnae remember it, but that's how I got a mark on my face. The range had a fender seat. Ma mother was bakin' girdle scones this day and ah had apparently sat on the fender seat and had made tae put both ma legs up on it. Ah'd always had a deformed right arm – born wi' it. Well, that day ah toppled and ma face struck the thing and got burned. Ma mother and ma sister Katie – she wis 11 years older than me – were in an awfy state. Ma mother was terrified for ma dad comin' home and what he'd say. He did blame her of course. Ma dad wis a great first aid man in the pit, and he looked after ma burn himself. There was no doctor. Ma dad says, 'If we get a doctor we'll get intae trouble.' There wisnae a guard on the fire in these days.

Ma mother did all the cookin' on the range. There wis no gas ring, and no hot or cold running water at The Square. We went tae the well at the bottom o' the back street and filled the pails. I didnae do that, but my older brothers and sisters did. Of course, there wis no flush toilet, jist a dry closet at the bottom of the garden. Oh, everybody in The Square had a dry toilet for their family. They were terrible things when you think about it now, though they were kept spotlessly clean.

The big houses in The Square, as I've said, were occupied by what we called gaffers – firemen, deputies, contractors, men like that. The big houses were at one side of The Square, and on the other side it wis the wee houses occupied by ordinary miners. If you were in the big houses you were a wee bit better off. Then The Saughs, the houses opposite the Lady Victoria pit, and the houses in Lothian Terrace, at the very top of Newtongrange, they were big houses occupied by gaffers – the like o' the chief electrician and the chief somebody else. They were all in these houses. They were a' men that didnae go down the pit, sort of bowler hat men.

The Ninth Street houses were lovely: three-bedroomed. Ma two older sisters Katie and Jean (Jean was five years older than me) and I (ma young sister Janet wisnae on the scene then, she was a latecomer) slept in one room. Ma five brothers all slept in the middle room, and ma mum and dad slept in the parlour, as they called it – the front room or livin' room, which had a suite in it but also a bed. So we were very lucky to have three rooms. We thought we were well off. Ma dad made a good livelihood, and we were comfortable compared to a lot of other people.

When in 1928 we came to Ninth Street it was gas lighting, and it was quite a while before we got electric light. But it was a more modern house than the one in The Square had been. Ma mother had a gas cooker right from the beginning, and Ninth Street had hot and cold running water, a bathroom, and a flush toilet. And bein' miners, our fires were kept on mornin' and all night so that we always had hot water. A gatherin' coal wis put on at night, because ma mum wis up at five in the mornin', puttin' the men out tae their work. Ye had a right miners' house. Oh, what a work for womenfolk like ma mother, wi' ma dad, ma five brothers, all colliery workers, as well as, includin' Janet, four sisters of us.

Well, ah began school at Newbattle, the old school. We went there till you Qualified. If you Qualified to a certain standard you could go to Dalkeith High School for either commercial or languages. Well, ma mother at that time for some reason or other thought ah should take a domestic course. When you think back now you were naïve. Ah thought, 'Oh, well, ah'm no' fussy about goin' tae the High School.' So ah stayed at Newbattle and took domestic, which ah've never regretted. We got sewing, embroidery, housewifery, laundry, and subjects like English and history, etc. Ah wis there till ah wis 14, and when ah left school ah wisnae asked what ah wanted tae be. Ah wis jist told, 'You're going tae the Scott Christie's College in Edinburgh.' And you just accepted that. There was no discussion. Ma parents thought that wis best for me. Ah would have liked to be a milliner. That wis ma ambition. Ah've always been fond o' hats. Ah never got the chance, but ah don't suppose ah wis very disappointed.

The Scott Christie College wis a right wee private college in Hanover Street, Edinburgh. Ma mother took me in. Mr Scott did the typin' side, Miss Christie the shorthand. Another man (ah forget his name now) did the book-keepin' side. Ah met Miss Christie, a nice person. 'Oh,' she says, 'your sister Jean was here. You'll be all right here.' You only got one afternoon o' book-keepin'; it wis shorthand and typin' all the time really. Ah wis there for a year. Ma parents had tae keep me.

After you were at the College about nine months they used tae put you out to do temporary work. Ah worked, for instance, for a fortnight at the North British Hotel. Oh, it wis a disgustin' place. You were down in the basement, and the greasy smell that wis comin' from the kitchen! Ah used tae think, 'Oh, what a place this is!' And yet it wis such a posh hotel.[7] And then ah worked in a lawyer's office for a fortnight. The College sent ye out tae things like that.

When ah left the College ah got a permanent job at Traill & Fletcher, wholesale grocers, in Rose Street in Edinburgh. Their office and warehouse wis right opposite John Menzies's warehouse, the wholesale newspaper distribution place. Traill & Fletcher had a big office. I was a correspondence typist. There wis a dozen other girls there. Most of them looked after ledger accounts. And there wis maybe five or six [commercial] travellers. Each traveller had a typist that looked after his accounts. In the office there wis a wee step up, wi' two desks. And there was Mr Gibbons, the old secretary, lookin' over the top o' his glasses at you a' the time. You were frightened. Mr Gibbons's assistant, a younger man, sat at the other desk. And there wis two directors. We were all upstairs, the warehouse wis downstairs, and there wis two or three different floors.

The hours at Traill & Fletcher would be, ah think, nine till six, and nine till one o'clock on a Saturday. Ah travelled to work in the train, it wis cheaper than the bus. Ah had a monthly season ticket, and Newtongrange station was just down the main street. Then in Edinburgh ye run up the Waverley station steps and ye were nearly there at Traill & Fletcher's office. The journey took only about 15 minutes. I enjoyed that job, I really enjoyed it.

Ah used tae get something like 6d [2½p] a day from ma mother, and ah went to the YMCA or YWCA in Coates Crescent and got a bowl o' soup and a roll or somethin' at lunchtime.[8] When ah first began, in 1938, aged 15, at Traill & Fletcher ma wages were 25s [£1.25] a week. Most folk in these days started with 15 bob [75p]. But at the Scott Christie College Miss Christie said tae me, 'Now you're going out for an interview for a job, Miss Weston, and I've had a word with Mr So-and-so, and I've told him, "Now this young lady's coming from the country. So you can't offer her any less." So when he asks you what pay you want you'll say 25 shillings.' So when at Traill & Fletcher I said 25s, he says, 'Oh, well, but you've got to travel, right enough. That's fine.' So that was good news, and I started with 25 bob.

Well, ah wis at Traill & Fletcher for two years. Then I had to stop working a'thegither, because ma oldest sister Katie got married that year, 1940. That meant ma mother wis left without help. And there again ma father just said, 'Now somethin' has tae be done, because your mother needs help.' Jean, ma older sister, said, 'Well, ah could come in tae the house, dad, tae help.' He says, 'Oh, there's no point you comin' in. You're goin' tae get married next year. It'll have tae be Elizabeth that helps her mother.' So ah never got any option, and I just accepted it. Ah wasn't weepy or broken-hearted about givin' up ma job. Ye see, our family were just brought up that we a' helped one another, and what ma mum and dad did was for the best for us. And even though they'd put that money out tae train me, ma dad still thought ma mother needed help. Ma five brothers were still at home and were all on differ-ent shifts, and ma mother had a busy life. Ma dad wasnae retired then: he worked on till he was 71 or 72. And, as ah've said, ma brothers were late marryin'. Alex, the oldest, wis about 48 when he married. David, Stephen, Wullie, and Henry were unmarried in 1940. David, the second oldest, was 36 when he died in 1954. So it was in 1940 ah wis brought intae the house tae help ma mother.

Ma mother did a' the food mostly: she hadnae time tae be runnin' cleanin'. She was makin' the beds, goin' for the shops – of course, vans came tae the door in these days. The baker came, the butcher came, the fish man came. But ye were sent down to the Store [Co-op] for various things, and sent to Dalkeith for things. And once the war broke out ye had tae go tae Dalkeith if there wis anythin' special goin'. A baker called The Clydesdale there had great pies, but ye had tae queue for them. They were so good – but ye were only allowed maybe half a dozen. Ma mother would say tae me, 'Take the bus tae Dalkeith and try tae get half a dozen pies.' Of course, half a dozen pies wouldnae go far in a big family like ours. But it helped, though ye didnae get a whole pie each, ye got a half one! Well, ah didnae get paid for workin' in the house tae help ma mum. But ah got pocket money. Ah think it wis somethin' like five bob [25p] a week. That would take me tae the pictures.

Pictures and dancing were among ma main interests as a young lassie. We loved dancing. Ah met Tom Herriot, ma future husband, when ah wis young. And Tom and I both loved the dancin', so we went dancin' together. We went to the dancin' most weekends. Oh, it wis a very popular pastime in the 1930s. We went to the dancin' at the Rosewell Miners' Institute because it wis the best dancin' in the district at that time. Rosewell's about three miles from Newtongrange. We used tae go there on a Saturday night, or to Vogrie, Gorebridge, or to Craigesk, underneath the old railway viaduct near Newtongrange. Craigesk wis a beautiful dance hall. We loved goin' to the pictures too. We went to Newtongrange pictures or to the Dalkeith Palace picture house. Tuesday we went to the pictures, on a Saturday it wis the dancin'. On Sunday we walked, walked for miles. We walked away up the hill tae what we called The Camp. We walked away round Gorebridge or else away roond by Bonnyrigg, round by the Glen, by the viaduct there. Oh, there were plenty o' walks round Newtongrange.

And then the Sunday night courtin' place wis The Ropes. That wis the pavement from the Lady Victoria pit up to the garage at the Auld Toll, where the main road tae Galashiels crossed wi' the road from Bonnyrigg and Dalhousie Castle and the road from Gorebridge. There was a fence along the pavement and it wis posts and wire ropes. Young people from Newtongrange, Gorebridge and Stobhill met there. Before I went with Tom Herriot, my girl friends Betty and Isobel and I would walk up there, because you knew you'd meet the boys there. 'We'll go up and see if any lads are up there – Bob Steel or Matthew Weir, or any of them.' The crowd that we went wi' were an Arniston crowd. But there wis no harm in it – no sex or anything. It wis jist friendly – laughs, and ye sat and blethered, then ye went your way. Sometimes they chummed ye down the road, sometimes ye didnae bother. It could be that's where boy met girl, but it didnae always happen that way. Ah didnae meet Tom Herriot there.

Then in these days the folk in Gorebridge were known tae folk in Newtongrange as The Germans. And in Gorebridge the folk in Newtongrange were known as The Chinese. I don't know why that was. I think it began possibly after the First War, when there were already a lot of Polish or Lithuanian people in Newtongrange.[9] Lithuanians are connected to ma own family actually, because ma oldest son's wife, her grandparents came from Lithuania. Ma mum and dad used to tell us that when they were younger they set up house at Dean Park in Newtongrange. The houses there are jist room and kitchen. But at that time couples brought up their families in them. And ma mother used tae tell us about the Dean Tavern there, and she said the Lithuanians used to come out the Dean Tavern the worse o' drink and they always ended up fightin'. The ones that stayed near mum and dad in Dean Park would end up fightin' in the garden. It wis nothin' but pandemonium on a Saturday night wi' the Lithuanians. A lot o' the Lithuanians – or Poles, as they were often called – took Smith for their name. But ah've heard ma dad and ma uncles sayin' the Lithuanians or Poles that all came and worked in the mines here at Newtongrange were a' good workers. They used tae say they worked like pigs.

* * *

Well, as ah've said, ah had tae give up ma job wi' Traill & Fletcher in Edinburgh in 1940 and work at home tae help ma mother. And that – damn it all – wis how ah wis called up. Because the next thing, in 1942, wis the call-up. Ah got this letter tae go tae the Dalkeith Labour Exchange. Ma brother Wullie, the joiner, had already been called up to the army in maybe 1940, because his trade wasn't termed a reserved occupation. Later in the war Wullie got married, then he went to the Far East, to the jungles. He always declared that's where he got his feet poisoned: he lost both his legs. So it wis intae 1942 when ah got called up.

When ah went to the Dalkeith Labour Exchange to register, quite a few other girls were there. The man that interviewed me there said tae me: 'You're unemployed.' 'Yes', ah said, 'but not because ah've been looking' for a job. It wis because ah had tae give ma work up.' And ah explained what had happened. 'Well,' he said, 'ah'm afraid, ma dear, that disnae make any difference. As far as we're concerned you're on the unemployment list here.' Now ah didnae get any money, ah wasnae claimin' any dole or anything. 'But,' the man says, 'you're unemployed and that's it. So,' he says, 'the war needs ye.' Ah says, 'What can ah do?' 'Well,' he says, 'you'll get a choice.' Ah said, 'What's the choice?' He says, 'We need women for the munitions in Birmingham.' Ah think ma face fell. He said, 'But you're a trained shorthand typist?' 'Yes,' ah said, 'ah went to college and trained. And,' ah says, 'ah had tae give up ma work because ma mum needs iz. Ah've got four brothers working in the pits, and the other one is in the army.' 'Ah, well,' the man says, 'you're alternative is the Services.' Ah says, 'As a typist?' He says, 'They need women in the offices to release the men.' Ah wis taken aback. Ah'd never even thought aboot that. And ah'd never even thought ah wid get called up. And ah'd never thought about volunteerin'. None o' ma friends had volunteered and none o' them were conscripted. Ah mean, ah wist jist brought up tae help ma mother. Ma friends were jist workin' and they werenae called up. Ah wis the only one among them that went intae the Services. Ah wis called up because ah wis on the Labour Exchange books as unemployed.

Anyway, ah said tae the man at the Labour Exchange, 'Ah don't fancy munitions.' Ah would have liked the WRNS. Maybe it wis jist their uniform, ah don't know. He says, 'Well, there's no vacancies in the WRNS. But the Air Force is open and the army.' It wasn't because goin' tae munitions and bein' away from home put me off. It wis jist the idea o' workin' in a factory. Ah didnae think ah could cope wi' it. Ah'd never worked in a factory. And, ah mean, doin' a repetitive job, puttin' a wee bit thing, passin' it on a conveyor belt – ah couldnae see myself doin' that. But as it happened ah never got the choice. It was taken out o' ma hands. The Labour Exchange man said to me, 'Well, you go home and discuss it wi' your family. And ah'll expect you back here tomorrow to give me your answer. But it's either one or the other, ma dear.' So that was all the time ah got.

When ah come home and told ma mum and dad, ma dad said right away, 'Well, ye're not goin' intae any munitions factory, Elizabeth. Your mum and I sacrificed to give you a training. And if you can get into the Services and do what you were trained to do, that's a' right. But ye're not goin' intae a factory.' So that wis it.

Of course, a' this came as a bit o' a blow tae ma mum and dad. But, as ah've said, ma oldest sister Katie wis married by that time, stayed locally, didnae have a job herself at that time, and said she would come and help ma mother. Ma other older sister Jean wis married in 1941, and jist gave her job up – in these days women didnae work after they were married – and so Jean used tae help ma mother while ah wis away in the Services.

Well, ah chose tae go tae the Air Force, ah jist fancied it. Ah jist didnae fancy the idea o' the army. It wis said a lot o' girls joined the army – the ATS – jist tae get a man. I think that wis a lot o' nonsense because, ah mean, the same could apply tae the Air Force – the WAAF. Certainly, in our area there were ATS down the road at Newbattle Abbey. They frequented the dance halls and they jist got that name. So that's what put me off joinin' the ATS. And by the time ah joined the WAAF ah wis goin' of course wi' ma future husband Tom Herriot, an engineer in the pit. But actually Tom wis very unhappy because he wis in a reserved occupation and they wouldn't let him away to join the navy. So ah wis in the WAAF before Tom got away tae join the submarines.

Well, within weeks o' registerin' at the Dalkeith Labour Exchange ah got the papers: 'Report to the Assembly Rooms, George Street, Edinburgh', on a certain date at 10 o'clock in the mornin' for joinin' the WAAFs. Ah didnae get any medical before ah went, ye didnae get anything like that. Ma older sister Katie came tae the Assembly Rooms with me tae help, supposedly. Ah reckon there must have been 50 other girls there that day. We were put into twos, and we were marched along George Street, down Hanover Street, along Princes Street, down the Waverley Bridge, and down the carriageway into the Waverley station. There wis somebody led us, somebody from the RAF probably, ah cannae mind who it would be. We were in our civilian clothes and carryin' our wee cases. When we got down into the station the train was there. We got on it and we were just told: 'Sit!'. It was terrible. Ah've never forgotten this. Ah've never seen so many women and men – mothers and fathers – crying as what was on that platform at the Waverley station in Edinburgh. Well, we were only young girls, 19 or 20 years old . . . .When the train set off they left a' these folk on the station platform cryin' – mothers greetin' and dads wipin' their tears away. They knew that we were goin' down tae Gloucester tae join the Women's Auxiliary Air Force. Gloucester was the WAAF record place. It wis October 1942, the same month as the battle of El Alamein in North Africa.

We weren't all just from Edinburgh and round about it. The girl that sat beside me on the train was from Glasgow. Dorothy Green was her name. Mary was from Helensburgh. Ah cannae remember where big Kathleen came from. But they were from different places. It must have been a special train, reserved for girls goin' intae the WAAF. It wis a corridor train, wi' only six in each compartment. You're sittin', six strangers in this compartment. And these girls were a' cryin', not all the way to Gloucester but for a good hour tae start wi'. And ah'm sittin' lookin' out the window, tryin' not tae cry. Eventually Dorothy Green, a nice-lookin' girl, and I told each other our names and where we were from. By this time an hour had passed, and the other girls sort o' dried their tears, and they were tellin' each other how they'd been called up or had volunteered, and how their parents had come tae see them off and that.

Ah cannae remember gettin' any food on the train. But we probably had a sandwich with us. It wis a long journey down to Gloucester. And when we got there it wis dark – wi' the blackout ye didnae have any lights anyway – and absolutely teemin' rain. Ah'll never forget it. There wis two trucks wi' canvas tops waitin' for us. We were herded on tae them – just hustled on – by these RAF sergeants: 'On, girls!' It wis RAF men drivin' the trucks. They took us intae the camp, wherever it wis. And it wis still teemin' wi rain. When we got there it wis long wooden huts we were put intae. And as ye came up: 'Jist file in, girls. Get a bed. Put your things down and come tae the cookhouse. There's a hot meal waitin' for you.' We got this hot meal, then we were told: 'Intae your hut – and intae your bed.' And oor breakfast would be at a certain time the next morning. And, ye know, ye hadn't a clue where ye were. We jist knew it wis Gloucester where the Receiving Centre was for us anyway.

In the wooden huts there wis, oh, ah think, 24 girls at least tae each hut, maybe 30, for they were long huts. They were single beds, and ye'd jist taken the first bed you'd come to. Funnily enough, ye sort o' stayed thegither wi' those girls that ye were on the train with, because you knew their first names. Then ye went and got your knife, fork and spoon given to you. Ye didnae have a mess tin, and ah cannae mind if we got a mug or a tinnie. Then the next day you got medicals of a kind, because ah don't think they were very thorough. Ah'll tell you right now I don't think I would ever have got into the Services, because ah can't salute. Ah've got a right arm ah can't do that with. Ah'm slightly deformed in my right arm, ah can't use ma right hand very much, ah can't turn it. Ah'm left-handed, so ah can do everything wi' ma left hand. But ah can't raise ma right hand over a certain height – ah've got to lift it up wi' ma left hand. Ah definitely should have been rejected on medical grounds. That's what ma father said: 'How have they taken ye?' I can use the fingers o' my right hand, and ah can type with it, but ah can't raise that hand. Well, at the medical exam at Gloucester ah didn't ask tae be released on medical grounds. Ah jist said tae the man, 'Ye know, ah'll not be able to salute.' He sort o' looked at me and he says, 'Why?' Ah says, 'Well, ah can't.' And ah showed him. 'Oh,' he says, 'that won't matter. You can type. We need you to type.'

Well, that didnae cause me any trouble at the Receivin' Centre at Gloucester. You got your uniforms and everything there, and ye got lectures about everything: health (VD and everything – the lot), and 'Walls Have Ears', and what ye were tae do – all the rules and regulations laid out to you. That's what ye got for that week. It was boring really. We were at Gloucester only about a week, then we were sent tae Morecambe tae do six weeks' square-bashin'.

It wis in November intae December 1942 that we did our six weeks' square-bashin' at Morecambe. We got it on the promenade there. An RAF sergeant, a great man, yelled at us: 'Left, Right, Left, Right', and you're marchin' up and down. Fortunately, we had trousers, navy blue flannel trousers, that we had to wear for that.

We were in private billets at Morecambe. They took over the boardin' houses, and these women must have made a fortune out of the Air Force. The RAF took over these houses and put in as many bunk beds as they could squeeze in. The room we were in wis jist a wee tiny room wi' three double bunks – so there were six of us in that room, jist crammed in. And ye got bubble and squeak for your breakfast. That wis the potatoes and cabbage left over frae the day before. Aye, that was what ye got for your breakfast – bubble and squeak fried. It wis the landlady that provided the food. It wis the army that provided these bunk beds – made o' iron. Then you were out on this damned parade all morning. There was a baker's shop on the prom, and we used to spend all our money in that baker's shop at lunchtime. We were starving. Sometimes, if we were lucky, we could get a cream cake there – that wis good for your morale. Then when ye got back to the billets in the evening ye got a slice o' spam and half a lettuce, and a bit tomato. When ah think about it now, those Morecambe landladies made a fortune out o' that. The RAF would give them enough money for good food, or they would give them supplies of food. And a' thae big houses on the prom had girls livin' in them.

Well, for six weeks we were there at Morecambe. It wis purely and simply square-bashin'. There wis no typing, shorthand, office routine, nothin' like that. You were jist doin' marching, turning, and saluting, and whatever else. Well, there wisnae so much salutin', because there wis no officer there: ye jist salute an officer. There wid be about 100 WAAF girls there, because, ah mean, there wis the 50 o' us, and there wis other units there before us.

When we were at Morecambe, even though we were doin' the square-bashin', we would go out in the evening. After about five o'clock we went to the Winter Gardens. You could walk about and go into a café and have a packet o' chips. You were not paid very much, though we'd gone away from home wi' a wee bit of money. The pay to start with was 2s 8d [13p] a day, plus 8d [3p] – a subsidy for somethin' at lunchtime. So that gave me as an ACW [Aircraftwoman] 3s 4d [17p] a day – about £1 3s 4d [£1.17] a week. And ye only got paid fortnightly, ye didn't get it weekly. It wisnae a lot o' money, we certainly werenae well paid. For your lunch you could get a bowl o' soup, a roll, and a cup o' coffee for 8d [3p]. Then you got a meal at night in the billets. We could go to the NAAFI at night; it was quite good and it wis cheaper than the shops. Well, if ye had spare cash it wisnae much. And ah think we had to send a wee allowance home to our parents: 7s [35p] or somethin' it wis. Later on, when ah wis an LACW [Leading Aircraftwoman], ma pay had gone up to 4s 4d [22p] a day – 30s 4d [£1.52] a week.

Well, you were homesick at first. But ah knew ah wis in the Forces and had tae make the best of it. So by the time the six weeks at Morecambe wis ending ah wis settled. While we were there the girl Dorothy Green from Glasgow got out medically because she had a weak bladder. She wet the bed once or twice. Of course, our landlady reported that, and Dorothy got discharged. She was quite sad, because she had settled down. And when Dorothy told us she said, 'Ah'm sorry. Ah would have liked to have gone on.' It wis surprising how quickly a sense of comradeship had developed among the girls. Once you're in the Forces you've got to make the best of it. There's no use sitting crying. So ah can't say ah wis one that pined tae go home.

When we got our postings we were taken to this big hall in Morecambe. I reckon there must have been at least 300 or 400 girls in that hall. The officers doing these postings were on the stage, and the girls' names and their numbers were called out. And you'd maybe get four or five at a time posted to certain units up and down the country. Only two of us out of all the girls in that hall were posted to Scotland, and ah wis one o' them. That's how ah came to Drem airfield in East Lothian.

* * *

When ah wis posted tae Drem, oh, ah thought that wis great. As the crow flies, Drem is only about 10 miles from Newtongrange. When you think about it the organisation was terrific in the Air Force. They must have informed Drem that Aircraftwoman Weston was arrivin' off a certain train. So there wis a van waitin' at Drem station tae take ye the mile or two up tae the camp. Ah wis the only WAAF from our lot at Morecambe that came to Drem. Ah don't know where the other girl posted tae Scotland went tae. Well, when ah got there, there wis the airfield. Then ye went roond the corner tae the next field, tae the WAAF site. It wis further up, nearer Fenton Barns farm. The RAF men were down in the airfield part: there wis a field between us. And then in the next field was the cookhouse. So all the girls were supplied wi' good bikes. Some o' the RAF men had bikes as well. They had tae cycle up tae the cookhouse for their breakfast and their meal at night. The cookhouse wis a couple o' hundred yards away from our WAAF hut. We didnae go up the road tae the cookhouse; we used tae cut through the hedge. On a wet day it wis quite a distance to go to the cookhouse. And ah remember it wis damned cold in the mornin'. And at first ah felt a bit lost at leavin' the girls at Morecambe.

When ah got tae Drem ah'd tae report at the main gates. The WAAF officer on duty in the guardroom said, 'Oh, yes, we were expecting you, Weston. Come along. We'll take you along to the huts.' It wis a nice wee site, the WAAF site at Drem. But they were Nissen huts. There'd maybe be 12 beds in the hut ah wis taken intae, six beds a side. In the centre wis a black stove wi' a pipe that went up through the ceilin': that wis the heatin'. Then the WAAF officer said to this WAAF: 'Dougan, I want you to take Weston under your wing. Take her up to the cookhouse in the morning for her breakfast, then bring her down to the main office.' 'Yes, ma'am.' So that wis how ah met ma great friend Isa Dougan, and we remain friends still. Isa arrived at Drem a fortnight before me. She wisnae awfy big, so she wis nicknamed Tiny.

At Drem there would only be about eight or nine huts as WAAF billets. There definitely wouldnae be any more than that. The women's camp wasn't a huge big camp. I remember it wis very, very cold. There wis brown linoleum on the floors o' the huts. On a Wednesday night – it wis called Domestic Night – we didn't get out, and you had to polish your section o' the floor till your face nearly shone in it. You got supplied wi' cleanin' material. We had no mops, we had jist tae do it wi' dusters. And ye cleaned your shoes, and cleaned a' your buttons wi' Brasso. Though nobody wis allowed out on a Wednesday night, you could go into the ablutions and do your wee bit washin'. We didn't send things to a laundry, we did our own washin' and ironin'.

For the stove or fire ye only got one bucket o' coal a day. Honest, it wisnae enough. It took a bucketful tae fill the stove. But you didn't get any heat until it started tae go red on the top and the pipe got hot. Oo were ready tae go tae oor beds by that time. So ma friend Isa Dougan and I used tae go to the compound and pinch coal! If we'd been caught we'd ha' been put on charges. It wis a serious offence. Emily, the Glasgow girl that wis the corporal in charge o' our hut, used tae say, 'Ah don't know anything about it. But we're needin' coal for the fire.' And Isa would say, 'Come on, Liz, we'll go.' So we'd take the bucket wi' us and creep away in the dark – there wis no lights at the time. Ye jist had tae watch that the duty officer wisnae about anywhere. There wis a wee bit in the fence where one o' us could get under. We jist put our hand in and drew the coal out bit by bit. Oh, we did that often. We probably werenae the only ones that did that of course. Though ah cannae remember now, we must have had a ration o' sticks tae kindle the fire wi'. What ah do remember is wakenin' up in the morning in the wintertime and icicles hangin' from the wee shelf at the top o' your bed. Ah often think now if they'd fell on top o' us they could have stabbed us tae death! You had three blankets, and these white cotton sheets – freezin'. But we used to make the bed up so that one of the blankets was like an envelope, so there was no cold got in. We were issued with Service flannelette pyjamas. They were warm, and ye wore socks in your bed, then after a while you'd take your own hot water bottle to the camp.

At Drem I wis allocated tae work for the signals officer. He needed a typist. The offices were a' long wooden huts, but they were divided. One part wis Signals, then there wis the main orderly room, the typists' office, the adjutant's office, and the CO's [Commanding Officer's] office. Then you came out the door and in the next door, where there wis a wee office I sat in. Then there wis the signals officer's office, and then the long wireless operators' and teleprinters' place. The orderly room was a big office, wi' maybe four or five typists. So there were a lot of WAAF girls working in the offices. And of course the WAAF officer – ah think there wis only one in the camp, and she wis a flight officer in rank – had her own office somewhere else in the camp. And the padre, a nice old gentleman, had his office. He was Church o' Scotland. He was given a WAAF girl, not a typist but a general duties girl, tae help him. She lived in our hut and became a friend o' ours, in our circle – Mary from Helensburgh. Mary was a staunch Catholic. But she thought there were nobody like the padre.

Us WAAF girls mostly worked day shifts. Wireless operators and teleprinter girls worked on three shifts. And that wis the kind o' work I did – saw the rosters were right, who was on night shift, back shift, day shift. And if somebody wis off sick ye'd got tae find a replacement. The signals officer ah worked for at first was a squadron leader. He came from Manchester and, honest to God, ah could hardly make out a word he was sayin'. Ah jist used tae guess a lot o' the dictation ah took from him. But the second signals officer ah worked for, Flight

Lieutenant Brochter, he wis different altogether. He was a very shy person. He had a batman, but ah think he wis frightened tae ask the batman tae do anything for him. Once he came to me and said, 'Weston, I wonder if I could ask a favour?' 'Well,' ah says, 'ye can ask and I'll try.' He says, 'Well, the lining of my jacket's come away. Do you think you could sort it for me?' Ah says, 'Oh, yes. Bring it down and ah'll take it up to the hut and stitch it.' He could have got his batman to do that, but he wouldnae. And there were other times he asked me tae do things like that for him.

As well as the WAAFs that worked in the camp offices ah've mentioned, there were one or two girls who were truck drivers, others that dished out equipment or clothing from the stores, and them that folded up parachutes – that wis a trade on its own of course. So the number of WAAFs at Drem when ah wis there in 1943–4 wis maybe 100 to 120, no' any more. There were nine or 10 billets for us, wi' 12 girls in each hut. Ye maybe didnae become friendly with everybody, but you got to know them. There weren't that many that you didnae know them all by sight. Then there wis maybe two sergeants, and one or two corporals, like our Emily from Glasgow.

There would be two or three hundred RAF men at Drem. Oh, there would always be more men than WAAFs there. There were transport men, teleprinter operators, and you got pilots, gunners, radio operators. The WAAFs and the RAF men were kept quite separate, except when you worked together or were at a dance in the camp. Our camp was quite separate from the men's camp – there was a field between them. There was no question of the men slippin' into our camp. There wis none o' that. I can honestly say there wis never any jukery-packery wi' the men in the camp. If it went on it went on outside the camp. But ah remember Jessie, a wee girl fae Edinburgh, met Leslie Paltryman, one o' the sailors in the Fleet Air Arm at Drem, and they got married at Drem. They settled eventually after the war at The Inch in Edinburgh. Another WAAF at Drem – Dickson wis her name – also married a sailor fae the Fleet Air Arm. He belonged tae the Kyles o' Bute, and later they went away tae live there.

The Fleet Air Arm at Drem jist shared the airfield wi' the RAF. The base at Drem wis Fighter Command – Spitfires. And a lot of squadrons came in there. There wis Polish and French squadrons came in – maybe boys who'd been on active service and came intae Drem for a period o' rest. It wis a quiet station. German bombers had come up the Firth of Forth in the earlier years o' the war, but when ah wis at Drem in 1943–4 Drem wisnae so active as it had been then. There were no army folk or anti-aircraft guns at Drem or round about us. And the barrage balloon folks were up at the Forth Bridge and that. We didnae have them either at Drem.

Ah wis quite lucky bein' at Drem, because it was so near Newtongrange and Edinburgh. Ah wasnae home every weekend, but if ah had no duties on Saturday or Sunday ah could get home by bus on a Saturday and back to Drem on Sunday night. There wis a special bus for Service people left Edinburgh on a Sunday night for Drem. Ah had tae leave Newtongrange on a bus for Edinburgh about seven o'clock that night. So ma friend Isa Dougan said, 'Liz, come tae ma house in McDonald Road in Edinburgh and we'll go together to Drem on the special bus.'

It was a good life in the camp at Drem. On the WAAF site we had a wee NAAFI [Navy, Army & Air Force Institute] of our own, just for the WAAFs. The camp food was not bad at all, oh, ah had no complaints. Then right outside the main camp gate wis the Parachute Café, which was a great place. It was run by the two spinster ladies that owned Fenton Barns farm. Ah cannae mind their names. But the Parachute Café wis where we spent oor money. Not jist tea and buns – you could get ham and egg there. Well, they had the farm, so there wis no shortage o' eggs. You could get a lovely meal there. When Tom Herriot, ma future husband, came home on leave one time he came down to the camp. And the Parachute Café wis where we went for a meal. He couldnae get over it, bein' able durin' the war, wi' the rationin' and a' that, tae get there ham, bacon, egg, and home-made scones. It wis run by the two ladies purely and simply for the camp – and it wisnae expensive. It wis really great. If we were feelin' a bit low we used tae say, 'Oh, we'll go tae the Parachute Café and get our tea. We'll no' go up tae the cookhouse tonight.' The Café wis great for our morale.

Then we had a picture house thing outside the camp. It maybe wisnae very great, but twice a week ye got a film. They werenae war propaganda films, but jist ordinary films. And there were dances in the camp. Sergeant Ryder, one o' the wireless operators, he organised the dance band. They called themselves The Squadronaires.

At Drem you had tae do night duty about once a month, overnight, in the orderly room. Even the WAAF typists had tae do it. It was in case anybody was posted in durin' the night, or signals came, or the teleprinter went durin' the night, or anythin' like that. There wis a teleprinter in the orderly room too, ye see. But you weren't allowed to stay overnight by yourself. You had to have a friend with you. So when I was on night duty Tiny Dougan stayed with me, and when she was on I stayed wi' her. So really it wis like twice a month we had tae be on. And the one who was actually on duty had to clean out the CO's fire in the mornin', take the ash away, and set the fire. And there wis two wee iron bed things you could lie and doze on a wee bit, but you didnae sleep: they werenae comfortable. Well, ah'll never forget this early mornin'. Isa wis cleaning out the fire, when the teleprinter went. It said: 'LACW Dougan posted Records, Gloucester'. Ah shouted through tae Isa, 'Oh, Isa. You'll never guess who's posted!' She says, 'Yes, it'll be me.' Ah says, 'Yes, you're right. And you'll never guess where you're goin'.' Isa said, 'Don't tell me it's Records, Gloucester?' 'Aye,' ah said. 'Oh, my God!' Isa was beside herself. But there was nothing she could do. She had tae go. Records, Gloucester, was the dreaded place. Nobody wanted tae go there, because once they got you to Gloucester you never got out. But, fortunately or unfortunately, when Isa got to Gloucester, an awful wet, damp place, she developed a terrible chest cough she couldnae get rid of. So eventually they posted her tae the isle of Tiree in the Hebrides, and that's where she finished her time in the WAAF.

Well, ah expect in the WAAF or other Services you could be posted somewhere else. But ah never thought for a moment after ah wis posted tae Drem that ah would be posted anywhere else. Ah never gave it a thought. Well, ah'd been at Drem about 15 months in 1943–4 when I was posted to the Air Ministry in London, to the WAAF Directorate no less. Ah wis beside myself. As a country girl, ah'd never been tae London in ma life before. Ah'd only been once in England, visitin' a friend in Derbyshire. The only holidays ah'd had before the war ah went wi' ma sisters to Rothesay or Dunoon, or somewhere like that. So when ma postin' from Drem came through, the WAAF officer there sent for me and said, 'Well, Weston, you're going to the WAAF Directorate in London – Air Ministry.' Ah says tae her, 'Can ye no' get it changed?' 'Weston,' she says, 'do you know the honour you've been given? You're going to work for Lady Welsh.' Ah didnae know who Lady Welsh was.[10] Ah wis really upset. Ah'd been so happy in the signals place at Drem. I thoroughly enjoyed bein' at Drem, even the cold winter was all part of it. So ah arrived in London at the WAAF Directorate no' long before D-Day.

* * *

The WAAF Directorate was in Adastral House, Kingsway, High Holborn, in London, Air Ministry headquarters. Air Chief Commandant Lady Welsh wis the Director, the most senior woman officer in the WAAF. Adastral House wis a buildin' with about seven floors. The WAAF Directorate had the sixth floor. The floors were in squares, the stairs went down the middle. So you had offices there, there, there, and here, and ye could walk round them. Our girls' office was Room 610. Eileen wis the corporal, and there wis Frankie, Kay, Frieda, Rita, and myself – the five typists. We served all the officers. We never saw Lady Welsh directly. But she had a PA [Personal Assistant] who gave her work to us. Then there wis flight and squadron officers – ladies who had all the different sections of the WAAF to deal with: welfare, changes in King's Regulations, main operations, administrative stuff. Then there wis Group Officer Woodhead, second in command tae Lady Welsh, and Flight Officers Montefiori and Lady Armitage-Smith.[11] These were the ones I dealt with mostly. Some of the officers ah never dealt with, because it wisnae ma work. But they were all commissioned officers in the WAAF Directorate. They were a' very nice. It wis jist us girls in the office that were plain WAAFs.

At Drem ma problem wi' salutin' never bothered me. Well, at the WAAF Directorate in London the medical officer gave me a card saying, 'This Aircraftwoman is excused salutin' with her right arm. Please accept a left-hand salute.' Ah carried that card in ma top pocket everywhere. But ah thought it wis goin' tae be terrible. London wis teeming wi' officers – and they were a' seniors. Well, one day ah wis comin' back fae ma lunch and I heard this shout: 'Air Woman!' And this WAAF officer said to me, 'Don't you know you salute with your right hand?' 'Yes, ma'am,' ah said, 'ah do know. But ah'm excused.' And ah gave her ma card. She looked at it and said, 'Where do you work?' When ah told her, she said, 'How do you work at that?' 'Well, I do,' I said. 'I'm a shorthand typist. I work in Lady

Welsh's department.' 'Does Lady Welsh know you can't salute?' 'Yes,' I said. 'All right,' she said. But she never apologised. And it really upset me. The street round about was millin' wi' people, and they'd be wonderin' what on earth wis goin' on. When I got intae the office I told Eileen, our corporal, and ah said, 'Ah knew this would happen.' Eileen must have told the PA that I was really upset. Well, Lady Welsh sent for me. 'Now, Weston,' she says, 'tell me what happened.' Ah just told her. 'Well,' she says, 'you're not to worry about it. It doesn't mean a thing. Your work here is much more important. Don't let it upset you. I'll put it right with the officer.' Now this officer that had shouted at me was herself in the Directorate, but I'd never dealt with her, though I knew her by sight. She didn't know me. But that was the only time ah wis ever pulled up for salutin' wi' ma left hand.

Ah liked the work we had. Mind, we worked hard: nine o'clock till six. And two of us had to be on all day one Saturday in four. We didn't work on a Sunday. If ye wanted a cup o' tea in the office ye had tae be on the hop, because the rest o' the building was filled wi' civil servants. And outside our office door there wis a wee sort o' cabinet with an electric ring for boiling the kettle. Wi' all the civil servants comin' in, oh, God, there wis a queue at that kettle.

Our billets were in Bentinck Close, St John's Wood, Regent's Park. They had been luxury flats and they were requisitioned. There were four or five storeys. Ah wis up on the fourth or fifth one, ah cannae remember now which it wis. But, oh, it wis lovely. We were right opposite Regent's Park, and at the end wis the Zoological Gardens – the Zoo. The windows in the flat were all out of course wi' bomb damage, and they were boarded up wi' wood tae about a foot from the top. So if it wis sunny ye got the best o' it. But the beds were underneath the windows, so if it was rainin' or snowin' ye got the rain or the snow on the top o' ye!

But actually the accommodation was good, because there wis a certain amount of heatin' in these flats. The flat we were in had four or five rooms, and there wis four beds tae a room. And there wis a huge kitchen wi' a huge table in the middle o' it – ye could dae your ironin' on it. And you could make a cup o' tea in the kitchen. And there were bathrooms. The room we were in had maybe been the sittin' room. It had beautiful wallpaper like a herbaceous border o' flowers. At one time the flat had belonged tae Florence Desmond.[12]

Then the dinin' room wis down on the bottom floor. And the food wis marvellous – plenty of it and good quality. The WAAF girls that worked at Whitehall, like teleprinter operators and plotters, all worked different shifts. So the kitchen functioned 24 hours a day. It wis about seven o'clock at night when we got back tae the billets, by the time ye got maybe the Underground tae Baker Street and then up tae Regent's Park. Sometimes we would take the Underground tae Camden Town, then a bus brought us tae the door. But we had tae get two transports tae get tae the office. You were allowed your travellin' expenses, and ah think we were allowed 9d [3½p] a day for our lunch. We got that in the next building tae Adastral House. The Air Ministry had a canteen there and we were allowed in wi' our passes. Ye could get a bowl o' soup and a cup o' something for 9d [3½p]. But when ye got home tae the billet at seven o'clock you'd get a lovely hot meal. There were girls there as cooks, and you could get lovely bacon, sausages, potatoes, and whatever. The food wis lovely.

On Sundays ye'd jist relax and ye got out of town. Ah wis fortunate. Among the girls in the office ah made awful good friends. Frankie lived out at Epsom. She used tae say, 'Elizabeth, come home wi' me for the weekend.' She wis from a frightfully posh family. Ah'd say, 'Aw, are ye sure?' 'Yes. Mummy says you've to come home for the weekend.' Frankie's father wis the director of a fleet o' buses. Mummy was a buxom woman, absolutely full o' life. They had a beautiful home. So mummy used tae say, 'Now, girls, get into the room. I've put clothing out for you. And get these uniforms off.' She hated them, and would have frocks and things laid out for us. She used tae say tae me, 'Ah'm so fond of you, Elizabeth, because your fiancé is a mariner.' (By this time I was engaged tae Tom Herriot.) And she'd say, 'You see, long ago I went with a submariner. Unfortunately, he was lost at sea.' But, oh, Frankie and her parents were good tae me. Now that wis very much a wartime experience. At Newtongrange ah'd never have met people like that, never!

Another of the office girls that became a good friend wis Kay. Kay lived out in Ilford. Then Rita, that also worked in the office, lost her fiancé at the Normandy D-Day landings. Rita always wore his ring on her forefinger. He was presumed lost, and Rita was so sad, not knowing whether he was dead or not. She never ever got official word that he was dead.

Occasionally on a Sunday, maybe once a month, Frieda from the office and I used tae take the train down tae Kent tae visit one of our WAAF officers, Lady Armitage-Smith, that wis in a wee RAF hospital there. She had a spot on her lung. When she wis goin' away tae this hospital she said tae Frieda and I, 'I hope you will come and see me.' Now it wasn't really the done thing for ordinary WAAFs to go and visit officers. But she said, 'Oh, but ah want you to come and see me.' She wis just herself in one o' these huts that circled round, followin' the sun. And she was so pleased tae see us. So ah felt that social class barriers were definitely breakin' down durin' the war – not with everybody: you did get some snooty-nosed ones. But the genuine gentry, they were great.

As ah've said, ah arrived at the WAAF Directorate in London no' long before D-Day. Then from jist after D-Day we were bein' bombed by the V1 flying bombs – we called them doodlebugs – and a bit later by the V2 rockets. It wis pretty horrible, frightening. You didn't get very many nights when you hadn't to get out of your bed. It didn't matter how often the siren went, the rule was you had to go down to the basement. Ye got so tired of it, you said, 'Oh, ah'm not goin'. If it's goin' tae hit me it's goin' tae hit me.' But the duty officer came up all the floors, 'Come on, girls. Get down to the basement.' And the lifts werenae workin': they wouldnae let ye go in the lifts anyway. Ye had tae get down the stairs. So ye were down in these cellars wi' your greatcoat on and your trousers. You'd maybe just be there half an hour and the All Clear wid go. So you'd climb up the stairs and intae your bed again. Ye'd just be in it when WWWOOO – the siren again. Oh, God! But, well, ah think ye jist got used tae it. But we never had any narrow escapes. Ye used tae hear them goin' over. Wis it the doodlebug or the rocket that whistled WWWHHHEEE? And they always said when the whistle stopped it jist dropped. And that's what you listened for. Ye jist waited, and you thought, 'Oh, it's passin' over.' Well, it wis jist something that ah wis fortunate tae come through.

The other thing that really used tae go for me was when we came off the Underground every night to change trains, families were lyin' on the platforms. They were shelterin' wi' their children from the raids. Oh, it wis heart-rendin'. When ye stepped off these Underground trains there wisnae much room. The families wid be lyin' there, maybe the mother and father sittin' against the wall, their covers round them, and maybe their three children in sleepin' bags and sound asleep, and ye were steppin' over them. It wisnae jist a few. It wis the whole length o' the platform. Every night these folk came down there tae the Underground platforms for safety, not knowin' when they went up again whether their homes would be still there or no'. And ye never heard them complainin'.

So ah came through a' that. And ah wis outside Buckingham Palace on D-Day and outside the Palace again on VE Day. Everybody went down The Mall to the Palace then. We were at the railins, but we had tae stand up on the wall, because otherwise ye were goin' tae get crushed tae death – huge crowds.

$$* * *$$

Well, Tom Herriot and I had met and were courting before the war, got engaged durin' the war, and as Tom, a submariner in the navy, wis comin' back from Trincomalee in Ceylon [Sri Lanka], we arranged tae be married in November 1945, when we were both still in the Services. Lady Welsh gave me a beautiful big canteen of cutlery as a wedding present from the officers of the WAAF Directorate. And ah still use a' the different kinds o' knives and spoons, carvers, servers and everything. Ah've used them every day since ah wis married.

Durin' the war, marriage didn't get you out o' the women's Services. You only got out if you were pregnant. But after the war was over and you were married you could get out, you didnae have to be pregnant. So ah jist applied for demob and ah got out in February 1946. Tom didnae get demobbed till after me. Ah got a job in a wee office in Frederick Street in Edinburgh. Ah wis there three months, then Tom asked me to go back wi' him to Gosport at Portsmouth, where he wis still in the navy. So ah wis wi' him there for three months. When I came back tae Newtongrange I got a job as a shorthand typist with the Lothian Coal Company. Ah worked there for a while, but left before it wis nationalised in 1947. Ah wis married four years before ah had any family. Then by about 1953 ah had three boys. When the youngest one was six ah got a part-time job in a wee shop in Newtongrange, until ah started in 1971 – at first part-time, later full-time – as a shorthand typist at Newbattle Abbey Adult Residential College, just down the road from Newtongrange.[13] Ah wis there at the Abbey nearly 16 years until ah retired.

Bein' in the WAAF durin' the war wis a great experience, it really was. Ah think ah wis possibly lucky tae land in London of course. The experience gave me a much broader outlook on life altogether. You saw things you wouldnae otherwise have seen, and you met people you'd never have met. You met all classes of folk. It wis an experience and one ah've never regretted. Maybe ah didn't want it at the time ah went tae the WAAF, but ah never regretted havin' it.

Elizabeth Weston (Mrs Elizabeth Herriot) died on 8 October 2013.

Jean Robertson

When the war broke out in September 1939 I was 17½, and I was scared stiff. Night after night I was scared to go to sleep in case the Germans came and got me!

I was born in Aberdeen on 21 March 1922. I had a brother and a sister. My brother Robert was three or four years older than me, my sister Gertrude was two years, nine months, and one week younger than me.

My father belonged to the village of Echt, about 12 miles from Aberdeen. He'd begun work on his father's small farm at Echt. I believe he went very early as a volunteer to fight in the 1914–18 War. I think he was in the Gordon Highlanders.[1] He was wounded in the leg in France, so that leg was 1½ inches short. After the war he worked shifts in Aberdeen first, I think, as a tram driver, then as a bus driver. But he often went for medical attention to Edenhall Hospital at Musselburgh in Midlothian. In fact, he died aged 48 at Edenhall in January 1941 while he was being operated on. I think he had worked on his father's farm from about 1908 till he went to the war. Though he never went back after the war to work full-time on the farm, he used to go there on his day off in Aberdeen to help his father.

I remember my grandfather Robertson. He was an Aberdeenshire man. They didn't move far in those days, did they?! My grandmother Robertson had died in childbirth. She had two sons, the older one my dad, and two daughters older than him. I remember them telling me that when the minister came to grandmother's funeral, the baby was baptised over her funeral. Then a housekeeper came to look after the four children, and my grandfather married the housekeeper. So there was a second family Robertson.

My mother belonged to Fyvie, near Turriff in Aberdeenshire. I think she may have been in domestic service before the 1914–18 War. But when the war broke out she came from Fyvie into Aberdeen and worked as a bus conductress during the war. Her father worked as a groom. I remembered him as 'looking after the horses'. When I knew him and my maternal grandmother they lived in Rothie Norman village, near Fyvie. So he worked around the farms there.

The first house I remember living in was in Northern Road, Aberdeen. It was a wee cottage-type house on the main road. You opened the front door and walked straight into it. It was ground floor only. I can't remember how many rooms or what form of lighting it had. I left there when I was five and a half. We moved then about 1927 or '28 to 105 Willowbank Road in Aberdeen. They were tenement flats there. There were shops on the ground floor, then three storeys of flats. We were on the third, or top, floor of the flats. We had three rooms in that house: a living room-kitchen, and two bedrooms. My brother Robert slept in one of the bedrooms, my sister Gertrude and I in the other one. Mum and dad slept in a recess in the living room-kitchen. It was gas lighting to start with. Then about 1930 it became electricity. That was something, because my dad had to get sunray treatment for his leg. We didn't have a fixed bath there. So it was the usual – you bathed either in the sink, or in a tin bath in front of the fire. The toilet, an indoor flush toilet, was halfway down the landing. It was shared between two families – us and our neighbours on the landing. Everybody in these days lived in those sorts of conditions. We never thought there was anything wrong with it. So the flat in Willowbank Road was my home until just after the war.

I began school aged five at what, I think, was just called Woodside Public School in Aberdeen. But I was only there six months. Then, because we flitted to Willowbank Road, I moved to Holburn Street School, another primary. I liked that school, though some teachers were better than others. I always liked English and geography, and you went through the whole lot – drawing, music, and so on. I enjoyed most things. It was ok there, a good school.

I sat the Qualifying exam there when I was about 11. I can remember I was frightened to death during the exam. I would have walked it at any other time. You didn't get to sit the Quali in your own school at Holburn Street. You had to go to another school in Aberdeen that was called the Central. You had to go up a spiral staircase there to the class-room where we sat the exam. By the time we got there I was shaking with nerves. Well, I pretended I'd passed the exam but I knew I hadn't. So I failed the Quali.

So then I went to Ruthrieston Intermediate School, right on the river Dee in Aberdeen. I liked that secondary school and most of the teachers. English again I found most interesting. We didn't do science, but we did domestic subjects: laundry, cooking. I was no good at maths – not my strong point! Then the year I went to Ruthrieston they dropped Latin. They thought it was more important for the girls to learn domestic science. Miss Mackay (we called her Kayanne), our English teacher, was furious Latin had been dropped. Her attitude was if we learned the derivation of words from Latin we would know English better. So she forced us to learn Latin – though I don't think she was supposed to do that. Miss Mackay came from the west Highlands. I suppose she must have been a native Gaelic speaker. She was a super teacher, and Latin was her interest, her language, her preference. But we didn't get French or any other foreign language at Ruthrieston. I quite enjoyed the cooking, and because we were allowed to bring home the stuff we cooked my dad used to be sitting waiting for it. He used to laugh at the stuff. But he didn't care what it was as long as it was edible! So at school we had cooking every week, and we also learned how to wash and iron.

Normally, you had to leave Ruthrieston at the age of 14. But I was allowed to stay on till I was 15 in 1937. That was because I got a scholarship. You got £3 a year for staying on, doing an extra year. Out of our class of at least 30, it was maybe 10 of us that got a scholarship. And it was good to be able to stay on. That must have been the result of passing an exam, a school certificate, in our third year when we'd be 14. I was always about third or fourth in our class. I was never top. My friend Dorothy Stewart was always top. Dorothy lived beside me. She and my other friend Dorothy Kynoch, who later became a minister's wife, were always top of the class. I wasn't too bad, but I wasn't as good as them. Anyway, in that extra year at school we must have studied the same subjects as before, but also we spent a lot of time going round museums, art galleries, and places like that – outside educational visits. Oh, I enjoyed that.

As a girl I was always a keen reader. I read, oh, *Anne of Green Gables*, that sort of stuff.[2] I remember getting comics, but I think you used to get them from your friends, and visitors, like your mother's friends, would bring you one. If you weren't feeling well they'd bring you a comic, that sort of thing. One I think I did read was called the *Girl's Own* or the *Girls' Only*.[3] But we didn't get a regular weekly comic. We didn't have that much money. My mother wouldn't be able to afford giving us a penny for a comic. And my dad's pay as a tram or bus driver would not be very big. I don't think he ever had more than £3 a week wages.

When I was still at school I joined the public library. My dad took me there. He was a keen reader himself of all the Zane Grey stories, all the cowboys stuff.[4] But he started me in the libraries. So I would say reading was my principal interest as a girl at school. I spent a lot of my leisure time reading. But we also used to play games, oh, in the street: hide-and-seek, and all sorts of things, chasing each other. The street was our playground. You didn't have to worry in those days about cars. Then when I was a bit older I was in a tennis club and I joined the Guides, though not the Brownies.

Every Sunday, or most Sundays, I went to Sunday School. My aunty Chris (her name was actually Christian), my father's sister, used to come for me and take me to church. My mother was a fairly regular churchgoer, but not so much my dad. He worked shifts. Our church was Holburn Central, Church of Scotland. In our family my dad was the important one, the family man. My mum looked after dad, getting meals and sandwiches for him and all that. Oh, I remember sometimes taking my dad's piece to him. Ma mother had to make it every day for him. Another thing she had to do in the summertime was to iron the white cover for his driver's hat. There was elastic all round the cover, and I can remember having to do that for him myself. Mum had everything ready for him before he left the house. So we didn't have to go to the tram or bus stop with my dad's piece or anything, unless occasionally he or we had forgotten something. Then we'd go with it for him to the bus terminus near the theatre and hand it in there. Generally, if dad was free mum was free, but otherwise . . .

As a girl I didn't have a bicycle. Gertrude, my sister, had one and I got to borrow it. I don't know why I didn't get a bicycle – possibly when I didn't pass the Qualifying exam: that's when you got your bicycle! Probably I suffered from being the middle child in the family, rather than the youngest one.

So I left school in 1937 when I was 15. I hadn't any ambitions to become a nurse or a teacher or a doctor. I wished to become a hairdresser! But you had to pay to be a hairdresser. You paid them, not the other way round. But my parents had no money for that. So I ended up in a shop, a big department store, in the china department. I left school on the Friday and started there on the Monday. The big store was Isaac Benzie's, in George Street in Aberdeen.[5] I didn't see an advert for the job. I think Benzie's just recruited youngsters at the school. I think they came to the school and offered us jobs. Several other employers did the same. My aunty Chris had worked for Benzie's as housekeeper. So I think it was the fact we knew the set-up, or my mother did, that was how I started there. At that stage I didn't have any particular interest in working in shops. It was just money wasn't it? You had to earn your living.

We had to be at Benzie's before the shop opened at nine o'clock in the morning. You had a card you had to stamp on your way in. If you were late there was a red mark on your card, and you had to report to the lady who made up the wages. And she always threatened to hold your money back. But I don't think she ever did, unless you were seriously late. I couldn't have been seriously late, or even a bit late more than occasionally, because I don't remember being fined. Benzie's store was maybe less than a couple of miles from my home. That's not very far, so I used to walk to work. It took me maybe about 20 minutes. So I'd be up in the mornings about half past seven or so, have my breakfast, and be out of the house by about half past eight. There was a canteen at Benzie's. But I don't think we got a tea-break in the morning or afternoon. I can't remember what we did for lunch. Oh, I don't think Benzie's would have given you a free meal! I think sometimes we went home for lunch, because we had to take turns about going home, relieving each other. But other days we must have gone for lunch in Benzie's, because I certainly remember using the canteen. Possibly we took our own sandwich for lunchtime. I remember sometimes at lunchtime we used to go out and buy a bar of chocolate, because at times you didn't get your lunch until two o'clock: if you were junior in the department you were last. Then I think we finished work at six o'clock.

When I began work at Benzie's in 1937 my wages were something like 10 shillings [50p] a week. I think that would be a fairly standard wage then for a girl of 15. Then you got it up. But you had to go every year and ask for it to be put up. You went to ask the middle-aged woman – I can't remember her name – that would report you if you were late. She was in charge. She seemed ancient to me as a young girl. She was unmarried: not many married women in these days were allowed to work, unless they were widows. Once a woman got married she lost her job. And the oldest ones missed that if they were in charge of a department. But in Benzie's she was the one who could report you to the boss himself. He didn't want to have anything to do with it. He just strolled around, greeting the important visitors.

I started work at Benzie's on the lifts. I was a lift operator. I think everybody started that way. You got a wee bit of training. Somebody showed you what to do. Oh, there wasn't much to it. So I must have done about six months, I think, on the lifts. By then I was quite used to it. Then I was moved into the china department and I was there all the time until the war came and I went to the WAAF. I didn't choose to go to the china department: we were told to go.

Benzie's was really quite a large department store. In the basement there were toys – it was all toys there. The next floor was the china. It was a big, big china department. Then there was a hosiery and under-wear department. And further upstairs there was millinery, and ladies' dresses and coats and things. And on the top floor was hairdressing. It was a pity I hadn't been moved from the lifts to the hairdressing. That's really what I wanted to do. But the stumbling block was you still had to pay to learn the work. However, I did find the china department quite interesting, and I'm still interested in china.

I discovered in Benzie's the different makes of china and so on. Some of it was quite valuable – Wedgwood, Mason's, and so forth. For a while I was down unpacking china that came in to the store. It used to come in great big barrels, huge things. And sometimes, when you had to take the top off the barrel, there would be mice in there. Luckily, there were two men who used to pack all the china when you sent it out to people. So we used to get those two men to lift the top off the barrels. Oh! And then of course you had to unpack all the china. If any of it was broken, you had to keep it aside. A man used to come from the railway company and inspect it all, and he paid compensation for breakages. Sometimes he would insist on taking all the breakages away with him. But the next time he would say, 'Keep it.' If there were only little chips in things you were allowed to keep that yourself. There wasn't much we got to keep, but I've still got a plate at home that I got in that way at Benzie's.

In the china department there were at least seven of us workers – all women. Every other department at Benzie's had at least three or four workers. There were six or seven departments, and there must have been several delivery van and lorry drivers. There were a lot of men and they delivered an awful lot of stuff. It was not a high class shop, I don't mean that. But a lot of customers had their stuff delivered to them by Benzie's. They didn't take their shopping home with them. Many of the customers were sort of middle class people, better off people. We had a few who came into the china department who had their own estates. They would come in for china for the servants' quarters, which was completely different from the stuff they used for themselves. Benzie's was something like Jenners in Edinburgh. Most of the customers would be better off people – but we had all different kinds of customers. Some people would come to Benzie's if they wanted something special, maybe wedding presents, that sort of thing and, oh, for the china. So I worked in the china department for about five years. Once you were in a department you were stuck there. There was no attempt by Benzie's to give you a wider or different experience by moving you round other departments.

* * *

I remember the outbreak of the war on Sunday, the 3rd of September 1939. We heard it on the radio, Mr Chamberlain's broadcast. And I think my aunty Chris came in from church afterwards. I certainly wasn't in the church myself. I can't remember if my dad was in Edenhall Hospital at Musselburgh then. Oh, he always went there, it was an army hospital. I wanted to volunteer as soon as the war broke out. I was 17½, and I was scared stiff! I was scared stiff in case the Germans would get me! I wanted to defend Britain against them. But not only that: my hair was black, and it seemed that heaven help anyone with black hair who was found by the Germans. We all thought they were going to invade. And of course the Nazi German attitude was that anybody with black hair was for the chop. (Aryan types – blonde hair and blue eyes – would be ok.) My sister Gertrude's hair was blonde, but mine was jet black. So I can remember when the war broke out, night after night I was scared to go to sleep in case the Germans came and got me. That was the only reason I was scared stiff of them. And, you see, we didn't really hear about what was happening to the Jews in Germany before the war. It was just my impressions from the radio and reading the newspapers, and of course listening to my dad. I approached my dad once or twice about me volunteering into the Forces. You needed your parents to sign the papers to do that. But my dad wouldn't sign for me to go. So I had to wait till I was called up.

Well, my dad died in January 1941, and I was called up toward the end of 1942. We had to register first, and then you got your calling up papers. You went to the Central School in Aberdeen (where I had sat and failed the Quali exam), and you got an interview there. You had to say what you were good at and what you'd had experience in, if you could type or maybe write shorthand, or drive. That was the sort of thing you were asked. So that must have been when they decided which sort of work you were going to be sent to.

I think I must have got a choice of women's Services. We had an aerodrome at Dyce, about five miles from Aberdeen. And we saw a lot of airmen – had dates with them as well! I may have been influenced by that. So that's probably why it was I went into the Air Force. And of course the Air Force was very popular at that time, and it was the newest of the Services. And the WAAF uniform looked better than the ATS or WRNS. You didn't see many WRNS in or around Aberdeen. I think they were down in Edinburgh and also further north than Aberdeen. And my dad put me off the army and the ATS. He didn't think women should be in the army, or have anything to do with soldiers. So he did influence my choice of Service. If I got a preference the WAAF was the one.

Then you got a letter telling you to report a week before Christmas to an RAF place down in Hereford. It wasn't in the city of Hereford, but up country. I can't remember now the name of the place. Anyway, you went down from Aberdeen by train. We left Aberdeen at nine o'clock in the morning, and we didn't get to the place till the following afternoon at four o'clock.

Well, my mum and, I think, my younger sister Gertrude, came to the station to see me off. I'm not sure, but I think three of us recruits went from Aberdeen on that train. I didn't know the others. And there were other girls who joined the train on the way down. We were all in the one carriage together. I think we were told where to sit. In war conditions, the trains ran if they could, and our one stopped and started. Och! We fell asleep, I think, half the time. But you kept waking up. The windows of the trains were all blacked out. And when you got to a station they'd removed the name of the station. So you couldn't tell where you were. Well, we got down as far as Crewe. I'd never before been further south than Carlisle, and I did think, 'One of these days we're going to fall off the end of England!' I really did.

As a girl, and after I'd started work at Benzie's, I'd only gone Sunday School picnics and family holidays, mainly in the Aberdeen area, visiting aunties and uncles. We never got to, say, Cruden Bay or Elgin, Montrose or Arbroath, for a summer holiday on the beach. Three of the women in Benzie's, much higher up and much better paid than me, they used to go on holiday to Switzerland and all sorts of overseas places. The workers at Benzie's, including me, did all get a week's paid summer holiday. But the furthest I'd ever been, as I say, was down to Carlisle after the war broke out, to visit Robert, my brother, who was married there. But that was most people's experience in these days: you didn't go far.

Well, when on our way to join the WAAF our train from Aberdeen landed at Crewe near the end of 1942, we'd to stay on that station until six o'clock next morning. There was nothing to eat, nothing. If we'd brought a sandwich with us we'd have eaten it long before then. So we were to wait at Crewe until the canteen there opened at six o'clock. But as soon as it did open then we'd to get on the train and continue the journey to our destination. As I say, it was four o'clock in the afternoon that day when we got there.

When we arrived at last at the WAAF camp it was Nissen huts. They were separate beds in them. You got a bed which you had to make up yourself, and three grey blankets. I can't remember if they gave us sheets or not. There was a little chest of drawers alongside the bed. That's all you had to keep your belongings in. I put the case I'd brought with me under the bed.

There were, I think, 12 girls in our hut. There weren't any others in it from Aberdeen. They came from all over Britain. You didn't understand what they were saying! And they didn't understand you: I had a fairly strong Aberdeen accent myself. I always remember there was one girl from Yorkshire. We had to do our own cleaning. And this Yorkshire girl walked down the centre of the aisle, shouting, 'Where's t' broom?!' Nobody had a clue what she was asking for. But after a time it became a friendly grouping in a sense, but they were all different. Some of them had a lot more money than the others. And, oh, some of them were a lot more experienced, too. So there was quite a mixture. But I think there was a spirit of camaraderie grew up, because we were all in it together. As we were in the same hut we all knew each other. Oh, we were all together on parade, and we did everything together – exercises, drill. We got each other up, and that sort of thing.

We got our uniform there. You got skirts, and all the underwear: golly, they were thick! And you got thick stockings, lisle stockings. You'd a tunic, and I think it was two or three blue shirts, a tie, and shoes. Even years later I never needed to go to a chiropodist, because when we got them in the WAAF you were asked what your size was, and if you said it was size six you got size seven. And if you said, 'That's too big,' you were told, 'No, it's not. You'll need them.' And they reckon it was because of that we've all got good feet! All the marching about, and the thick socks of course, spread our feet. They were flat-heeled shoes, and you'd to spit on them, rub stuff on them to polish them and get them shiny like patent leather. They had to be like mirrors when you went on parade.

And you were introduced to the various drills and parades, medicals, inoculations, and all that. Oh, every minute of the day was regimented. You didn't get time to yourself. And you'd be marched to the cookhouse. I suppose it was one way to keep us all in together. And, oh, I remember we all broke down in tears, especially on Christmas Day. Because we'd only been in the WAAF about a week, and it was the thing in the Forces that on Christmas Day the officers served the other ranks. That Day I think it was the saltiest soup I've ever had in my life! We were all in tears, and the tears were rolling down into this soup. I don't think any of us enjoyed that Christmas Day! That first Christmas was terrible. And what also wasn't funny was that I had whitlow on one of my fingers, and I had the nail taken off. That was severely painful.

Another thing was that when you got your pay you had to queue up for it. You were on parade, and you had to go forward to the table where the pay officer sat, and salute. Well, my finger was bandaged with this whitlow business, and I didn't know whether I was supposed to salute with this great big bandage on my finger.

There was an NCO, a corporal or a sergeant, had a little room at the end of our hut. She was in charge of us, gave us our orders, and marched us up and down: 'Stop talking,' 'Put the lights out,' and all that. A lot depended on how agreeable or disagreeable such an NCO was. You'd be reported at the drop of a hat if you came in late, that sort of thing. But in those first weeks you really weren't allowed out the camp anyway.

So I was in that first camp at least three weeks, maybe longer. And then I think you were just told what work, trade, or job you were going to do in the WAAF. And then you moved on to another camp or airfield. So I was moved to Jesmond, a district in Newcastle-upon-Tyne. There was a big aerodrome there. The first one was a camp, not an aerodrome. I don't remember if at Jesmond it was Fighter, Bomber, or Coastal Command. My job there was charging the big batteries – accumulators they were called – for the planes. I don't really know what these huge batteries or accumulators were. The men used to go out and collect them up. You were supposed to charge them up in this great big hangar. And you used to get acid all over your uniform. You'd get a new uniform every day. I think you had gloves. I did that job only a couple of times, then the men decided I'd be better in the office looking after other things and making the cocoa. I must admit the men were very good. They looked after the WAAFs. They were sort of protective, especially the older ones if they were married; and if you were in their section they looked after you. Oh, those great big accumulators were horrible things. The men had to bring them from the planes to this hangar, they were all charged there and taken back again. But I never had to take them back. I suppose I must have been shown along with another WAAF what we were to do. There was a sergeant in charge of it all. But he certainly didn't approve of the women being in the hangar. That was how I got to work in the office instead. The office work was easier. Well, it was January in 1943, so the hangar was cold and draughty. And we could hear Newcastle being bombed by the Germans at night.

I was in a Nissen hut at Jesmond with other WAAF girls. You had a great big stove in the middle of the hut. Somebody'd get up during the night and try to feed the stove to keep it going. It was coke it burned. The hut was reasonably warm as a result of the stove, and we all sat round it in the evenings. At night, you'd lie in your bed first with your blankets, then you got undressed. And by the time you got into bed, the bed was warm. Then we used to put our clothes under the blankets, to keep them warm for the morning. I think there was a door at either end of the hut. If the door was opened – oh! So the Nissen hut was not the most comfortable accommodation.

Jesmond was a big RAF station. I don't know how many WAAFs would be there, but there must have been quite a number. I think it was there that the cookhouse was terrible, the food was awful. There was a lot of maggots. Oh, that was terrible. You were scared to eat. If an officer came round at meal times and asked us, 'Is everything all right?', you didn't dare say no. They'd stop giving you anything next time you went to the cookhouse!

And then at Jesmond, as well as at the earlier camp, there were no showers, just baths. But the baths were in another hut. You had to leave your own hut and go to it – freezing cold and all that. And no sooner you got in the bath than somebody was banging on the door: 'When are you getting out?!'

The work I did in the office at Jesmond was writing up which batteries they'd been doing, and that sort of thing. And also I would make the cocoa for the men who were moving the batteries. So I learned how to make cocoa! Oh, it wasn't just in the morning or evening. There was always cocoa there. I think we just boiled the water for it in a kettle. There wasn't a big boiler that kept boiling up the water. We just had a little office, and the men would come in there for their cocoa. They showed me how to make the cocoa. So I was the cocoa girl. Oh, you were always learning something in the WAAFs!

I'm not sure how long I was at Jesmond. But I had my 21st birthday at Cranwell in Lincolnshire, so I was there by March 1943. I must have been at Jesmond therefore about a couple of months. I didn't volunteer to go to Cranwell. My name and my WAAF number 472899 came up on orders: 'You're going to Cranwell.' You got a rail ticket, you were taken down to the station and put on the train. No other girls went with me. I was on my own. Oh, you got used to that. Anyway, at Jesmond I think they realised I was hopeless, and they probably got a terrible report on me!

At Cranwell they moved all the married families out, and the WAAFs used the married quarters. We were all in three-bedroomed houses, so it was far more comfortable. I suppose Cranwell was quite a prestigious posting. It was an RAF headquarters and the RAF college was there, where they trained pilots. But not long after I arrived there we certainly had food poisoning. Almost all the WAAFs had food poisoning. I was lucky, I wasn't affected by it. Again, we all ate at the cookhouse. So something there must have . . . The ambulance came round every night, knocking at the door: 'Bring out your sick.' It was pretty grim. I remember some nights in particular.

At Cranwell I was put on a course of training in direction finding. You trained at that for several weeks. If you were training that's all you did. There were other WAAFs on the course. We learned Morse code – which was a laugh – and all sorts of things, like soldering. So Cranwell was quite a different experience from Jesmond. I felt I was doing something useful and worthwhile. I quite enjoyed learning the various things. And the girls were friendly. At Cranwell my best friend was Jessie Murray. She came from near Buckie in Banffshire. Jessie had her 21st birthday at Cranwell, and her mother sent her a clootie dumpling. Jessie and I were the only two there who knew what a clootie dumpling was. You can imagine the rest of the girls: 'What are we supposed to do with that?' But they managed to get through it all right. Later on, I was Jessie's bridesmaid.

So Cranwell was a nice posting. It was a bigger place than Jesmond, and it was quite different: there was a lot of flying going on all the time. And you seemed to get a lot more visitors from other places. It was more civilised living at Cranwell for us WAAFs. For instance, we had baths in our house there. In our house there were maybe only six of us, and we all got on well together. Oh, you got used to each other, you looked after each other. And if you were on shift work, they'd bring cups of tea and things like that to each other. You were still having to eat in the cookhouse. But you could go into town and have a meal if you could afford it. Grantham was the nearest town to Cranwell. It was nice in Grantham.

Then in the camp we'd concerts – operas that were ENSA concerts.[6] You were allowed to go to them. They brought the performers in. And you were also able to go to the pictures and dancing in Grantham. Oh, there was bussing in and out. You'd to be back in the camp by half-past ten. When you think of it, they did look after us. And there was an officer in charge of us WAAFs – someone you could go to and speak about welfare matters, and who'd keep an eye on you, especially if you came in late! Oh, there was a fair strictness about that. The WAAFs were kept in separate accommodation from the men's accommodation. Oh, they were never together. So in spite of the war and all the wartime conditions, and being so far from home, we did enjoy a certain amount of entertainment – pictures, dancing, that sort of thing. You never seemed to be long on your own. And there was always something going on.

You got leave every three months. I think I got home leave from Jesmond – or, because I didn't have long, did I go to Carlisle that time? I think I went and stayed with my brother and sister-in-law at Carlisle. It wasn't that far away. I think we got seven or nine days' leave at a time. And you got a day off every week. I seemed always to be on shifts. I seemed never to have a nine-to-five job in the Forces. The shifts varied. I think you used to go on duty about eight o'clock in the evening. I know you'd to go to the canteen before it closed, to get whatever you needed for the night. And then you were on duty till the next morning. You worked right through the night. That was a sort of regular shift. Actually, I think there were just two shifts – day shift and night shift. Oh, they were quite long hours. But it wasn't hard work. It was something different. I quite enjoyed it. You could see what you were doing.

What I did in my work in directional finding was, well, there were three stations outside each Air Force base. And inside the office you had a thing you turned till you got it opposite your bearing. You could hear your bearing. There were three different things, and when the three of them reported one point – that's where the plane was. We had to bring them back. These were sort of navigational beams. When the pilots were coming back from sorties half of them got lost, they didn't know where they were. So we could direct them to our place. And you could hear them come across when they did it right. You had to know what you were doing. It was very important and responsible work. But it wasn't difficult. Our room where we did that work was quite small. There were always at least two of us together on duty. There wasn't an officer or an NCO, just the two of us. I was an LACW (Leading Aircraftwoman). I never got further up than that!

As an LACW I think you got a little bit more pay. I've a funny feel-ing I got 21 shillings [£1.05] for a fortnight. We got paid every fortnight. So my pay wasn't an awful lot more than I'd had in Benzie's in Aberdeen when I'd started work there when I was 15. But then in the WAAF we got free food, accommodation, transport – everything, as well as our pay. We also got a ration of cigarettes – and a bar of choc-olate. But I think we did have to buy our own cigarettes and chocolate. I smoked at that time – we all did, like chimneys, when I think of it. *Passing Clouds* – that was the name of the cigarettes. They weren't round, they were oval, and they were in a pink packet. And then, when you couldn't afford anything else, you bought Woodbine. Everybody turned to them in moments of stress!

Among the WAAF girls at the RAF bases, including Cranwell, that I was at there were all different kinds. Oh, we were all about the same age, mainly in the early 20s. Some of them looked lovely in their uniform; others looked absolutely falling apart! I remember one girl went in for a commission. She was a nice girl and we were quite friendly. She had the next bed to me at Cranwell. She became an officer. She wasn't one of your pushy, terribly ambitious people. But I think some of the other girls were making fun of her. They would maybe see her as rising above her social class. I can't remember her name, and I don't know what happened to her.

A terrible thing I always remember that happened at Cranwell was when two planes crashed into each other right overhead the aerodrome. There was eight killed. And it was the usual thing: one plane coming in to land, the other taking off.

* * *

Well, I never seemed to last long at any of my postings. After I did all my training in direction finding at Cranwell I was moved to Fraserburgh, 30 miles north of Aberdeen, my home town. I'd been at Cranwell maybe about six months, as it would be autumn 1943 when I was sent to Fraserburgh. The aerodrome there was at a place called Cairnbulg, along the beach road and just outside Fraserburgh. I was quite a long time there that included D-Day in June 1944 and VE Day in May 1945. I came home to Aberdeen on leave from Fraserburgh. But there was a terrible snowstorm in that winter of 1943–44, and I couldn't get back to the camp. Everything stopped, the trains as well. I was in trouble if I was absent without leave. But I was stuck at home. And it was easily a week later before I got a lift from a lorry going to Fraserburgh. It was an ordinary civilian lorry. I sat in the middle in the cab, between the driver and another fellow. As we were going through the villages on our way, people were coming from their houses and waving to us, because we were the first transport they'd seen. It was a terrible storm.

So I think I was at Fraserburgh, or at any rate Cairnbulg, longer than at any other of my postings in the WAAF. And I met my future hisband at Fraserburgh. He was an English lad, from Liverpool. He was in the RAF. He'd volunteered immediately war was declared in September 1939, when he was 18. He was a pilot in Fighter Command, then he became an instructor and was instructing over in Canada. He'd been at Cranwell, but not at the same time I was there. Then when he came back to Britain from Canada, he was instructing Poles at Fraserburgh. I remember him telling me when he was in charge of a big parade on the square at Cranwell, he'd got all the men lined up awaiting the arrival of senior officers. When the officers arrived the men all had their backs to them, because he had thought the officers would come through a door on the other side of the square!

At Fraserburgh on VE Day, oh, we went mad! There was a big party in the sergeants' mess, that sort of thing. I don't remember anything else. We didn't go into Fraserburgh itself that night, we stayed in the camp. Of course, at other times we used to walk into Fraserburgh for meals and things. It was quite a relief when the end of the war in Europe came in May 1945, though there was still the war against Japan of course, until it ended in August.

Another thing that happened at Fraserburgh: a German plane landed on the airfield there one night. It was either just before or just after the war ended. Their plane got in the circuit, came in at the same time as our planes did, and landed on our airfield. When they got out the plane they must have held their hands up. They were speaking German of course. But there was nobody in our camp who could speak German, except one fellow who was a German Jew. So he questioned them. It turned out that they'd flown over us deliberately in order to surrender.

Some weeks before VJ Day – Victory over Japan – in August 1945, I'd been posted again. This time it was from Fraserburgh/Cairnbulg to

Turnhouse aerodrome at Edinburgh. I was at Turnhouse by the time of the Parliamentary general election in July 1945, when the Labour got in. We did directional finding at Turnhouse. I remember there were German and Italian prisoners of war near there, and we used to go past them on the road to the direction finding place.

Turnhouse proved another short posting for me. After only a few weeks there I was sent to Bonchester Bridge near Hawick. We were direction finding there. But we weren't in a camp. It was just a hut and a generator. The hut was our billet. It was next to the village pub. When we went to the direction finding tower a taxi, driven by a lady from the village, used to take us there. We had to go along a country road to the tower, which was in the middle of a field. Well, I was at Bonchester Bridge on VJ Day, the 15th of August 1945. There weren't really any celebrations by us at Bonchester Bridge, because there were only eight of us there. And the villagers didn't really want to mix with us. We didn't find them very friendly. The lady who used to take us in the taxi up to work was a farmer's wife, and she was all right. When we had time off we used to go into Hawick, about six miles away.

Two or three miles on the other side of Hawick there was a big army camp at Stobs, where the Irish Guards were stationed. My fiancé was a Catholic, and because I kept moving camp in the WAAF it took me a year to get instructions from a priest about being received into the Catholic Church. So the priest used to come across from Stobs to Bonchester Bridge, and he received me into the church. I got married in October 1945 in Aberdeen. Then I went back to Bonchester Bridge, and my husband to Cranwell. But of course Servicewomen were being released then within a month of getting married. So I was demobbed in November 1945, and we lived in Grantham, where my husband was allowed to live out, until he was demobbed in February 1946. Then we went to live permanently in his home town, Liverpool.

Looking back now on my wartime years in the WAAF, I'm glad I did it. I feel sorry for people who weren't then in the Forces! It was probably the camaraderie with the other girls that I found particularly enjoyable. Of course, we were all over the country, which we wouldn't normally have been. If I'd still been in Benzie's store in Aberdeen I wouldn't have been wandering all over the country. And you learned to stand up for yourself and do things for yourself. You became more self-reliant and more self-confident. I wouldn't have met so many interesting contemporaries. And I certainly wouldn't have met my husband.

Jean Robertson (Mrs Jean Rooney) died on 1 November 2003.

Margaret Campbell

The doctor's daughter in Taynuilt was a friend of mine, and just when the war broke out she said, 'I want to join something.' And she thought it should be the Women's Royal Naval Service. So we both agreed to apply for the WRNS.

I was born on 14 October 1918 at Inverliever farm, a sheep farm, six miles up Loch Etiveside from Taynuilt.[1] My earliest memories are of growing up there: idyllic, absolutely idyllic surroundings. I think our house there had five rooms. Well, my father inherited Inverliever farm. He wasn't keen on farming. He was more or less an academic. But, I mean, he was the son that was left, because one of his brothers went to Canada, one was a doctor, one was a banker, and my father was the one that was left at home. He did farm, but he was never as interested in it as he was in how roads went on, and things like that. Oh, he was never professionally employed as a university lecturer. But he was a Gaelic scholar and he was very good at it. Oh, he was absolutely a native speaker of Gaelic, and could read and write in it. But Gaelic was never spoken to us, my brother and me, because my mother had no Gaelic.

My mother died when I was eight. Well, my grandmother was alive, so I remember her much better. My brother, Archibald, was two years younger than I. When we were growing up at Inverliever farm there were no other children there for the two of us to play with. We were just our two selves. But we imagined – we had an imaginary lot of children. The shepherds and other workers on the farm weren't married and had no children. The men lived in a bothy. But life at Inverliever wasn't lonely for Archibald and me. Incidentally, none of my family were in the 1914–18 War.

We had no school at Inverliever. The nearest school was six miles away, and there was no road or anything like that to it from Inverliever. I was eight when I 'went to school'. But before then my brother Archibald and I got a tutor to ourselves in our house. So I always thought I learned more there than I ever did in six years later on at Oban High School. Our tutor was a woman, and she lived with us in the house. But we had to wait till I was eight before the tutor came. My brother would then be six and old enough to have the tutor. Before then my father and mother would teach me. So I could read and write and everything long before I was eight and the tutor came. Then when our tutor, Miss McLaren, came she was straight from college, and young and enthusiastic, and we were very keen to learn. So then we had school every day at home. We were never off school of course. But we had homework and everything, just a normal school day. We had a room that Miss McLaren taught us in. She was enthusiastic and, oh, she must have been a good teacher, because I sat and passed my Qualifying exam when I was 10. The usual age for the Quali was 11 or 12. But I was too young at 10 to go to Oban High School. I had to wait another year.

After I passed the Quali Miss McLaren left us. She became Mrs Kent eventually. We got another tutor, Miss MacDiarmid. She belonged to Greenock, Miss McLaren to Tighnabruaich on the Kyles of Bute. Miss MacDiarmid lived with us in our house. She was a good teacher, too. She started teaching me French and things like that. Well, I was keen on languages. But we only had Miss MacDiarmid for a year.

My mother had had a big house in Taynuilt called Springbank which had been in her family since it was built in 1884. So about 1929 we moved from Inverliever farm to live down there. It was the Depression, and my father had decided to give up the farm, because wool was only 6d [2½p] a pound, and lambs were 2s 6d each [12½p], and you couldn't believe it. Another reason for our moving was because my brother and I both needed to go to school. So my brother went to a local school in Taynuilt, and I travelled to Oban High School.

I travelled by train. There was a scholars' train that started from Dalmally, about 12 miles up the road from Taynuilt, and picked people up on the way to Oban. It ran about eight or ten past eight in the morning. Oh, I used to be up about eight and run to the station! It was three quarters of a mile from our house. But I had a bike and could jump on the bike. Then after school was over for the day we had to wait till six o'clock or something for the ordinary train back to Taynuilt. It was a long day. In the winter it was dark when you left home and dark when you returned.

It was very strange to go to Oban High School and be in a class of 40-something after never having been in school before. And they didn't know what class to put me in. There was just A, B, and C in those days and not any more. They're E, F, G, and something now. But they just put me in B to see where I'd be. And of course I was away ahead of anybody else there because I'd been taught at home. So I was first in English, French, History, Geography, and all the rest of the subjects. And then at the end of a term they wanted to put me into A, the top class. I was always sorry that I didn't join it. But I didn't want to move from B because I'd made friends with the people I was with there. So I didn't move and I never did move. I just stayed with them in B. The only difference was that in B you didn't have Latin, which I would have liked.

Because I was at Oban High School for a term before we moved down from Inverliever farm to Springbank house in Taynuilt, I lived with an old lady in Oban. I was just a wee girl of 11, but there were three girls in the fourth year at the High School who used to call for me every morning and take me to school. They seemed like adults to me. They were wonderful to me. I wasn't homesick at all. When I hear of people going away at 18 and thinking it's terrible, I think, 'Goodness, I was away when I was 11.' Many children in the Highlands have to move away from home when they go into secondary schooling.

Oban High was a big school. I think there would be about 800 pupils. You moved from room to room. You went to No. 13 for French, and to No. 21 for maths. And, oh, there were some very, very enthusiastic, good teachers. There was Miss Maryann Skinner, who taught French. She'd taught everybody's father and mother too. She was teaching till, I think, late in the 1950s, though she was elderly when I was there in the 1930s. The head teacher then was Mr Angus McLeod. He came from Lewis. Trigonometry was the only thing he taught, I think. I took French for a long time, even afterwards when I'd left school. And I took German in the fourth year. I stayed on to the sixth year. We had to stay in the sixth year then. We could have sat our Highers in the fifth year, the way they do now. But I think it was all from the point of view they wanted good passes. So they would insist on pupils staying on until they got a better pass. There was one boy, a minister's son, Willie Young. Oh, you couldn't compete against him. He was a brilliant boy, brilliant at everything. Well, he was allowed to sit his Highers in the fifth year, because they would know that he would pass. But nobody else was allowed to do that.

Oh, I enjoyed school very much. I was quite happy there, and had plenty of friends. It was only the first term I stayed in digs. After that I travelled to and fro between Taynuilt and Oban. Oh, there was a hostel in Oban for pupils, a girls' hostel and a boys' hostel. That's usual in the Highlands. But probably the girls' hostel at Oban must have been full, otherwise I think I would have been in it.

In my own class at Oban High School there weren't a lot of the pupils who were native Gaelic speakers, but just the ones from the islands. And even then in the 1930s, not all of them from the islands might be native Gaelic speakers, but a lot of them would be. The ones from Ardnamurchan and Mull and places like that would be. But that would be all.

As a girl my interests included the Guides, once we came down from Inverliever to Taynuilt. I was in nothing at Inverliever itself. Mine was a very religious family. My father was an elder in the United Free Church of Scotland in Taynuilt.[2] And, oh, we were always in Sunday School. I was at two Sunday Schools in fact each Sunday, probably just so that you would get the treats and picnics, etc. I went to the Baptist one and I went to our own one – just for the trips, not for the teachers. I was able to attend Sunday School at Taynuilt even when we lived on the farm at Inverliever, because my people came down to the church at Taynuilt by boat. We had a motor boat. My brother Archibald came to Sunday School as well, though we didn't come in the winter. Years later the United Free Church was converted into a house.

Then I read a great deal. Och, we had an awful lot of books in the house. I liked to read every sort of book. I remember reading *A Tale Of Two Cities* when I was about nine. I didn't really understand it all that much.[3] And then my brother and I played all sorts of games – cards, dominoes, draughts, and that sort of thing.

When we left school we didn't get great guidance at all in those days. As far as I remember there were three possibilities: you could teach, you could nurse, or you could go to university. That last one was something I do regret very much that I didn't go when I could have gone. But I didn't have any strong ambition to become a nurse, a teacher, a doctor, or a missionary. I didn't know what I was going to do. So I left school when I was 17 not at all sure what I was going to do. I was quite keen on games and on gym, and somebody thought that perhaps I should be a gym teacher. In those days the women's college for physical education was in Dunfermline, so I went there for an interview. But they wouldn't take you before you were 18. I didn't want to wait another year before I did anything. So instead I went to the Glasgow and West of Scotland Commercial College. It was in Pitt Street, Glasgow, and years later the College became part of the University of Strathclyde.

At the College I took the usual commercial subjects: shorthand and typing, book-keeping (the class for which I never attended at all), arithmetic, and French. Oh, I hated book-keeping. The Regal cinema was just opposite the College, and we used to go there instead of to the book-keeping class. It was 6d [2½p] to get into the Regal. So we were always there in the afternoon!

I was in digs in Glasgow – friends of friends of the family. They were very, very happy digs. Oh, I loved it. There was a dental student and a medical student staying there as well. So I was at the College for a year and passed the course, and even got something (though it wouldn't be anything very startling) in book-keeping. But it's funny: nobody has ever asked for my certificate, never in my life. It makes you wonder what you have them for. So then I came home and I got a job in Oban.

Though I can't remember how I got that job in Oban, I must have applied because I remember when we left college we were told that if we could ask for £1 a week to start with, then we'd probably get more later. That was a sort of minimum, £1 a week. Well, that was what I got when I went to that office in Oban, D. & J. MacDougall. I was the only girl in their office. They were big builders. They built the cathedral in Oban, and various other places like that. Anyway, I got this job locally, as I don't think I would have preferred to have got a job in Glasgow, and I was able to travel in to Oban by train from Taynuilt.

At D. & J. MacDougall there were three partners. But one of them died and there was some kind of share-out. I don't know what the rest of them got, but I got an envelope with a £5 note in it as part of the share-out. And I was over the moon. That was a lot of money. And after a little while my pay was increased to 25 shillings [£1.25] a week.

It was a very small office in Drimvargie Terrace, Oban. The only people who worked there were the two partners, the son of one of the partners, and myself. One of the partners did the architecture and the other two men did the routine work. My work was letters and filing, and just general office duties – answering the phone, and stuff like that. I never had any book-keeping! Somebody else kept the books. Oh, I found the work there interesting. And they were very, very nice to me, quite kindly and sympathetic. I would be 18 or 19 at the time I started there in 1936–7. So it was a good place to start. But after a bit I got bored with it. So I was maybe a couple of years with D. & J. MacDougall and then I left. I think that was either just before the war broke out or just when it had broken out. Anyway, I went from D. & J. MacDougall into the Women's Royal Naval Service. I didn't have another job in between them.

* * *

As I've said, the doctor's daughter in Taynuilt was a friend of mine, and just when the war broke out she said, 'I want to join something.' And she thought it should be the Women's Royal Naval Service. So we both agreed to apply for the WRNS. What I found only afterwards, however, was that she didn't even post her application! She did go into the WRNS eventually, but she never applied at that time. Anyway, I did apply then. But nothing happened and nothing happened. And then I think I wrote and asked them what had happened to my application. When I think of it, they put every obstacle in your path, They said you have to come to Glasgow for an interview and would have to pay your own fare, and all that sort of thing. So I said, well, that was no trouble, because I went to Glasgow from time to time. So anyway I eventually went to Glasgow for an interview.

The interview was at, I think, the Central Hotel at Central station. But I can't remember for sure. I had a medical examination. It would be a naval person in uniform that would do the colour blindness test. That's a thing they're most particular about in the navy, whether you're colour-blind. But whoever interviewed me was, I think, a civilian, a civil servant of some sort. I don't think she was in the WRNS. She didn't know much about anything at all – as usual. Having been in a secretarial college I knew the different speeds of typing and shorthand. But she was expecting people to have, oh, ridiculous sorts of speeds, like 100 words a minute for typing, or something that you could never have. She really didn't know much about it. Anyway, this woman wasn't very good, she hadn't a clue about anything, I didn't think.

Well, I heard nothing about joining the WRNS for ages after that medical and interview. I wasn't working, I was at home. I was unemployed really, though I never had any benefit paid me. Anyway, I kept writing to the WRNS, asking them what was happening. Nothing, but nothing, was happening. And then out of the blue I got a telegram saying, 'Report to Dundee', I think it was, as a coder. Then hard on the heels of that came another telegram saying: 'Cancel my so-and-so and report to the naval officer in charge in Oban.' I didn't know there was a naval officer in Oban. However, I duly reported and found this old Commander A.G. Boyce, RN, who'd been in the navy before the war, then retired, and had now been taken back into it. Commander Boyce was in a room in the Station Hotel in Oban. There was just him and a borrowed typewriter, that was all. So I was the first WRNS girl in Oban. And that wasn't until May 1940, as late as that. So they didn't really encourage you to join the WRNS. I'd applied in September 1939, or something like that. And I'd obviously been keen to get into the WRNS, otherwise I would have gone off somewhere else – maybe into the WAAF or ATS.[4]

I don't know what attracted me to the WRNS. It was my friend in Taynuilt that had encouraged me. She thought the WRNS was the nicest of the three women's Services. But the delay of about eight months in getting me into the WRNS was typical of all the Services. They muddle through, they really do. I think in those early days of the war a lot of girls trying to get into the WRNS would have had a bit to wait. But once it started it fairly grew. At the beginning there was Commander Boyce and myself. Then by Christmas 1940 there were a hundred – an awful lot more.

I lived in digs again in Oban, and I was very happy in them. I was still in digs even after they opened the Palace Hotel as quarters. And Commander Boyce used to say to me, 'Have you moved into quarters yet, Margaret?' I was not his secretary to start with. But then he got a naval officer, Lieutenant Eric E. Staples as his secretary. And we were just in the office after that. Commander Boyce continued to ask me if I'd moved into quarters, and I'd say, 'No, sir.' And he would just laugh. I didn't want to go into quarters, and I kept out of them as long as I could, because I had far more freedom in digs. In quarters they had to be in by 10pm, and do all sorts of things. But I was free, and I didn't have inspections, nothing like that. But eventually, well into 1941, I did have to move into quarters.

Both Commander Boyce, the head naval officer, and his secretary, Lieutenant Staples, wanted me to go in for a commission. I didn't want to, because I was quite happy where I was. And what I'd seen of the administrative staff, the ones that were saying you'd got to be in by 10pm and you've got to do this and the next thing, I wasn't impressed with them at all. I didn't want to be one of them. But by about September 1941 both Commander Boyce and Lieutenant Staples were leaving Oban. Both were being sent abroad, one to Freetown in Sierra Leone, the other to Takoradi in the Gold Coast [Ghana]. I was friendly with both of them, because I had known them so well from the very beginning. As I say, they'd kept on telling me to go and get a commission. So I thought, well, if they're leaving I'd better accept their advice and pursue a commission. So then I went to London for an interview. At the interview you'd got three formidable women sitting in front of you. One was the Marchioness of Cholmondeley. She had the brightest blue hair that I'd ever seen in my life. Another one on the panel was the Director of the WRNS, Vera Laughton Mathews. She was a sister of Charles Laughton, the actor. She was just as big as her brother – huge. But she had a wonderful memory.[5] She would remember people wherever she met them. Well, after the interview you came back to work, and then you waited a bit. Then they said you'd passed your interview. Then you had to go to the Royal Naval College at Greenwich.

Oh, Greenwich was a wonderful place, absolutely wonderful. It was obligatory to live in quarters. You got lectures in naval history. I've still got copies of the lectures. Then you could get office procedure, naval sort of things, and confidential books – just everything about the navy. Afterwards I did a signals course because I was admin. Well, you'd do that for a fortnight. Now they have it for months; these courses that used to be a fortnight are now much, much longer. My recollection of that fortnight mostly is that we had divisions and everything every morning, and you'd chapel and all sorts of things. You had to be watching the board all the time if you were supposed to be in a different place. I think we were up quite early in the morning. We had to be somewhere every minute of the day more or less. At the end of the course I thought I would be posted in a secretarial capacity, because that was what I was trained at. But the navy had a surplus of them at that time, and I was told to stay behind and do the cipher course. We did the cipher course in a fortnight or so – now it takes months and months. But I found that course very interesting, even though it was a cram course. Well, I knew a lot of people at Greenwich Naval College and made friends quickly. Then at the end of the course I was appointed to Greenock.

And of course when you arrive anywhere after Greenwich, they say, 'Oh, we weren't expecting you.' That's the navy all over. Once you graduated from Greenwich, for six weeks or something like that you were a cadet, and you wore a white band in your hat. You were in your ordinary uniform. You didn't have a commission until after that period of about six weeks. Well, the cadets were less than the dust, as far as everything was concerned. They got all the dirtiest jobs and everything that was worst. The cadets used to say, 'Oh, but we were told at Greenwich we had to do this.' The reply was, 'Well, this is the way we do it here. Forget about Greenwich. This is the way we do it here.' So when I arrived at Greenock in October 1941 I was still a cadet. You'd no status as a cadet. But after six weeks or whatever was up you became a fully recognised commissioned officer. As a commissioned officer I started off, of course, in the lowest rank, as Third Officer. On the men's side the lowest naval commissioned rank was sub-lieutenant. WRNS officers' ranks went from Third to Second then First. Later on, by the time I left the WRNS, I was a Second Officer.

Greenock was a big, big station. Their signals department was second to the Admiralty's because of all the bombing in Liverpool and Plymouth and Portsmouth. Greenock had a huge teleprinter room down below, manned by WRNS. You were sent down with a big basket of supposed-to-be secret messages to send. But nobody would give you a machine! When you went down with this basket they were all busy and nobody, none of the girls, would give you a machine. So you'd come back up again, and at the end of your watch they would say, 'What on earth were you doing down there? Why did you not . . . ?' But you couldn't get a machine. It was very frustrating. But eventually one of the girls would relent and give you a machine.

It was a wonderful machine the teleprinter. You pressed a key that said, 'Who are you?' And you could talk to somebody in Orkney or London or anywhere at all. I remember at the end of a message you got on the teleprinter the letters TMOG, which meant, 'Thanks very much, old girl.' But I didn't do a lot of teleprinting. You only did that when you were a cadet, not once you were an officer. But we used to have chats. If you knew someone in another place, you could ask, 'Is So-and-so there?' And they would say, 'Yes.' And then you could talk to that someone. But then the supervisor would come rushing in, and your someone would say, 'Stop talking. Supervisor here!' Then there were so many naval bases of course during the war that you used to have to go through an awful lot of places to get to somewhere. You went to Donibristle in Fife, then somewhere else, then somewhere else again.

I've said Greenock was a big, big station. There were a thousand WRNS there, and over a hundred WRNS officers. We officers lived in a beautiful house called Belair, in Newark Street. It was one of the big, big houses, with grounds all round about it. Then in Greenock we were lucky: we didn't have any air raids there. By the time I got there in October 1941 it was all right. But I remember when I was in Oban they'd been bombed in Greenock, Glasgow, and Clydebank. The Clydebank raids in March 1941 were terrible.

Greenock was a major shipping base. A lot of troopships left from there, and a lot came in there as well. And, oh, the convoys! Oh, we were very, very busy in Greenock. A lot of American soldiers came in there from 1942 onwards. Poor souls, arriving in the rain. When I think of the sort of receptions we got later on in New York – bands playing, hooters going and everything – and they got nothing but rain and misery at Greenock. It was terrible.

Once I ceased to be a cadet and I wasn't any longer on the teleprinter, I was moved then on to ciphering. That meant secret messages in the signals department. It was a very busy place. There were supposed to be eight people on a watch, but there were never eight, because there were always people on leave or off sick. I would say there was normally only about six on watch. There was a head of watch who was responsible for everything that happened. Eventually, of course, I became a head of watch because I was at Greenock for such a long time – more than four years, from October 1941 to January 1946.

The secret messages were concerned with all sorts of ship move-ments, war movements – everything. Even Enigma and stuff like that was all on. The worst thing about secrecy was that when you were head of a watch, you have messages pouring in from all sides. They were coming off the teleprinter. You were getting them, and you were also getting all the stuff that the people in the cipher room were unbutton-ing. And you had to decide who was to get it. So you were just writing like mad. The messages were piling up. Who was to get it? And if you missed somebody off, there was hell to pay. People did make mistakes. There was no doubt about it. Because, if you're terribly busy . . . If there was something going on, like Churchill meeting Roosevelt, or the start of the North Africa landings, the messages were even more secret.[6] There was one thing called Hush, Hush. When I was head of a watch the girls in the cipher office would shout, 'There's a Hush message!' Well, it was only the head of watch that could handle it. So you had to go and decipher it, type it, roll it off on one of these Ormig machines – a duplicating machine. You did that by hand. Every message went off on the Ormig. There was only four or five copies made of the message. And you had to go round personally with a copy to the Admiral, the Chief of Staff, and the operations room, and one was locked in the log. Meantime, your own desk was this height – with papers pouring in all the time you'd been doing that. And then the girls would shout: 'There's another Hush!' And, och, it was awful. When there were things like that going on it was very, very difficult. Oh, when a thing like the North Africa landings were on, these push things, you were working long hours. We were in three watches then. You doubled up, and you were on morning, evening and night, sort of things. You were very exhausted. If you had a good night you got sleeping. But you never, never, never had a good night when these things were on. They were very good hours when I think of it: nine to one, and six till eleven. Then the next day you were on one to six, nine to one, six till eleven. Then you'd two days off. I used to come home to Taynuilt, or go up to Glasgow, or do something else.

Among the cipher staff and between the watches, there was good camaraderie, unbelievable, unbelievable. Relations were very good, wonderful, and a sense of all of us being in the war together. I've got friends in London still from the wartime. In fact Becky, a WRNS with me in Oban, phoned me last night. We've been friends all those years. I've had lots of friends who were WRNS who've kept in touch with me. Mind you, a lot of them are dead now. Some of the girls during the war would be older, even a lot older, than me and aged 40, even when I was in my mid-twenties. Oh, there were lots of characters among the WRNS I knew during the war. Our Chief Officer was a Lesbian for one thing. I'd never heard of such a thing. We didn't know what that was! She was a theatrical, very, very theatrical, and from a theatrical home. She'd been in a lot of films. She was a character. She smoked cigars and wore patent leather shoes, which we thought a bit odd. But we were very naïve in those days. Some girls were even more naïve than I was. Most young people didn't get holidays in those days, didn't go away from home. But the WRNS girls and women we were with were more experienced, more sophisticated. There were a lot of more or less titled people. Oh, very much upper social classes, most of them pretty well-educated. Oh, there was Lady This and Lady That. But, I mean, they were just the same as anybody else, not snobbish or unfriendly. And there were lots of WRNS girls from naval families, admirals' daughters, and people like that.

At Greenock the same admiral was there all the time I was there. I can't now remember his name. When I was in the WRNS at Oban the admiral at Tobermory, Stephenson – I remember him – used to come and see us. He was known as 'The Terror of Tobermory'. Everybody, even our Commander, was worried sick when Admiral Stephenson was coming over to us in Oban from Tobermory. He'd got whiskers away out here.[7]

So I was at Greenock for more than four years. But in the middle of it, in 1943, Archibald, my brother, who was in the RAF, was killed in a Lancaster bomber.[8] I'd like to have gone abroad, but I didn't want to go because my father was old. My father had been nearly 50 when he married, so he was old. But then, in 1943 or 1944 I think it was, they took naval crew men off the troopships and put WRNS on instead, so that the men could go and fight. For the WRNS that was a sort of perk. And because I was senior and all that, I applied to go on the troopships as cipher staff. The *Queen Mary* and the *Queen Elizabeth*, peacetime civilian passenger liners, used to come in every fortnight during the war with troops. Well, I was appointed to the *Ile de France*, a former

French passenger liner. There was myself and another WRNS officer, who'd been before. You know, you went on as a junior. There were also three Other Ranks WRNS girls. So that was the cipher staff on board the *Ile de France*.[9]

I'd never been abroad before. My first voyage across the Atlantic on the *Ile de France* troopship was in February 1945. American troops were going back then to the USA. That first voyage was very rough, and the ship, which was quite an old one, sprang rivets. So instead of coming straight back as usual we had six weeks unexpectedly in New York. We were put into the Barbazon Plaza Hotel for six weeks. Oh, we were very short of cash. Of course, we didn't have a lot of money anyway – about £10 a month or something like that. But we got cash. There was a place where we could get it. The navy was quite good. And of course we were fêted beyond belief, beyond belief. We were taken to every show. We never had to pay for anything. And we were taken for what they said were weekends to people's houses out in the country. It was lovely. It was the English-Speaking Union and people like that who acted as our hosts.[10] But ordinary people were so friendly. They would stop you in the street because you were in uniform, they didn't know the uniform, and they wondered who you were and where you came from. Somebody said to me, 'Do you know my brother Paul? He's in England.' It was a great experience. Oh, it was lovely. Then we came back to Greenock after six weeks.

Well, I was three times back and forward across the Atlantic on the *Ile de France*. I was still on board her when VE Day came on the 8th of May 1945. That was my second voyage. On board on these voyages the troops were packed like sardines, very, very overcrowded. I'm sure it must have been very uncomfortable for them. But of course I was never anywhere near there. We WRNS had no dealings with the troops at all. And, oh, we had lots of scares about U-boats until VE Day. But you had them when you were coming in to port. Two destroyers came out and met you and escorted you into Greenock – and out of Greenock. Because it was in the Irish Sea and the English Channel that the U-boats were waiting. The greatest dangers lurked there. You weren't in danger when you were really out into the Atlantic. Anyway, you never thought anything of danger when you were that age. You don't think about it. But, I mean, it was exciting. The captain of the *Ile de France* used to send for us, and when I think of it we knew absolutely nothing about it. I had a book called *Atlantic Convoy Instructions*, which was just my Bible. I used to be looking it up for things all the time. If the captain didn't understand something about a signal, we were supposed to be able to tell him what it was all about. And really and truly at that age you really didn't know. You didn't know a lot about it yourself. So we had quite a responsible job on those voyages. The captain of the *Ile de France* was a British merchant navy officer, not a naval officer. They were all merchant navy on the troopships. And there were no French naval or merchant navy men on the *Ile de France*. The ship had been taken over by the British.

So the sort of cipher messages we WRNS were sending and receiving on the *Ile de France* were to do with the ship and the personnel. There were thousands of American troops mostly going back to the USA by the time I joined the *Ile de France* early in 1945. The fact that on VE Day in May 1945 I was on board 100 miles off Ireland and heading back to Greenock, meant we missed all the victory celebrations. When we got back everyone said, 'Oh, you should have been here yesterday.' We'd been duly met by the destroyers that escorted us in. The destroyers dropped a lot of depth charges then, too. It was, I suppose, a dangerous time still. But after that I had one more trip on the *Ile de France*, and then ciphering was finished completely.

* * *

Well, I was sent on leave. They didn't know what to do with you then. Anyway, I got sent to the photographic department in the Admiralty in London, and I was already in London on VJ Day in August 1945. And that work was so tame compared with an operational station. It was just different altogether, and boring, very boring. I wasn't actually in the Admiralty building; we were farmed out all over different places in London. And we were in digs there. I shared a flat with Lesley, a WRNS friend of mine. Perhaps I was in one of the first groups to be demobbed, because I was in the WRNS quite early. Lesley and I were demobbed about the same time, and we went to Belfast and Dublin for our demob leave. I'll never forget seeing the lights in Dublin, and food – butter and cream and steaks. And nylons, though we used to get nylons from people in America, and we brought nylons back with us.

So for five and a half years I was in the WRNS. It was a long time out of your life. Yet you felt guilty that you enjoyed the war so much, because it was such a happy time. Personally, I wasn't in any great danger, apart from the voyages back and forth to USA on the troopships. Those years were the central experience of my life. You met so many different people from so many different walks of life. It widened your horizons. And I didn't feel anything difficult at all, including getting on with people. But I never thought of becoming a Regular in the WRNS. I couldn't wait to get out. I was so fed up with the photographic department and, the war being over, I never thought of staying on.

During the war I hadn't developed any interests or ambitions about what I might do after it. A lot of people went, or went back, to university or did something like that. I didn't do that, and yet that's something I should have done, I suppose. So when I came out the WRNS in January 1946 I worked in London in an office. It was quite an interesting job with a public relations firm. Nobody knew what public relations was, and I found it very difficult to explain to people what it was. Colonel Williams ran the firm. He had recruited people he thought would be useful. John Buchan, Lord Tweedsmuir, had two sons, Alastair and William, who worked with me in the office.[11] We were very friendly, and it was a very, very happy office. Oh, another man the Colonel had there for his connections was the Russian Prince George Galitzine. Well, many a time the Prince borrowed 30 bob [£1.50] from me, because he never had any money.[12] Colonel Williams was promoting industry. He was hoping that people from abroad would come and buy British. We used to have people from India and different places, delegations that came over to buy British machinery and things like that. He would take them to the theatre, the cinema, and to all sorts of places, and dine and wine them, in the hope they would buy British. But the British economy was right down at bedrock bottom, and everything was so slow. It would take three or four months for machinery, etc., to be delivered. So potential customers would go to Switzerland or somewhere else they could get goods much quicker. So after about two years, the Colonel's firm folded up.

Well, I didn't want to come back to Taynuilt or Oban. I was very happy in London and had lots of friends, and I knew a lot of people. I was sharing a flat with a WRNS friend. But she died of cancer when she was 30. It was like losing a sister. But the thing was my father lived in this big house Springbank in Taynuilt. A couple who were waiting for a house of their own looked after him all the time. Then they got a house, so I came up from London to try and find a housekeeper or someone to look after him. He was old, but fit and perfectly all right – and so pleased to have me home after I'd been away so long and my brother had been killed in the war. So I felt I couldn't leave him, and I just stayed on at Taynuilt and looked after him. But I was so unhappy there: I didn't know anybody now in Taynuilt, and I'd all my friends in London. However, I got a secretarial job, Monday and Friday, with two different local landowners. That would be from 1948 to about 1951. Then I married in 1952, and my father died in 1954. I went abroad. After that I was in Nigeria for three years but came back in 1961. My husband, an electrical engineer, was killed out there, and I was left with three children aged eight, seven, and three. I came back to Taynuilt, and I was fine. My husband had been away from home a lot before he was killed, so I was used to coping with the children. And I got a chance to send the two older ones to John Watson's School in Edinburgh.[13] The young one went to Oban High School and she stayed with me. I took in boarders who worked at the big hydro-electric scheme at Cruachan. Then I got a job at the Hydro Board scheme, as secretary to a succession of generation engineers there. I retired from that job in 1979, but even then I was going until 1991 to fill in for anybody who was off on holiday. That was quite easy for me, because it was only for a fortnight. But the minute they got computers and fax and all that, I couldn't go back. I couldn't cope with that. It's a different world. By then I was 72 or 73. So I had a variety of experience.

Margaret Campbell (Mrs Margaret Harris) died on 20 January 2014.

Isa Allan

Probably about 1941, maybe before that, I volunteered to go into the WRNS. I'd then be 18 or 19. I can remember fillin' up these forms and that, but nothing ever came back, the papers never arrived from the WRNS. I suspect they went into our fire – put in by ma mother. Oh, ma father wouldnae do that. Because ma parents said, 'Oh, no, ye can't go into the WRNS. It's full o' . . .' 'Well,' I said, 'I'm no' goin' anywhere else.'

I was born at Westruther in Berwickshire on the 20th of September 1922. Ma father was actually ex-army. He'd been a Regular in the Scots Greys.[1] He was away in India for about 11 years. Well, I wisnae born then. The rest o' my family, all older than me, missed out. I can remember them saying 'There was a man in our house', when he came back. The soldiers didn't get home on leave from India, and, well, he went just on leave up in the Himalayas and that. He was out the army and then he must have gone back. He'd be recalled maybe as a reservist, because he went through the First World War. He didn't serve long enough in the army for a pension. He missed out by about two or three months. There was some problem anyway. But he didn't speak much about it. Though he wanted to go to the Second World War, too, by then he was too old. But he was annoyed. And he didn't want me to go to the war! But I was dying to get away!

I think my father and I were chummier than the rest of the family were with him, because he was out the army and home while I was just growing up, whereas he'd be away when my sisters and brothers were growing up. He was actually born in Glasgow. His mother, a McLeod from Skye and a Gaelic speaker, died when he was born. He was brought up in Glasgow and at first worked in some sort of gents' shop there which he didn't like. So he pared off and came to the Borders to some relatives. When he left the army he must have taken up farm work, and he was always working on the farms. He moved from farm to farm as just an ordinary worker. He had nothing to do with cattle, but worked with horses.

Before she got married I think my mother had just stayed at home and helped, because there was 13 children in her family, and I think she was the youngest. So she never really went out to work before she got married. I don't think she would have much choice. She was definitely a Borderer. But I couldn't really tell ee where she belonged to in the Borders. I'd say it was Kelso area. But she spoke a lot about Dryburgh, living at Dryburgh. And she went to school at St Boswells.

My grandfather – my father's father – was a tailor, a master tailor, in the Borders. You know how they went round. They stayed wi' people and made their suits – bespoke tailoring, took orders on the hop. And they sat there while they made the suit. But my grandfather is supposed to have thrown his thimble over the bridge at Kelso, and he went off to Glasgow. He was originally a Glasgow man, and then he must have come to the Borders and done this business, and then he just packed it in, gave it up. I don't remember him. He was dead before I was born.

My other grandfather – my mother's father, I think he was something to do with, would it be that sort o' horse-driven delivery things – a roundsman, something like that? Not a baker's roundsman, I think it was more goods – a railway carter, some of thae kind o' things. Maybe that's why they were at St Boswells, because o' the railway junction there. But as far as I know that's what he always did. Then there's nothing I know about my mother's mother. She was dead by the time I came along. Being the youngest in our family I missed out on the grandparents: by the time I appeared I had no grandparents! And I don't know anything about my great-grandparents.

I had two brothers and four sisters. Walter was the oldest of the family. I think Walter and I had about 21 years' difference in age between us. Walter was a chauffeur with titled people. He started off at Lauder and he went to a gentleman in Stow. And he finally went down to Hampshire, why I don't know. Then he just got into a good job wi' the Lord Lieutenant o' the county. Walter even went into the army with him as his batman in the Second War. After the war Walter was there in Hampshire till he died from a massive heart attack. Walter was more like a father to me, and he always wanted me to go into teaching. He was going to pay for this teaching. But I didn't want to become a teacher: I wouldnae have the patience!

The next in the family was my oldest sister Jean, who would maybe be about two years younger than Walter. I think I would maybe be about seven when Jean got married and went down south to live in Hampshire. Then after Jean it was my brother Sandy. The next one was, oh, I think, Jessie, then Effie, then Christine, then me. There was eight years between Christine and me. So I was, or was supposed to be, the baby of the family! Well, the older ones were all away from home either working or married when I was aged about eight and at the primary school.

Though I was born at Westruther I don't remember anything about living there, because I was just maybe weeks old and we moved to Lauder. And I was at the school there to begin with. Then we came to Galashiels, and later to Melrose. But I finished school at Galashiels Academy. The reason we moved from places was because my father had finished working there, and moved on from one farm to another. I just remember us being at Lauder. The farm he worked on there was Wyndhead, just as you go in to Lauder from the south end, just opposite Thirlestane Castle. The farm cottages were just in the town.

Oh, I quite liked the school and got on well. There were good teachers who encouraged you. The subjects I was interested in at the secondary school were mostly geography and arithmetic. I have happy memories of the primary school, but I preferred Galashiels Academy. Oh, I don't know why. It was just more relaxed somehow. It was maybe ma father having been in India made me interested in geography. And I've always fancied travelling, though I haven't done a lot of it. At the Academy there was book-keeping but not shorthand and typing. So I learned shorthand and typing privately. Some of us went to night school for that – well, that's not strictly true! We joined the night school, but we didnae go to it! We were out, though we were 'back home at the right time'!

I was at Galashiels Academy three years and left when I was 15. As a girl at the school I didn't have any particular ambitions. I quite enjoyed the school, but I was just excited to be getting out. I didn't have any ambitions to be a nurse, a doctor, a teacher, or a librarian. It wasn't because I'd made up my mind to do commercial work, office work, secretarial work once I left school. No, I think taking shorthand and typing at night school would just be a fad at the time – two or three of us wanting to do something.

The first job I had was in a grocer's at Earlston – which was terrible! It was boring. The job wasn't advertised. I got it by self-contact. I wasn't really interested in working in a shop, working among onions and ham and stuff: 'Tippence worth o' carrots'. It was Rutherford's shop, a general grocer. They had jist everything. It was licensed and had china and everything. It was a fair-sized shop, but I wouldnae think it was the biggest shop in Earlston at that time. I think the Galashiels Co-operative branch there was maybe bigger. The hours I worked were nine till five – not till six: I had to get the bus back to Galashiels, you see. And I worked Saturday mornings nine till 12. Mr Rutherford, the owner and manager, had a shop in Lauder as well. He was quite a good man. He didn't reduce my wages because I didn't work on till 6pm during the week as I had to get away earlier to catch the bus back home to Galashiels. The journey by bus took about half an hour anyway. I could have cycled – I had a bike, but I was too lazy!

As well as Mr Rutherford there was three of us workers in the shop. There was a younger fellow called the apprentice, myself, and another girl. The shop was busy in these days maybe, but nothing extraordinary. There werenae queues outside on the pavement! As I say, 'Tippence worth o' carrots', or something like this. Of course, folk were poor in those days. The folk in Earlston itself came into the shop, but, oh, country folk too. They a' seemed to patronise it. Of course, they hadnae cars, or so many cars, in these days. And they would depend on the vans going out to them. Mr Rutherford had just the one delivery van, which went round the countryside, maybe to Birkenside and round about that way, and the farms round about Earlston.

My wages when I first began at Rutherford's were 9s 4d [46p] a week. Well, I got 10s [50p], but they kept 8d [4p] off for insurance. I gave my mother the 9s 4d and I got 10s back! So I gained the 8d. Most youngsters in these days would give all their wage to their parents. But in my family there were so many older ones than me. As the youngest one I was spoiled, ruined! But possibly my brothers and sisters would occasionally send my mother and father something or buy something for them. Oh, my parents werenae gasping on my wages! And then I had money to pay out on bus fares, though then they werenae so dear as they are now. I think then it was 9d [3¾p] to Earlston return. I just got a daily return ticket. And then sometimes ye got lifts. Somebody – maybe the baker – came along and said, 'Right. Are ye goin' tae Earlston?' So you'd save a wee bit on fares then. So I worked at Rutherford's grocery in Earlston for maybe about six months.

That had been my first full-time permanent job. But even before then, when I was still at school, I'd had a job during the summer holidays in the *Border Telegraph* newspaper office in Galashiels.[2] I could maybe have had a permanent job there once I left school. But, oh, it was a boring job, too. Oh, it was terrible. You checked everything, the dots and the commas and a' this. You had to read it out. I was a sort o' proof reader. But I wasn't interested in that, and I didn't really want to get a permanent job there. That was just for some pocket money! I suppose in a way it was quite good experience. And then I got the full-time permanent job in Rutherford's grocery.

Well, from Rutherford's I went to work at a garage in Earlston. I got in there because Agnes Blair, my cousin, worked there in the office. I don't think there was a vacancy. But Agnes needed a bit of assistance. She had been there for years and years, working to the man (I can't remember his name now) that owned the garage. I got in there because of my shorthand and typing. There'd be two garages in Earlston in these days. One was on the main street, and the other one, where we were, was in the back street. Ye got off the Edinburgh road into it. The hours o' work there, oh, just the usual, nine tae five, Monday tae Friday. You didn't work on a Saturday morning. My wages at the garage were just similar to what I'd had at Rutherford the grocer's, but lucky if I had 10 bob [50p] a week. Again I travelled to work mostly by bus, but sometimes I stayed at Earlston overnight at my cousin Agnes's place, because it was just suitable. At the garage I was just helping with anything – answering the phone, accounts, the post. The phone rang a lot, but Agnes was very deaf and she wasn't able to answer it.

Then in the autumn of 1938, when I'd be 16, I got into the same line as I wanted: shorthand typist, at Langlands Mill, a spinning mill at Newtown St Boswells. My future husband's father, Mr Hall, was the owner of the mill. That was how we met. My shorthand speed was still about 100 words a minute. That was more than adequate for what I was doing at the mill. I was the shorthand typist to the secretary of the mill company, Mr Dickson, who came from Peebles. There were about 30 workers employed at the mill. My hours there were again nine till five, and sometimes you worked on a Saturday if they were hard-pressed. But the mill workers themselves worked till 12 on a Saturday. My wages there was a wee bit better: I think I had about £3-something. And there were holidays and everything. Ye got two weeks' paid holidays. They were factory holidays just. And at the end of 1938, I can remember getting £3 for my Christmas! At Rutherford the grocer's and at the garage at Earlston you might get a trades holiday. But if you wanted to go away for a holiday it was unpaid! There were no set annual holidays. At Rutherford's I remember you got a half-day on a Wednesday, but no half-day at the garage at Earlston.

Another thing I remember about Earlston in these days was the hiring fairs for farm workers.[3] I didn't see the fairs when I was working there but I can remember them. The hiring fair was held in The Square, in front o' what was the Town Hall. They took up the whole Green. And I can remember the shows and a' that at the hiring fair days. We would go at nights to the shows. That would be all. I can't remember the farm workers standing waiting to be hired. But I can remember them going to Ma's, an aunt o' mine, and havin' meals – mince and tatties sort of thing. She used to do meals on the hirin' days. Ma had a house on The Square in these days. And I can remember it was a great day. It was a public holiday for the farm workers! As I say, we went tae the shows of course. That wis all we were interested in.

Ah actually met ma future husband before ah started work at Langlands Mill at Newtown St Boswells. Margaret, the girl that was there at the mill, was leaving. This is how I got the job. I was on my own in the office. And, oh, I found the work more interesting and satisfying. It was more in line with what I'd been training for. I had no problems with typing, and my speed in shorthand was more than adequate to cope with Mr Dickson's dictation! Well, of course, I was only at the mill about a year or less before the war broke out. But by then things had been beginnin' tae brew. Ah wisnae a bit interested then though. I was more concerned about what dance was on the next night!

As a young girl ma interests were, well, I was in the Brownies and the Guides, but ah wisnae terribly active or committed to them. I went there, but just if it was suitable. I didn't like campin' or anything like that, so I never did go campin'. As a girl I went holidays with my parents jist to relatives. Well, my oldest sister Jean, bein' married and down in Hampshire, we went there every summer. My mother and I went there. She would stay for so long, and I stayed the six weeks of the school holidays. For the seaside we went for a day trip to Portobello at Edinburgh in what we called the Maggie Lauder train! That was your day out. Sometimes we went to Glasgow to my father's aunts. And there was a Spittal trip, but for us it wisnae Spittal: we went to Portobello! But that wis aboot it.[4]

As children we had to go to the Church of Scotland and Sunday School. Every Sunday you had to go. My mother was keen for us to go. You had to get yourself ready, and you used to get a penny for the collection. You used to get two ha'pennies, and put one ha'penny in the collection and keep the other one! Then we used to buy was it a potato ginger thing, sort of cinnamon stuff, and you hoped to find a ha'penny or a penny inside it. There was a little shop in the middle of Lauder and we used to go there, and ye got twenty a penny. And if you counted with the shop woman and then stopped her countin' you got a whole lot more! We used to muddle her up with her countin'. But the potatoes were the best buy if you could get another ha'penny. Or you could go for my oldest brother Walter's cigarettes, and you could get a ha'penny in the packet.

I didn't play hockey. I wasn't interested in sport. But just after I left school I became interested in dancing. I went everywhere to dances: Earlston, Lauder, Redpath, and so on. They were in the evening, but, oh, I got there! I went with girl friends. It was just the normal ballroom dancing – waltzes, quicksteps, foxtrots – not eightsome reels or other country dancing. When I was little I can remember my mother taking me with her to – it would be a Women's Rural thing – and they would be having a night of dancing of jist eightsome reels. But that wasn't the sort of dancing I went in for. The dances were held in village halls, town halls, that sort of place. The Melrose Shillingly Hop was one you should never go to![5] My parents didn't really approve of me going to the dances. But I just went! I used to say to my father, 'You'll walk me up to Redpath. But don't come back for iz!' But he did as I asked him. He used to push me up there. I was frightened. I was a right coucher. It was a long way for a young lassie. And there were no lights on the road. I wouldnae go myself, I was a right coucher. But that was my great interest, going to the dancing.

Then I went to the cinema. There was no cinema in these days in Galashiels, but they had one in Melrose, though that was later on. And I read, but really I'm not a reader, it wasn't a major interest, and neither was knitting or sewing. So my main interest was dancing and meeting with my friends. But as long as you could get out ..!

* * *

I was working at Langlands Mill in Newtown St Boswells for several months before my future husband, the son of the millowner, was called up to the RAF in the spring of 1939, even before the war broke out, and just before his 21st birthday that year. The call-up was supposed to be only for six months, but he was actually away for more than six years.[6] He remembers that he went first to Uxbridge, then he was at RAF Catterick, then at Invergordon, where he was with flying boats in Coastal Command, then in Wales, in Shetland at Sullom Voe, at Prestwick, then Egypt, then through the North African, Sicily, and Italian campaigns, and at the end of the war in 1945 he was at Udine near Trieste.

I remember hearing Mr Chamberlain on the radio in September 1939 about the outbreak of the war. But, oh, we didn't feel anything. Of course, you're thinkin', 'It'll have nothin' to do wi' me.' So I remained at work in the mill. But then, probably about 1941, maybe before that, I volunteered to go into the WRNS. I'd then be 18 or 19. I can remember fillin' up these forms and that, but nothing ever came back, the papers never arrived from the WRNS. I suspect they went into our fire – put in by ma mother. Oh, ma father wouldnae do that. But they both said, 'Oh, no, ye can't go into the WRNS. It's full o' . . . ' 'Well,' I said, 'I'm no' goin' anywhere else.' But it was a bit funny, because the next thing ah wis into the WRNS! Oh, ma mother just wouldnae think it was suitable for young girls to gaun into the Services – terrible! Oh, I don't know what she wanted iz to do, but I wasnae to get away intae a thing like that. But as time passed she must have had her thoughts. Ma sister worked for Sheriff Boyd at Whiterig in Bowden, two miles up the road from Newtown St Boswells. Sheriff Boyd's daughter-in-law was the superintendent for the WRNS for the south of Scotland.[7] So I think somebody paid a visit there, because I did get into the WRNS! I think my mother was vexed that she had burnt the papers I'd expected to get from the WRNS. So I'm sure my mother would gin up and see Mrs Boyd, because there wis no other way it would have happened. I didnae have anything tae do with it. But that was how I got into the WRNS. I mean, I'm supposin' that. But it's the only thing that comes up. Oh, ma mother wouldnae own up!

What made me volunteer for the WRNS was – just to get away. The ATS and the WAAF didn't appeal to me. I just always fancied the WRNS. I can't remember why, but I just fancied it. If I was going anyway I'd like to have gone to the WRNS. I didn't have any relatives in the WRNS or in the navy. I had cousins in the merchant navy, as wireless operators and these things. But I hadn't much connections with them. So it wasn't that, and I don't think it would have been the WRNS uniform either. I don't know if my interest in geography would come intae it, so that I would maybe see the world if I joined the WRNS. Possibly it was because I wasnae bein' allowed tae get in to the WRNS that made me so adamant that that was where I was goin'. Because there wasnae many girls round Galashiels, Newtown St Boswells or Earlston that were in the WRNS. It was more difficult anyway to get into the WRNS than into the ATS or WAAF. All my friends got into the ATS no bother. Anyway, it wouldn't have mattered whether it was the ATS, WAAF or the WRNS ah wanted to join, ma mother was, oh, definitely determined to stop me. So it was 1941, I think, when I'd volunteered, I got away in November 1942.

Ee had tae go away for a medical to George Street in Edinburgh. I think it was the Music Hall. I got through the medical no bother. Then it wis probably within weeks jist, you were in the WRNS. Well, I went to HMS *Cochrane* on the 30th of November 1942. That was a shore station at Dunfermline in Fife. It was on a big estate that we were actually billeted – Hillend in Aberdour, about four miles from Dunfermline and on the Firth of Forth. We were taken by bus between the billets and the shore station. Our billets was really a big mansion house, the navy must jist have commandeered it. It wis big rooms wi' these bunk beds. I maybe suffered from homesickness for the first two or three days, but that would be all. Once I got to know the other girls I was ok. I was the only one, as far as I remember, there from the Borders. There'd be aboot maybe a couple o' hundred WRNS at HMS *Cochrane*. Girls came there from all over Scotland, that's where ee would report. It was jist a training place. Ee were there for three weeks. Ee got kitted out. Ee got eer first lot of uniform, but after that ee had to buy eer own. The uniform was just a kind o' – not nap, but it was a smooth material, navy. There was a jacket and skirt, no trousers, and no sort of denims or overalls. You got your first lot o' shoes – flat-heeled. After that ee had tae buy them. And ee got stockings, lisle stockings, and one hat. Everything was just the one. Ee didnae get underwear. Ee had to provide your own. And when ee were at HMS *Cochrane* ee had tae wear the uniform – regulations. And ee got drill, marching, all these kind o' things. But no weapons, ee never had weapon training.

But I didnae like it there at HMS *Cochrane*. I don't know what the problem there was. I jist didnae like it. Of course, I was just newly in the WRNS and it wis a big change. I'd never lived away from home before. When I'd gone on holiday I'd always been with family. I was worrying about my future husband as well. He'd been away in the RAF for three and a half years by the time I got into the WRNS in November 1942. Oh, it was a change in ma life a' right. But, oh, on the other hand it wis great tae get away from home. Now there wis nobody to say where are ee goin', or where have ee been, or who have ee been with? Oh, ee couldnae get out the house without a great harangue, ee know. I used to tell ma parents fibs and everything! Once away from home I had a great sense of freedom. It wis great tae get away. Of course, at HMS *Cochrane* they had set rules – signing out, signing in, and this carry-on. It wis something new, but it wisnae really bad – though three weeks there wis long enough!

Well, from HMS *Cochrane* I wis posted tae Buckie in Banffshire. There was only three of us WRNS there in Buckie. Two of us were in my office, and one in the other one. It wis jist a very small naval office. And the three of us were billeted out in digs in private houses. This couple that I was billeted on, Mr and Mrs Geddes, the husband was a tailor. And we used to get clothing coupons because, well, I wis in the office there and ee could write your stuff out, the coupons and that. So he used to make us suits and, oh, he didnae charge ee for them. Well, we had to pay for the material, but not for his labour. And of course the suits werenae regulation style as well, because there was a bit flare in them.

There wis no WRNS officer at Buckie, jist two naval officers and some other ranks, and the three of us WRNS. So there wisnae much discipline, no marching, no nothing. So it wis jist intae the office and home to the billet at night. So it was really good at Buckie.

The work I was doing there in the office was everything – unfortunately. I joined up as a typist, but, well, ee did everything. You did signalling, ye had tae do decoding, ye had tae do a' the things they needed for goin' on leave. The ships came in and ee had tae kit them all out. Ee had tae be a dogsbody. Ee'd everything to do.

I think the naval officer in charge o' us would be a reservist. I suppose he was compos – but eccentric: you can say that again! He was Commander Cadogan, quite a senior officer. He was English and he came from – was it Querrington? His wife was a titled lady. He lived in a hotel him. And there was at the Royal Naval Office, Buckie, a Lieutenant Ooster, I think his name was, who was on the engineering side. And then there was a third officer, a kind of joiner – an artificer. I think they'd all been Regulars in the navy but they'd just been brought to Buckie as reservists.

I remember there was one ordinary seaman that did a' the washing, mine as well – well, the shirts and everything. There was an electric fire in the stores and he used to turn it upside down and boil the clothes! Oh, he was a right character. He had been a Regular, recalled as a reservist for the war. He'd been out in the East and he had connections wi' the Chinese. Oh, he had travelled the world. We finished our education there at Buckie! Oh, for us it wis a new world that wis openin' up. I enjoyed it.

The three of us in the WRNS got on well together, we were all friends. Jean, the other WRNS in Mr and Mrs Geddes's digs with me, came from Scone near Perth. Jean and I shared a room, but of course were in separate beds. There was no canteen at Buckie for us, so we went back from the office to the Geddes's for our lunch and at tea time. Mrs Geddes was a housewife, and had two daughters who were schoolgirls when we were there.

At the office we worked from nine to five. We didn't work on a Saturday. What we did at the weekends, oh, that's a thing! But it wis jist what wis goin' around. We were invited out a lot, maybe because we would be conspicuous wi' our uniform. But then at night we could change into our civvies, because there wis nobody there to check us. We weren't supposed to wear our civvies, we were supposed to be in uniform. But if we were goin' somewhere – say it was an RAF base, where it wis officers only – well, other ranks WRNS like us wouldnae be allowed in. But, ee see, we were there in our civvies so we got in. Then Jean, ma roommate, got loads of parcels from relatives she had in Canada, and it was all dresses. So she shared them with me, and we used tae negotiate coupons wi' a man that worked in the Dundee Equitable shoe shop (he came from Selkirk actually). And when he gave us the coupons we went to other shops and bought, well, if you wanted something special in clothes . . . We got plenty coupons – and there was plenty of entertainment, dances and so forth.

So for me Buckie was a very happy place. Of course, there was a lot of fishing there, and a' the fishing folk were ever so kind. If you were in wi' them you were a' right. They were very good to us. And Mr and Mrs Geddes couldn't have been better.

But I remember at Buckie Commander Cadogan just took it into his head ee'd to get away: 'Get yourselves away.' So he'd phone up the officer along at the Air Sea Rescue base and tell him, 'Take these girls away out, and rescue this box.' Some box or other, ee know, that would be dropped into the sea. It wis supposed to be just an exercise for us. So we were taken about 11 miles out on the North Sea in this RAF speed launch. And when they shut the engines off – well, we'd been as well sitting on a cork! It wis a' right when the speed launch wis movin', but when ee stopped and ee'd be lyin' there, oh, it really wis jist like a cork. And ee'd be lyin' there for nearly three-quarters o' an hour. The boy that was supposed to be the medical man, he was sick. I was sick. My roommate Jean was sick. Even the mascot – a dog – was sick. So they finished up spreadin' the RAF flag over us and bringing us back in to the base. Oh, it wis terrible! But that wis Commander Cadogan. He just took notions. He did some silly things.

Well, I was at Buckie for about 16 months, from December 1942 till April 1944. Commander Cadogan went and promoted iz. That's how I had tae move. I didn't want promotion. I think the Commander wanted iz to get on. He was sorry, but he felt I should go. I don't really know why. I got on with him all right personally, though ee had tae humour him. He really thought it wis in my interests to go. But I would have preferred to stay. Oh, I wis quite sad tae leave Buckie. I went then to Scapa Flow in Orkney.

At Scapa Flow I was based at HMS *Prosertine* at Lyness, on the island of Hoy. The billets there were, oh, jist Nissen huts. There'd be about 16 of us WRNS in a hut, eight beds down one side and eight down the other. It was not an ordinary hut: ours was haunted. And that's true! By gum! It would make your hair stand on end! The hut was haunted by the Grey Lady. I don't know if she was a WRNS who'd died, I don't know who she was. But there was a something – you could feel it. In the night time ee felt like there wis somebody leanin' over ee. It wis terrible really. One of the girls was from Edinburgh. She wis a right hard nut. And she'd shoot up in bed and put her light on. She'd always a torch, she wis always equipped: 'Who's there?!' And, I mean, if it had jist been myself I would have said, 'It's all nonsense.' But that Edinburgh girl wis a hard nut, as I say. You could feel it, that somebody wis coming! You would waken up in the night and feel it. But apart from the Grey Lady, the huts at HMS *Prosertine* were quite warm and comfortable. They had central heating, like water pipes.

The food was very good. Oh, there was a great big kitchen and cookhouse. You went to a dining room. Oh, we had plenty o' everything at breakfast, lunch and tea. I suppose if you wanted it could you could go for cocoa at suppertime.

As I've said, when I went from Buckie to Scapa Flow I was promoted to Leading WRNS. That gave me a wee bit extra money. I don't know if the pay I had got as an ordinary WRNS is recorded in papers I've got here, but I think we had about £3-something. But if ee wis comin' home on leave ee had your flight fare. We used to come down in the plane from Orkney to Inverness. We went over from Lyness to Kirkwall and got a commercial plane, maybe a three- or four-seat thing. And we had tae pay for that. I was never nervous about flying. We took the plane because crossing by boat on the Pentland Firth was terrible! I've seen me really sick comin' across on the boat. Oh, it wis terrible. We'd probably get to Scrabster on the Caithness side of the Firth but couldn't get any further, and then have to turn and go back. It was really terrible! That happened to me more than once. The ambulance used tae be waitin' at Scrabster tae take ee. Then after that ee'd a' this train journey on the 'Hell Train Jellicoe' from Thurso down to Inverness.[8] Then you had to change at Inverness for Edinburgh. It wasnae too bad at Inverness, waitin' for the train tae Edinburgh. But it wis a long journey. It took you about two days from Lyness before ee got to Galashiels or Melrose station. You had ten days' leave or so, and they gave you travelling time. If ee'd had a very rough crossing over the Pentland Firth, I've seen me get into bed and my bed would rock back and forth for aboot two days. You felt ee were still bein' seasick. Oh, it wis a horrible feeling. But it wis no' as bad as when I was on the RAF speed launch at Buckie!

I had leave four times a year. There were shorter passes for 24 hours or 48 hours. Well, it was no use that. There was nowhere you could go. Well, you could go to Kirkwall and these places. But, I mean, there was nowhere ee could go and stay. And of course the Orkneys were full o' Service folk – sailors, soldiers, and airmen. It was very crowded there durin' the war, but I suppose ee jist got accustomed to it.

Oh, in Orkney during the war there were very good entertainments for Services people. A lot of artistes were brought up from London, Edinburgh, Glasgow, and elsewhere. I remember a violinist – a Russian was he? – who was very good. He played on Flotta island for the Forces. But ee had tae get boats across to there, because we were on Hoy. Then there was a camp cinema, if you wanted tae go. Films were shown most nights. And there were dances. Oh, there wis always somethin' goin' on. And then ee would have eer days away tae Kirkwall and that, and do your shoppin' there. But they did put themselves out to entertain ee. And that wis good for morale. It'd have been hopeless if ee'd been left lookin' out the window at stormy seas every night. Then ee didn't go down near the front and that. They had sheds and docks there for all these people, members o' the crews, that had come off boats with diseases. They were all lookin' out the windows o' the sheds. Yon was terrible. They were sort o' isolation units. I don't think they were small-pox cases – it wis venereal diseases and all that sort o' thing. Ee'd see them gettin' their food shoved intae them. It wisnae even a hospital. It wis jist huts. It would give you the creeps.

Then of course we could go anywhere on the boats round all the different islands. And ee sometimes got the chance to do that. When you had time off you could just hop on to a Royal Navy boat. We could go to Kirkwall or the island of Flotta, which was just across from Lyness, or to Scrabster on the Caithness mainland, or to Stromness, just north of Hoy. Oh, it wis a different world for me, coming from the Borders where we didnae see the sea much, apart from our day trip to Portobello. So bein' at Scapa Flow wis great, I enjoyed that. Though I'd been a wee bit homesick at leaving Buckie. But once you were there at Scapa Flow and on Lyness you just had to get on with it.

There were about 500 WRNS, I think, there. It took a bit of adapting after being used to just three o' us at Buckie. It wis terrible really to go from three to 500! But, oh, ee soon made friends once ee got to know the girls. They were very mixed and, oh, ee had to be double-barrelled up there: Morgan-Nevilles, and names like that! Oh, it wis a wee bit . . . But, you know, there was that little . . . And these were jist the ordinary WRNS, no' the officers. Some o' them were kind o' silly, well, no' silly, but they werenae very worldly like! I'd had several years working in shops and offices, so ee knew something aboot the world! So at Scapa ee were mixing wi' girls from a different social class. But, oh, there was no snobbery, and people mixed.

We hadnae had any WRNS officers at Buckie, but there were a lot at HMS *Prosertine*. But, oh, they were a' right. Ah didnae have much tae dae wi' them. The most senior WRNS officer there wis the Superintendent. She belonged here in the Borders, well, she wis married tae a man up at Bowden, Sheriff Boyd's family. And he was a naval man. I can remember the Superintendent coming round, because we had some photos of the Eildon Hills at Melrose and that, and she wis on about it. Oh, she wis quite approachable. I remember the officer who was under the Superintendent bein' called out once to see what wis goin' on. There had been some WRNS signallers that worked nights, and some o' them were sleeping during the day. And there must have been some sailors got into the billet. There wis doors at each end, ee know. And, I mean, nothing happened. But this officer wis called out and she says to one of the girls, 'What happened?' 'Well,' the girl says, 'he wasn't suitably dressed.' And the officer says, 'Did he not have his hat on?'! So that's what you were up against! But there were no nasty incidents that I can remember. Even when ee were travelling down in the train on leave, half the train was locked off, oh, segregated. Sometimes it was the Air Force that were in charge of patrollin' the train. We, the WRNS, were locked away, I would think. But nothing ever happened.

Maybe some of the WRNS met their future husbands when they were up there in Scapa. But I don't remember anybody in my own hut that married a naval rating. There were WRNS that met other people's husbands. That was sad, that was the worst. We had access to a' their history. It must have been awful during the war with husbands away in the Forces. But I think it wis jist something ee had tae handle. Then if girls became pregnant they were out. I think they were just shunted out right away. But there was nothing made public, oh, nothing. They would just say, 'Oh, she's been posted, she's been posted.' But I don't think there was very much of that actually, not that I knew of anyway.

At HMS *Prosertine* there wis discipline. Ee jist had tae flout it if ee could! Oh, there was a lot more o' the signin' in: there was no comparison wi' Buckie. Then there were other camps, further out from where we were, where naval ratings were stationed. As I've said, there were loads of different Services on Orkney of course. Earlier on in the war the Germans had attacked Scapa Flow. A U-boat had sunk the battleship *Royal Oak* there. But after that they couldn't get in by sea or air to Scapa because of the boom and the barrage balloons. Well, there maybe would be air raids on Orkney when we were there, but we didnae have any at Lyness. I think there was once a bomb dropped about the Old Man o' Hoy or some o' these places, but otherwise nothing. We never had to get out of bed at all at night. So I don't remember in 1944–5 hearing guns firing or bombs exploding. But we saw the results of German attacks on ships comin' in that had been away on the Russian convoys or out in the Atlantic. I remember seeing the Royal Naval fleet often in Scapa Flow during the war. Sometimes you saw only halfboats – the other half had been blown away. I mean, half the crew were buried at their battle stations, because they shut the doors in action so that the ship didnae sink. Half the boat then could keep watertight and afloat. Us WRNS didn't have to attend funerals o' the men killed. Our job was tae deal wi' a' the work o' notifying the next of kin and that kind of thing. And many were young fellows. Sometimes some of them you would know. I remember there were some lads from the Borders killed on HMS *Berwick*. It'd been badly battered coming from the Azores. I jist knew somebody, a relative actually, on the *Berwick*, and ee felt, well, what next? He was a rating, but he wasnae killed. I wouldnae say the casualties were severe, but the ship had been in conflict.[9]

The work I actually did at HMS *Prosertine* was all code, all Top Secret work. Our contact was with the Admiralty and with ships and fleets at sea. And we had a' these direct lines and everything. We didn't deal so much with merchant navy convoys, it was more the fighting ships – destroyers and everything, submarines, and warships, and the Fleet Air Arm, too. We were sending messages and receiving them. So HMS *Prosertine* was a very important centre of communication for the

Admiralty, the fleet in the North Atlantic, and mostly for the Russian convoys and everything. In my job I'd know what was goin' on, more or less at the time it wis happenin'. There were some upsettin' experiences. But, well, it's a' right when ee're no' really in contact with it. But it's there. And, as ah say, ee got no variety. It wis jist the same kind o' old job the whole time. I think after a time it wis jist a bit wearin', even borin', because there wis no variety.

So I was at HMS *Prosertine* from April 1944 until November 1945. Then I came back down to HMS *Cochrane* at Dunfermline in Fife, and then ah wis sent to Pitreavie, about three miles from Dunfermline. At Pitreavie we were in these houses. It was Fleet Air Arm, about which I knew nothing. So that was a new task for me in communications. But ee jist had tae muddle eer way through. There wis no training or instruction – just thrown in at the deep end. Well, we hadnae the experience or anything. I didnae half feel a dope tae begin with. Half the time ah didnae want to bother! Ee jist had tae look intelligent. It wis all ee could do. Ee lived at, or jist outside, Pitreavie, as well as workin' there. So I wis there until I wis demobbed in July 1946. By then I'd been in the WRNS for three and a half years, from November 1942 to July 1946. Long enough!

But ah wasnae really glad to get out the WRNS. I was quite happy. I thought on stayin' on, becoming a Regular – and then I thought no. Oh, they did ask ee to sign on, but there wis no pressure for that. But I think if it hadnae been for the circumstances I would have preferred to have stayed on in the WRNS. By then, well, we were gettin' married. We'd got engaged durin' the war when he was abroad in the RAF. I knew I was getting married by the time I left the WRNS. And we got married in the summer of 1947.

I would have got my old job back in Langlands Mill at Newtown St Boswells. But I didn't want it. Oh, I'd outgrown that. I never went back. But I did go back to the garage at Earlston before I got married and helped out for a week or two. Then my sister Jean was ill down in Southampton and I went away down there and stayed wi' her for a time. Then ah come home and got married and that was it. No more work! Women in these days didn't go back to work once they got married. Oh, at times, at times, I felt restless and it wis difficult to settle down. Oh, it wis a different life altogether from bein' up at Scapa Flow with 500 other girls in the WRNS! I mean, I really didnae enjoy comin' back – which was maybe not a nice thing tae say, but I didn't. It wis especially difficult to settle down in the likes of Melrose. Well, I never regretted bein' in the WRNS. It was a good life – had other people no' been sufferin'.

Isa Allan (Mrs Isa Hall) died on 1 August 2002.

Elizabeth Stewart

Oh, I don't know why I volunteered into the WRNS. But it wis nothin'
tae do wi' ma dad bein' in the merchant navy. Ah jist fancied the
WRNS.

Ah wis born at Kelton, a hamlet on the banks o' the river Nith, about
four miles south o' Dumfries and about two miles north o' Glencaple
village. Ah wis born on the 21st o' January 1922. Ah didn't have any
brothers or sisters. Ah wis an only child.

Ma father was in the merchant navy. When he gave that up he went
on to workin' on the railway at Dumfries, and he worked there till he
retired. My father had ran away to sea. He sailed all over the world.
Oh, the stories he used tae tell, ye know. He used tae be wi' Halliday,
a local shippin' company. They've got a place at New Abbey now,
across the Nith from Glencaple and beside Sweetheart Abbey. Ah'll
tell ee the boat ma father used tae go on: *The Havelock*. We've still
got an old mug that came from that boat. As a girl ah've had ma tea
wi' ma father on the old boat. Ma father was an officer, first or second
mate, in the merchant navy. The officer above him, Richardson wis
his name, and, oh, they were very good pals. But one day Richardson
died on board the boat. Ah remember that ma father wis awfy upset.
By the time he retired from the sea ma father was a captain, aye, he
was a captain. He was 65 when he died. He didnae get long tae enjoy
his retirement.

Ma mother was about the same age as ma father. She died the year
after him. Before she was married ma mother worked as a domestic
servant wi' people that were at the Clydesdale Bank in Dumfries.
They'd also been at Stranraer and Portpatrick when she worked wi'

them. I don't know anything about my grandparents. I never knew any o' them. By the time ah wis growin' up they were dead.

The first house ah can remember livin' in was at Kelton. Oh, it wis an old house. It belonged to the farmer. It had two rooms and the kitchen and a back kitchen. I slept in one o' the rooms, and ma mother and father in the other one. Ma father never worked on the farm. It wis just that we lived there. The house wis in a row wi' other farm cottages. In the old days we didn't have runnin' water in the house there. There wis jist a tap outside. We had to share the tap wi' the other folk in the other houses. There was just that one tap for everybody. The lightin' in that house wis, oh, paraffin lamps. There wis a dry toilet outside. It wis the usual sort o' farm cottage. Ma dad would never move from there, ee see. He widnae move. He'd grown up there himsel', before he ran away tae sea. I don't know if his own father had been a farm worker. He may have been, but ah don't know. Well, ah lived in that house at Kelton till the war came and then I went away to the war.

I'd be five when ah started school. Ah started at Brownhall Primary School. It was down the Glencaple road. You were there till you were of age to go tae the next school. Oh, I liked the school fine. Ah jist got on fine with the subjects. There wis nothing particular that interested me. I got on fine with everything. Then I sat the Qualifying exam and I came tae Dumfries High School when I was 11 or 12. I got on a' right at the High School. Ah liked it there. Ye got all the subjects, and again there wis none in particular that interested me. The teachers were quite good.

I didnae have any ambitions, whether to become a dressmaker or somethin'. Ma first job wis, well, sales assistant jist in a shop. The shop wis the actor John Laurie's sister's. His sister was Miss Lily Laurie. She had the shop in Church Crescent in Dumfries. It was nearly opposite Greyfriars Church. So John Laurie was a Dumfries man, a very nice man. He was Private Fraser, supposed tae be the funeral undertaker, in the TV programme *Dad's Army*. He was in and out o' his sister's shop. I used to see him quite often, aye, a nice chap.[1]

In the mornin' ah started work in the shop at nine o'clock, and ah finished at five. You got an hour off at dinnertime. Miss Laurie used to jist tell me tae go upstairs and get something tae eat. They had a flat, ye see, above the shop. Oh, ah cannae remember now what ma wages were when ah first began in Miss Laurie's shop. But they werenae very much. You wouldnae get rich there! But Miss Laurie was very good, she was very good. And you were able to buy stuff from the shop at reduced prices. Oh, it wis quite a busy shop. And then she used tae get a' the big bugs o' the town, ye know, in the shop. Oh, Miss Lily Laurie wis an awfy nice kind woman. She would do anything for anybody. She had a terrible bad leg, though, wi' an ulcer. Then there wis another sister, Gracie Laurie, and she was a singer, and a lovely violinist she was. Oh, they were a talented family. So I got on well in Miss Laurie's shop and, oh, ah met some interesting people there.

Ah stayed workin' in the shop till early in 1943, when I volunteered into the WRNS. I wasnae conscripted, I volunteered. Ah'd just had ma 21st birthday, so it must have been about January or February that year. Oh, I don't know why I volunteered into the WRNS. I jist fancied it. And of course ma dad at that time wis all for me goin' there. But it wis nothing' tae do wi' ma dad bein' in the merchant navy. Ah jist fancied the WRNS. I don't know why it wis, ah jist fancied it. So ah went along to somewhere in Dumfries where there wis a recruitin' office. Ah cannae remember clearly now. Anyway, then ah went tae Liverpool first. What ah did there wis, oh, all sorts o' things, jist learnin', jist talkin', lectures and so on. Ah wis only a fortnight there anyhow.

Then ah went on to Wales – Pwllheli in North Wales. It was, oh, a Butlin's Holiday Camp there! It was a camp, with huts. It was called HMS *Glendower*. The huts, or chalets, were built for Butlin's.[2] I was only a fortnight there when, jist in the street, I met Ted Breese, a Welshman. We got married the following year. I was in uniform when I met him.

HMS *Glendower* was a big camp. Oh, there were a lot o' WRNS there. The accommodation was quite comfortable. The chalets were clean. There were two WRNS girls in each chalet. Though I hadn't been away from home on my own before – as a girl I'd gone away with my mother on holidays. But I didn't feel homesick at HMS *Glendower*, because there wis a lot of WRNS girls there and a lot of things to take up your attention. And in the chalet ah had a nice quiet girl with me. She wis an English girl. Ah never ran across other girls from Dumfries there, no' in that camp.

When I arrived at HMS *Glendower* I was already trained as a WRNS stewardess. As a stewardess, well, ye had tae dish out the food. Put it all ready for them and dish it out, and one thing and another. And ah used tae do some o' the WRNS officers, because they asked me, ye know, when the other girls were away somewhere else. The officers were quite friendly and pleasant. They werenae the sort o' bossy type, oh, no. They didnae say, 'Ah want this, ah want that.' They were jist friendly, they were very good. The rank and file WRNS had a big mess, and the officers had their mess next to ours. So I saw the girls coming in for their food. And, oh, I would say there'd be two or three hundred girls there at HMS *Glendower*. They had different jobs – telephonists, and one thing and another.

It was an awful big camp. There were a lot o' sailors an' all, not jist WRNS. I felt that this really was what I wanted to do when I volunteered. Well, ye see, ye kept goin', and had somebody tae talk to all the time and everything. As ah say, ah didn't feel homesick, well, ah missed ma mother and father. But ah got home on leave. Oh, the leave was quite reasonable. Well, ah think we had seven days maybe at a time. And ye werenae long comin' up home on the overnight train. There were weekend passes as well. And then of course ah wis only there a fortnight at Pwllheli when ah met Ted Breese. So that wis a' right! And Ted's home wis jist near HMS *Glendower*, next door to it! So ah wis able tae visit Ted's home and his parents. Oh, ah got a good meal there when ah went! But the food in the camp was good, too, and there wis plenty of it.

Ted was a railwayman, and the train he was on used to go through our camp, right through the middle of it! So ah was able to wave tae him as he passed through, and he waved tae me and gave me a toot on the whistle. The other girls used tae double up laughin' at this.

Well, ah stayed in the camp till ah got married in 1944. Then Ted and I got a house near the camp. We were lucky. And, ah mean, well, Ted wis at work, so we jist carried on there. So ah carried on in the WRNS for maybe jist a few months after ah got married. Actually, we got married at the time o' D-Day in June 1944.. But they widnae let me leave the camp because o' the restrictions on movements at that time. However, Ted and me went and got married in the registrar's office in Pwllheli. Then Ted wis able tae get me a ticket pass tae come up tae Dumfries tae have the weddin' there as well. Ma mother had everythin' ready at the Dumfries end, ye see. They – the navy – wouldnae let us travel, but we outwitted them. So the same night we got married in Pwllheli we jumped on the train – wi' Ted's mother an' a'. Ah had ma civvy clothes on: that's how Ted got the pass. So really ah jist jumped the camp. But, ye see, by the time we went back tae the camp the restriction wis lifted. It'd jist been a couple o' days. So ah didnae get intae trouble for gettin' married twice tae the same man!

Well, as ah say, ah jist remained in the WRNS for maybe a few months after ah got married. Then ah jist gave it up. Ah jist notified the officer ah wis married and ah wanted tae leave the WRNS. So ah wis in the WRNS for about two years, from early 1943 to early, ah think, in 1945. Ah cannae remember the exact dates. Ah certainly was out the WRNS before VE Day in May 1945.

So ah'd been almost about two years at Pwllheli, then Ted and I came up to Crewe, and we were lucky tae get a house there. We got a flat first then we got a house, and then in 1952 we came up to live in Dumfries. So by then ah'd been away from Dumfries for almost 10 years, though Ted and me had come backwards and forwards there on visits.

So lookin' back on ma two or so years in the WRNS, well, ah widnae have met Ted Breese, ma husband, if ah hadnae gone in the WRNS. The war changed life for a lot o' people. A lot o' girls, like me, met their husbands as a result o' it. So ma time in the WRNS wis an experience, wisn't it? Ah met a lot o' people, no' jist ma husband, that ah wouldnae otherwise have met. Oh, there wisnae a hard discipline in the WRNS, nobody bossed ye about. Since the war ah've never kept up wi' anybody ah knew in the war. Ah've not been at any reunions. Well, Ted and me had two children to bring up. They take up your time.

Elizabeth Stewart (Mrs Elizabeth Breese) died in April 2003.

Christina Millaney

When I was 17, in 1941–2, I wanted to volunteer into the Forces. Even before I had finished my apprenticeship as a tailoress I wanted to go into the WRNS. But my mum wanted me to finish my time before I joined up.

I was born on the 16th of April 1924 in 67 Links Street, Kirkcaldy. My mum and dad both had a shop in Links Street. My dad had his shop, but my mum had a shop within the house, if you know what I mean. I can only remember vaguely about that, because my mum, my brothers and sisters and I left Links Street about 1931 when I was seven. We went then to live in Percival Street in Kirkcaldy.

My father was an apprenticed and skilled cabinetmaker by trade. He used to repair furniture. But I think he didn't do his cabinet-making in his shop in Links Street, he used to just buy and sell. I suppose it was people coming to his shop with stuff and they sold it. But don't ask me what it was, I haven't a clue. I think my dad had been born in Dundee, but I don't know. He was actually an alcoholic. But when he wasn't drinking he was fantastic. He used to take us to the pictures on a Wednesday, his half-day. And he was always super. We had a lot of fun. But then it had come to a point where John, my oldest brother, had said either he or dad would have to go. But I don't remember a lot about my dad. I never saw him again after I was 11.

My mother was born in Dunfermline. I don't know what she did for a living before she was married. You never asked these things. It must have been a struggle for my mum bringing us up on her own after the troubles with my dad. But she was very strong. We had a very happy childhood and we were a very close family. And probably those troubles brought us closer together. We were a Catholic family, and my mum was very devout. She wanted us all to go to university. I think that was her ambition, that we would get a good education. But it didn't work out. She couldn't afford it. So we had all to leave school at 14. Well, she said she couldn't give us an education but she hoped that we could all get a training. And that's what we did get.

I had three brothers and two sisters. My oldest brother was John. He was 16 years older than me. John left home when he was 19, and later once told me it was because 'he couldn't take any more.' He got married in London and remained there but he returned often on visits to us. My second oldest brother was Joe, 14 years older than me. Then came Mary, 10 years older than me. Then Freddie, eight years older than me. Then Esther, three years older than me. So I was the youngest of the six. Joe, from what I could remember, was very fond of my father and had always stuck up for him, so they were very good friends. After Joe got married he went to stay in Edinburgh. Mary got married and had a family by the time the war came. Freddie married as well, but he stayed in Kirkcaldy. Esther was called up to the ATS during the war. My mother's ambition that we should have a good education had succeeded at least partly for John and Joe. They both attended St Joseph's, the Catholic boarding school at Dumfries, but came home when, I think, John was 14 and Joe was 12.[1] They all did very well actually. John became a painter and decorator in London and had his own business. Joe was a fully apprenticed upholsterer and became head of the carpet department in the well-known firm of C. & J. Brown in Edinburgh. Freddie became a baker to trade and he ended up being general manager of seven shops in Kirkcaldy. Esther became an upholsteress and actually started in business for herself. She got the contract for all the curtains and all the stains round the beds at the Victoria Hospital in Kirkcaldy. I became a fully apprenticed tailoress. Mary didn't get a trade, though I don't know why, and she became a bus conductress. But my mum's ambition that, failing a university education, we should get a training, was very successful.

Then I remember our aunties but I don't remember any grandparents. I didn't know them. But my father's father belonged to Dundee, and he was a cabinetmaker. I don't know what my other grandfather had done for a living. It was never mentioned to me by my mother. Maybe it was taboo or what, but nobody ever talked about it! I think our forebears on my father's side had come over from Ireland but, ach, I don't really know. Millaney is my maiden name. It should have been Mullaney. Everybody else was called Mullaney. But my father was called Milleney. He knocked the -e-y off, and we were called Millen then.

Our house in Links Street was quite a big place actually. It was on three floors. The shop was downstairs, and you went upstairs and there was a big huge kitchen and a back door. Well, we had upstairs again. Then there was three bedrooms, if I remember. Then there was a door and upstairs again was an attic, quite a big attic that covered the whole lot. But we didn't have a bathroom or a bath. Well, we just had one of these big portable baths, and you got a bath in it once a week on a Friday or a Saturday in front of the fire, which was quite nice! We had our own toilet, we didn't share it with anybody. It was a flush toilet, but it was an outside toilet. It was gas lighting in that house. My mother had no range there for cooking on, it was just a gas cooker. I don't remember a range or an open fire for cooking on at all. Then there was a huge garden at the back.

As I've said, we moved from Links Street to Percival Street about 1931, when I was seven. That was a council house. It was actually a flat, in a four-in-the block. We were on the ground floor. There we had two bedrooms, a sitting room, a huge kitchen, a bathroom and bath, a flush toilet, running hot water, electricity, a gas cooker, and I think my mum had a big double sink in her kitchen – all mod. cons, and a great boon for all of us. And we had a garden.

By then I had already begun school at age five in 1929 at St Mary's in Dunnikier Road in Kirkcaldy. It was quite a fair journey for a wee girl. We got a tram from Links Street – but we had to walk home! I didn't come back home at dinnertime. The school janitor – we used to call him Daddy Reilly – and his wife had a house at the school. His wife made soup, and you got a plate of soup. Oh, you had to pay something for that, but I cannae remember what it was.

I got on well at St Mary's. I got a prize every year! I liked the school and I've always had a very good memory. I never thought I was clever, but I could remember what I was taught. I just liked every subject. I was quite good at sums. I never had any difficulty. In fact, I made a few enemies at the school because they used tae call me a swot. But I wasn't. I think it was at 11 or 12 you sat the Qualifying exam, but I sat it when I was 10 and passed it. That meant I could have gone on to a secondary school. But, well, there wasn't a Catholic secondary school then in Kirkcaldy. There is now but not then. So you had to go to Cowdenbeath Catholic secondary school, which was about eight miles away. Our mum said she couldn't afford it. There'd be bus fares to pay. So we never got to go there. So I stayed on at school in Kirkcaldy and went then into what they called the Advanced Division, and you did get a higher level of education. But, I mean, it wasn't the same as going to a High School. Actually your education was stopped. Though I stayed on for three or four years I knew everything, because I was getting it over and over again. I probably lost interest then. So none of us in my family went to a secondary school, though my brother Freddie was dux at St Mary's, and my sister Mary was very clever as well. As I'd got older I'd really wanted to go to university but I never got the chance. Well, that's all you could do – stay on till you were 14. When you're a child you don't realise there are those difficulties. I used to think my mum was dreadful because she wouldn't let me go to Cowdenbeath High School. It was only later on that she explained the reason. I wanted to go to the non-Catholic High School. Actually, there was one in Kirkcaldy and I wanted to go there. But because it was non-Catholic and she was very devout, my mum wouldn't let me go there. So that stopped that. But I got to be a teacher years later! Anyway, I left school at 14 in 1938.

Well, I was very good at sewing. From when I was 10 I wanted to be a teacher of sewing. Ah wanted tae go intae that. What happened, when I left school, was that my mum, having had a shop business, had a lot of contacts. And she knew the manager of the Alexander's bus company factory up at the top of the Gallatown, a suburb of Kirkcaldy. So she got me a job with them, to learn to be a French polisher. And that was my first job after I left school. But I didn't like it, in fact I hated it. There was only four women there: two young girls, myself and another – I was 14, she was 16 – and two older women. And there was about a hundred men. To be quite honest, I got frightened in that place. Oh, it was a big place, the bus company's works. And I didn't like the job, which was to do with all the French polishing of all the windowsills, sort of thing. It just didn't appeal to me at all.

We started at eight in the morning. You got free bus passes – that was a perk, I suppose. You worked five days: I don't think we worked on a Saturday morning. I think we only got half an hour for lunch, because you were actually in the place of work. It was like a canteen they had there. Then we worked till I'm sure it was about six at night. I'm not sure about the time we finished, but I know we had to work later because we were getting Saturday off. But of course you werenae getting Saturday off. You were actually working Monday to Friday the five or so hours you would have been working on Saturdays that most people would in those days. My starting wages at Alexander's were 7s 6d [37½p] a week.

Then I hated all the men at Alexander's. They were always trying to get you in corners. I was only a wee girl, only 14, and very naïve. I didn't join a union. I haven't a clue if the men were in a union or if it was a non-union place. We didn't need a lot of friends, because you had your family – your family was your friends. I remember one girlfriend. But I went most places with my older sister Esther because she was that wee bit older than me. I did have one friend at Alexander's. I used to come down from Percival Street in the morning, and there was a young lad. He was 16. I can't remember his name. But him and I used to get the bus. And he was always sticking up for me. If he saw anybody that was trying to be stupid and silly he would say, 'You leave her alone. She's a nice girl.'

I was at Alexander's for a year. I was glad to get away from the place. Oh, gosh, I hated it. I'd actually just got a rise in my wages and had got up from 7s 6d to 10s [50p] a week. But then I saw this advert in the paper for a tailoress apprenticeship. I didn't tell my mother, but because I didn't work at Alexander's on a Saturday, I went down to this tailor's place on my own. I was 15 by this time and I got the job. I went home and told my mum I'd got the job but I'd be dropping 2s 6d [12½p] in wages – back to 7s 6d a week. My mum said I wasn't to go to the tailoring job, that I couldn't take it. This is very vivid in my memory. But then Freddie, my brother and whom I doted on actually, said that he would pay my mum the 2s6d extra so that I could go to the tailor's. Freddie wouldn't have had much pocket money for himself. But that's what he did for me.

This tailoring shop was named Fisher. Mr Fisher did clothes for Michael Nairn and all these people and for an awful lot of business people in Edinburgh.[2] So it was a high-class shop. The shop was in Hunter Street, Kirkcaldy, opposite the Post Office. The shop's not there now though. I just had to run down from Percival Street, through the railway station, and into the shop. So it wasn't far to go – no bus or tram fares, just five to ten minutes down the road.

We really got a good apprenticeship at Fisher's. We started there at nine in the morning. But you worked till six. And you worked on a Saturday till half past 12. I used to go home for lunch. We didn't get a tea break for ten minutes in the middle of the morning, we never got anything like that. But I loved it there at Fisher's, I just loved the job. I started, as I say, with 7s 6d [37½p] a week, and I ended up, I think, with 35s [£1.75]. I had four years' apprenticeship there. I started at 15 and finished my apprenticeship as a tailoress when I was 19 in 1943. I don't know if my mother signed an indenture on my behalf, I can't remember anything like that.

Mr Fisher used to do his cutting out in the front shop. And as you got older he would ask you to come through and give him ideas about what you thought. So I learned quite a lot from him, quite a lot about cutting. I suppose I was quite quick in doing things. Well, as I say, I just loved it.

Mr Fisher kept strict discipline in his shop. As I say, he didn't do anything like having a tea break. He used to be in his front shop and he would keep the door open to where we were in the back shop, so that you never got to speak either. But when he went home for his tea at five o'clock we went daft, mad! We used then to send out for fish and chips and we sat and ate them in the shop. So we got our own back on him.

Mr Fisher was in his forties. He was very dapper, very, very well-dressed. As I say, he did all the cutting. Then there was three time-served ladies in the shop. There was Peggy – I forget her second name. Her father was the chauffeur to Michael Nairn, the boss of Nairn's linoleum factory in Kirkcaldy. And there was Barbara, though I can't remember her second name either. And there was another little lady, too, worked in the shop. Mr Fisher wasn't the only man there, because he did have one man that worked through in another room. That man did a lot of the men's stuff. But I did men's suits as well. Mr Fisher put me on to everything. Then there were three apprentices. I was the youngest of the three when I first started at age 15. Isabel Beveridge from Falkland was one of the three of us. I think her father was the manager of a factory. Isabel was about a couple of years older than me. I got on very well with her. The third apprentice was there when I started, then Mr Fisher started another one. But I can't now remember the name of either of them.

So Mr Fisher had his front shop and he had his fitting room for his customers. The front shop was all decked up with a three-piece suite in it. He had a big long table, and all his fabrics were up at the back. That's where he cut out. Then the fitting room was where he used to take the mirrors for fitting his suits and things. Me and the other workers worked in the workshop. It was like two tables. We used to sit on the table actually with a seat. You put your feet on the seat. But the man that worked in the shop he worked cross-legged in the traditional tailors' way. He did that, but we girls and lady workers didn't. The way we sat was quite comfortable.

I suppose I was a pretty quick worker. Some of them didn't learn as much as I did. I actually learned how to do ladies' and gents' suits, and I was working on gents' jackets. So I did everything. I got a really good training there at Mr Fisher's shop. And, as I say, I ended up within four years with 35s [£1.75] a week. I think that was the maximum. But when you think about it now it wasnae very much! But I also used to do sewing at home at night. I did that for money, not for the shop. I made suits and that for people, and made all my mum's clothes as well. So I had a very good training and I got on very well with Mr Fisher.

I didn't join a trade union at Mr Fisher's shop. He was a non-union shop. So none of the others there was in a union. If you wanted a rise in your wages you had to go and ask Mr Fisher for it. And I used to be the spokesman for asking for rises, because Mr Fisher wasnae very good at giving us rises. Well, you did get a rise until your time was out. But once your time was out, as I found later on, I felt you weren't getting enough pay.

When I was working with Mr Fisher, oh, aye, you got holidays. I think you got a week. But you didnae get paid. Then when I was a girl at school, well, my dad's brother, Uncle Joe, lived in Dundee and they were very close to my mum. Uncle Joe never took a drink. He was the opposite of my dad. I think Uncle Joe worked in a factory. It was actually him that gave me away when I got married after the war. So Esther, my sister three years older than me, and I went to Uncle Joe's in Dundee for the seven weeks school summer holidays. Though I remember one summer when Esther and I stayed the seven weeks with an aunty on my mother's side of the family. She lived in Pittencrieff, just up from the glen, at Dunfermline.

* * *

I remember the actual outbreak of the war in 1939. It happened on a Sunday and we were all at church. The priest made an announcement from the pulpit that war had started. And he said that if anybody wanted to go home . . . So most of them ran out the church! You were frightened in case there were bombs going to be coming across you! Well, ma mother's generation had gone through the First War, and it was very, very upsetting to find themselves in another one. That's what happened to ma dad. Well, I was one of them that came out the church that day and went home. You wanted to get home. That was all you thought about, just getting home. And later that morning there seemed to be an air raid. But I think it was probably just a practice with the sirens to check they were working.

My brother Joe was called up. He was in the Air Force. My brother Freddie was called up, and my sister Esther was called up. She was in the ATS. Well, when I was 17, in 1941–2, I wanted to volunteer into the Forces. So even before I had finished my apprenticeship I wanted to go to the WRNS. But my mum wanted me to finish my time before I joined up. I thought it would be glamorous to join up! I just wanted to get away. Everybody was going away to the Forces. There was nobody left, you know. And I felt it was an exciting thing to do. So when my apprenticeship was finished and I was 19 I volunteered into the WRNS with my friend, a girl called Hannah Dempsey. We'd been at school together. It must have been the naval recruitment place in Kirkcaldy where we joined up. They said there was only vacancies for stewards in the WRNS. We said that was all right, we would go as stewards. We didn't try the ATS or the WAAFs. We didn't want to. We wanted the Senior Service! What attracted me to the WRNS, I just think, was it was a nicer uniform for one thing. I didn't want to go to the ATS because my sister Esther said it was horrible. She didn't like the ATS at all. I might have gone to the WAAFs. Maybe I did volunteer for the WAAFs, but I can't remember now. Probably Hannah and I just got into the WRNS because they had vacancies. Anyway, I volunteered. I was 19 in April 1943, so I think it was the summertime that year that we got in.

Well, you got your papers sent to you. And you went to your posting. My sister Mary, who was by this time married and had a family, and my mum came to see me off. I wanted to join the navy to see the world – and I got stationed at Crail![3] My friend Hannah Dempsey wasn't with me. We'd been hoping to keep together, but she got posted down to England. I suppose we were disappointed, though we kept in touch just by letters. But you were just excited about doing something different.

Crail was just a Fleet Air Arm station. I can't remember now much about the camp there. I can't remember if there were wooden or brick or Nissen huts there. I'm now quite mixed up about this. You had a training, six weeks' training I think it was. You were taught all about the WRNS, and you had all this marching to do – left, right, about turn, and everything. And you got your uniform issued. You were taught what the navy stood for. You had to salute the quarterdeck. The quarterdeck was a flag somewhere and you had to salute that. It was as if every camp was a ship. I do know I was at Crail and I became ill with something and I was in sick bay. When I came out of sick bay, I remember, I was a steward and I loathed it. When you were a steward you were actually dishing out food to the men. And you then had all this washing-up to do. And they didn't have any washing-up liquid or anything. What they had was this tin can with holes punched in the bottom and bits of soap were put in this can. You put the water in it and had to shake it up to make a froth to wash up these dishes. And it was thick grease and, oh, I absolutely loathed that.

We worked in Kellie Castle, near Pittenweem, because it was a hospital. There were seven of us WRNS there, and there were doctors and nurses. What we were doing was looking after the staff, not after the patients. The seven of us WRNS shared two to a room. It was a Glasgow girl that I was with. Her and I got friendly, but she married an American and left the Forces. At Crail I'd met this other girl who'd come from Peterhead. She used to go and see the First Officer to try and get her category changed from being a steward. And I thought, 'I'm going to do the same!', because I didn't like being a steward either! So I went and saw the First Officer until she got fed up looking at me, because I went every week. I'd had that kind of experience with Mr Fisher in his tailor shop, asking for better conditions. So the First Officer actually got fed up with me. She says, 'The only vacancy I've got is for a parachute packer. What can you do?' I says, 'I can take a machine to bits and put it up again!' It was a lie – I couldn't. But I said I was very good with my hands and could do this job with parachutes. I was a trained tailoress. So then I got sent on a training course to Eastleigh, near Southampton. The course was six weeks, training to be a parachute packer. You went to school every day. There was men and women did the job. There was about three or four New Zealanders on our course. You were taught everything about 'chutes. It wasn't only 'chutes you packed. You packed K-type dinghies too. That's the little ones that they used to take into the plane with them. The planes we were involved with were Hurricanes and Spitfires. The packers were all naval packers, Fleet Air Arm, not RAF packers. So in the training you were taught how to pack a 'chute. You were taught how to pack a small dinghy. You were taught how to put the big dinghies in the kites – the planes.

Then in the training course there was a school place we went to. There was a very high ceiling there, and you had to go up on this thing. It was like a seat you sat on, and you had your Mae West on. This was called wet dinghy drill. There was a big pool of water. You had to thingmy your quick release and just drop into the pool. You had a bathing suit on, but you also had these dungarees on. So when you dropped into the water everything clung to you. Of course, all the boys went 'Oooooh!' I can't remember if the water was warm or freezing. But when you dropped into it you had to do your quick release on your Mae West so that it blew up.

Then because we had to teach the pilots and other aircrew wet dinghy drill, we went to the baths and did that with them. Having had to do that sort of work yourself was the best way to understand and teach it. You had to inflate the dinghy and all the rest of it in the water. Oh, gosh, that was quite skilled work. It was far more interesting than washing dishes at Kellie Castle! It was fantastic. I enjoyed that. We had a written exam at the end of the six weeks. And I came top of the class!

And then you were posted. I was always in Scotland, except for that six weeks' course at Eastleigh and a later one. I was posted to Peterhead as a parachute packer. Then from Peterhead we used to go in one of the Service's lorries to Aberdeen public baths for wet dinghy drill with the pilots and other aircrew. We used to take these men there to keep them in training in case they had to bale out or anything. The men had to sign for their 'chutes as well. And they had to return them and sign them in again. Then you hung the 'chutes up for a time. I suppose that was just to take creases out of the 'chutes or to dry them. I remember the pilots used to call me Scottie. And there was some men wouldnae let anybody else touch their 'chutes except me. I suppose they'd feel safe if I'd folded their 'chute. So 'I want Scottie to do my 'chute', you know. So I had my own sort of wee gang of men!

One of the pilots that used to come to me – I can't remember his name now – says to me one day, 'Scottie, have you ever been up in a plane?' I says, 'No.' And he says, 'Would you like to go up in one? Write and tell your mum I'm goin' to take you up in a plane.' So I went up with him in his plane. He was in the pilot's seat and I was the co-pilot, I sat beside him. I had told my mother when this flight was going to happen. The pilot flew the plane over our house in Kirkcaldy. And my mother was looking up and saw us. I waved down to her. I was quite excited. The flight was definitely against regulations! But, oh, it was so exciting. It was really fantastic.

So once I got into parachute packing it was really interesting. And you met all the aircrew and everything. At Peterhead there were between 10 and 20 WRNS girls. They did various jobs. One I was very friendly with was a girl called Barbara who came from Leicester. She was actually a writer, which meant she did office work, clerical, typing. Some of the girls drove lorries. There might have been about half a dozen to a dozen of us who did the parachute packing.

The parachutes were quite long, because you had all these strings as well. What you had to do was, you had to put the 'chute on this great big long table. And you had to sit on the edge of it on one side of the table, and do one half of the parachute, folding it over – one, two, three, four – until it was finished. Then you went to the other side, and did that again, folding over the other way. Then you rolled it up to go into a wee pack. And then you had all these strings. There was sort of hoops that you hooked it into. You had to be very careful to do it in the right way, otherwise it wouldn't unfold properly. It was very responsible work. But you didn't lie awake worrying about all that, because you were very well trained. You had to pack the dinghies as well, because you had the big dinghies that you had in the aeroplanes. They used to do DIs – daily inspections – in the mornings, to see that all the planes had their dinghies in properly. The pilot sat on his 'chute. It was a bigger one; though I don't know why. It was just like a seat thing he had attached to him. The observers and that they just had small ones. The observers and air gunners just carried their packs; their packs were maybe about two feet by one foot, something like that. And they put them under their knees or somewhere when they were in the plane. Oh, it was a very skilled job altogether, very responsible work. You'd to sign everything as well. One time it went all over the camp that somebody had baled out and it was me had packed his 'chute. So he came and gave me £1 for saving his life. Thank God it had worked!

I was never in an air raid shelter at Peterhead. Well, I went into the WRNS in 1943 when, I think, the war was nearly finished.[4] But when I was down at Eastleigh in England on the first parachute course we spent most of every night in the air raid shelters. You were never in bed. You were always down in the shelters. During the war I went down twice to London, once in 1941, when I stayed with my oldest brother John, before I joined the WRNS; and once when I was on leave from, I think, the parachute course at Eastleigh. In 1941, when I was 17, there were air raids all the time. Even as we were coming into London on the train to King's Cross there was an air raid on. And at my brother John's house we actually slept in a shelter. He had one of these Morrison shelters inside his house, in his dining room, and we slept in there.[5] John stayed in Wembley. They were in a street of bungalows. One of the bungalows had gone – obliterated, just a blank space in the street. So we were very lucky, because we were just not far from there.

At Peterhead, on the lighter side of things, I remember we used to have our civvy clothes with us. So we used to get dressed up in these at night, climb the fence, and go across to the petty officers' parties! It was strictly against the rules. But we went in civvies, we didn't go with our uniforms on. Of course, the WRNS were always kept separate from the navy men, the ratings and petty officers, and the Fleet Air Arm officers. Oh, there was quite a bit of ground to cover over from our place to theirs, and there was a fence. But the petty officers, if they were having a party, used to say to us to come to it. They were a mixture of petty officers, chief petty officers, and sub-lieutenants. And you met them all because you were doing the parachutes and things. Of course, if we'd been caught going over to their parties we'd have been disciplined. In fact, in those days I was awful naïve when I think of it. I was stupid! I hadnae much . . . But, I mean, there I met a lot of nice lads and they were gentlemen. So I don't remember anything that was out of order, I don't remember any girls in the WRNS leaving because they were expecting a baby. There was a WRNS commissioned officer in charge of us, a First Officer. And she would keep an eye on our welfare and so on, and make sure all was going well. So I don't remember anything ever being . . .

Well, I never even knew what was happening in the war. You just did your job, you know. And I never felt homesick. Then, after a time, I did another and more advanced course at Eastleigh, this time for three months. And again at the end of it I was top of the class, and I was automatically made a Leadin' WRNS. And then I was to wait for so many months and I was going to be made a petty officer. But, well, I was at Eastleigh doing that second course when the war finished on VE Day, 1945. And I was demobbed before I got that promotion to petty officer.

When the end of the war in Europe came on 8 May 1945 we all went out to the pub. I think there was about 10 of us went to this pub to celebrate, because we'd all been on the same course. Everybody in the pub was coming and throwing money at us. We had a pile of money!

I can't remember exactly when I was demobbed. I know that I had my 21st birthday on the 16th of April 1945 and, of course, I was still in the WRNS then. But I think I was home by the time I had my 22nd birthday in April 1946. So I probably came out the WRNS early in 1946. Anyway, I went back to working for Mr Fisher in his tailor's shop. I didn't think then of going anywhere else, or trying other employment, or trying to get into college or university. I just wanted to get back and earn some money. We werenae in a position to do anything else but get a job. Oh, gosh, I hadnae been able to save much in the WRNS during the war. My pay when I got back to Mr Fisher was about 35 shillings [£1.75] a week or something! I gave everything to my mother and got some pocket money back from her. But I was awful lucky! Boyfriends used to take me out, so I didnae need an awful lot of cash! I had a lot of different boyfriends!

Well, I worked then at Mr Fisher's for about three years till July 30th 1949, when I got married. Once I got married I had to give up my job at Mr Fisher's. Because you were a married woman you weren't allowed to remain at work. You got the sack. They didn't employ married women. So I stayed at home with my mum for six weeks. But what Mr

Fisher did was he used to cut out suits and things for me sometimes. He was very good, quite sympathetic. So I actually did quite a lot of sewing at that time. I did that on my own. Mr Fisher didn't pay me. But he used to help me to cut out things if there were difficult pockets and things like that. When I had to leave my job in the shop and I told him I was going to do sewing at home until I went to England, Mr Fisher says, 'Well, if you've got any problems just let me know and I'll see what I can do to help.' He kept his word on that and was very good. But they weren't allowed to employ married women, they said. It was just the custom that when a woman got married she more or less automatically lost her job.

I'd met my husband, a Kirkcaldy man, before he got a job down in Corby [Northamptonshire]. I'd met him actually on a blind date when I came back home out the Forces. My friend was going out with his friend and she asked me to make up a foursome, and I did.

So I had started up at home on my own making suits for people. I had got plenty of work. But, oh, gosh, when I went down to Corby that was a different thing altogether. I got a job down there in a factory. I'd never been in a factory in my life. It was a Co-op clothing factory. You were doing the same thing all the time. It was boring. I was working there for three years before I had any family. Then I started working in the house again doing tailoring work. I think being a tailoress it was like that, you could always do work at home. So I remained in Corby for eight years then I came back to Kirkcaldy. My husband didn't want to come back to Kirkcaldy, but he did and he became an inspector of works on the motorway. He actually fell 27 feet off the Forth Road Bridge when he was working on a road into the Bridge. He was then off work for ages. So I carried on doing tailoring jobs. I happened to make a suit for my niece June. And Mrs Bolam, head of the Home Economics department in Fife, saw this suit. The next thing she was at my door asking me if I would like a job teaching. I says, 'Oh, gosh, no. I've never done anything like that. I'll never be able to teach.'

At that time I'd be 35. I actually started at Templehall School in Kirkcaldy, but also I went to night classes for English and everything, and got some Highers. Then when I was 42 I went for three years to Atholl Crescent College of Domestic Science in Edinburgh, which was really what I'd wanted to do when I was a schoolgirl. I got a permanent job teaching Home Economics in Glenwood Junior High School in

Glenrothes, and was there until I retired when I was 62. So I was 17 years a teacher. During those years, about 1982, when I was 58, Andy, my husband, had a very severe stroke. He didn't know where he was or anything. He couldn't speak. He was paralysed. All he had was his left hand. So I looked after him for 16 years.

As teachers of Home Economics we were all the lowest of the low, I suppose. You had cookery and laundry – and sewing, which I think the girls particularly liked, because they were all getting suits made that they'd never got before. Naebody else could teach them to make suits!

Well, looking back on my wartime years in the WRNS, oh, I think it was great. I had a great social life as well. And the girls were great. They were all different – all doing different jobs. And from all walks of life. But you chose your friends, like you would do any time. And I had a lot of friends and a lot of good times. And I was a volunteer – there by my own decision. I think most of them were.

Christina Millaney (Mrs Christina Morrison) died on 1 May 2004.

Olga Matthews

I was 17 on the day after war was declared on the 3rd of September 1939. Well, the first thing I did then was I went for a year to the Edinburgh College of Art. That's what I wanted to do. Well, I was only there for a year – which I often regret. But all my friends were joining up. And you felt it would be more fun just to be in it. But what I did was, in the first summer vacation from the College, in 1940, I went and worked on a farm in Berwickshire. So it was terribly late in the war when I volunteered into the WRNS.

I was born on the 4th of September 1922 in Edinburgh. My father, well, that is rather relevant actually, because my father was in the navy, a Regular naval officer, in the First World War and called back in the Second War. In the First War he was at the battle of Jutland, and he was certainly on HMS *Warrior*, which sank there.[1] When the *Warrior* sank, the captain (whose name I can't remember) heroically came off the ship last, as he was supposed to do. Now what really happened was that my father, who was a paymaster and secretary to the captain, as soon as he got off the ship, the captain suddenly said, 'Oh! We've left the confidential box behind. Back you go, boy, and get it.' So it was actually my father who was last off HMS *Warrior*!

After the First War a lot of the naval officers were encouraged to leave. And they all thought they were going to make a fortune once they left the navy. My father and mother lived in London for a bit. But he couldn't get nice jobs. Then my mother's father in Edinburgh said that if my father would like to come up and go to law school there and come as an apprentice in his legal firm, he'd get on. My father, himself an Englishman, went up to Edinburgh and eventually became a Scottish solicitor there in my grandfather's firm of Bell, Belleron & Findlay. Well, I don't think it was a full university course in law my father took. He just sort of went to law classes, but worked with my grandfather in his office. Apprentices all had to get practical experience. I don't know how long it took, perhaps about five years. By the time my father joined the firm other partners had died, and the firm was then called Dudgeon, Farmer & Matthews. The 'Matthews' was my father's name. In the Second War my father was called back into the navy. He went to Glasgow first, then down to Warrington in Lancashire.

During the time my father was training to become a solicitor, my mother did some teaching. My mother had done, oh, a lot of very interesting things. As a child in Edinburgh she was sent to a French school, a private school, in Manor Place, run by some ladies. And it was compulsory to talk French all the time. The pupils arrived at eight years old or something, and you just had to talk French. I don't think my mother had a smattering of French before she went there. They had some teachers, English or Scottish teachers, who taught subjects like maths and English, and they were allowed to speak English in those classes. But with the ladies who kept the school you had to speak in French all the time, no matter what the subject. And the outcome of it was that my mother was the most beautiful speaker of French.

When the First World War came I think she did some land work or something, and then got a job in the Foreign Office in London. She was able to translate, and she was at the Peace Conference at Versailles in 1919. And of course whenever trouble comes up nowadays with Bosnia or something, my husband and everyone else says, 'That was all your mother's fault. She arranged things at Versailles'! She was a typist of 22 or so. And she went to be secretary to the ambassador in Constantinople [Istanbul]. And my father had some job as a naval attaché, and that's where they met, in Constantinople. They were married there just after the First War. Once she married, my mother was no longer employed full-time. But she did a certain amount of writing and, as I've said, some teaching.

I had one brother, Robin, younger than me. He went to Oxford University and then to Cambridge, and eventually became Master of a College in Cambridge. His subject was economics. Robin was entirely intellectual; practically – absolutely useless.

So I grew up in Edinburgh. I started school at what was called the PNEU School. I think it meant Parents' National Education Union or something. It was sort of modern ideas, I think. I remember very little about it now. Then, as I've mentioned, when my father was training to become a solicitor, my mother started teaching; and it was at a boarding school outside Edinburgh in Midlothian: Oxenfoord Castle.[2] She used to come out daily there from Edinburgh, so I was there, too, as a day pupil, presumably at reduced rates of fees. When my father qualified as a solicitor, my mother stopped teaching at Oxenfoord. I was then 13 or 14, and that's when I went to St George's School, a private fee-paying school at Murrayfield in Edinburgh. I started there more or less at the secondary stage, maybe in the second year of it. I remained at St George's till I was 17 and did the Highers exams. The subjects at St George's that particularly interested me were art, English and mathematics. If I'm not being too immodest I could say I was good at maths. I was very interested in mathematics.

As a girl I didn't really have any particular ambitions, maybe to become a teacher or a mathematician. The only ambitions I had were mad ones, like being a mountain climber! I didn't feel I wanted to become a doctor or take up nursing. I just went on from day to day. So I left school in the summer the war broke out. I was 17 on the 4th of September 1939, the day after war was declared. Well, as I've said, the first thing I did then was I went for a year to the Edinburgh College of Art. That's what I wanted to do. I was only there for a year – which I often regret. But all my friends were joining up. And you felt that it would be more fun just to be in it. But what I did was, in the first summer vacation from the College, in 1940, I went and worked on a farm in Berwickshire. It was supposed to be for the harvest and for whatever was happening. But I didn't go back to the Art College as I should have done. I'd made up my mind by then not to go back to it.

The farm I was working on in Berwickshire was called Chalkielaw, and was between Duns and Manderston. Lord Palmer or somebody lived in the big house at Manderston. I think eventually Lord Palmer got all his tenants out except one.[3] The farmer we worked for was a very stubborn old man who stayed alive till he was about 95. We girls were in the bothy. There were some other girls there, too, to start with. After a time, however, I was left the only girl there. But by that time I'd made friends with the people in the two cottages next door to the bothy. I worked a lot with the lady in the next cottage to me. She worked in the fields. She had three of a family: a boy of 17 or so, not much younger than me, a younger boy about nine, and a younger girl. They all walked to school in Duns, about a mile away. They were quite happy and much healthier, too. The little boy was called Willie. Years later, I went down there and tried to get in touch again with Willie. He had become Lord Palmer's manager for the whole Manderston estate. I was awfully pleased, because Willie's family were such a nice family, and they worked so hard. Farm workers in those days lived on very little. It was a poorly paid job. They did have a few perks, such as potatoes, and they had a little vegetable garden. In some ways, so far as food was concerned, they were maybe better off than people living in the towns.

Oh, I enjoyed working on Chalkielaw farm. It was a worthwhile job, because of rationing, the shortages of food, and all that. And Mrs Rankin, who lived next door to me, was my best friend. She was the farm worker's wife. I worked with her. She worked on the season, not all the time – a seasonal worker. And if this doesn't sound patronising, what I can say is that she was so intelligent. She was quite uneducated but very, very intelligent. She was born before her time, as many ordinary people were. She'd never had a chance to stay on at school after the age of 14.

Well, after that spell at Chalkielaw farm, I went down to the south of England. An aunt of mine was an artist, and she was living near this farm in Sussex. She thought it would be nice if I came down and worked there. The farm in Sussex was a very nice place. From that time on I went from one farm to another. I can't remember now really how it happened that I kept going to different places. I would have liked to say I was in the Women's Land Army. I thought about joining it, and I actually tried to join it. But they wouldn't have me because I was already registered as an agricultural labourer. I was a full-time farm worker and had been since going to Chalkielaw farm in Berwickshire in 1940. So I couldn't really volunteer into an allied force like the Women's Land Army.[4] I can't remember now when I applied, but I think I may have applied more than once. It's such a long time ago that I can't remember. Well, I'd left Chalkielaw to go down to England because I'd been quite lonely. The other girls at Chalkielaw had gone by then. They were all students, as I had been. One of them was a medical student. She wouldn't have been called up until she qualified as a doctor. There were two other girls who were students of English. But they would be called up once they graduated.

Anyway, I do remember that I had a sort of bout of bronchitis, and I went and stayed at home in Edinburgh for a bit to recover. My parents were keen on me giving up farm work. They thought it was strenuous work. And my father, being of course in the navy himself, thought I should volunteer into the WRNS: 'Do apply for the WRNS, because it's so good.' So I suppose it was really he that put the idea into my head. I can remember thinking myself that I could join the women's Services, and that if so it would be the WRNS. Oh, I would certainly go to the WRNS. I wouldn't go to the ATS or the WAAF. All the talk at home had been of the navy, the sea, rather than the army or the Air Force; although one of my sort of lifetime friends that I'd been at the Art College with had gone into the WAAF right away after, you know, that first year at the College. I formed the impression that the WRNS was the most prestigious and the most attractive. The WAAF came next, then the ATS. I think the poor ATS had for a time in certain quarters an unsavoury reputation! Oh, it never occurred to me to think of the WAAF or the ATS.

So it was terribly late in the war when I volunteered into the WRNS. I wasn't actually in until about January or February 1945. All the time before then since the summer of 1940 I was doing farm work, and then latterly working in market gardens. So I suppose I must have written or gone into a hall somewhere in Edinburgh to register and volunteer for the WRNS. Some things are just blank. But I think it's very likely I would have gone to the Music Hall in George Street. I'd have had a discussion with somebody in the WRNS, most likely an officer. I think it may have been on that occasion that they said, 'Was there any reason that you want to be near home?'. You know, in case I had an ill or widowed mother or someone. And I said no. And I think I'd have had a medical examination: they wouldn't have taken me without one, especially as I'd had a bit of trouble with bronchitis. And I've always been a bit asthmatic, though I've got over it now. So I joined the WRNS certainly several months before the war in Europe ended in May 1945.

I was sent first to Millhill in London. It was a huge institution there. You had three weeks there just to introduce you to the WRNS and the navy. Then they decided what category to put you in. Here again, I've got little recollection of what happened at Millhill. I mean, we're talking about 60 years ago now. I do remember one or two lectures about Nelson and so forth, and all the things we were going to do in the world. Anyway, one thing I do remember is that it was rather dreary.

Millhill was a huge building. I think it was a naval barracks. We weren't in huts there. We got uniform and we had to wear it all the time. The uniform I remember with horror. It was just a sort of serge suit. I think if girls today had to wear that, what a fuss they would make! There was a white shirt, and rather a nice little hat, black stockings and black shoes. The person who was sort of helping us with the shoes was very nice and said, 'They're uncomfortable at first, but they get very comfortable.' And it was true, they did. I suppose our feet flattened out with all the marching up and down! But I didn't find the uniform positively uncomfortable, and you got used to it. And everyone else was wearing the same. I don't suppose it was so bad. The officers' uniform was nice.

At Millhill we were occasionally allowed to go little trips, bravely to go to a tea shop or something like that. We were divided in some way into groups, whether it was by education or what it was . . . I think it was something to do with our qualifications. I had my Highers and had been to a college. Few other people there had done that. I think that's the way we were divided. Anyway, in my group there was a very nice girl called Louise. She was older than me. I'd be 22 by then. Louise had been to art school, and had done some designing work in a factory. And then, like me, she'd wanted a change. Anyway, since all those years ago, though we lived in different places, we kept up, we kept up until she died three years ago. I called my daughter after Louise.

After three weeks at Millhill I went to a station, which was Yeovil [Yeovilton] in Somerset. Yeovil [Yeovilton] was a Fleet Air Arm flying training place.[5] My job there was to be what was called an Aircraft Direction (AD) Wren. We worked at what must have been some big house that had been taken over. The object of this Aircraft Direction job was that these pilots were learning to fly. And at the same time there were people learning to direct them from aircraft carriers. It seemed a bit late in the war to be doing that. But never mind. We were learning a little bit about radar, and a little bit about plotting, and that sort of thing. What we did when we got to work were the same jobs that naval ratings would do at sea when the enemy was being chased about. There was no question of us going to sea, or still less of us as WRNS going into action. Oh, we wouldn't be sent into action.

The work was interesting, because I was quite good at maths. Then there was a thing called DR [Detection Range] you sometimes had to deal with. It meant you had to calculate where the enemy plane was. I can't remember the details, but I enjoyed doing it. We didn't work very long hours. It was like office hours really, a sort of nine to five job, and then we were free in the evenings.

I think there were eight or ten of us WRNS who were working at the air station there. And at this place at Yeovil it was lovely because, after all the barrack rooms, we were in dispersed quarters. There were a few of us in different houses. There were two or three to a bedroom. At Millhill we'd been in larger rooms with maybe a dozen or two dozen girls, something like that. And I suppose it had been double bunks there. And you hadn't had a chance to get to know the other girls, except for Louise. I think we had one or two others who came with us to Yeovil, but I can't remember them now. At Yeovil it was civilian digs we were in that had all been taken over by the navy. It was actually an old vicarage that we were in, in a tiny village called Rimpton. And I think there must have been a WRNS cook for the whole thing.

It was beautiful countryside there. And, oh, we were on bikes, everywhere on bicycles. We went out to work on bicycles in fact. They were provided by the navy, and they were big, heavy, sort of Post Office bikes. So we could explore the countryside on our bikes. On one outing I'll always remember I was biking with a boyfriend called Frank to Wookey Hole, where there are lovely caves. It must have been 20 miles there and 20 miles back. We didn't think anything of it. And I was accustomed to cycling. I think I'd had a bike when I was at Chalkielaw farm near Duns earlier in the war. I'd love to go back to see that bit of the country again around Yeovil, and all these quiet little streets. The next village to Rimpton was Marston Magna: they're lovely names. We went to the pub at Marston Magna. That's where I discovered real cider – scrumpy.

Though there were only eight or ten of us WRNS doing this particular work at Yeovil, there were, oh, more than that Fleet Air Arm personnel there. There were about that number in each house, and I think there were four houses. So altogether there'd be about 40 there.

In our leisure time I think they had dances occasionally at the air station. For one thing you met other men there! You met pilots. But I didn't pursue my interest in art when I was at Yeovil. I hadn't been able to do painting or drawing at the various farms I'd worked at earlier either. Just at that time I think I dropped all that. And then communal life is different. You didn't get much peace. I mean, I shared the room at Yeovil with two or three other girls. So there wasn't a lot of space to do painting or drawing.

As for leave, I'd met some cousins in London when I'd gone there for a weekend. But I don't think I had home leave at all when I was at Yeovil, because we weren't there very long. But if I did have a leave I just had to take a long and rather uncomfortable train journey to Edinburgh. I think you went up the west coast. The trains were awful, the stations all dark and crowded, and you were sitting on your bag. Unless I had a week's leave it wasn't worth going.

Another thing I remember about the Aircraft Direction Wrens was that they were, in a way, horrible, awful snobbish, and exclusive. To my knowledge no AD Wren ever went out with an ordinary naval rating, an ordinary sailor. It sounds awful. Of course, that was the case throughout society. There was class consciousness. People felt uncomfortable with other people whom they thought belonged to a different social class. So I think, in that society, if you'd met an awful nice naval rating you wouldn't tell. You'd be breaking protocol if you did anything like that. Some of the other girls didn't like this sort of thing, and there was supposed to have been a big laugh when one of the girls asked another, 'What does AD stand for anyway?' And the answer came: 'Admirals' Daughters'! But it was quite a small group of 'Admirals' Daughters' who seemed to see the other girls as just there to do the cooking for us. And then there were some of the older Wrens who despised those of us who had come into the WRNS so late, though of course in my own case I'd been doing war work by working on the farms. So there were these differences between groups of the girls. One girl who lives in Edinburgh, well, if I see her now and talk to her she says, 'Weren't we awful? Weren't we horrible?'

I was still at Yeovil when the war in Europe ended in May 1945. But when VE Day was over I went to this place in South Wales. It was a small village called Dale, right in the south-west corner of Pembrokeshire. Again it was lovely country, but of a different sort. The air base there was called after the village, just Dale. The camp, which was built entirely of Nissen huts, was called Kete. It was the same thing: the fliers were in one place and the fighter direction in another. All these places were called HMS-Some-Bird, and I wish I could remember what our HMS was called. Some of the WRNS girls remained at Yeovil; others of them, as well as the flying and training instructors, came down to Kete. I think most of the ones who'd trained with me came to Kete.

I was never promoted in the WRNS. Wren Matthews – that's what I was and that's what I remained! But I was in a very superior service! For a short time, when I was at Yeovil, I began getting keen about applying for a commission. I think we had one Wren who gave us an awfully interesting lecture about aircraft. I wasn't normally into that, and I thought I must work hard and get to it. But it didn't work out like that: I think laziness. I sort of gave up. So I didn't apply for a commission. But in this Aircraft Direction category I was in, we were all sort of well-educated.

At Kete the living was quite rough because we had these cold cabins – Nissen huts. And there we were all in double bunks. There were ten double bunks, so there must have been about 20 girls in the hut. There was a stove in the middle of the hut. We made toast on it. The floor was concrete, and you had to polish it every week. You did your own little bit. But we never seemed to mind.

Well, at Kete it was interesting work and it was a beautiful place. It was near the islands of Skomer and Skokholm, and there were great bird sanctuaries along there. You could walk for miles round the coast. I already had an interest in nature, partly through working on the farms. So it wasn't a new interest that developed for me in the WRNS. Then, once the war was really over with the defeat of Japan, quite a strong dramatic group developed in the camp at Kete. I think three officers who were instructors had been actors in civil life. And they got together and encouraged the development of the drama group. My friend Louise and I did the scenery painting. So I suppose that helped renew my interest in painting. Louise and I were the only two people there who had art school experience. So that was really about the only painting I did during the war years or in my whole time in the WRNS.

I remained at Kete until I was demobbed about February or March 1946. I'd been in the WRNS about a year, or just over that. Well, you're suddenly rather lost. I missed the company, because I'd been with other people of my own age, some of whom shared my interests. A girl called Rosemary, for instance, was interested in archaeology. I think we travelled up together to Edinburgh when we were demobbed. After she was demobbed she went to Edinburgh College of Art as a mature student. She qualified as a teacher of art and she did some beautiful pictures. So I kept in touch with her. I've forgotten what my WRNS friend Louise did after the war. But she got married pretty soon, to one of the pilots she'd been training with at Yeovil. I think Louise was painting all the time. Her husband did all sorts of jobs, wasn't very contented, and he decided to become a clergyman in the Church of England. But I never see Louise and she's never been up in Scotland.

Well, I didn't go back to college. I wondered what to do. Then I took a secretarial course in Edinburgh. But I wished I'd done something more than that, like going back to College. I can't remember now which secretarial college it was I went to. But it was for shorthand and typing and book-keeping, and the course lasted about a year. And then I did various secretarial jobs. I was private secretary to a consultant doctor at Edinburgh Royal Infirmary. Then I had a job at the medical school, in the chemistry department. I met my first husband there. He was a demobbed RAF fellow. After he'd finished at Edinburgh University he got a job at Newcastle. So we went down and lived there. We had two boys and a girl. But I'm afraid my marriage broke down. My aunt had died and she'd left us a house in Richmond in London. I went down there with the children, and we were there for a while. Then they grew up and moved away. While I was there I trained to be a teacher. I was teaching art and maths. I did that for several years. By then my daughter Louise had a partner, my elder son was married, and the younger one was still at university but he liked coming up to Scotland. So I got a teaching job in a primary school at Fodderty, north of Inverness and near Dingwall. So I was happy in primary. I had the older primary children, so I had a lot of fun with them, too.

Well, often when I had worked on the farms during the war I thought it would be nice to marry a farmer. When in the 1970s I was staying with friends at Strathpeffer near Fodderty, a neighbouring farmer came over one day to help with their sheep. He became my second husband!

Looking back now on my time in the WRNS, one thing I want to say which is not personal but more political, is that nowadays people will say how dreadful it was when we dropped the atom bomb on Japan. When that happened I was in the navy. They weren't blood-thirsty people, or anything like that, in the navy. But nobody regretted the dropping of the bomb. It was relief that the war was over. My husband was out East in the navy then, and they were told that they might have to go in, and that the Japs would just fight to the end. Probably if that had happened more people would have been killed than were killed by the bomb. Of course, we didn't know at all then about the genetic effects of the bomb.

So that year I was in the WRNS, well, it was an experience. Yet when I think about it I somehow find it all very painful. I knew people who were killed, some of the fellows at Yeovil who didn't return. Oh, it certainly was a distinctive year that, it certainly was. I often think back on it. And I wish I'd kept up with more of the people I met then.

Olga Matthews (Mrs Olga Clarke) died on 31 March 2008.

Alexina McGlinn

Eih wis in ma twenties when Eih had tae go, when ah wis called up. So it wid be in the later part o' the war. Ah didnae want tae go tae munitions or anythin' like that, no, ah didnae fancy it. And ah didnae fancy the ATS. Well, when ah wis called up ah fancied the forestry, that's what ah fancied. Ah'd never heard o' the Timber Corps before then.

Ah wis born on the 14th o' October 1922 at home in Dundee. Ma father wis a labourer, well, what ye'd call a hod-cairrier, a builder. He wis always in the buildin' trade. When ye think aboot it it really wis a hard job. Ma father wis a Dundee man, born and grew up in Dundee. He was 86 when he died. My memory's a blank aboot when he died. But it wis efter the Second War. Eih wis married then and he wis still goin' strong. It wis jist Jimmy – that's ma laddie – wis born. He's 57 now. Well, ma father wis in the army at the First World War. He wis under age for the 1914 War, but he jist went. There wis nae work. He volunteered – that wis the answer. He wis 17 when he went off tae the army. But he came back safe frae the war. And ah think he wis in Russia at the end o' the war. Ah'm sure he was.[1] Well, he came back and then he went intae workin' as a labourer again – when he could get work, because there wis an awfy lot o' Means Test at that time. It was really bad.[2] Ah mind o' ma mother and father causin' a lot o' trouble at home because there wis nae money comin' in. It wis really terrible. In fact, ma mother had tae go tae work tae keep us. Well, there wis always work in the mills.

Ma mother wis a spinner in the jute mills, always, always in the works. Ma mother wis 14 when she started work. There wis long hours, poor pay. They jist had tae accept it. Folk said in Dundee it wis often the man that couldnae get a job, so he stayed at home and got the tea ready. He biled the kettle. Ma dad did that when he got leave, if the twa o' them werenae fightin' wi' yin anither. Oh, hard times.[3]

Ah dinnae ken much about ma father's faither. But he came frae Greenock. He wis sort o', kind o' Irish. He worked on the land – like wi' the tatties and the turnips, the harvest, and so on. He wis a farm worker – when he could get work as well. Ah dinnae ken what part o' Ireland grandfaither McGlinn came frae. In fact, there wis a mix-up wi' his name. It seems that that's no' his name. His name wis MacAlyn. But he had sich a strong brogue that's the name that come oot. They thought he wis sayin' McGlinn. Eih dinnae ken when he came tae Scotland. But it wid be before the First War, because to me he wis always an auld man. He was a typical Irishman and never lost his brogue. Eih dinnae ken anythin' aboot ma grandmother McGlinn. She wis dead. She wis Irish as well, but ah'm no' sure o' her ain name. But ah never saw her.

Ma mother's mother, her merried name wis Angus and she belonged Fife. Ma grandfaither Angus, oh, he had a horse and cart. Worked for hisself. He sold fruit. But they werenae well-off, jist quite ordinary. He wis a Dundee man. Ah don't remember these grand-parents much, because we lived in a different part o' Dundee from them. And ma mother never, never really mixed. And the money wisnae there tae travel back and forrit. But, oh, ah mind o' seein' ma grandfather and ma granny Angus. He died when ah wis quite young, and ma granny later on.

I'd three brothers and three sisters, seven o' us a'thegither. James was ma oldest brother. Then came me, ma brother Alex, then ma sister Jenny. Then a sister, Helen, that died when she wis jist aboot four year old. She had that – is it scarlet fever? One o' these kind o' . . . Ah'm sure it wis scarlet fever. After Helen came ma sister Williamina – a fancy name, eh? And after Williamina came Michael. So that wis seven o' us a'thegither, three boys and four girls.

The first house Eih lived in wis in Brook Street, Dundee. It wis a tenement, doon a great big . . . We lived in a pend.[4] And there wis a lot o' buildins, ken, there wis a lot o' people lived in the one area. That wis the west end o' Dundee. We were on the top flat o' the tenement. It wis a room and kitchen. The toilet wis on the stair. It wis a flush toilet. It wis a shared toilet. Well, on our flet it wis three families shared the toilet. And there wis three families underneath us. So that wis six families in the block o' two storeys. The three families below us had their own shared toilet.

The lighting in our house wis a gas mantle. We didnae have runnin' hot water. You got a bath at the end of the week, in a big tub in front o' the fire. That wis the usual. It wis the girls first or the boys first. But it wis the same water for us a'. Ma mother and father couldnae afford tae keep bilin' the kettle. Friday night wis bath night. It wis like a routine. As ah say, I'd three brothers and three sisters, seven o' us a'thegither. That's how we lived.

The sleepin' arrangements were ma mother and father slept in the kitchen. And all of us children were in the room. There wis a division – a curtain – put up between the boys and the girls in the room. But all of us children were in the room – except when the baby wis new. Oh, aye, when the kiddie wis new, when there wis a new baby it slept wi' ma mother and father in the kitchen. That wis the situation. They were a' big families then.

How ma mother did her cookin' in Brook Street, well, we had a coal fire. And she used tae keep a pot for keepin' the water warm. There wis a gas ring, but no' a gas cooker. It wisnae a range, it wis jist a hob. One gas ring, that's all there was. And ah dinnae think ma mother had an oven. Oh, ma mother wisnae a baker. She wis too busy workin'. As ah say, it wis an open coal fire, and always we had a pot on top o' the coals. To have one o' these big ranges wi' an oven, ah think ye had tae be a wee bittie better-off for that. Ye were considered a toff if ye had one!

Ah lived in Brook Street till ah wis about 12, in 1934–5. We went up then to Moncur Crescent, near Dundee Football Club's ground. This is when they started buildin' a' the new council houses and gettin' rid o' the slums. Oh, there wis quite a difference for us. There wis too many rooms: we didnae ken what tae dae wi' them! In Moncur Crescent we had two bedrooms and what we would call like a sittin' room, and a kitchen and a bathroom. Electricity – what a difference frae the gas mantle and candles! Oh, we had every convenience. And ma father had a garden, though he wisnae much o' a gardener. But it was there. Though we never had the time tae sit in the garden, we were too busy workin'. But Brook Street and Moncur Crescent houses were the complete opposite o' each other. And by the time we arrived in Moncur

Crescent we were beginnin' tae get older, and in a few years after that ma brothers were workin'.

I started school at St Andrew's School in the Overgate. It was quite near where we lived in Brook Street. St Andrew's wis always jist the one school I wis at. Ah wis there from the age o' five till ah wis 14. I always remember leavin' at 14, because ma mother was expectin' another baby. That would be Michael, the youngest o' us.

Ah wisnae that bright! Well, tae be quite honest, there wis more . . . Long ago ye were awfy feared, ye were really frightened o' the teacher. And if ye're frightened o' the teacher ye jist cannae learn anythin'. And that's it. And, well, ah suppose there wid be aboot 40 in ma class. It was a mixture, boys and girls. They came frae roond aboot the West End. Oh, the children were a' pair. Oh, it wisnae as bad as the children comin' tae school without boots or shoes, it wisnae as bad as that. If ye were really destitute ye got school shoes and school stockins. And you really felt terrible wi' them on, ken. Well, ah used tae get them and, well, ah used tae feel embarrassed wi' the shoes ah got. They were big, heavy, clumsy things. Well, ah didnae like them. But ah had tae wear them, or else ah had nothing tae put on. You sort o' accepted it. As ah say, ma father couldnae get work and, oh, it wis ma mother that had tae work. Oh, a' the time we lived in The Burn – we kent Brook Street as The Burn – ma father couldnae get work.

Well, at St Andrew's School we had, oh, a horrible woman teacher, Miss McGettrick. Ye see, ah've never forgot her name. She whacked the children. She used a stick on our hands. Oh, ah got that often. Ye couldnae concentrate on the work because you were hungry. If ye're hungry ye're no' interested in anything.

Ah didnae have a job when ah wis at school, no' deliverin' papers or milk or anythin' like that. Ma older brother James had a job. He delivered milk. Then ah think he went away tae this home for poor children. It wis in Fife. What d'ye call it? Cromarty or Cromarton Home. It wis supposed tae be a holiday.[5] But ah dinnae think James enjoyed it. And it wis in the winter. Ah wis never there myself. Anyway, ah wis on James's milk run for two weeks. Ah got paid two shillins (10p) a week. Ah started at six in the mornin'. Ah wis up aboot half past five. It wis jist a fellow on his own wi' a horse and cart. He worked for a company. Ah cannae mind the name o' the company. But it wis a small affair, jist one horse and cart and a load, a load o' milk. He had one o' these cans or pitchers and a lid on it. Sometimes he filled the can from the cart, and sometimes he had bottles o' milk. Ah didnae enjoy that job, let's put it that way. Ah delivered the milk before ah went tae school. Ye just worked till ye were finished, maybe aboot eight o'clock. Then ye went home and, oh, ye were lucky if ye got a slice o' bread and a cup o' tea. That wis your breakfast. Ye didnae get porridge. And, oh, an egg? We didnae ken what an egg was. But ye accepted all these things. On our bread we had margarine, oh, no' lard, but margarine. Ye got a piece on margarine or sometimes jam. Ma mother didnae have time tae make jam, and, oh, ma mother didnae bake, she didnae cook. Well, that wisnae the fashion, no' among these kind o' people. Everything wis bought. We were jist ordinary working people.

Well, ah wis jist haudin on for ma brother James until he came back from this home for poor children. This milk company took him back again. But, as ah say, ah never had a job o' ma own like that, deliverin' milk or papers, when ah wis at school. And ah didnae have a Saturday job either. Ah never heard o' anybody havin' these jobs at that time. Where we lived people wouldnae get anythin' delivered because they wouldnae have been able tae afford it.

And then, as far as food went, we never got toast. It wis jist bread and margarine. Toastin' bread at the fire, well, that wis a luxury. When ah came in frae the school at midday, well, it would be soup or broth. And a cup o' tea and another piece on margarine. That wis your dinner. And then when ah came in again after school, maybe a piece on cheese: no luxury. Ye didnae get anythin' cooked at night, no meat, no fish. Ye never got fresh fruit, no apples. We used tae get spulters – that's bad fruit, a pennyworth o' spoiled fruit. That wis a luxury. Well, there yist tae be a market in Dundee. And at the end o' it it wis sealed. When they put away their tents and that anythin' that wis left over ye could buy it for ha'penny or a penny. Ye thought it wis great. Ah went tae the market wi' ma auldest brother James. We did a bit o' scroungin'. Oh, ah didnae have pocket money as a girl. Ye were lucky if ye got a ha'penny. Ye were frightened tae spend it.

Anyway, the food we ate week by week wis soup and kail, and potatoes and mince if you were lucky. The mince wis once a week. Then we had a fish and chip shop nearby, and you could get a fish supper for 2d (1p). We'd get a share o' that. And we'd get some chips on a piece. But ah don't remember, as ah say, fresh fruit or much in the way o' vegetables except for the soup and the kail. It was soup and very plain food. Never got an egg. But ye accepted it because that's the way it was.

When Eih wis a girl at the school ah had tae go for aulders. Have ye heard o' them? Well, that's stuff like breid that's been left frae the day before. Ah had tae get up at six o'clock in the mornin' tae go for bread – auld teabreid – for wir breakfast. Ye went roond the back o' the baker's shop where they sold the stuff off cheap frae the day before. Well, that's what Eih used tae do. We didnae think nothin' aboot it. Ye'd tae stand in the queue at six o'clock in the mornin' and wait tae the shop opened. And it cost 6d [2½p]. Ye took your pillae slip and filled it wi' breid. As Eih say, Eih did that as a girl when ah wis at school. Well, once again, ye didnae think nothin' aboot it. Ye didnae like it, but that wis it.

Then, well, ma brother James went tae school dinners, but he didnae like it so he didnae go back. He wis the only one o' us that went tae school dinners. Ye had tae put in for that, like puttin' in for shoes or clothing. It wis mainly tea that we drank. Oh, we didnae drink much milk. There wis nae milk at the school in them days. Efter ma ain bairns were born, efter the Second War, that's when ye got the milk. Well, Eih think there wis big improvements efter the war, wi' school dinners and milk. But there was more work then. And Eih always worked.

When ah wis a girl ma parents were never able tae take us away on a holiday. But the hale family went tae the berries. We had tae go tae the berries tae get claes for the school. Every year we went tae the same place: McDonald's farm at Blairgowrie. It wis jist beside the railway station. Well, ye had tae walk aboot a mile frae the station tae get tae the camp. So there were a lot o' folk there, and a lot o' dormitories. There wis a mixture o' folk, mainly frae Dundee and Glasgow, some frae Fife. So every summer we went for a fortnight tae the berries. That wis the only holiday . . . Well, actually it wisnae a holiday. Ah didnae like it, but there you are. Ah had tae pull the berries. And many a time a bang on the ear ah got because ah got fed up o' it! Aye, ah didnae like it.

It wis raspberries. Raspberries were easy: you could stand. Strawberries wis horrible, because ye had tae get doon on your knees in the wet and the thistles. Well, wi' raspberries ye had the big bucket in front of you, and it wis gettin' heavier and heavier and heavier. And you were hungry and you werenae interested. And we were paid a hawpenny – a ha'penny [¼p] – a pound. Ye were paid when they weighed them up. Oh, no, ah didnae like the berries. But ye had tae go. Well, it wis tae get your school shoes and gymie apron. Well, goin' tae the berries wis healthy, and there wis good fun at night. Because there was what we called The Big Hotplate, where everybody came in wi' their sausages and their eggs and their ham. And they were boilin' their clothes on it, tae. And it wis a mixed crowd o' people. Ah dinnae ken if we played wi' the children. We maybe fought wi' them! But ye accepted it, because that's what wis there. Nowadays the young yins want everything right away. They dinnae ken the benefit o' having tae really strehve for it.

Ah never had any ambitions tae be a nurse or a teacher or anythin' like that. That wis never in oor circle. It wis jist a case o', 'Ah wish ah wis 14 and could get oot tae work.' Ah think it wis jist the eidea o' gettin' away from the school, and you thought work wis great adventures. But efter ye were at your work ye discovered it wisnae any better than bein' at school. It's jist the same. But, as ah say, mei ambition wis jist tae leave the school and get a job.

So as soon as ah wis 14, roond aboot 1936, ah left the school and got a job right away. Well, ah wis a spreader in the calender – tae do wi' bags. But ah wis only there for half a day. Later, ah went tae the weaving. It wis Grimond's jute mill at the Top o' Hilltown in Dundee, no' far frae Moncur Crescent where we lived. Oh, Grimond's wis a big mill. There'd be maybe hundreds o' workers employed there. When the gates opened at dinnertime everybody breenged out.

In the mill there wis the winding and the weaving and there wis the spinning. The work ah wis involved wi' as a spreader wis, well, there wis a woman sat on a machine and she sewed up these bags. You'd tae turn them on to the right side and spread them out. And it wis hard work because it wis piece work – piece work for the woman that wis on the machine, but no' for you. Ah wis paid an hourly wage – and badly paid. When ah began ma wage wis 12s 6d [62½p] a week. It would be eight o'clock in the mornin' when ye started, and ye worked until half past five. Ye got a break for your dinner at 12 noon tae one o'clock. Oh, there wis no tea breaks in that time. So ye worked straight on frae eight till 12 noon, and then back again frae one o'clock tae 5.30pm. It wis hard work. At that time aboot 1936 when Eih started ye were workin' on a Saturday; but then later on – before the war, maybe in 1937–8 – workin' on the Saturday stopped, and it wis jist a feive day week till the Friday. But Saturday work wis frae eight till 12 noon. So then that would be 46½ hours a week, somethin' like that, for 12s 6d. Ah didnae get any increase in ma wages as a spreader. Then Eih left that and Eih went on to the weaving, and ah made ma own wages at that. That's tae say, ah wis on piece work at the weaving. Piece work wages varied frae week tae week, but as ah got older maybe some weeks ah would have 28 shillins [£1.40] a week. So as ah got aulder the situation changed, and ye really could make money. It depended on the work ye got done. But, oh, you worked all the time, you were workin' all the time.

Well, actually Eih did the work in what you called the factory. There wis a distinction between the mill and the factory. The weavers thought they were different. It wis a class thing. The weavers, not the spinners, were thought o' as havin' a sort o' plum job in the mill, because as a weaver you made your own wages. And they dressed differently. They wore their hats and their gloves. And it wis a wee bit poshy. Ah didnae get a hat, ah wis too young. The weavers were all women. There were no men weavers. The men that worked in the factory were called tenters. They mended the looms. If your loom broke down ye went and told the tenters and they come and fixed it. Well, the tenters wis a wee kind o' trade, a wee bit o' a textile mill trade. And ye didnae get men spinners either. It wis all women that worked in the factory and the mill. Any young laddies startin' work in the mill when they left the school at 14 were paid off whenever they were 18. The bosses wouldnae pay them the wage: like ye got a different wage when you become an adult. That wis how in Dundee when the wife went out to work in the jute mills the men stayed at home and made the tea. Ma mother had tae go out tae work tae keep us, if ma father wis at hame tae look after us. It wis really bad in Dundee. Men were unemployed for years and years.

Ah wis working in Grimond's mill for maybe about a year when ah began as a weaver from the age o' 15. And fundamentally ah wis a weaver for the biggest half o' ma life.

When ah started work when ah left school ah gave every penny o' ma wages tae ma mother. Ah got a shillin' [5p] back from her for myself. And ah had tae bei ma ain stockings, and the rest o' ma clothin'. Well, sometimes, like if there wis something special in clothin', ma mother would bei it for me. But ah always mind ah had tae buy ma own stockins. It wis lisle stockins ah wore, no' stockins like what they have the day.

Then in ma leisure time ah went tae the dancin' and the pictures. Ah couldnae go tae them both in the same week, oh, no, no. If ah bought a pair o' stockins ah couldnae go to the dancin', 'cause ah didnae have the money. Ah jist had a shillin' [5p] a week. Then we walked down tae the mill. When ah come home for ma dinner at dinnertime ah got the bus – a penny [½p] for the bus. But ah had tae walk back tae ma work. That wis the only time ah got the bus.

Well, ah had ma friends in the mill, girls that ah worked beside. We were all on the same level. There wis no social club at the mill, oh, nothing like that – jist work. Ye had tae find your own entertainment if ye had time or energy. And that wis your main choice, dancing and the pictures. Well, that wis the thing in them days.

* * *

When the war came in 1939 ah jist mind the declaration wi' Chamberlain on the wireless, and a' that. Oh, ah never volunteered. Well, Eih didnae join. Eih didnae want tae go tae the Forces. But we were conscripted. Eih wis in ma 'twenties when Eih had tae go, when ah wis called up. So it wid be in the later part o' the war. It wis most likely in 1943–4. Ah didnae want tae go tae munitions or anythin' like that, no, ah didnae fancy it. And ah didnae fancy the ATS. Well, when ah wis called up ah fancied the forestry, that's what ah fancied. Maybe it wis the name Forestry Commission that made me fancy it. Ye had tae go tae Perth tae register. That wis where the office was. Ah'd never heard o' the Timber Corps before then.[6] Ah don't remember havin' a medical examination. Then after Perth we had tae go tae Shandford Lodge near Brechin, jist for sort o' a wee bit o' trainin'.

Well, Shandford Lodge, eight miles frae Brechin, had been a shootin' lodge. There were huts in the garden. Well, there they gave ye a trainin': how tae drive a tractor, and how tae fell a tree, how tae use your implements – you know, your saw and a' the rest o' it. They gave you a long-handled axe and a band saw: they used tae call them six-foot saws, crosscuts. There wis somebody at the other end o' the saw and ye'd pull the upright handles at either end o' it back and forward. Ye shared the saw wi' your partner. Ye didnae always work wi' another girl. Sometimes ye worked on yer own when ye were sneddin' the trees – that wis, takin' off the branches. And then ye worked wi' men and they showed ye what tae do. Oh, they didnae have films or pictures, nothin' like that, jist word o' mouth. You'd stand at a tree and they said, 'This is what you do.' You chopped a wee bit out the front o' the tree and then put your saw in – and down the tree came! Timber!

Shandford wisnae a camp, it wis a lodge. So you didnae say, 'The camp'. It was a big house and it'd been turned into dormitories. Ye had single beds. There'd be aboot 20 girls when ah wis there. That wid be one intake o' us. The girls didnae jist come frae Dundee and Perth, oh, no. They came from different places – some o' them from Fife, some o' them from Glasgow. But only from Scotland, no' England. But mainly the girls, like myself, were from Dundee. There werenae girls from the Highlands there as well, because the Timber Corps had camps all over the place. And, och, I would say we all got on well together. We had some good laughs. It wis a rough living, but it wis good. All the girls were in one dormitory. And there wis a fire or stove in the middle o' the room for tae take the chill off the air. It wis murder in the winter. Well, ah'd always lived at home, but ah really liked it there at Shandford Lodge.

Ye started work at eight o'clock in the mornin', because there wis men from the town – Kirriemuir. They used tae come in then wi' the lorries. And we worked wi' the men. The hours were eight till five. Ye didnae work there on a Saturday mornin'. Ye came home on a Saturday for the weekend. So ma parents were pleased tae see me – sometimes!

The wages, oh, they were very poor. Ye didnae get as much as ye did in the jute mill, oh, nothing like that, nothing like that. Maybe it wis aboot £1 a week or somethin'. And ye had tae pay your board.[7] We got wir food but it wisnae very good. She wisnae a very good cook. Ah cannae mind now what we got, but ah know it wis . . . But we jist had tae accept it. And, well, you had tae hand in your ration book. Oh, ah dinnae think the food wis a balanced diet o' meat, fish, soup, vegetables, fruit, cheese. Oh, ah dinnae think it wis as good as that. We were away in the country, so we didnae get fresh fruit, no' even apples. No, there wis nothing, nothing like that. Raspberries – there wis nane. We werenae at the raspberries, we were jist in the woods. The ferms roond aboot jist grew tatties. We were at the tatties. We helped the farmer oot when he couldnae get workers tae howk oot the tatties. That was a murderous job. It wis like the strawberries – your back, oh, terrible! And the tractor wi' the digger came roond before your basket wis full from his last run. But ye got through it. It wis wonderful how you did. But we got through it. We didnae get anythin' for howkin' the tatties. We were jist helpin' the farmer. But Eih liked ma time at Shandford Lodge. Ye wis there for six weeks.

In the Timber Corps ye got a uniform that wis almost the very same as the Land Girls' uniform. But instead o' their broad-brimmed hat we wore a tammy, a green tammy. It had a badge on the front that said 'Forestry Commission'. It didnae say 'Timber Corps'. And usually you said you were in the Forestry. You didnae say you were in the Timber Corps.

After Shandford Lodge ah went tae Kinnordy estate, aboot a mile frae Kirriemuir. Lord and Lady Lyell lived there. They were living on the estate then.[8] We were in the dormitories. We got oor water frae Lintrathen, aboot six miles beyond Kinnordy. The camp wis in that area. They were wooden huts in the camp there that we lived in. They were drei toilets. But the girls that looked after them looked after them well, so they were quite good. They were clean. Oh, there wis nae baths there though, jist the shower. In them days we werenae so hygienic conscious.

The girls at Lintrathen were the same girls Eih'd been at Shandford Lodge wi'. They moved up, because the camp wis already opened. There wis girls already in the camp. And we came and filled in the places that were empty. So ah kenned maist o' the girls at Lintrathen because Eih'd already known them at Shandford Lodge. Then Eih'd made up wi' Jean Graham and a friend. Jean wis Dundee. But ah cannae mind now the other lassie's name. So we had quite a good time. Eih knew Jean in Dundee but not to speak to. But Eih knew who Eih wis lookin' at. She wis a weaver, but she didnae work in the same mill as me. Ah think ah got to know her through the dancing.

In the camp there wisnae any kind o' recreation room. There wis nothing. There wis only one night – Wednesday – that wis the night for goin' intae Forfar. You could either go tae the pictures, go tae the canteen, or go tae the dancin' in Forfar. Everybody went in a lorry into Forfar for the night, then we were brought back to camp. It wis good, well, you looked forward tae goin' tae the canteen and gettin' some chocolate, because everything wis rationed. The sweet ration wis actually nothing at all. But in the canteen you could get quite a bit. So we used tae get chocolate and sweeties. And then Eih had a bike at the camp. It wis ma ain bike. Ah must have saved up and bought it off ma pay. Ah didnae hae the bike in Dundee, ah jist had it at the camp. It wis a few mile frae Kirriemuir, and Eih used the bike for goin' frae the camp tae Kirrie. There were nae transport, no buses, jist the lorry tae take us tae Forfar on a Wednesday. Forfar wis six miles or so beyond Kirriemuir. But there wis nothin' much in Kirriemuir – no pictures, no dancin', nothin'. There wis more in Forfar. Kirrie wis like a village, Forfar's a wee town. Kirrie used tae be a braw place. It wis great goin' in there and seein' a' the ploomen and a' the fermers gathered in The Square on the hirin' or feein' days. That wis durin' the war. But that's a' finished now.[9]

Though ye were in the Timber Corps durin' the war ye didnae get extra food rations because it wis heavy work. If we did get extra the cook must ha' kep' it, because we never got it! Oh, the food wis terrible. It wis bad. We used tae get some soup made wi' beetroot! Some folk say it's nice soup. Oh, well, our cook wisnae very good at it. Maybe she forgot tae wash the beetroot first! But, oh, ah managed tae survive. Ah never lost weight in the Timber Corps and ah didnae get heavier. Ah wis always the same. And ah felt fit, workin' wi' the saws and axes. Ah really liked it out in the fresh air and sunshine. And then ye were workin' wi' these men from the town. It wis quite a change. At times it wis a bit rough, but ye'd get a joke. Aye, it wis good.

Ah dinnae mind o' any accidents happenin' Ah never had any injuries maself. Ye had tae be careful. Ah don't remember anybody that dealt wi' first aid. Possibly there wis, but ah never came in contact wi' it. Ah don't remember any o' the girls havin' tae go tae hospital. We were away in the country. Well, if ye had tae go tae hospital ye had tae go tae hospital. But there wis nothing like that. When it wis wet ye could slide a' ower the place. But we were pretty careful. And we were good at standin' at the fire, burnin' the brush, especially in the winter! Aye, Eih liked that. Well, ah think the forestry wis better than the munitions or the army. Ye see, a lot o' people picked the munitions because they made a lot o' money. But Eih wisnae really interested in the money. Eih wis interested in what ah wis doing.

Then if ah come home at the weekend ah used tae go tae the church on a Sunday, though ah wisnae really a churchgoin' person. As a matter o' fact, actually ah wis supposed tae be a Catholic. But there wisnae a Catholic church in Kirriemuir. And, well, as a young girl, ah wisnae really a regular churchgoer, because ah wisnae really that interested in religion. It wouldnae bother me if ah missed it. Ah wisnae that interested that ah got upset aboot it. And there wis no priest or padre visited the camp. There wis nothing like that.

One or two of the girls in the camp married when they were there. Oh, Mary Edwards, she married a Kirriemuir boy. He wis in the timber. He wis involved wi' it. And they had twins and ended up livin' in Kirriemuir. But it didnae mean she could leave the Timber Corps when she got married. If she didnae have a child she jist worked on, unless something cropped up, like she become pregnant. And even the cook, she married a man in Kirriemuir and she ended up there. But even when Eih left the Timber Corps she wis still in it.

As ah've said, we didnae work on Saturdays. So ah got the bus home and come back from Dundee at the end o' the weekend. Ye didnae get any extra money once ye'd completed your trainin' at Shandford Lodge. It wis jist the same money. The money, as ah say, wis very poor. Ah tried tae give ma mother some money when ah got home at the weekends. But it wisnae much, it wisnae much. It was a case ye had tae do it or else . . . Of course, the pound went far in them days. But we got our food provided at the camp, we didnae have tae pay for it. That wis part o' the deal. The £1 pay wis really pocket money. And you got an outfit, you got your uniform. Then ah never went in for lipstick and rouge or red paint for your nails! Ah wis a wee bit backward that way. Then because ye couldnae get silk stockins girls used tae put sort o' brown paint on their legs. Oh, ah put some stuff on ma legs and put a seam up the back – sun tan!

So ah liked Lintrathen tae, and ah liked forestry. It wis fine when it wis good weather. And then we worked wi' Italian prisoners o' war. They worked in the woods wi' us. Ah suppose they were in a camp in the Kirriemuir area, but no' beside us. Ah think the prisoners made the best o' a bad job. And then we also worked through the local men that lived in Kirriemuir, ken, people that belonged Kirriemuir. Ah made contact wi' local families. Jim Redford, jist a man that came out – he hired oot his lorry, he wis awfy good tae us. He used tae bring us some pieces, sandwiches. Well, it wis always a change tae get something nice tae eat. There wis boiled ham on Jim's sandwiches – quite a treat. Well, it wisnae Jim that did the sandwiches, it wis his wife. When Jim came in wi' his horse and cart he always had something for us. Eih wis there occasionally at Jim's house when his wife and him invited me. So ah really enjoyed my time at Kirriemuir. Eih wis there for almost a couple o' years till near enough the end o' the war. Then, still in the Timber Corps, ah wanted back tae Dundee.

Eih jist felt that Eih'd like tae get oot. Even though it wis sich a short distance away ah jist wanted hame. There wis maybe a wee bit o' home-sickness, though ah didnae suffer much from that, no' really. But by that time ah'd had enough. You know how you like changes now and again. And, oh, ah'd aye been at hame, where ah had ma brothers and ma sisters. And ah quite enjoyed bein' at home.

Well, as ah say, still in the Timber Corps, ah worked in MacGregor & Balfour's sawmill in Loons Road in Dundee. It was quite a big sawmill. There wis no roof on it. But there wis different parts tae it. There wis where ye got the saws. It wis open at the sides but there wis a roof. Working in the sawmill, well, it wis different from workin' in the open in the forestry. It wisnae sae friendly. It wis people that come from their houses tae their work there, where in the forestry you were there, already on the site.

Well, it wis jist after the war – after the atomic bomb wis dropped and after VJ Day – that ah left the Timber Corps and ah went back tae the weaving, in Ferguson's factory. And ah carried on as a weaver, but jist for a wee while. The notion for weavin' then disappeared, and that's when we started tae move around. Oh, ah had quite a few different jobs. Ah wis in the Post Office – in the dinin' room; and ah wis in . . . But the grass wis aye greener. Oh, ye could go fae job tae job, nae bother at a'. It wisnae so much the money. It wis jist tae get a choice o' changin'. Ah wisnae unsettled after the war. It wis jist there wis sich a big choice o' jobs, that ah liked movin' around. But ah always worked and ah always remained at home until ah got married when ah wis, we'll say, 25 in 1947 (when things are past ah forget dates). Ah married a Dundee chap and we settled down in Dundee. Ah worked all the time ah wis married. Efter ah'd had ma son Jimmy and ma daughter Maureen ah always went back tae work. Ah worked, oh, at different jobs, as ah say, no' in factories. And then when ah left ah got a job cleanin' in an office. And ah worked there till ah wis 75. Ah worked for the money but also tae put in ma time.

Lookin' back on ma wartime years in the Timber Corps I would say it wis a happy experience for me. Ah've no regrets, none at all. Oh, ah didnae want tae go tae the munitions or the ATS. Ah didnae fancy them. Ah didnae find the skills ah'd learned in the Timber Corps useful later on. When you say tae somebody now that you took doon trees they laugh and they say, 'Och, you're bletherin'.' It's like a joke. Well, the forestry job maybe gave me more self-confidence, but ah wisnae aware o' it. It wis certainly quite different frae the factory, a different thing a'thegither. Even your outlook wis different. The men ye worked wi' in the forestry were a wee bittie coorse. But you thought nothing aboot it. So, oh, Eih enjoyed ma time in the Timber Corps.

Alexina McGlinn (Mrs Alexina Bolger) died on 10 July 2012.

Glossary

a' – all
aboot – about
afore – before
Ah, ah – I
ain – own
an' a' – and all
a'thegither – altogether
a'thing – everything
auld – old
Auld Year's Night – 31 December; Hogmanay
awfy – awful, awfully
aye – yes; always

bairns – children
bei – buy
besom – a disagreeable woman
biled – boiled
bilin' – boiling
bittie – a small bit
bletherin' – conversing loquaciously and/or nonsensically
braid – broad
braw – fine
breenged – rushed, plunged
breid – bread
burn – a small stream

ca' – call
ca'ed – called
cairry – carry
canna, cannae – cannot
catched – caught
claes – clothes
clootie – a cloth
coorse – coarse
coucher – a coward
couldnae – couldn't
cowp – rubbish tip

dae – do
didnae – did not
dinnae – do not
doon – down
drei – dry

ee – you
ee'd – you'd
eer – your
efter – after
eidea – idea
Eih – I

fae – from
fa'en – fallen
fa'in' – falling
faimly – family
faither – father
feared – afraid
feenishins – finishings
feive – five
fither – father
flair – floor
flet – flat
follaed – followed
forrit – forward

frae – from
fund – found

gars – causes, compels
gaun – go, going
gey – rather
gie – give
gin – go
girdle – griddle, a flat iron plate for baking on
greet – weep
guid – good
gymie – gym
gyte – mad

ha' – half; have
hadnae – hadn't
hae – have
hale – whole
hame – home
hand-doon – an item passed on
ha-penny – half penny
haudin' – holding
hen – a familiar and/or affectionate form of addressing a girl or
    woman
hoor – hour
hoose – house
howkin' – digging out, gathering

ingiein' – ingoing
intae – into
iz – me; us

jined – joined
jist – just
jukery-packery – roguery, trickery, jiggery-pokery

ken – know
kep' – kept

laddies – boys
lassie – girl

ma – my
mair – more
maist – most
masel' – myself
meenit – minute
mei – my
merried – married
muckle – big

nae – no
no' – not
noo – now

o' – of
och – an interjection expressing feeling
oo – we; us
oor – our
oot – out
ower – over; too

pair – poor
peenie – pinny, pinafore
pend – a vaulted passageway or entry from a street to the back of a
    block of houses
pillae – pillow
plitterin' – plowtering, muddling
ploomen – ploughmen
pridefae – prideful

rither – rather
roond – round
roosed – enraged

sae – so
sair – sore

seeck – sick
shair – sure
sich – such
skelped – smacked
stooks – sheaves of grain set up on end, in an inverted V of four or so
    a side, to dry in a harvested field
stravaiging – roaming about
strehve – strive
swee – a sway or swing; a hinged horizontal bar over the fire

tae – to, too
ta'en – took, taken
tattie – potato
thae – those
thame – them
thegether, thegither – together
theirsels – themselves
tippence – tuppence
tooken – taken
totty – tiny
troosers – trousers
twa – two

wasnae – was not
wee – small, little
weel – well
werenae – were not
whaever – whoever
wheeched – whisked
wi'- with
wid – wood; would
widnae, wouldna, wouldnae – wouldn't
wir – our
wis – was
wisnae, wisn't – was not

yaised – used
ye – you

yer – your
yersel' – yourself
yin – one
yist – used

Notes

Abbreviations and contractions used in these notes are: AFC – Air Force Cross; ATS – Auxiliary Territorial Service; b. – born; Bart – Baronet; Bn/bn – Battalion; Brig. – Brigadier; c. – circa; Capt. – Captain; CBE – Commander of the Order of the British Empire; CO – Commanding Officer; Col. – Colonel; CWGC – Commonwealth War Graves Commission; Coy – Company; contd – continued; Cpl – Corporal; d. – died; ed. – edited; est. – established; DBE – Dame of the Order of the British Empire; FRGS – Fellow of the Royal Geographical Society; Infmn – Information; JP – Justice of the Peace; L/Cpl – Lance Corporal; Lt – Lieutenant; m. – married; MC – Military Cross; MM – Military Medal; regt – regiment; RAFVR – Royal Air Force Volunteer Reserve; RAOC – Royal Army Ordnance Corps; RASC – Royal Army Service Corps; REME – Royal Electrical & Mechanical Engineers; rev. – revised; RN – Royal Navy; Sgt – Sergeant; SQMS – Staff Quarter Master Sergeant; TA – Territorial Army; WAAF – Women's Auxiliary Air Force; WRNS – Women's Royal Naval Service; WOI – Warrant Officer, First Class; WOII – Warrant Officer, Second Class.

Margaret McLeod, pp. 15–23

1. The Territorial Army (originally titled the Territorial Force) had been est. in 1908 as a second line of defence to the Regular army, and many TA bns had fought in the 1914–18 War. The TA in peacetime was composed of volunteers who trained twice a week, and attended an annual camp for which they were paid. See, e.g., Trevor Royle, *The Flowers of the Forest* (Edinburgh, 2006), 52–4. The Seaforth Highlanders, formed in 1881 from

the earlier 72nd of Foot (raised in 1778) and the 78th (raised in 1793), merged in 1961 with the Cameron Highlanders to form the Queen's Own Highlanders, which merged in 1994 with the Gordon Highlanders to form The Highlanders. In 2006 The Highlanders became the 4th Bn, Royal Regiment of Scotland. Trevor Royle, *Queen's Own Highlanders: A Concise History* (Edinburgh, 2007), 211–12.

2. Rangers: the senior echelon of the Girl Guides.
3. Founded and edited 1919–43 by Arthur Mee (1875–1943), journalist and author, *The Children's Newspaper* was published weekly, 1919–65.
4. Brora and Rogart, both also in Sutherland, are respectively about six and eight miles from Golspie.
5. Fort George, built 1748–69, following the Jacobite rising of 1745–6, is on the Inner Moray Firth, nine miles north-east of Inverness.
6. Neville Chamberlain (1869–1940), a leading Appeaser; Conservative Prime Minister 1937–40.
7. Dixies were army camp kettles or cooking pails.
8. The ATS (briefly at first titled WATS – the Women's Auxiliary Territorial Service) was est. in Sep. 1938. By 1940 it had enrolled 34,000 volunteers. In the 1914–18 War there had been a similar body – the Women's Army Auxiliary Corps, which enrolled 41,000 volunteers, but which had been disbanded in 1920. Arthur Marwick, *Women at War 1914–1918* (London, 1977), 169; Carole Harris, *Women at War in Uniform 1939–1945* (Stroud, 2003), 5, 19.
9. Dunkirk was the main Channel port from which, between 26 May and 4 June 1940, some 338,000 Allied troops (about two thirds British, a third French, and a few Belgian and Dutch) were evacuated by British and French warships, some merchant vessels and a host of small boats, in face of the overwhelming conquering might of the Nazi German army and air force. A disaster for the Allies in that the evacuation showed how decisively they had been defeated in Europe, Dunkirk was also a miracle in that so many troops were rescued. Via other French ports such as Saint-Nazaire, Brest, Le Havre and Cherbourg, a further 160,000 troops, British and French, as well as some Belgian, Polish, Czech and Canadian, were also evacuated to Britain. Some others, in much smaller numbers, succeeded in escaping into Vichy France, from there into Spain and then to safety at Gibraltar. See, e.g., Winston Churchill, *The Second World War* (London, 1949, vol. II), 88–102; Hugh Sebag-Montefiore, *Dunkirk. Fight to the Last Man* (London, 2015, rev. edn); Sean Longden, *Dunkirk: The Men They Left Behind* (London, 2009).

10. Unspecified numbers of residents of the Edinburgh district of Morningside were said to speak in distinctively 'refined' or 'genteel' accents.

Christina Chisholm, pp. 24–51

1. Raised in 1793, the regt became in 1806 the 79th Cameron Highlanders, with 'Queen's Own' added to its title in 1877. In 1961 the regt merged with the Seaforth Highlanders to become the Queen's Own Highlanders. The latter was merged in 1994 with the Gordon Highlanders to become The Highlanders, which in 2006 became the 4th Bn, Royal Regiment of Scotland. Royle, *Queen's Own Highlanders*, 211–12.
2. James Scott Skinner (1843–1927), b. Banchory, Kincardineshire, a composer and fiddler known as 'The Strathspey King'.
3. The battle of Atbara, Apr. 1898, was fought in the second Sudan War. In Sep. that year at the battle of Omdurman General Kitchener's army defeated the jihadist army of the Mahdists, which included militant groups called Dervishes. The Mahdists were led by the Khalifa Abdullah, successor to the Mahdi (a devout Muslim religious and political leader who had died in 1885 after driving from the Sudan Egyptian forces controlled by the British in Cairo). Omdurman confirmed the addition of the Sudan to the British empire. The battle of Diamond Hill, Jun. 1900, was in the second Boer War, 1899–1902.
4. The Pipe Line Under The Ocean (PLUTO) was created to ensure safe arrival of the huge quantities of petrol needed by the Allied forces landed in Normandy from D-Day, 6 Jun. 1944, onwards. The petrol was carried through pipes laid under the English Channel from the Isle of Wight and Dungeness to France.
5. General (later Field Marshal and Earl) Wavell (1883–1950), b. Winchester; an officer in the Black Watch; in Boer War, 1899–1902; wounded and lost the sight of an eye in 1916 during the Great War, 1914–18; Commander-in-Chief, 1938–41, of British Forces in the Middle East; commander from 1941 of Allied Forces in south-west Pacific; Viceroy of India, 1943–7; published an anthology of poetry in 1944.
6. The Ministry of Economic Warfare (or 'Ministry of Ungentlemanly Warfare' or 'of Dirty Tricks') was established by Winston Churchill as Prime Minister in May 1940, with the Labour MP Hugh Dalton as minister in charge. The work of the Ministry – all very secret – was to conduct sabotage and guerrilla warfare against Nazi Germany and develop

resistance movements in occupied Europe. The Special Operations Executive, also very hush-hush, was the directing and co-ordinating body for those undercover activities. See, e.g., Churchill, *Second World War*, Vol II, 572; Giles Milton, *Churchill's Ministry of Ungentlemanly Warfare* (London, 2017), M.R.D. Foot, *The Special Operations Executive 1940–1946* (London, 1999).

7. In the last confused days of the fighting in France in Jun. 1940, the 51st Highland Division was driven back and surrounded by the Germans at Saint-Valery-en-Caux on the English Channel coast west of Dieppe. Forced to surrender, 8,000 men of the Division became prisoners of war; only 1,350 other men of the Division, including Christina Chisholm's brother Alex, succeeded in escaping to Britain. Churchill, *Second World War*, Vol. II, 130–5.

8. From Dec. 1941 the National Service (No. 2) Act made single women and childless widows aged between 20 and 30 (lowered from 20 to 19 in 1943) liable to service in the Forces or in industry; Christina Chisholm's sister Marie opted for the latter. Angus Calder, *The People's War: Britain 1939–45* (London, 1969), 267–8; Juliet Gardiner, *Wartime Britain 1939–1945* (London, 2004), 433.

9. Tilley lamp, a type of oil- or paraffin-burning lamp, was named after its manufacturer.

10. Hugh Ross was Provost of Inverness, 1945–9.

11. Dugald MacEchern, *The Sword of the North: Highland Memories of the Great War* (Inverness, 1923), 669pp. The author's father, Rev. Charles MacEchern (1842–1924), was a Church of Scotland minister in Inverness, 1874–1923. Dugald MacEchern (1867–1946) was himself a Church of Scotland minister in Caithness.

12. Dame Myra Hess (1890–1966), English pianist, famous in America as well as in Britain; made a Dame of the British Empire for her lunch-time concerts during the 1939–45 War. The wartime concerts were actually held in the National Gallery, near St Martin-in-the-Fields church in Trafalgar Square, London.

13. Fees at the Royal Academy were abolished: about 1920 for the upper school (pupils aged 16 and over); from 1948 for the lower or middle school; and on or about 1961 for primary pupils. Infmn: Inverness Royal Academy.

14. Robert Louis Stevenson, *Treasure Island* (1883). Ian Hay (pen name of Major-General John Hay Beith, MC (1876–1952)), novelist and playwright, educated and subsequently employed as teacher at Fettes College,

Edinburgh; author of *The First Hundred Thousand*, about rank and file soldiers in the early part of the 1914–18 War.

15. *Film Fun*, 1920–62; *The Wizard*, 1922–63, contd 1963–9 as *The Rover and Wizard*; *The Beano*, 1938–; *The Dandy*, 1937– (from Aug. 2007 to Oct. 2010 retitled *Dandy Xtreme*); *Rover*, 1922– became *Rover/Wizard*, 1970–3 as *Wizard (Picture Stories)* and 1973–6 as *Wizard and Rover*.

16. Dr Kurt Hahn (1886–1974), b. Berlin, educated there and at Oxford University and four universities in Germany. An educationist, he fled from Nazi Germany in 1933 and founded Gordonstoun School, fee-paying and boarding, in Moray, where the School regime emphasised physical activity and character-building.

17. The Munich Agreement, 30 Sep. 1938, by Britain, France, Fascist Italy and Nazi Germany, followed the annexation of Austria six months earlier by Nazi Germany. The Munich Agreement may possibly have forestalled the outbreak then of war, but it handed over immediately to Nazi Germany a sizeable part of the Sudetenland of independent and democratic Czechoslovakia. The Czech government was excluded from the discussions leading to the Agreement. Russia also, which (like France from 1925) had a treaty of mutual assistance from 1935 with Czechoslovakia, was ignored in the negotiations leading to the Agreement. The British Prime Minister Neville Chamberlain claimed that by the Agreement an outbreak of war had been avoided and he had secured 'peace for our time', which was a great relief to many people in Britain. But many more critical people denounced the Munich Agreement as a disastrous betrayal of Czechoslovakia and a humiliating defeat for British diplomacy. Chamberlain's claim proved entirely unfounded, for six months later Nazi Germany overran and annexed the remainder of Czechoslovakia. Only then did the Chamberlain government's policy of appeasement of Nazi Germany begin to be revised while Europe slid rapidly down the slope toward war. See, e.g., C.L. Mowat, *Britain between the Wars 1918–1940* (London, 1956), 604–19; Martin Gilbert and Richard Gott, *The Appeasers* (London, 1963), 113–84.

18. Lady Maud Baillie (1896–1975), CBE (1945), of Dochfour and Ballindalloch, eldest daughter of the 9th Duke of Devonshire. Her first husband, Capt. Angus Mackintosh, Royal Horse Guards, d. 1918; her second husband, Brig. The Hon. G.M. Baillie, MC, d. 1941 on active service. She served in the ATS, 1938–45. Mrs Christian Fraser-Tytler (1897–1995), née Shairp, daughter of an advocate/sheriff in West Lothian.

She worked as a clerk at the Foreign Office 1917–19, attended the Versailles peace conference in 1919, and in that year married Col. Neil Fraser-Tytler (1889–1937) of Aldourie. After her husband's death Mrs Fraser-Tytler joined the ATS. In 1939–43 she was a member of staff of the Adjutant-General at the War Office, in 1940 became a Controller, and was appointed Director of Organisation of the ATS. Awarded CBE in 1941. In 1943 she was appointed Deputy Director, ATS, in Anti-Aircraft Command. After the war she was active in several public and voluntary bodies. *The Independent*, 19 Jul. 1995; *Daily Telegraph,* 24 Jul. 1995; *Oxford Dictionary of National Biography*, Vol. 55, 824–5.

19. Mr M. Cymbalist, tailor, lived, at least for a time, at 40 Waterloo Place, Inverness.

20. The poet William Wordsworth (1770–1850) lived in France in 1791–2 during the French Revolution. The lines come from his major poetic auto-biography, *The Prelude*, book xi, 1, 108, (1839).

21. Donald Alexander Fowler (1904–1975), articled to a firm of architects in Inverness 1921–5, a full-time student at Aberdeen School of Architecture 1925–8, became a draughtsman in Inverness in 1928 and then also an Associate of the Royal Institute of British Architects. In 1929–34 Fowler worked in Shanghai for the Public Works Dept. He worked as an architect in Inverness in 1934–8, when in 1936 he was involved in building *Over and Above*; then until his retirement in 1969 he worked successively in Oxford and Leeds. It seems most likely his Fascist activity in Inverness took place in 1934–8, but no evidence, such as local newspaper reports, has so far been found of such activity on his part. Infmn: Royal Incorporation of Architects in Scotland; *Inverness Courier*; John Gifford, *Buildings of Scotland. Highlands and Islands* (Penguin, 1992), 206.

22. Though Pastor Niemöller (1892–1984), like Dietrich Bonhoeffer (1906–1945), was a leading German Protestant pastor and active opponent of the Nazis he survived imprisonment, 1937–45, in two successive concentration camps (Sachsenhausen and Dachau), and post-war was awarded high honours by both West Germany and the Soviet Union for his untiring work for disarmament and international peace and understanding. His autobiography (1934), titled *From U-boat to Pulpit*, dealt also with his experiences as a German U-boat commander in the 1914–18 War. Dietrich Bonhoeffer was actively engaged in underground activities against Hitler and Nazism until his arrest in 1943. He was hanged by the Nazis at

Flossenburg concentration camp in Apr. 1945, a few days before the end of the war.

23. The Spanish Civil War, 1936–9, was fought between, on the one side, the Republicans, Liberals, Socialists, Communists, Anarchists, Catalonians and Basques, and the International Brigades – broadly, those from the political centre and the left, supported to some extent by the Soviet Union; and, on the other side, those to the right of centre, led by General Franco: Monarchists, Fascists, landowners, most of the regular army (including its Moroccan troops), aided and supported by Nazi Germany and Fascist Italy. If the Spanish Republic had survived the Civil War, its victory would have marked a severe setback to Fascism generally. And if also the 1939–45 War had nonetheless broken out, Spain might then have become an ally of, or at the very least a friendly neutral towards, Britain, France, the Soviet Union and the USA in that War.

24. John MacCormick (1904–1961), a leading figure in the formation in 1928 of the National Party of Scotland, of which he became hon. secretary, 1928–42. He became founder and chairman in 1942 of the Scottish Convention, and chairman, 1949–61, of the Scottish Covenant Association. He stood unsuccessfully six times for election as an MP. Author of *The Flag in the Wind: The Story of the National Movement in Scotland* (London, 1955). Wendy Wood (1892–1981), an Englishwoman brought up in South Africa; studied art under Walter Sickert (1860–1942); came to live in Scotland after her marriage; a founder, 1928, of the National Party of Scotland, but left the Party in 1949 to found the Scottish Patriots.

25. A Women's Royal Naval Service (WRNS) had been established in 1917, near the end of the Great War, and had enrolled 57,000 members. Dissolved in 1919, it was re-formed in spring 1939. At that stage, the WRNS was an exclusive body that sought references from applicants. But the Service expanded greatly by 1941, and during the war it had over 100,000 women in its ranks. Gardiner, *Wartime Britain*, 436.

26. Scapa Flow, a wide stretch of deep water in Orkney, enclosed, though not quite entirely, by islands, had been the main wartime base for the British fleet since before 1914. At the beginning of the 1939–45 War, however, it was not a wholly secure base as it lacked adequate anti-submarine and anti-aircraft defences. Thus the battleship *Royal Oak*, anchored in Scapa, was torpedoed in Oct. 1939 by a German U-boat which passed unseen in and out through an incompletely blocked gap between two of the islands. The *Royal Oak* lost 833 lives, almost its entire crew, in the disaster.

German air raids on Scapa Flow followed, and the fleet was forced to put to sea to ensure its safety. Scapa Flow was then made safe by the building of the Churchill Barriers that closed gaps on the eastern side of the anchorage. Airfields were also constructed to deal with any further German air raids, which more or less ceased in early 1940. Capt. S.W. Roskill, RN, *The Navy at War 1939–1945* (London, 1960), 22, 49, 50.

27. Lord John Lisle (1903–1997).

28. It is uncertain whether Christina Chisholm is referring here to the 13th Duke of Hamilton (1862–1940) or to the 14th Duke (1903–1973). The 13th Duke had four sons, the eldest of whom, Douglas Douglas-Hamilton, AFC, FRGS, Conservative MP from 1930, wing commander in the Auxiliary Air Force, was Marquis of Douglas and Clydesdale until he became 14th Duke of Hamilton on the death of his father in Mar. 1940. Some 14 months later, on 11 May 1941, Rudolf Hess, Hitler's deputy leader of the German Nazi Party, landed by parachute near Eaglesham in Renfrewshire (only a dozen miles from the Duke's residence at Dungavel in Lanarkshire), in an attempt, it seems, to persuade the Duke to use his influence in British government circles to bring about peace with Nazi Germany, which was about to invade the Soviet Union but, Hess hoped, without fighting a war on two fronts. As the 14th Duke's eldest son, Angus, was born in 1938, it seems more likely that it was the 13th Duke and his sons, including the future 14th Duke, whom Christina Chisholm had met through the Council for Physical Training & Recreation.

29. Overlord was the code name for D-Day, the Allied landing in Normandy on 6 Jun. 1944.

30. Enigma was a secret German machine, about the size of a portable type-writer, which by means of cogs revolving wheels or rotors could send top secret encyphered signals or messages. What the Germans never learned was that French, Polish, and British Intelligence had from before, but especially quite early in, the war broken into the secrets of Enigma, and went on doing so, through the British government code and cypher school at Bletchley Park, Buckinghamshire. The secret information thus acquired, as well as continuing developments at Bletchley Park, greatly helped the Allies to win the war and, conversely, Nazi Germany to lose it. For a full, detailed account of this aspect of the war, see, e.g., Max Hastings, *The Secret War: Spies, Codes and Guerrillas 1939–45* (London, 2016).

31. John Buchan (1875–1940), later Lord Tweedsmuir, b. Perth; prolific author; barrister, company director, employed in the 1914–18 War by both

the Foreign Office and the War Office as Director of Information; Conservative MP, 1927–35, for the Scottish Universities; Governor General of Canada, 1935–40. It may be that the 39 steps in his book of that title were those leading to the beach at Broadstairs in Kent where Buchan was on holiday in Aug. 1914 and where he began writing his most popular book, published in 1915. For his biography, see Janet Adam Smith, *John Buchan* (London, 1965).

32. Ghee – clarified butter.
33. Erwin Rommel (1891–1944), German general, later field marshal; in army from 1910 and fought in several campaigns in 1914–18; an early Nazi sympathiser, he later became commander of the guards at Hitler's HQ. In 1940 he distinguished himself as commander of a panzer division; in 1941 he was made commander of the Afrika Corps and sent to North Africa to strengthen the Italian troops there against the British and Commonwealth forces. Rommel was successful there until his defeat in Oct.–Nov. 1942 by the Eighth Army at the decisive battle of El Alamein. Shortly before the complete defeat of the Axis forces in North Africa in 1943, Rommel returned to Germany and was soon put in charge of defending the French Channel coast against the threatened Allied Second Front that took place in Normandy from D-Day in Jun. 1944. By then, Rommel had become involved in a secret conspiracy by some generals and others to overthrow Hitler, which culminated in the Jul. 1944 Bomb Plot. Rommel was given the choice by Hitler either of being tried and executed or of committing suicide. Rommel chose suicide.

General (later Field Marshal) Bernard Montgomery (1887–1976), fought in the 1914–18 War; commanded one of the divisions of British troops retreating to Dunkirk in 1940. In 1942 he became commander of the Eighth Army in North Africa, which defeated the Germans and Italians at the battle of El Alamein in Oct.–Nov. that year, and took a leading part in driving them out of North Africa six months later. Montgomery then led British troops through the campaigns in Sicily and Italy until he was made deputy commander under General Eisenhower of the Allied forces that landed in Normandy on D-Day in Jun. 1944. Montgomery sought to shorten the war in Sep. 1944 by the huge Allied paratroop landings at bridgeheads over three rivers in the Netherlands. The Americans were successful at Eindhoven and Nijmegen, but the British at Arnhem were opposed by unexpectedly powerful German forces, and Arnhem, with heavy losses of life, proved 'a bridge too far'.

During the dangerous German counter-attack in the Ardennes in Dec. 1944 Montgomery played a notable part in preventing a German break-through. After the war he held several senior appointments in the army and with NATO, and was awarded the title Viscount Montgomery of Alamein.

34. Lyons Corner House in The Strand was one of a chain of teashops estab-lished by Sir Joseph Lyons (1848–1917) and colleagues that became one of the largest catering businesses in Britain.

35. That during her night shift Christina Chisholm's path should cross that of the Prime Minister may well have been due to the personal regime he had adopted and to the constant enormous burdens of office he carried throughout the war. In his memoirs of those years he recalls that in 1914–15 during the Great War, when he was First Lord of the Admiralty, he had been forced into a daily routine which had greatly extended his daily capacity for work. That was, to go to bed for an hour as early as possible in the afternoon, when he fell always into a deep sleep. That rest enabled him to work on until the wee small hours of the morning. The next day he would then resume work between 8 and 9 am. In that way he found he could do within one day one and a half day's work. Churchill, *The Second World War*, Vol. I, 375.

36. Mrs Mopp, played by the actress Dorothy Summers, was one of the most popular characters in the revered comedian Tommy Handley's (1892–1949) weekly BBC radio comedy programme *ITMA* between 1939 and 1949 which did so much to help keep up public morale during the war.

37. Commander Sir Mansfield Cumming (1859–1923), RN, Head, 1909–23, of Secret Intelligence Service (MI 6). See, e.g., Alan Judd, *The Quest for C: Sir Mansfield Cumming and the founding of the British Secret Service* (London, 1999).

38. The Easter Rising by the Irish Republican Brotherhood, supported by the Irish Citizen Army led by the Edinburgh-born socialist James Connolly, began on Easter Monday, 24 Apr. 1916, and lasted almost a week. The main action was in Dublin, where the General Post Office and other build-ings in the city were fought over between the rebels and British troops. Very few risings took place then elsewhere in Ireland. The establishment of an independent Irish Republic was proclaimed by the rebels, along with a provisional government. But British government forces armed, unlike the rebels, with artillery, crushed the rising. Over 400 people – rebels, British troops, and civilians – were killed. Fifteen of the leaders of the

rising, including the two main leaders, Patrick Pearse and James Connolly, were executed. The Easter Rising and its severe suppression became a factor behind the later Anglo-Irish War of 1919–21. See, e.g., Desmond Greaves, *The Life and Times of James Connolly* (London, 1961); F.S.L. Lyons, *Ireland since the Famine* (London, 1973); Robert Kee, *The Green Flag* (London, 2000); *The Oxford Companion to Irish History*, ed. S.J. Connelly (Oxford, 1999).

39. Claridges in Brook Street, a leading London hotel and restaurant, est. 1812.

40. Edward Wood, Lord Halifax (Earl from 1944), Conservative politician; as Lord Irwin, Viceroy of India, 1926–31; Foreign Secretary, 1938–40; a leading appeaser of Nazi Germany; a candidate in May 1940 for the prime ministership, Halifax withdrew on the grounds that he was a member of the House of Lords, not of the House of Commons, the centre of decision-making. Halifax ceased to be Foreign Secretary in Dec. 1940 and became British ambassador to the USA, 1941–6.

    Joseph P. Kennedy (1888–1969), an American millionaire, US ambassador to Britain, 1938–40; father of President John F. Kennedy; Ambassador Kennedy believed, as Christina Chisholm says, that Britain would be defeated by Nazi Germany.

41. Moss Brothers, gentlemen's outfitters, est. 1851 by Moses Moss in Covent Garden, London.

42. Stirrup pump – a portable pump held in position by the foot.

43. The Blitz, which had begun in Sep. 1940, ended early in May 1941 when the Luftwaffe bombers prepared to fly east to bomb the Soviet Union in its invasion by Nazi Germany that began on 22 Jun. that year.

44. For nine months from mid-Jun. 1944 Nazi Germany launched one of its highly destructive secret weapons against Britain – the V1 pilotless plane, popularly known as the doodle-bug or buzz bomb. Before the end of the war in Europe in May 1945 some 7,500 V1s were fired at Britain, mainly against London and south-east England, though a few fell as far away as Yorkshire, Lancashire and Shropshire. Some of the V1s were released by the Germans from piloted planes. V1s caused thousands of deaths and injuries. A V1 that exploded on the Guards Chapel at Wellington Barracks in west London during a religious service killed 119 people and seriously injured scores of others. From Sep. 1944 another Nazi German secret weapon was launched against Britain – the V2 rocket, 45 feet long and weighing 14 tons. Some 1,100 V2s were directed against Britain – again,

almost all on the south-east and east of England, a quarter of them against London. The V2s killed 2,700 people and badly injured 6,000 others. See, e.g., Churchill, *Second World War*, Vol. VI, 34–49; Juliet Gardiner, *Wartime Britain*, 547–64; Calder, *The People's War*, 559–63.

45. Sir Archibald Sinclair (1890–1970), Viscount Thurso from 1952, a Regular soldier, 1910–21, Liberal MP, 1922–45, Secretary of State for Scotland, 1931–2, leader of the Liberal Party, 1935–45, Secretary of State for Air, 1940–5. The minister was Dr Robert F.V. Scott.

46. London Pride – a hardy perennial saxifrage (a rock plant).

47. Sir Murdoch Macdonald (1866–1957), Liberal MP for Inverness-shire 1922–50.

48. VJ Day – Victory over Japan Day: 15 Aug. 1945.

Nancy Cowe, pp. 52–73

1. Thanks are due to Pauline Smeed, secretary, Dunbar & District History Society, for confirming that East Barns farm and village no longer exist.

2. Sir James Hope (1898–1979), 2nd Bart, MM, JP, son of Sir Harry Hope; educated at Fettes College, Edinburgh; in Black Watch, 1916–19; District Chairman, East Lothian Agricultural Executive Committee.

3. The inscription actually reads: DISCE VEL DISCEDE – LEARN OR DEPART.

4. The poem, by Robert Burns, begins:

> My heart's in the Highlands, my heart is not here;
> My heart's in the Highlands a-chasing the deer;
> Chasing the wild deer, and following the roe,
> My heart's in the Highlands wherever I go

5. Exactly when Stark's Dunbar-based bus and taxi services began has not yet been confirmed, but they ended in 1964 when the firm was taken over by SMT (Scottish Motor Traction).

6. Grahame Budge (1920–1979) played for Scotland in 1950.

7. At Dunbar on 3 Sep. 1650 Cromwell defeated a Scots Presbyterian army that was fighting in support of Charles II.

8. To guddle – to fish with the hands.

9. Anna Sewell (1820–1878), novelist, wrote *Black Beauty: The Auto-biography of a Horse,* published in 1877. It was a plea for better treatment

of animals that became possibly the most famous fictional work about horses. *Pegasus* has not been further identified.

10. Grant's chemist shop was at the south end of Dunbar High Street and is now Lloyd's Pharmacy. Grant's operas were performed in Dunbar parish church hall, that was also near the south end of the High Street. Sir William Gilbert (1836–1911), was the English librettist, or writer of the book of words, for his and his partner the composer Sir Arthur Sullivan's (1842–1900) light operas. The two partners produced more than a dozen light operas during 1871–96, including *The Pirates of Penzance* in 1880. Giuseppe Verdi (1813–1901), the leading Italian composer of his era, produced more than a dozen famous operas, including *La Traviata* and *Otello*. In his early days Verdi was a strong Italian nationalist. Richard Wagner (1813–1883), an outstanding German composer though with anti-semitic views. His many operas included *The Flying Dutchman*, *Lohengrin, Tristan and Isolde, Die Meistersinger*, and *The Ring Cycle*.

11. The annual Hiring Fair in Dunbar was held in the main street on the first Tuesday in Feb. Beryl Robinson (ed.), *A Living from the Land: Reminiscences of Tom Porteous, Ploughboy and Forester, East Lothian* (Gullane, 1999), 1.

12. The Scottish Farm Servants' Union, founded in 1912, was never a strong union. The post-1914–18 War depression created still more difficulties for the Union, and in 1933 it affiliated to the Transport and General Workers' Union, then in 1942 merged into it and became its Scottish Farm Servants' Section.

13. Greco's ice cream shop and restaurant was at the north end of Dunbar High Street.

14. Known as Aitken's Lemonade Factory, and owned by William Aitken, it lay behind Dunbar High Streeet, with the factory entrance in Lawson's Place.

15. At 6am on 2 Jul. 1940, the 15,500 ton Blue Star liner *Arandora Star,* on its way to Canada with 1,500 German, Italian and other internees on board, was torpedoed and sunk by a German Nazi U-boat off the west coast of Ireland. This was the first news that the British public and relatives of interned 'enemy aliens' had that internees were being sent overseas. Almost half these 1,500 deportees lost their lives. Questions in Parliament indicated that at least 200 refugees from Nazi Germany and Fascist Italy (the latter of which had entered the war the previous month as the ally of Germany), as well as some long-standing German, Italian,

Austrian and other opponents of Nazism and Fascism were among these deportees. The loss of the *Arandora Star* showed the appalling muddle into which government policy on internment of aliens, including many Jewish, anti-Fascist and anti-Nazi and other refugees in Britain, had fallen. See, e.g., F. Lafitte, *The Internment of Aliens* (Harmondsworth, 1940), especially pp. 123–4.

16. A gimmer is a young ewe.

17. Miss Molly (or Mollie) Marrow (full name Mary Stewart Marrow) (1887–1949), was not English but was born at Newton Stewart, third daughter of an army major. She came to live in East Lothian in 1895, joined the Red Cross at the outset of the 1914–18 War and went as a Voluntary Aid Detachment (VAD) nurse to work in French hospitals. As well as the General Service and other war medals, she was awarded the Croix de Guerre, the Médaille de la Réconnaisance Française, and the Red Cross Service Medal with bar. Post-war, she reorganised the VADs in East Lothian. In the 1939–45 War she became County Director and Controller for East Lothian branch of the Red Cross Society. She became a leading figure in the West Barns branch of the Women's Rural Institute, and in 1937–49 was East Lothian county councillor for Dunbar and district. With the establishment of the National Health Service by the Labour government in 1948, Miss Marrow was appointed a member of East Lothian Hospitals Board of Management. She was a very active leading figure in the Conservative Party in East Lothian and was county chair of the Party for some years until shortly before her death. *Haddingtonshire Courier*, 17 Jun. 1949.

18. See above, Christina Chisholm, Note 28, p. 378.

19. Edward VIII (1894–1972) had become king in Jan. 1936 on the death of his father George V. Because Edward then insisted, against the Cabinet's advice, on marrying Mrs Wallis Simpson, a twice-divorced American, he abdicated on 11 December that year.

20. The North African campaign, in which the Eighth Army played the major part until the British and American seaborne landings in Nov. 1942 in Algeria and Morocco, lasted from Jun. 1940 to May 1943. The Eighth Army emerged as the Army of the Western Desert in Aug. 1941 from the former Army of the Nile. Alan Moorehead, *African Trilogy* (London, 1965), 181. The Allies invaded Sicily in Jul. 1943 and had captured it within five weeks. Allied forces then invaded Italy on 3 Sep. 1943. Rome fell to the Allies in Jun. 1944.

21. The WAAF (Women's Auxiliary Air Force) had had, like the ATS and the WRNS, a predecessor organisation in the 1914–18 War: the WRAF (Women's Royal Air Force), formed on the same day as the Royal Air Force itself, 1 Apr. 1918. By 1919 32,000 women had enrolled in the WRAF, but it was dissolved that year. The WAAF was est. in Jul. 1939, and by the end of 1943 the number of women enrolled totalled 182,000. Carole Harris, *Women at War in Uniform*, 7, 8, 63, 70.

22. Isobel Cumming, who joined the ATS at Newbattle Abbey in Nov. 1941, was the first of the nine ATS who recall their wartime experiences in this book to join at Newbattle Abbey.

23. Nissen huts, named after their designer, Col. N.P. Nissen (1871–1930), had semi-circular arched corrugated-iron roofs and concrete floors.

24. Sir Will Y. Darling (1885–1962), b. Carlisle of Scots parents, served in the 1914–18 War in France, Gallipoli, Salonika, Egypt, Belgium and Germany. During 'The Troubles', or Anglo-Irish War, in Ireland, 1919–21, he was on the staff of the Police Adviser in Dublin. He returned in 1922 to Edinburgh and worked in Darling's, his family's business. A Moderate or Progressive town councillor from 1933, city treasurer, 1937–40, he was Lord Provost, 1941–4. He was a 'National' government Parliamentary candidate, 1937, for West Lothian; Conservative MP, 1945–57, Edinburgh South; author of several books. The Chief Constable of Edinburgh, 1935–55, was William Morren (1890–1972), knighted in 1952. Of the two men, it was more likely to have been Will Y. Darling who gave Nancy and her friend a lift in his car.

25. When a squad was ordered to 'Fall in!' and was to be marching off to its left, the first member, or marker, to fall in took up position at the extreme left of the front rank of the three lines of those on parade – often, or usually, as Nancy Cowe says, the marker was the tallest member of the squad. The next order given would then be: 'Right dress!' Each member of the squad, from the marker rightward, would then fully extend her/his left arm to touch the shoulder of the person on her/his left. This ensured all members of the squad were equidistant from each other (if necessary by shuffling their feet) from right to left and from the front rank to the rear rank. The next order given would be: 'Left turn!'; then finally, 'By the left! Quick march!' If the squad, however, was to march to the right, the orders given would be adapted accordingly.

Lady Margaret Egerton (1918–2004), a daughter of the Earl of Ellesmere and a sister of the later Duke of Sutherland, grew up at Mertoun House, near St Boswells, Roxburghshire. She had joined the ATS shortly before the war broke out. At first a clerk with Scottish Command, she then became a commissioned officer and trained recruits in Edinburgh and Orkney. After the war, she became a lady-in-waiting to Princess Elizabeth and married Winston Churchill's principal private secretary Sir John Colville. *The Scotsman*, 12 May 2004.

Celia Sprot (1917–2011), a daughter of Major Mark Sprot of Riddell, Lilliesleaf, Roxburghshire, joined the ATS shortly before the war and became a clerk in Scottish Command at Edinburgh Castle. She married William Whitelaw in 1943. With her friend Lady Margaret Egerton, she led the ATS contingent in the Edinburgh Victory Parade along Princes Street in 1945. *The Scotsman*, 5 Dec. 2011.

William Whitelaw (1918–1999), MP, Viscount Whitelaw; Deputy Prime Minister to Mrs Margaret Thatcher, and leader of the House of Lords.

26. Garelochhead – a village on the shore of the Gare Loch, seven miles north-west of Helensburgh, Dunbartonshire.
27. The United States had entered the war in Dec. 1941.
28. The 'flail things' attached to the front of the tanks were for detonating mines.

Jean Crosbie, pp. 74–89

1. *Daily Express*, 1900 to date, for many years from 1917 owned by Lord Beaverbrook. The *Scottish Daily Express*, its Scottish edition, was published, 1928–74, in Glasgow, then in Manchester. The *Evening Citizen*, Glasgow, 1864–1974, was from 1940 also a Beaverbrook newspaper.
2. J.& P. Coats, founded at Ferguslie, Paisley, in 1826 by James Coats, b. 1774. It had become a huge firm by the end of the 19th century and dominated world production of thread.
3. The brothers Jacob (1785–1863) and Wilhelm (1786–1859) Grimm, philologists and collectors of German fairy tales such as *Rumpelstiltskin*, published three successive volumes of *Nursery and Household Tales* in 1812–22.
4. *Hotspur*, 1933–59, a weekly comic published by D.C. Thomson Ltd, Dundee.
5. A British film, 1942, about a destroyer and its crew, sunk by a German dive-bomber, and starring Noel Coward, John Mills, Bernard Miles and Richard Attenborough.

6. There are some similar comments made about the 'reputation' of the ATS by two or three other contributors to this book. Such comments had been made also in the 1914–18 War about women then in the Women's Army Auxiliary Corps. An official inquiry had found then that such allegations were untrue and had been spread partly by enemy agents. A similar inquiry whose report was published in 1942 found likewise that allegations of immorality in the ATS were unfounded. Carole Harris, *Women at War*, 5, 39.

7. Except for Esther Cowper, who joined the ATS at Glencorse Barracks, Edinburgh, all the other ATS recruits who joined after Jean Crosbie and who recount their experiences in this book, joined at Newbattle Abbey, near Dalkeith, Midlothian.

8. Square-bashing – marching, about-turning, wheeling, turning to left or right, saluting, halting, etc., usually done on the barrack square.

9. At first mainly cooking, driving, clerical, typing, laundry, stock-keeping work, the range of trades open to women in the ATS greatly increased as the war continued, and included anti-aircraft and searchlight duties.

10. The Clydebank Blitz in 1941 in fact took place on two successive nights: Thurs. and Fri., 13 and 14 Mar. It seems probable that her visit to Glasgow which Jean Crosbie recalls here was on the first of those two nights. These particular German bombing raids were not confined then to Clydebank but were spread widely over Clydeside, including Glasgow. The number of people killed and injured may never be known exactly, but it seems likely to have been more than 1,200 killed and about the same number seriously injured. Of those casualties more than 500 were killed at Clydebank and more than 600 seriously injured. Out of a total of 12,000 houses in Clydebank, 4,300 were totally destroyed or damaged beyond repair. Only eight houses out of the 12,000 remained undamaged. See Dr I.M.M. MacPhail, *The Clydebank Blitz* (Clydebank, 1974).

11. The Commonwealth War Graves Commission has confirmed that 26 ATS lost their lives in the German air raid at Great Yarmouth on 11 May 1943.

12. Sgt Charles Hamilton Crosbie, No. 1682055, RAF Volunteer Reserve, 547 Squadron, was killed aged 28 on 12 Apr. 1944. He is commemorated on the Scottish National War Memorial at Edinburgh Castle, and on the Runnymede Memorial, Surrey. Infmn: CWGC.

13. The CWGC has confirmed that W/171933 L/Cpl Anna Macleod of Stornoway was among the 26 ATS killed at Great Yarmouth by an enemy bomber on 11 May 1943.

14. Joyce Grenfell (1910–1979), entertainer, toured with concert parties during the war, and afterward she appeared in her one-woman shows, specialising in comic monologues.

15. By this time the trades or occupations open to the ATS had been extended to include working with searchlight units as well as on anti-aircraft (ack-ack) gunsites. In early 1941 an experimental all-women ack-ack unit had been formed; and later that year, by which time there were 170,000 women in the ATS, an extra 30,000 searchlight operators were recruited. In 1942 the 93rd Searchlight Regt became the first all-female ATS unit of its kind. Carole Harris, *Women at War*, 55–6.

16. VE (Victory in Europe) Day was on 8 May 1945.

17. The result of the 1945 general election held on 5 Jul. was not announced until 26 Jul., because the votes cast by men and women electors serving abroad in the armed forces would need time to arrive in Britain. Labour won a massive majority – 393 seats, Conservatives 213, Liberals 12, Communists 2, others 20. Yet more than half of the eligible 4½ million men and women in the Forces did not vote at all. Nonetheless the election was a turning point in British history.

Isobel Cumming, pp. 90–115

1. The Military Medal for bravery was created in Mar. 1916. It was awarded to both men and women. Marwick, *Women at War 1914–1918*, 109, 110.

2. Sir James Hamilton Ferguson (1894–1953), landowner, killed in Kenya.

3. A Primus stove was an oil-burning portable cooking stove.

4. The date of the hail storm remains presently unconfirmed.

5. A Jenny Wullock was an effeminate man.

6. Drochil Castle – a ruined 17th century castle, seven miles north-west of Peebles; Neidpath Castle, a 14th century tower, a mile west of Peebles.

7. Quartered meant that workers arriving late for work had their pay docked for every quarter of an hour of lateness.

8. The text is from Matthew, Chapter VI, verse 34: 'Take therefore no thought for the morrow: for the morrow shall take thought for the things of itself. Sufficient unto the day is the evil thereof.' The New English Bible, 1961, version is: 'So do not be anxious about tomorrow; tomorrow will look after itself. Each day has troubles enough of its own.' Infmn: Rev. Jack Kellett.

9. German Dornier and Heinkel bombers attacked the Forth (railway) Bridge and the fleet at Rosyth on 16 Oct. 1939, causing 60 casualties (16 killed

and 44 wounded) aboard the cruisers HMS *Edinburgh* and *Southampton* and the destroyer HMS *Mohawk*. Two bombers were shot down, four of their crew killed and another four taken prisoner. W.F. Hendrie, *The Forth at War* (Edinburgh, 2002), 90–3; Andrew Jeffrey, *This Present Emergency: Edinburgh, the River Forth and South-East Scotland and the Second World War* (Edinburgh, 1992), 27, 33.

10. The Royal Scots, oldest infantry regiment in the British army, was formed in 1633. In 2006 it merged with the King's Own Scottish Borderers, formed in 1689, to become the 1st Bn, Royal Regt of Scotland. PSI – Permanent Staff Instructor.

11. The origins of the Black Watch lay in the 17th and early 18th centuries, when the government began forming independent companies of Highlanders to police the Highlands. Uniformed in a dark blue, green, and black tartan gave these troops their title. In 1739 they became an infantry regt in the British army, and from 1751 were numbered the 42nd. In 2006 the Black Watch became the 3rd Bn, Royal Regt of Scotland.

12. See above, Jean Crosbie, Note 6, p. 387.

13. Of the nine ATS women who contributed their recollections (in chronological order of their joining the ATS) Isobel Cumming is the first to recall joining at Newbattle Abbey.

14. The National Service (No.2) Act of Dec. 1941 made Britain the first country in the world to conscript women. Single women and childless widows aged from 20 (19 from 1943) to 30 were made liable for war service. In theory, women could choose to join one of the women's auxiliary Services (ATS, WAAF, or WRNS), or be directed into industry (especially into munitions) or civil defence. Before the Act was passed, but also after it, many women volunteered into the auxiliary Services; but by the end of the war some 125,000 had been called up to join them. See, e.g., Juliet Gardiner, *Wartime Britain,* 433.

15. Ack-Ack – Anti-aircraft guns and their personnel.

16. Eton Crop – A women's hair fashion, popular in the 1920s, in which the hair was cut short and sleeked.

17. In 1939 pay for volunteers into the ATS was a basic 1s 4d (c.6½p) per day, rising to between 1s 10d (11p) to 2s 6d (12½p) per day for those who passed trade tests. Later in the war, basic pay was evidently increased to 2s (10p) per day. Carole Harris, *Women at War*, 2, 25.

18. A clootie, or cloutie, dumpling is a suet pudding containing raisins and currants, and steamed or boiled in a cloth.

19. POM was dried potato to which water was added to make it like mashed potato.

Esther Cowper, pp. 116–137

1. Sir Robert Lorimer (1864–1929). He designed the Scottish National War Memorial at Edinburgh Castle in the 1920s.
2. There were in fact three paper mills at Penicuik: Valleyfield, Esk Mills and Dalmore.
3. The result of an underground fire, the Mauricewood pit disaster on 5 Sep. 1889 cost the lives of 63 miners. Of those killed, 23 were aged under 20, and 11 of those 23 were aged under 16; the youngest was aged 12. Altogether, 102 children under age 14 were orphaned by the disaster. Two sons of Esther Cowper's grandfather William Meikle, William, jnr, aged 14, and Walter, aged 12, as well as William snr's younger brother Thomas were also all killed. Andrew B. Donaldson, *Mauricewood Disaster* (Roslin, n.d. [1989]), passim.
4. A shankie, on the other hand, was a lavatory named after Shanks of Barrhead, well-known manufacturers of lavatory equipment. A chanty or shanty was a chamber pot.
5. Rt Hon. Alex Salmond, PC; b. 1954; educated at Linlithgow Academy and St Andrews University, MA (Hons); an economist; a leading Scottish Nationalist all his life; member of SNP National Executive, 1981–; Deputy Leader, SNP, 1987–90, Leader, 1990–2000 and 2004–14; MP, Banff and Buchan, 1987–2010, Gordon, 2015–17; MSP, Banff and Buchan, 1999–2001, Gordon, 2007–2011, Aberdeenshire East, 2011–2016, Leader of the Opposition, 1999–2000, First Minister of Scotland, 2007–2014; author, *The Dream Shall Never Die: 100 Days that Changed Scotland For Ever* (2015).
6. The catechism, a summary of the principles of religion, in this case according to the Church of Scotland, was in the form of question and answer.
7. Cockleroy, the name given the hill on the Ordnance Survey map, is said to be 278 metres high there. Other names given the hill have included Cuck-le-Roi and Cocklerue.
8. Stravaiging – wandering about.
9. *The Rainbow*, 1914–56.
10. Plymouth Brethren: a Christian puritanical sect without ordained clergy,

founded in Dublin in 1825 and whose first congregation was est. in Plymouth in 1830–1.

11. Skerry's, near Surgeons Hall, Edinburgh, was a private college for post-school students. There were Skerry's also in Glasgow and Newcastle. The Edinburgh courses included Highers and Lowers, and commercial and professional subjects for national examinations.

12. The *Linlithgowshire Gazette*, 1891–1952, then merged with the *Bo'ness Journal* and continued as the *Linlithgowshire Journal & Gazette*.

13. A distinctive and critical view of the arrival and attitudes of at least a few of the ATS recruits at Glencorse Barracks was recorded more than half a century later by Mrs Lydia Neil, born, like Esther Cowper, in 1918, and who lived in the village of Auchendinny, close by the Barracks. Mrs Neil had worked from the age of 14 in Dalmore paper mill at Auchendinny. Aged 22, she married in 1940 and, as she recalled, 'As soon as you got married you stopped working.' But her husband was called up to the army soon after their marriage. So . . . 'Ye had tae take a job – wartime. So ah wis put to the ammunitions. Ah didnae want tae go. We had tae go. We were made tae go. We all got notified we would be put to the ATS or the ammunitions. We got no choice. We jist got told we were tae go to the munitions. And then we were put to the ammunitions down at the powder mill at Roslin. There were eight or nine o' us frae Auchendinny a' went. And there wis three o' us anyway frae the Dalmore mill.' Roslin gunpowder mill, founded in 1801, was within walking distance of Auchendinny; but there were also trains between Roslin and Auchendinny. Mrs Neil recalled that: '. . . we used tae get the train on a Friday, on wir day shift back intae Auchendinny station. . . . And the train used tae be packed wi' ATS. Ye had tae stand. That wis a' the ATS comin' in tae Glencorse Barracks. That wis the admission day for them. Oh, they looked at us – ye know, they used tae have their fur coats on and shrugged their shoulders at us when we came in the train. Oh! They were lookin' down their noses at us. And they were the scum! We went tae the church on Sunday because we were on night shift. And they were a' sittin' out at the wooden huts at the ATS camp – the North Camps is jist up there at the church at Glencorse – and they were a' sittin', but wi' towels round their head. They were a' gettin' searched – for lice! And they were the ones wi' their fur coats that turned their noses up at us! Oh! They looked down their noses at us! They were the ATS, the ATS. We done harder work than they ever done, ah think.' Ian

MacDougall, '*Oh, Ye Had To Be Careful': Personal Recollections by Roslin Gunpowder Mill and Bomb Factory Workers* (East Linton, 2000), 144, 145, 150, 151, 154.

14. William Wolfe (1924–2010), National Convener, SNP, 1969–79.

15. See above, Isobel Cumming, Note 17, p. 389.

16. Winston Spencer Churchill (1874–1965), eldest son of Lord Randolph Churchill; army officer, 1895–8, fought at the battle of Omdurman, 1898; a war correspondent in the Boer War, 1899–1902; MP from 1900 as a Conservative, then from 1906 as a Liberal; held successive offices, including Home Secretary, and, 1911–15, First Lord of the Admiralty. After the failure of the Gallipoli campaign in 1915, he served briefly in the army, then from 1917 he was Minister of Munitions, in 1919–21 Minister of War and Air, from 1924, when he had rejoined the Conservative Party, he was until 1929 Chancellor of the Exchequer. Out of office, 1929–39, he was a leading opponent of the appeasement of the Nazis (though critical also of the Republicans in the Spanish Civil War). First Lord of the Admiralty, 1939–40, he was Prime Minister of the Coalition government of 1940–5. Kept out of office by the Labour Party electoral landslide victory in 1945, he was Prime Minister again from 1951 until his retirement in 1955. A great war leader in 1940–5, he was a towering figure of the 20th century, though certainly not without his critics.

   Louis Mountbatten (1900–1979), Earl Mountbatten of Burma; a great-grandson of Queen Victoria; a naval commander, served at sea in the 1914–18 War. In the 1939–45 War he was, 1941–3, Chief of Combined Operations, and 1943–5, Supreme Allied Commander, South-East Asia. In 1947 he became the last Viceroy of India before it gained its independence and the sub-continent was partitioned between India and Pakistan. First Sea Lord, 1955–9, and Chief of the Defence Staff, 1959–65; he was assassinated in Ireland by the IRA in 1979.

17. Further details about *Freight,* including its years of publication, have so far proven unexpectedly elusive. Reuters itself, named after its founder Julius Reuter (1816–1899), a German journalist, was est. in 1851 in London as a speedier agency for providing news by means of telegraph and carrier pigeons. It has remained a leading agency for providing an accurate and speedy foreign news service.

18. *Picture Post*, an illustrated weekly news magazine, 1938–57.

May Kerr, pp. 138–159

1. In 1900–1, around the time May Kerr's father was sent to an Industrial School (possibly the one at 26 Greenside Row) there were six in Edinburgh (including Leith, then still a separate burgh). Est. from the mid-19th century by voluntary bodies, Industrial Schools were intended to meet the needs of children aged 7 to 14 who, as orphans, beggars or vagrants, were likely to become, if not already, delinquents. In 1932 Industrial Schools and Reformatories were renamed Approved Schools. See, e.g., S.L. Hunter, *The Scottish Educational System* (Oxford, 1972), 151; *Edinburgh and Leith Post Office Directory 1900–01*, 830.

2. The Royal Scots Fusiliers, raised in 1769, became the 21st of Foot, merged in 1959 with the Highland Light Infantry to form the Royal Highland Fusiliers, which in 2006 became 2nd Bn, Royal Regt of Scotland.

3. Holyrood Laundry was in Lower London Road at Abbeyhill, Edinburgh.

4. The air raid, on 16 Oct. 1939, is outlined above in Isobel Cumming, Note 9, p. 388.

5. Alexander's Motors, Motor Engineers & Body Builders, Semple Street, Tollcross, Edinburgh.

6. 'On the parish' meant relief given, 1845–94, to poor, destitute, disabled, unemployed or aged people by parochial boards. These boards were superseded, 1894–1929, by parish councils empowered to levy rates for the purpose. Even after the abolition of parish councils in 1929, 'on the parish' remained for some years in popular parlance.

7. James Clark Junior Secondary School (named after Lt Col. James Clark, CB, KC, Deputy Lieutenant of Edinburgh, who had been killed in action in 1915) was built in 1915 beside the King's (presently the Queen's) Park and Arthur's Seat, but was requisitioned by the army until almost the end of the 1914–18 War. The school was opened in 1919, but closed in 1972 and converted into housing. Thomas Nelson & Sons, printers and publishers, Edinburgh, 1798–1968. John Millar & Sons, confectionery works, 176 Causewayside, Edinburgh, 1844–2006.

8. The Battle of Britain, Jul. to Oct. 1940, was Hitler's unsuccessful attempt to destroy the RAF in order to make possible a Nazi German invasion of Britain.

9. A progress chaser ensures each stage of work is on schedule and is completed as and when intended.

Williamina MacNab, pp. 160–182

1. The General Strike, 4–12 May 1926, was called by the Trades Union Congress (TUC) to support the coal miners in their struggle against the private coal owners' demands for reductions in their wages, lengthening of their hours of work, and return to district rather than national settlements. After nine days, however, the TUC leaders suddenly called off the strike, and the miners, already locked out by the owners before the General Strike had begun, were left to struggle on alone for some six months and were eventually driven back to work on the owners' terms.
2. For J. & P. Coats, see above, Jean Crosbie, Note 2, p. 386.
3. The catastrophic Great Irish Famine, 1845–9, caused by a blight upon the potatoes on which millions of poverty-stricken Irish people were dependent for their staple food, resulted in the death of about one million through starvation and diseases such as typhus. Hundreds of thousands of other Irish men, women and children, some of them victims of eviction by landowners, were forced into emigrating to Britain, the United States, Canada, and Australia. British governments, by their laissez-faire policies, worsened the vast problems of the Famine.
4. A slipper bath was a partially covered bath.
5. *Perthshire Advertiser*, 1829 to date; amalgamated with *Perthshire Courier* 1929, and incorporated *Perthshire Constitutional* from 1951.
6. Lady Margaret Drummond Hay (1907–1993).
7. NAAFI – Navy, Army and Air Force Institutes.

Ann Baird, pp. 183–197

1. It was perhaps *Comic Cuts*, published weekly, 1890–1953.
2. For the *Hotspur*, see above Jean Crosbie, Note 4, p. 386; for the *Rover*, see above, Christina Chisholm, Note 15, p. 375.
3. *Red Letter*, 1899–1988; *Secrets*, 1935–91, retitled *Secrets & Flames*, 1940–9; *Women's Own*, 1932 to date; *Family Friend*, 1849–1921; *People's Friend*, 1869 to date. If Ann Baird read the *Family Friend* was she reading back numbers of it? Or, more likely, did she mean to say: 'No – the *People's Friend*'?
4. National Association of Girls' Training Corps, 1940–63, when it merged into (a) the Sea Cadets, and (b) Girls Venture.
5. Barr & Stroud of Glasgow had a world reputation as designers and manufacturers of range-finders for ships and on land. They produced submarine

periscopes, gunnery control fire gear, gunsights, optical reflector sights for aircraft, depth recorders, survey instruments and prismatic binoculars. C.A. Oakley, *Scottish Industry* (Glasgow, 1953), 101–2.

6. No German planes were actually brought down by anti-aircraft fire during the Clydebank blitz in Mar. 1941. But a Polish destroyer, in John Brown's yard there for repairs, fired a tremendous barrage from its ack-ack guns against the first German attack on the night of 13–14 Mar. MacPhail, *Clydebank Blitz*, 45.

7. The Allies had invaded Sicily in Jul. 1943, and the fall from power of Mussolini soon followed. Allied landings in Italy took place from Sep. and, after a prolonged struggle against stiff German resistance, Rome fell to the Allies on 4 Jun. 1944. In early May 1945 the remaining German forces in northern Italy and southern Austria surrendered.

8. Trieste, an important port at the head of the Adriatic, had been awarded to Italy at the end of the 1914–18 War. It was sought at the end of the 1939–45 War by both Yugoslavia and Italy. Almost a decade later, in 1954, a settlement was reached by which Italy received the city and port of Trieste, and Yugoslavia the adjoining coastal strip.

9. Clark Gable (1901–1960) was a leading American film star for 30 years.

10. Some ATS women, for example, served in France in 1940 with the British Expeditionary Force. Others went then to Egypt. Carole Harris, *Women at War*, 30.

Isa Dougan, pp. 198–220

1. Toffee-nosed – snobbish, conceited, supercilious.

2. Munrospun Ltd, a textile and clothing firm, est. 1830, ceased production at Restalrig in Edinburgh in 1970.

3. *The Scotsman*, 1817 to date.

4. Fairley's had a reputation as a rough, tough dance-hall.

5. The League of Health and Beauty was founded by Mary Stack, and after her death its leadership was continued by her daughter Prunella Stack. In 1999 the League was retitled the Fitness League.

6. *Daily Record*, begun in 1847 in Glasgow as the *North British Daily Mail*; bought in 1901 by Lord Northcliffe and retitled the *Daily Record & Mail*; acquired by Lord Kemsley (1888–1968), and *& Mail* dropped from its title in 1954; acquired, 1955, by the *Daily Mirror* Group. For *Daily Express*, see above, Jean Crosbie, Note 1, p. 386. As the *Leith Gazette* was not

published until 1952, the paper taken was probably (because of her family's connections with Stranraer) the weekly *Galloway Gazette*, published in Newton Stewart, 1870 to date.

7. See above, Christina Chisholm, Note 26, p. 377.

8. The CWGC has no record of an RAF casualty named Dougie (Douglas) Steel. Gunner Frederick F.S. Kinnear, Royal Artillery, d. 26 Jan. 1941, aged 19, and is commemorated at Warriston Crematorium, Edinburgh. Flying Officer William Francis, RAFVR, d. 17 Jan. 1944, aged 20, buried at Rosebank cemetery, Edinburgh.

9. The Women's Land Army, which had existed in the 1914–18 War, was re-established in Jun. 1939. By 1941 it consisted of about 20,000 volunteers. Their numbers increased from the end of that year with the introduction of conscription for unmarried women and married women without children, aged between 20 (later 19) and 30; and by Jul. 1943, when recruitment was ended by the government, there were 87,000 Land Girls. Calder, *The People's War*, 267–8, 428; Gardiner, *Wartime Britain*, 448–51.

10. For an early German bombing attack in Oct.1939 on the Forth Bridge and naval vessels in the Firth of Forth, see above, Isobel Cumming, Note 9, p. 388. Another German bomber, shot down in Feb. 1940, crashed near North Berwick at the mouth of the Forth estuary. See, e.g., Jeffrey, *This Present Emergency*, 54–7; J. Tully-Jackson and I. Brown, *East Lothian at War* (Haddington, 1996), 20–3; I. MacDougall, *Voices from Work and Home: Recollections of John Macvicar* (Edinburgh, 2000), 180–2.

11. What *was* a Great Fire of London took place on 29 Dec. 1940, during the Blitz and before Isa Dougan joined the WAAF. In a massive Luftwaffe raid 22,000 incendiary bombs and 120 tons of high explosives were dropped on the city. As firemen's pumps ran dry, many buildings, including eight churches built in the 17th century by Christopher Wren, were destroyed, and St Paul's Cathedral itself narrowly escaped destruction. That raid killed 160 people and injured 500. Gardiner, *Wartime Britain*, 310–14. Joe Loss's Band in Hammersmith Palais: Joe Loss (1909–1990); he preferred to call it his orchestra.

12. MacBrayne's shipping company, est. 1851; adopted, 1879, the name of its then principal director David MacBrayne (1814–1907). It became the dominant company in west Highland and the Isles sea transport; later amended its name to Caledonian MacBrayne (CalMac). From 1990 wholly owned by the Secretary of State for Scotland.

13. The Oak Leaf (or Leaves), in bronze or silver, was (or were) awarded to Servicemen and Servicewomen, and to merchant seamen, mentioned in despatches or who had already been awarded a medal or medals.

14. The RAF Regt was formed in autumn 1942 to take over from the army the defence of RAF airfields.

15. Mae West – an inflatable life-jacket, so-called after an American actress with a large bust.

16. Several of the Servicewomen contributors of their recollections to this book have some comment to make on this aspect of their wartime experiences: see, e.g., above, Jean Crosbie, Note 6, p. 387.

Nessie Lawrie, pp. 221–239

1. The 'wee policeman' was William Merrilees (1898–1984), who became Chief Constable of Lothians and Peebles Police, 1950–68. In 1933, two years before Nessie Lawrie's account of Mr Faust's club in Princes Street, William Merrilees, then a plain-clothes detective, had taken an active part in a police raid on the notorious Kosmo dance club in Swinton Row, off Elder Street, Edinburgh, which raid resulted in the conviction of the club's owner and two of its managers for living wholly or partly on the immoral earnings of the club's dance instructresses. The owner was sentenced to 18 months' imprisonment, the two managers to three months' each – but the latter two men appealed successfully. Nessie Lawrie's account of Mr Faust's Princes Street club suggests he was not deterred by the Kosmo club case. See William Merrilees's autobiography, *The Short Arm of the Law* (London, 1966), 83–106; *Edinburgh Evening News*, 1 Aug. and 17 Nov.–7 Dec. 1933.

2. It was an old Edinburgh tradition that girls and young women who climbed up Arthur's Seat, the city's 822 feet high extinct volcano, early on 1 May and washed their face in the dew would, or might, be lucky in love.

3. Deanna Durbin (1921–2013), a Canadian singer and actress who appeared in a score of films between 1936 and her retirement in 1948.

4. Nessie Lawrie was quite correct: it was a false alarm.

5. Two German bombers shot down on 16 Oct. 1939, after their attack on the Forth Railway Bridge and naval ships in the Firth of Forth, were the first to be brought down in Britain. A third bomber, which may have been the one Nessie Lawrie refers to here, was a Heinkel, which crashed on Kidlaw

Hill, near Humbie, East Lothian, on 28 Oct. 1939. Of its crew of four, two were killed by fire from RAF fighters and ships in the Firth of Forth. Jeffrey, *This Present Emergency*, 54–7; Jackson and Brown, *East Lothian at War*, 20–3. See also above, Isobel Cumming, Note 9, p. 388.

6. National Association of Girls' Training Corps, 1940–63, when it merged into the Sea Cadets and Girls Venture.

7. The Boeing Flying Fortress (B17), the Americans' largest bomber, could fly higher than the RAF Lancaster, and was therefore more difficult for German ack-ack guns to hit. The B17 had a crew of 10 men, as many as eight of whom could fire its guns when attacked by German fighter planes; whereas in the RAF Lancaster there were only three gun positions. See, e.g., Martin Middlebrook, *The Battle of Hamburg* (Harmondswoth, 1984), 45, 48, 49.

8. Pilot Officer John Gillespie Magee, whose parents lived in Washington DC, USA, was a member of 412 Squadron, Royal Canadian Air Force. He died aged 19 on 11 Dec. 1941 and, as Nessie Lawrie says, was buried at Scopwick Church cemetery, Lincolnshire. Lines from his poem *High Flight* were read by US President Reagan as part of his address to the American people after the disaster in Jan. 1986 to the spaceship *Challenger*.

9. Robert Taylor (1911–1969), a particularly handsome American film star.

10. *The Lambeth Walk* was a popular song and dance from the 1937 musical *Me And My Girl*.

Elizabeth Weston, pp. 240–265

1. The battle of El Alamein in Egypt, 23 Oct.–4 Nov. 1942, was a decisive defeat of the German and Italian Axis forces in North Africa, and a turning point in the campaign that had begun there more than two years earlier.

2. Elizabeth Weston's father appears as a more honest and principled contractor than many other coal pit contractors. Immediately after the 1939–45 War the Scottish miners, in a complaint to the Ministry of Fuel and Power, described the contracting system in the pits thus: 'It is the system where one man has a contract with the [private coal] company and has a few or several men working under him. He draws all the wages from the company and pays the men who are working with him individually. The workmen never know what the contractor has earned or the rates paid by the company. The system itself creates suspicion as some of these contractors have made huge sums of money at the expense of their fellow

workers, and in most cases have done very little work for it. We can say that many contractors are detested even more than some coal owners.' Very soon after the nationalisation of the coal industry in Britain in Jan. 1947, the contractor system was abolished. R. Page Arnot, *The Scottish Miners* (London, 1955), 299, 300. 'Mungo' was Mungo Mackay (1867–1939), agent and general manager of the Lothian Coal Company based at Newtongrange. A brilliant mining engineer, Mackay, until his retirement and death on the eve of the 1939–45 War, ruled with a rod of iron not only the Lady Victoria pit but also those other pits of the Lothian Coal Co. near Newtongrange. Through informants and toadies among the miners he also controlled the village of Newtongrange, its tied Company houses, and even relations among its inhabitants. See, e.g., Ian MacDougall, *Mungo Mackay and the Green Table* (East Linton, 1995).

3. Sandwich Islands was the 19th century name for Hawaii.

4. Weil's Disease, named after Weil, a German doctor who first identified it, was a bacterial infection transmitted by rats.

5. James A. Hood (1859–1941), a son of the coal master Archibald Hood, who founded the Lothian Coal Co. in 1890. James A. Hood, general manager of the Company from 1890 till 1902, then succeeded his father as managing director, then from 1911 to 1941 he was chairman of the Company. A Midlothian county councillor from 1889, Hood founded in 1924 the Hood Chair of Mining at Edinburgh University, in conjunction with Heriot Watt College. At his death, Hood left a total of £436,000, including investments in 103 different companies; but most of his wealth was invested in the Lothian Coal Co. See Hood's obituary by Dr Michael Cotterill in *Dictionary of Scottish Business Biography* (Aberdeen, 1986), Vol.1, 42–5.

6. The National Coal Board was formed to administer the industry upon its nationalisation in 1947.

7. The North British Hotel, at the east end of Princes Street, is now called the Balmoral Hotel.

8. The Young Men's Christian Association was founded in London in 1844 by George Williams, and became an international organisation aimed at self-improvement. The Young Women's Christian Association was founded in 1887 from a merger of two similar organisations that had been formed in 1855.

9. By the early years of the 20th century, a considerable number of Lithuanians (or 'Poles' as they were sometimes misnamed) had settled in Midlothian, especially at Newtongrange. The 1911 Census indicated a

total of 253 males and 109 females in the county. *Census of Scotland, 1911* (London, 1913), iii, 54–7.

10. Air Chief Commandant Lady Ruth Welsh, DBE, was the second Director (1943–6) appointed in charge of the WAAF.

11. Group Officer C. Woodhead; Flight Officers M.L. Montefiori and Lady P.T. Armitage-Smith.

12. Florence Desmond (1905–1993), actress and comedienne.

13. Newbattle Abbey had been gifted to the nation in 1933 by Philip Kerr (1882–1940), 11th Marquis of Lothian. It had opened, uniquely in Scotland, as an Adult Education Residential College in 1937, but closed in 1939 and during the war became, as has already been seen above, requisitioned by the army for the initiation of recruits to the ATS. It was restored as an adult education residential college in 1950.

Jean Robertson, pp. 266–283

1. The Gordon Highlanders originated from the 75th and 92nd Highlanders, raised respectively in 1787 and 1794. The latter were titled the Gordons from 1798. The two regtiments merged in 1891 to become the Gordon Highlanders. The regt merged in 1994 with the Seaforth and Cameron Highlanders to become the Queen's Own Highlanders, which in 2006 became 4th Bn, Royal Regiment of Scotland.

2. *Anne of Green Gables*, by Lucy Maud Montgomery (1874–1942), a Canadian novelist and writer of children's literature. Published in 1908, the book is about the growing up of an adopted orphan in Canada.

3. *Girl's Own*, 1880–1956.

4. Zane Grey (1872–1939), American novelist who from 1904 wrote more than 50 books, of which his *Riders of the Purple Sage* (1912) became the best known.

5. Isaac Benzie (?–1926) had opened his first shop in Aberdeen in 1894. Originally at 185 George Street, Benzie's main store was opened in 1906 at 143–151 George Street. After his death in 1926, the business was run by his two sons, Isaac jnr and Athol. Isaac jnr died in 1935, and the store was run by Athol until he retired in 1955. It was then taken over by House of Fraser Ltd, and in 1972 retitled Arnott. It closed c. 1986. Infmn: House of Fraser website; Local Studies, Aberdeen Council Central Library.

6. ENSA – Entertainments National Service Association. By early 1946 ENSA had given over two and a half million concerts to the Forces and

to industrial workers, and had employed more than four-fifths of the entertainments industry in doing so. Calder, *The People's War*, 371.

Margaret Campbell, pp. 284–299

1. Taynuilt, in Argyll, is nine miles east of Oban.
2. The United Free Church of Scotland was formed in 1900 from a union of
   the great majority of congregations and ministers of the Free Church of
   Scotland (itself formed in 1843 in a major breakaway – The Disruption –
   from the established Church of Scotland) with the United Presbyterian
   Church (formed in 1847 by earlier Secession churches from the Church of
   Scotland). The remnant of the Free Church of Scotland that remained
   outside the union of 1900 became known as 'the Wee Frees'. The United
   Free Church of Scotland and the Church of Scotland united in 1929.
3. A novel by Charles Dickens and published in 1859, originally as a serial;
   it is set in Paris and London at the time of the French Revolution, which
   began in 1789.
4. When the WRNS began recruiting in spring 1939 'Only women aged 18
   to 50 and living near naval ports were considered. References from serving or retired naval men were also necessary, making the Service the
   most selective and nepotistic of the auxiliary forces.' Harris, *Women at
   War*, 8, 9.
5. Sybil, Marchioness of Cholmondeley (1894–1989), Superintendent,
   WRNS. Dame Vera Laughton Mathews, DBE, (1888–1959), Director of
   the WRNS, 1939–46. Margaret Campbell is mistaken about Dame Vera.
   She was not a sister of Charles Laughton nor any relation to him. See her
   Blue Tapestry: The Story of the WRNS (London, 1948), 21. Charles
   Laughton (1899–1962) was a leading stage and film actor.
6. Winston Churchill, as Prime Minister, and Franklin D. Roosevelt, as
   President of the United States, met several times during the war, from
   Aug. 1941 onwards (though the USA did not enter the war against the Axis
   powers, Nazi Germany, Fascist Italy and Japan, until Dec. 1941). The
   Allies' North Africa landings, in Algeria and Morocco, took place on 8
   Nov. 1942.
7. Commodore (later Vice-Admiral, retd) Sir Gilbert Stephenson, based on
   HMS *Western Isles* at Tobermory, was indeed 'The Terror of Tobermory'.
   The reasons for his fame, or notoriety, are fully explained in the book of
   that title by Richard Baker (Edinburgh, 1999).

8. Margaret Campbell's brother, 1346811 Sgt Archibald Sinclair Campbell, RAF, was killed on the night of 22–23 May 1944 while flying over Germany, and is buried there at Hartefeld. Infmn: Mrs Jess Wilson, Sgt Campbell's niece.

9. The *Queen Mary* and the *Queen Elizabeth*, huge passenger liners built by John Brown Co., Clydebank, and launched in 1934 and 1940, respectively, transported several hundred thousand troops during the war. The *Ile de France,* built as a passenger liner at St Nazaire in 1926, was requisitioned by the British government in 1940 upon the Fall of France to Nazi Germany.

10. The English-Speaking Union was founded in 1918 by Evelyn Wrench (1882–1966), a British author, to promote fellowship of the English-speaking peoples of the world.

11. John Buchan, Lord Tweedsmuir (1875–1940), author, MP, administrator, Governor-General of Canada 1935–40. Among his many books were *The Thirty-Nine Steps*, *Greenmantle*, and biographies of Sir Walter Scott and the Marquis of Montrose. In the 1914–18 War Buchan became an officer in the Intelligence Corps, in 1917 the government appointed him Director of Information. Alastair Buchan (1918–1976), in the Canadian army in the 1939–45 War; in the Dieppe Raid, 1942; post-war, a journalist and author; Director, Institute of Strategic Studies 1958–69. William Buchan (1916–2008), 3rd Lord Tweedsmuir; author.

12. Prince George Galitzine, (1916–1992), author and lecturer; a major in the Welsh Guards in 1939–45 War.

13. In 1759 John Watson, a lawyer (Writer to the Signet) had bequeathed the residue of his estate to trustees, who were to apply the funds to charitable uses within Edinburgh. An Act of Parliament in 1822 allowed the trustees to establish and endow an institution for the care and education of destitute fatherless children 'of the better classes' (i .e., clergymen, army and navy officers, doctors, lawyers, and others). The children had to be aged at least 10 and not more than 15. The syllabus was to include English, Latin, French, maths, drawing, singing and instrumental music, gymnastics, etc. Originally there were places for 100 children. Designed by William Burn and built in 1825–8, John Watson's remained a school until nearly the end of the 20th century, when it became the Scottish National Gallery of Modern Art.

Isa Allan, pp. 300–317

1. The Royal Scots Greys, formed in 1681 as a dragoon regt by General Tam Dalyell, and so called because of their grey horses; amalgamated, 1971, with the 3rd Carabiniers to form the Royal Scots Dragoon Guards.
2. *Border Telegraph*, originally titled *Galashiels Telegraph*, 1896 to date.
3. Earlston hiring fair was always held on the last Monday in Feb. Other Borders hiring fairs were held annually at Kelso, Hawick, Duns, and Berwick-upon-Tweed. Until at least the mid-1920s the hiring fairs were held outdoors; from then the Scottish Farm Servants' Union began to succeed in urging the fairs be held indoors. Until the Agricultural Wages (Regulations) Scotland Act, 1937, farm workers were hired for a year at a time. The Act also led after a few years to the disappearance of the hiring fairs, though one appears to have been held at Earlston as late as 1941. Joseph F. Duncan (1879–1965), general secretary of the Scottish Farm Servants' Union, had in 1913 described the hiring fairs as 'simply a relic of barbarism'. See, e.g., I. MacDougall, *Voices from Lilliesleaf* (Edinburgh, 2015), 367.
4. The beach at Spittal, beside Berwick-upon-Tweed, attracted many summer outings by Borderers.
5. The hazards (if that's what they were) of the Melrose Shillingly Hop have so far proved elusive to identify.
6. For the first time in peacetime, conscription had been imposed in Britain on all men between their 20th and 21st birthdays, under the Military Training Act passed in Apr. 1939. The first young men affected registered early in Jun. and began training in Jul. 1939. As Isa Allan says, the term of service was to be six months. But the war began on 3 Sep., and those pre-war conscripts, like her fiancé, had to serve for the duration of the war.
7. Sheriff John Boyd (1856–1943), a son of Sir John Boyd, Lord Provost of Edinburgh, 1890–3, was an advocate and editor, *Scottish Law Reporter*; appointed a Sheriff Substitute of Lanarkshire 1897; an active Conservative. His daughter-in-law, Mrs Violet Boyd (1894–1982), was an early volunteer into the WRNS on its formation in 1917; m. 1919 Lieut. Commander John Boyd, son of Sheriff Boyd; shortly before the 1939–45 War began, she was asked by Dame Vera Laughton Mathews, Director, to take a senior appointment in the WRNS and became Area Officer then Superintendent at Rosyth, and later Superintendent, WRNS, at Chatham naval base; awarded CBE in 1945; post-war was county commissioner for the Girl

Guides Association for a decade from 1948. Obituary in *Southern Reporter*, 29 Apr. 1982; infmn from her grand-daughter, Caroline Boyd.

8. Admiral John Jellicoe (1859–1935), Commander-in-Chief, 1914–16, British Grand Fleet; fought the German navy at the battle of Jutland, 31 May to 1 Jun. 1916.

9. HMS *Berwick*, a cruiser built in 1926 at Fairfield shipyard, Glasgow.

Elizabeth Stewart, pp. 318–322

1. John Laurie (1897–1980), stage and TV actor, with appearances in 25 films between 1930 and 1971.

2. Billy Butlin (1899–1980), passed some of his early life in Canada but became involved in fairgrounds in Britain, and from 1936 pioneered holiday camps in several parts of the country, including Skegness, Ayr and Pwllheli, where very popular all-in family holidays were provided. HMS *Glendower* was no doubt named after Owen Glendower (c.1350–c.1416), Prince of Wales and Welsh national leader.

Christina Millaney, pp. 323–337

1. St Joseph's College, 1875 to date, was founded as a boarding school for boys.

2. Sir Michael Nairn, Bart (1874–1952), chairman, Michael Nairn & Co., linoleum manufacturers, Kirkcaldy. The first factory in Scotland to make floorcloth was built in Kirkcaldy in 1847 by Michael Nairn, whose son, Sir Michael Nairn (1838–1915), had carried on the business.

3. Crail, a picturesque old fishing burgh on the east coast of Fife, is about 20 miles north-east of Kirkcaldy as the crow flies.

4. Although 1943 proved a turning time in favour of the Allies, the war was far from finished. Heavy fighting on the eastern front continued for a further two years; the Western Allies did not land in Normandy until Jun. 1944; and the war against Japan was abruptly ended only with the dropping of the atomic bombs on Hiroshima and Nagasaki in Aug. 1945. So the Second World War ended then.

5. There were several different kinds of air raid shelters, including the large public ones built of brick. Anderson shelters, named after Sir John Anderson (1882–1958), Home Secretary and Minister of Home Security, 1939–40, were made of corrugated iron and were dug two or three feet

down into the gardens of householders (if they had a garden). Each Anderson shelter could house about eight persons seated. Another family shelter was the Morrison, named after Herbert Morrison (1888–1965), successor to Sir John Anderson in 1940 as Home Secretary and Minister of Home Security. The Morrison shelter could be erected indoors. It had a steel plate on top, usable as a table by day, and wire mesh sides. See, e.g., Calder, *The People's War*, 54, 187; Gardiner, *Wartime Britain*, 6, 317–18, 527–8.

Olga Matthews, pp. 338–348

1. HMS *Warrior*, an armoured cruiser, was heavily damaged on 31 May 1916 during the battle, and sank the next day.
2. Oxenfoord Castle, four miles from Dalkeith, ceased to be a school some years ago.
3. Lord Samuel Palmer (1858–1948).
4. The Women's Land Army, which, like the ATS, WAAF and WRNS, had had a forerunner in the 1914–18 War, was re-established in Jun. 1939. By 1941 it consisted of about 20,000 volunteers. With the introduction of conscription for women at the end of 1941, the number of Land Girls increased to about 87,000 by the middle of 1943. Calder, *The People's War*, 267–8, 428; Gardiner, *Wartime Britain*, 448–51.
5. The Fleet Air Arm, est. 1909, had been greatly reduced towards the end of the 1914–18 War by the transfer in 1918 of many hundreds of its airplanes and thousands of its personnel to the newly formed Royal Air Force. As a result at the beginning of the 1939–45 War the Fleet Air Arm was in a weakened state, with out-of-date and inadequate aeroplanes (some of which were of the old double-wing kind). It took some time before the strength of the Fleet Air Arm became more adequate to deal with its distinctive tasks. These were to act as eyes for the fleets of warships, to help protect them against enemy air attacks, and to attack enemy war and merchant ships. Fleet Air Arm planes were based on aircraft carriers, but also on aerodromes such as at Yeovilton and Drem. Fleet Air Arm planes also took part in the Battle of Britain against the Luftwaffe, and in the North Africa campaign in 1940–3. The Fleet Air Arm also attacked the great German battleships *Bismarck*, *Gneisenau*, and *Tirpitz*; and had successfully bombed the Italian fleet at Taranto in Nov. 1940 and kept it out of action for many months.

Alexina McGlinn, pp. 349–363

1. In the civil war and the war of intervention by several European and other states, including the USA and Japan, which began immediately after the Bolshevik Revolution in Russia in Nov. 1917, British troops were sent to Murmansk, Archangel, Baku, and Vladivostok and one or two other places in Russia. If Alexina McGlinn's father was indeed in Russia at that time he was presumably at one or more of those places. See, e.g., Lionel Kochan, *The Making of Modern Russia* (Harmondsworth, 1963), 259–64.

2. The mass unemployment of the early 1930s in Britain (between Aug. 1931 and Jan. 1933 it reached virtually three million) was made even less bearable for all those unemployed by the 10 per cent cut in unemployment benefits imposed by the so-called 'National' government in 1931, which also introduced the Means Test. Because of the inquisition that accompanied it the Means Test was bitterly resented not only by the unemployed but by working people generally. 'The Means Test reduced the payments of half a million persons and removed a quarter of a million from the registers, as well as deterring thousands more from applying. . . . What made the Means Test hated and loathed by the working classes was its form and its administration. It was a household means test. It took account of any earnings by members of the household (sons and daughters, for instance), as well as of savings, pensions, income from house property or any other assets. Thrift was penalised and improvidence rewarded. Family solidarity was undermined: growing sons and daughters were forced to support their parents in a way which frayed the tempers of both generations and might break up the family: sons and daughters would move into lodgings in order not to be "dragged down" by having to support their parents. The test was an encouragement to the tattle-tale and the informer, the writer of anonymous letters and the local blackmailer; to all sorts of unneighbourliness. It stimulated petty tyranny and insolence on the part of Labour Exchange clerks and managers; the weekly visit to the Exchange would bring the sudden, curt announcement by the clerk: "They've knocked you off the dole." ' Frank McCusker who, like Alexina McGlinn, belonged to Dundee, recalled years later in the 1980s how he had worked there in the jute industry from the age of 12 in 1918 until he was 18. 'Then I was paid off. They told me I was too old – which meant I had to get bigger wages. So they paid you off and they got another one at 14 years of age to take your job. And when he come to 18 he was paid off as well.

And that's the way it went right through the system. . . . Dundee was what they called a woman's town. The women did all the work. The men did makin' the teas and looked after the house, because there was no jobs for them. But they [the jute millowners] had the women workin' because they were cheaper . . . than a man.' When Frank remained unemployed he was put on the Means Test . . . 'and because my father was workin' I got half-a-croon [12½p] a week for to keep me. Actually my father had to keep me. He was a general labourer but he was always in work 'cause he was a big hefty bloke. And that's what I got right up till I was practically married. I had to live off my father, he kept me goin'. And then after I got married in 1932 I got a pound. I got a pound for myself, ten shillings [50p] for the wife, and then after the kids came on two shillings each for the kids. And that was to keep me in rent, coal, gas and everything. So you'll know how well off we were at that time.' Four National Hunger Marches by unemployed men and women from many areas of Britain took place between 1930 and 1936, and a fifth March from Jarrow to London. At a Hunger March demonstration in London in Nov. 1936, Mrs John Harley from Greenock, one of the marchers, declared that her husband had been employed for only nine months in 12 years. She had £1.90 a week to maintain her family, which included four children. She said, 'We live in a single apartment house. I am ashamed to confess it but my husband, three sons and myself are compelled to sleep in one bed.' Their single apartment was in a building where there were only two lavatories for 65 people. Her daughter slept with an aunt two miles away from home. After paying for groceries, rent, shoe repairs and clothing, her weekly budget left her with just over 10p a week to buy meat and vegetables. National Archives of Scotland, DD 10/246/2; Mowat, *Britain between the Wars*, 432, 471, 484; *Daily Worker*, 12 Nov. 1936; Ian MacDougall, *Voices from the Hunger Marches*: *Personal Recollections by Scottish Hunger Marches of the 1920s and 1930s* (Edinburgh, 1990), Vol. I, 29.

3. Dundee, where the 1921 Census showed that in the population aged 15 and upwards females outnumbered males by 19,000 or 37 per cent, 'was of a character which reflected the substantial reversal of male and female economic functions: a city where men were frequently dependent on the earnings of mothers, sisters, or daughters . . .' William M. Walker, *Juteopolis: Dundee and its Textile Workers 1885–1923* (Edinburgh, 1979), 40.

4. Pend – a vaulted passage; a vaulted entrance to a passageway.

5. Cromarty, or Cromarton, Home has not yet been identified.

6. The Forestry Commission, founded in 1919 by the government, sought to ensure reafforestation after the huge demands for timber during the 1914–18 War and also during the industrial revolution before that. Forestry was to be massively extended and developed by the state and, to a lesser extent, by private landowners. The Commission's headquarters were based in Edinburgh, in recognition of the extent of forestry in Scotland. Formed in England in Apr. 1942, the Women's Timber Corps, in effect an extension of the Women's Land Army, emerged the following year in Scotland also. In the course of the war some 1,500 women and girls joined the Timber Corps in Scotland. In the 1914–18 War a section of the Women's Land Army was engaged in timber-cutting. There was also then a Women's Forestry Corps, which was controlled by the Board of Trade. Marwick, *Women at War 1914–1918*, 101, 124.

7. Wages of Timber Corps girls appear to have varied according partly to age, whether food and/or board had to be paid for, and where there was any additional payment for piece work. Specific sums are given in Affleck Gray, *Timber!* (East Linton, 1998), 11, 37, 39 and 44, thus: First, at age 17, 35s (£1.15), at age 18, 41s 6d (c. £2.07), at 19 and over, 46s (£2.30); for accommodation provided 3s (15p) per week. Second, basic wage £2 12s 6d (c. £2.62); on piece work, payment was 10p for each tree felled, snedded, cross-cut into lengths for coalpit props, and all brush burned. Third, approx. 38s (£1.90) per week, but no food provided. Finally, £2 5s 0d (£2.25) per week.

8. Lord Charles Lyell, VC (1913–1943), killed at Tunis. Lady Sophie Lyell.

9. See also above, Nancy Cowe, Note 11, p. 383; and Isa Allan, Note 3, p. 403.

Index